Too Much Information

More by Gene Ambaum & Bill Barnes:

- Unshelved
- What Would Dewey Do?
- Library Mascot Cage Match
- Book Club
- Read Responsibly
- Frequently Asked Questions
- Reader's Advisory
- Large Print

More by Bill Barnes:

- Runtime Error

Too Much Information

an **UNSHELVED**® collection
by Gene Ambaum & Bill Barnes

OVERDUE MEDIA
Seattle

Reprinting *Unshelved* comic strips originally published on the *Unshelved* website from April 27, 2010 to December 1, 2011, and *ALA CogNotes* newspapers in June 2010, January 2011, and June 2011. Individual comic strips copyright © 2010 and 2011.

ISBN-13: 978-1-937914-00-4

First printing: January 2012

Printed in China.

FOREWORD

There are things in life that just go better together. Rainbows and unicorns. Popcorn and monster movies. But without a doubt, the best combination of all is comics and librarians. Which makes *Unshelved* the ultimate mash-up of the universe. It is the monster movie where a popcorn-eating unicorn jumps over a rainbow. (Just try and top that one.)

Brought to the page and computer screen by the dynamic duo known as Bill and Gene, *Unshelved* sweeps us into the intriguing world of the stacks that is the Mallville Public Library. We see the whole parade of life drawn together with all its warts (and lost library cards). And the heroes are truly heroes of the first order: the fearless librarians who battle to serve their patrons by providing them with knowledge, books, and, of course, a place for the kids to run around like maniacs on a rainy day.

The only question you'll have after reading *Unshelved* is how to catalogue it. Satire and Humor (817)? Drawing and Drawings (741)? Good and Evil (216)? You may even want to shelve it in—gasp!—the Graphic Novel section. Whatever you do, be sure to face it out. Because this, my friends, is pure Dewey gold.

Jennifer L. Holm,

New York Times *bestselling author and three-time Newbery honoree, writes the* Babymouse *and* Squish *graphic novel series with her brother, Matt, and amazing historical novels on her own (*Turtle in Paradise, Penny from Heaven, *the* May Amelia *books, and the* Boston Jane *series). She's made of sugar and spice and everything nice.*

illustrations © Matt Holm

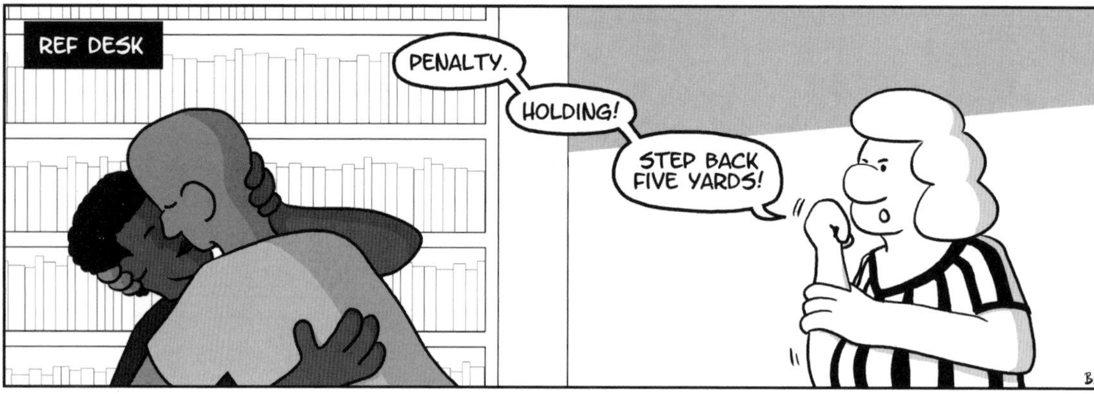
REF DESK
PENALTY.
HOLDING!
STEP BACK FIVE YARDS!
BB

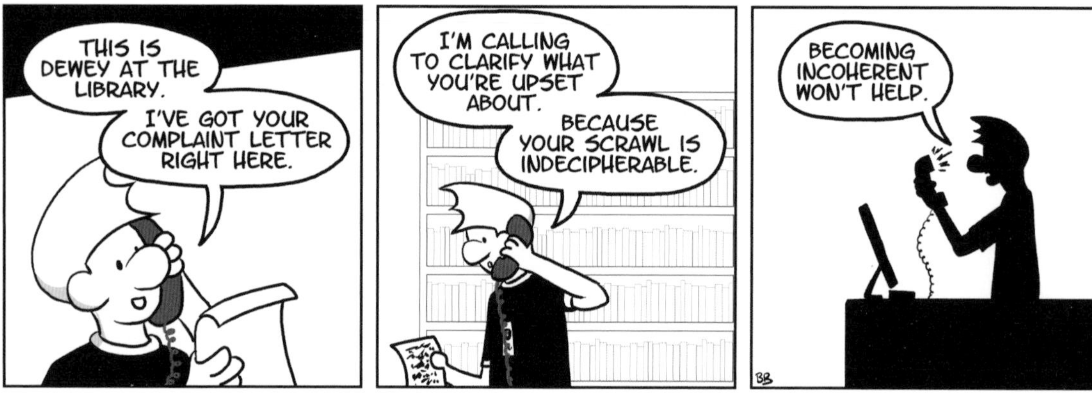
THIS IS DEWEY AT THE LIBRARY.
I'VE GOT YOUR COMPLAINT LETTER RIGHT HERE.
I'M CALLING TO CLARIFY WHAT YOU'RE UPSET ABOUT.
BECAUSE YOUR SCRAWL IS INDECIPHERABLE.
BECOMING INCOHERENT WON'T HELP.
BB

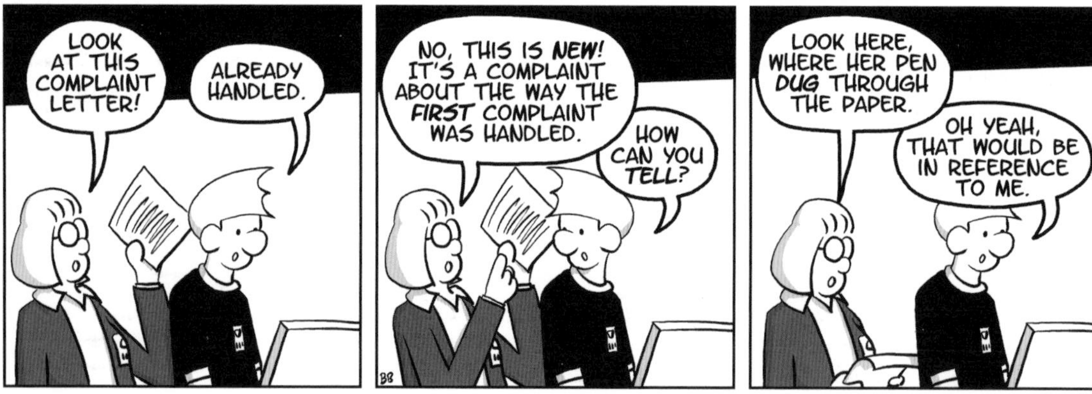
LOOK AT THIS COMPLAINT LETTER!
ALREADY HANDLED.
NO, THIS IS *NEW*! IT'S A COMPLAINT ABOUT THE WAY THE *FIRST* COMPLAINT WAS HANDLED.
HOW CAN YOU *TELL*?
BB
LOOK HERE, WHERE HER PEN *DUG* THROUGH THE PAPER.
OH YEAH, THAT WOULD BE IN REFERENCE TO ME.

Too Much Information

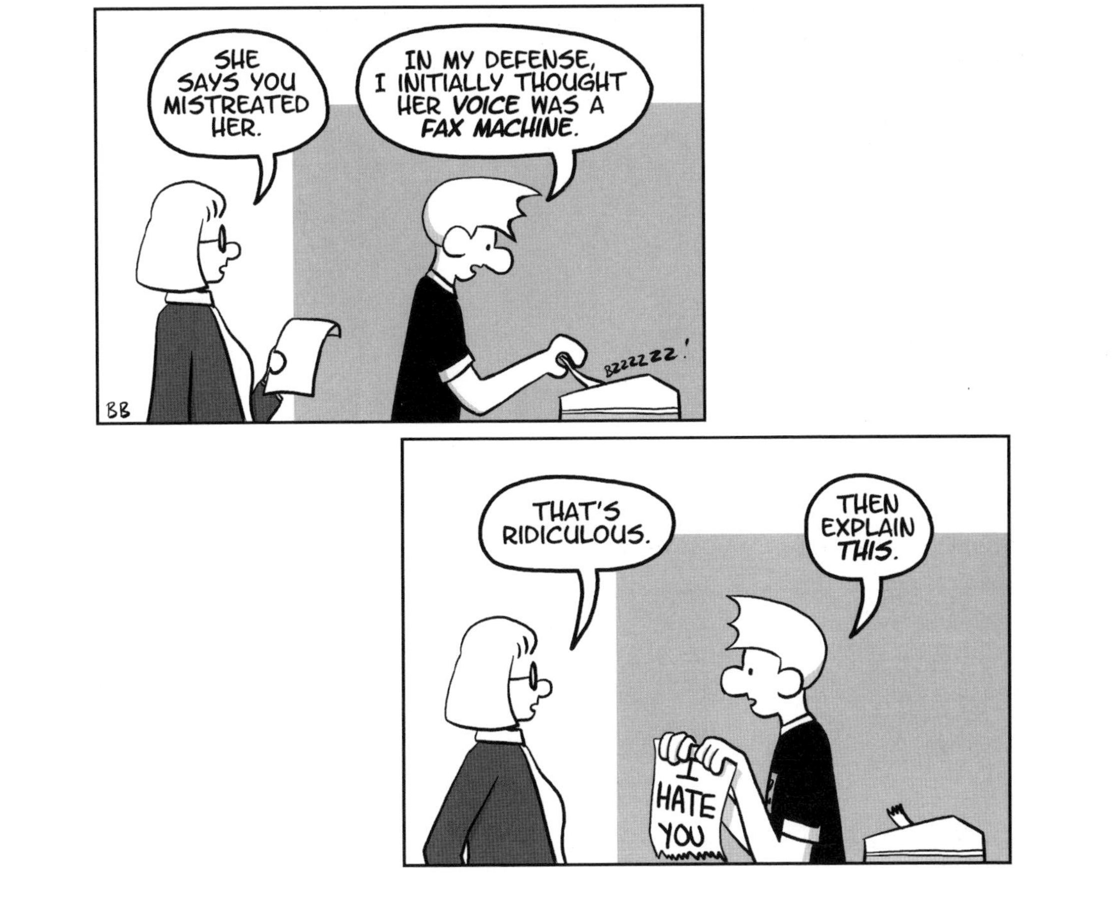
SHE SAYS YOU MISTREATED HER.
IN MY DEFENSE, I INITIALLY THOUGHT HER VOICE WAS A FAX MACHINE.
BZZZZZZ!
BB
THAT'S RIDICULOUS.
THEN EXPLAIN THIS.
I HATE YOU
I'M GOING TO SHOW YOU HOW THIS IS DONE.
HELLO, THIS IS THE MANAGER OF THE LIBRARY.
YES I --
NO I --
YOU DON'T --
IS THAT HOW IT'S DONE?
WITH PEOPLE LIKE HER, YES.

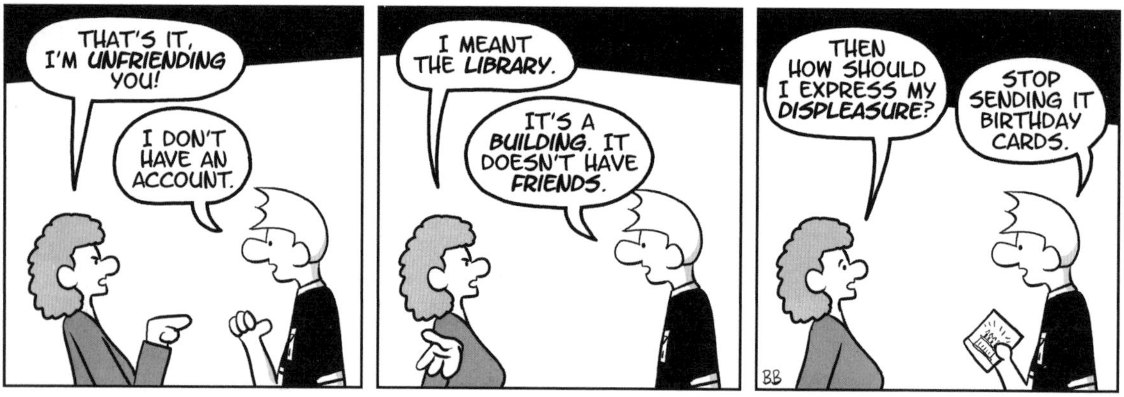
THAT'S IT, I'M UNFRIENDING YOU!
I DON'T HAVE AN ACCOUNT.
I MEANT THE LIBRARY.
IT'S A BUILDING. IT DOESN'T HAVE FRIENDS.
THEN HOW SHOULD I EXPRESS MY DISPLEASURE?
STOP SENDING IT BIRTHDAY CARDS.
BB

LIBRARY TIP #72: BE KIND, REWIND

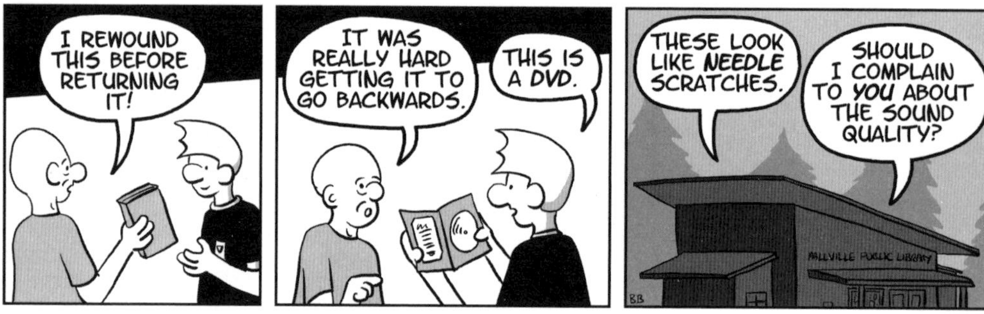
I REWOUND THIS BEFORE RETURNING IT!
IT WAS REALLY HARD GETTING IT TO GO BACKWARDS.
THIS IS A DVD.
THESE LOOK LIKE NEEDLE SCRATCHES.
SHOULD I COMPLAIN TO YOU ABOUT THE SOUND QUALITY?
BB

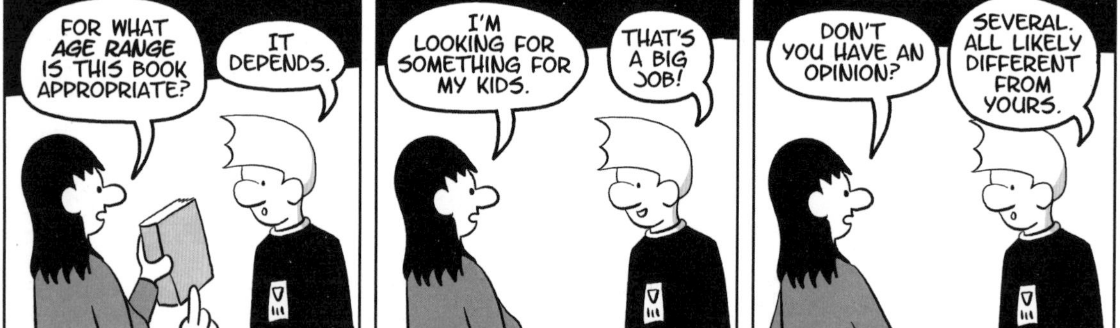
FOR WHAT AGE RANGE IS THIS BOOK APPROPRIATE?
IT DEPENDS.
I'M LOOKING FOR SOMETHING FOR MY KIDS.
THAT'S A BIG JOB!
DON'T YOU HAVE AN OPINION?
SEVERAL. ALL LIKELY DIFFERENT FROM YOURS.
BB

Too Much Information

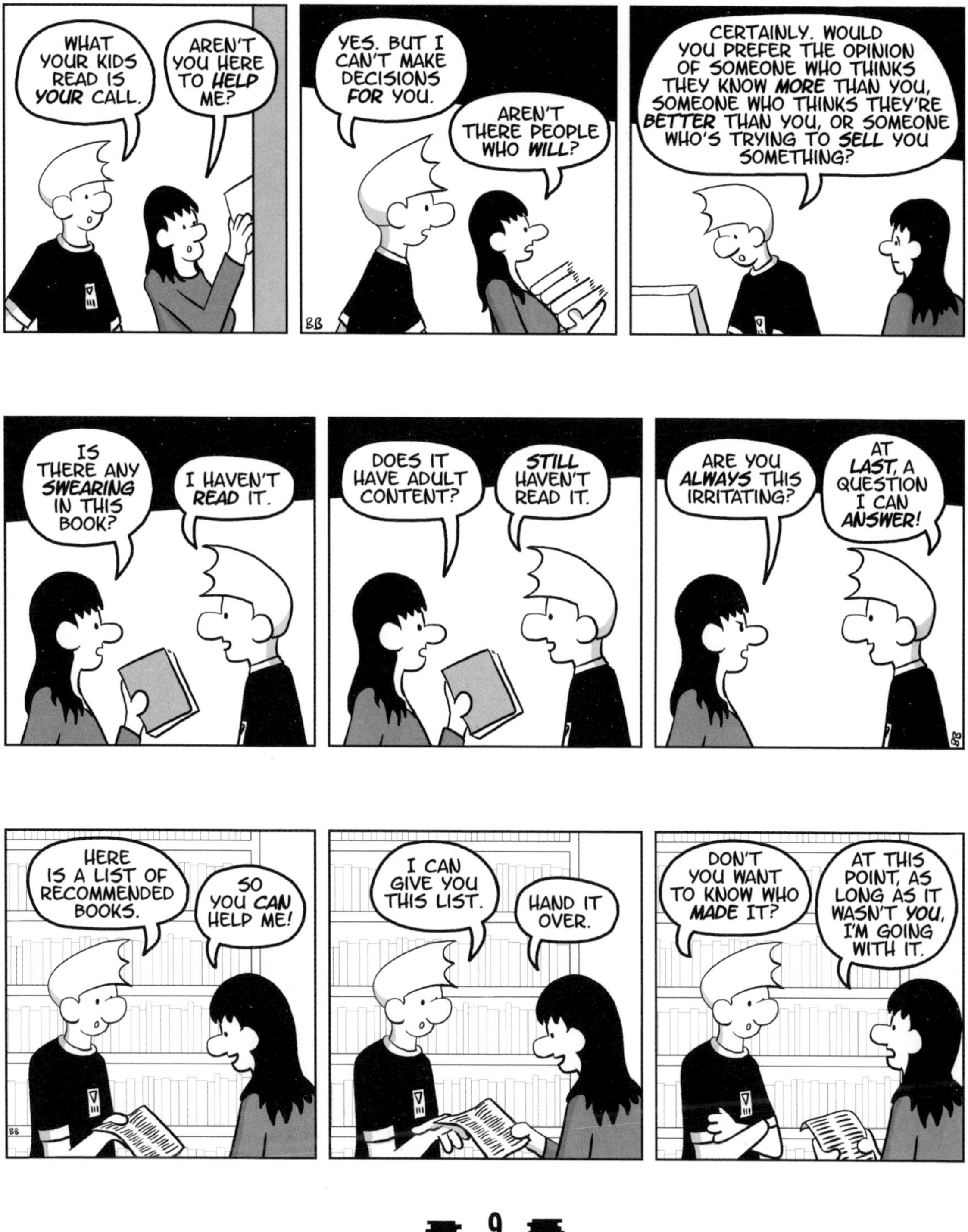

WHAT YOUR KIDS READ IS YOUR CALL.
AREN'T YOU HERE TO HELP ME?
YES. BUT I CAN'T MAKE DECISIONS FOR YOU.
AREN'T THERE PEOPLE WHO WILL?
CERTAINLY. WOULD YOU PREFER THE OPINION OF SOMEONE WHO THINKS THEY KNOW MORE THAN YOU, SOMEONE WHO THINKS THEY'RE BETTER THAN YOU, OR SOMEONE WHO'S TRYING TO SELL YOU SOMETHING?
IS THERE ANY SWEARING IN THIS BOOK?
I HAVEN'T READ IT.
DOES IT HAVE ADULT CONTENT?
STILL HAVEN'T READ IT.
ARE YOU ALWAYS THIS IRRITATING?
AT LAST, A QUESTION I CAN ANSWER!
HERE IS A LIST OF RECOMMENDED BOOKS.
SO YOU CAN HELP ME!
I CAN GIVE YOU THIS LIST.
HAND IT OVER.
DON'T YOU WANT TO KNOW WHO MADE IT?
AT THIS POINT, AS LONG AS IT WASN'T YOU, I'M GOING WITH IT.

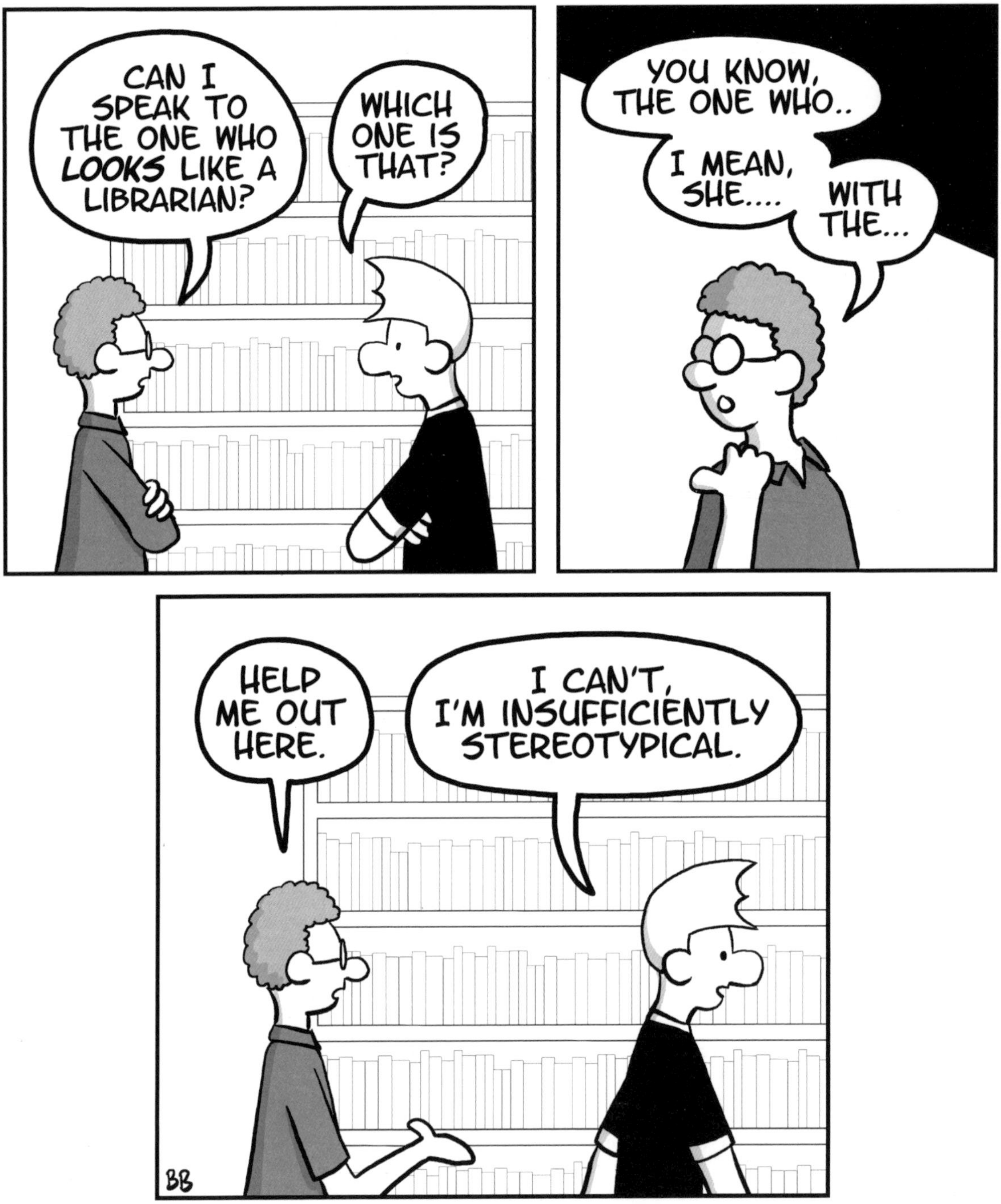
CAN I SPEAK TO THE ONE WHO *LOOKS* LIKE A LIBRARIAN?
WHICH ONE IS THAT?
YOU KNOW, THE ONE WHO..
I MEAN, SHE....
WITH THE...
HELP ME OUT HERE.
I CAN'T, I'M INSUFFICIENTLY STEREOTYPICAL.
BB

Too Much Information

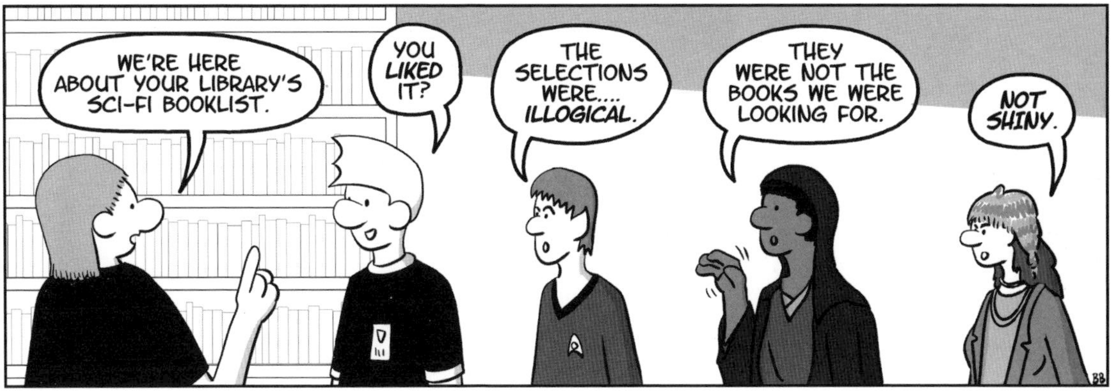
WE'RE HERE ABOUT YOUR LIBRARY'S SCI-FI BOOKLIST.
YOU LIKED IT?
THE SELECTIONS WERE.... ILLOGICAL.
THEY WERE NOT THE BOOKS WE WERE LOOKING FOR.
NOT SHINY.
BB

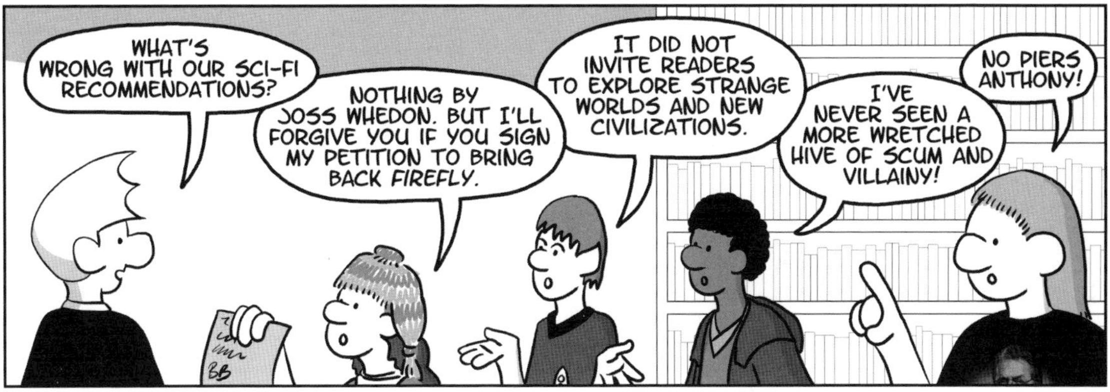
WHAT'S WRONG WITH OUR SCI-FI RECOMMENDATIONS?
NOTHING BY JOSS WHEDON. BUT I'LL FORGIVE YOU IF YOU SIGN MY PETITION TO BRING BACK FIREFLY.
IT DID NOT INVITE READERS TO EXPLORE STRANGE WORLDS AND NEW CIVILIZATIONS.
I'VE NEVER SEEN A MORE WRETCHED HIVE OF SCUM AND VILLAINY!
NO PIERS ANTHONY!
BB

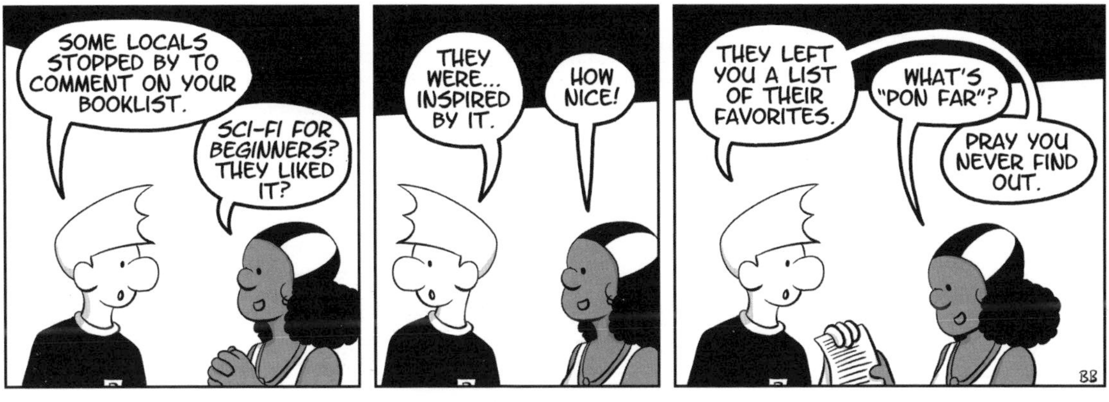
SOME LOCALS STOPPED BY TO COMMENT ON YOUR BOOKLIST.
SCI-FI FOR BEGINNERS? THEY LIKED IT?
THEY WERE... INSPIRED BY IT.
HOW NICE!
THEY LEFT YOU A LIST OF THEIR FAVORITES.
WHAT'S "PON FAR"?
PRAY YOU NEVER FIND OUT.
BB

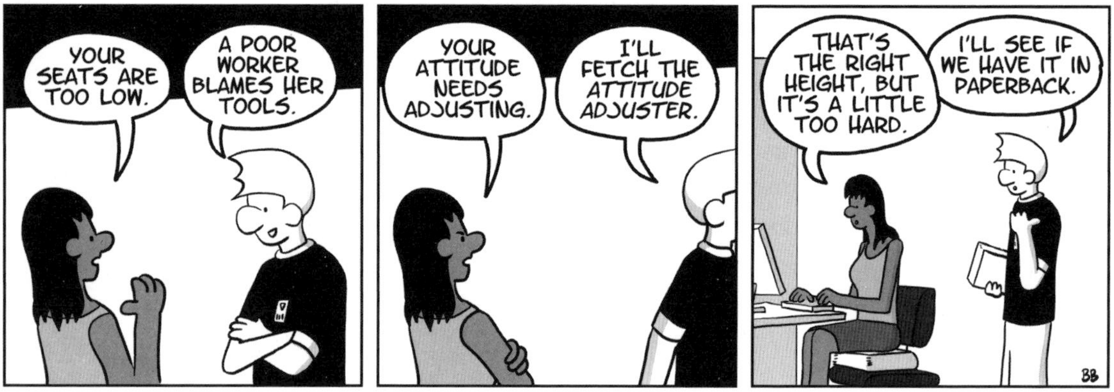
YOUR SEATS ARE TOO LOW.
A POOR WORKER BLAMES HER TOOLS.
YOUR ATTITUDE NEEDS ADJUSTING.
I'LL FETCH THE ATTITUDE ADJUSTER.
THAT'S THE RIGHT HEIGHT, BUT IT'S A LITTLE TOO HARD.
I'LL SEE IF WE HAVE IT IN PAPERBACK.
BB

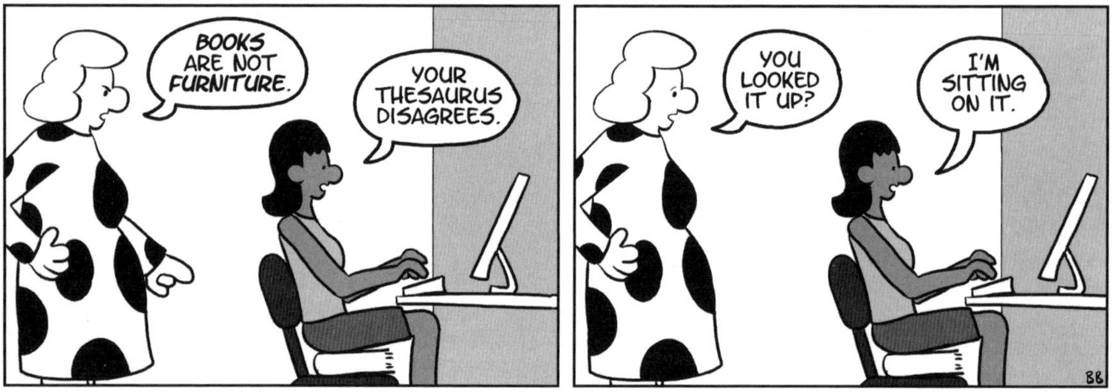
BOOKS ARE NOT FURNITURE.
YOUR THESAURUS DISAGREES.
YOU LOOKED IT UP?
I'M SITTING ON IT.
BB

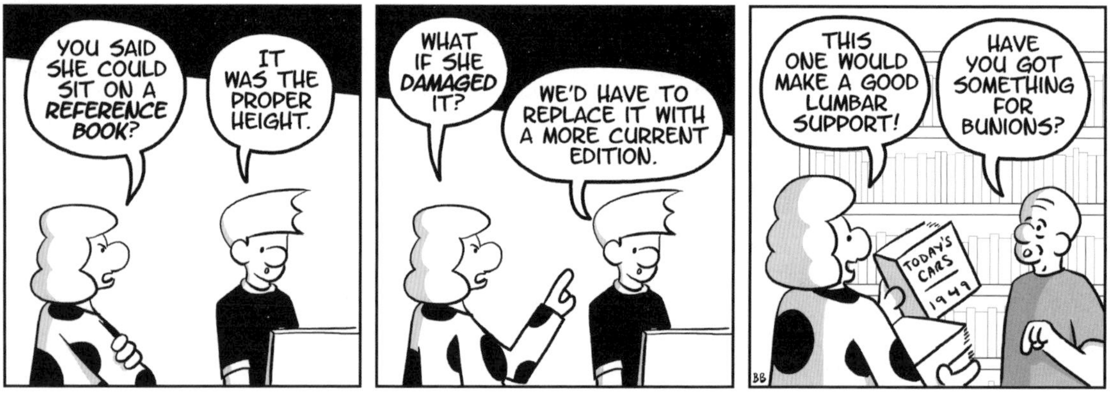
YOU SAID SHE COULD SIT ON A REFERENCE BOOK?
IT WAS THE PROPER HEIGHT.
WHAT IF SHE DAMAGED IT?
WE'D HAVE TO REPLACE IT WITH A MORE CURRENT EDITION.
THIS ONE WOULD MAKE A GOOD LUMBAR SUPPORT!
HAVE YOU GOT SOMETHING FOR BUNIONS?
TODAY'S CARS 1949
BB

Too Much Information

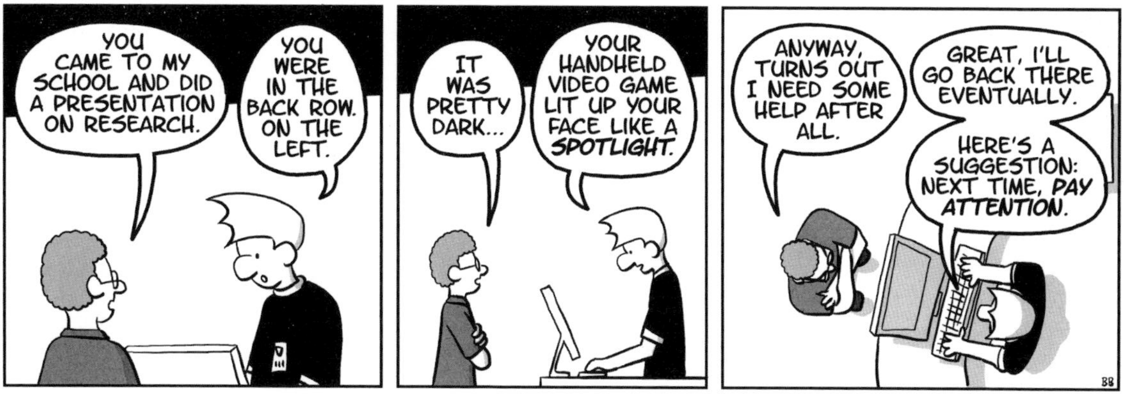
YOU CAME TO MY SCHOOL AND DID A PRESENTATION ON RESEARCH.
YOU WERE IN THE BACK ROW. ON THE LEFT.
IT WAS PRETTY DARK...
YOUR HANDHELD VIDEO GAME LIT UP YOUR FACE LIKE A *SPOTLIGHT*.
ANYWAY, TURNS OUT I NEED SOME HELP AFTER ALL.
GREAT, I'LL GO BACK THERE EVENTUALLY.
HERE'S A SUGGESTION: NEXT TIME, *PAY ATTENTION*.
BB

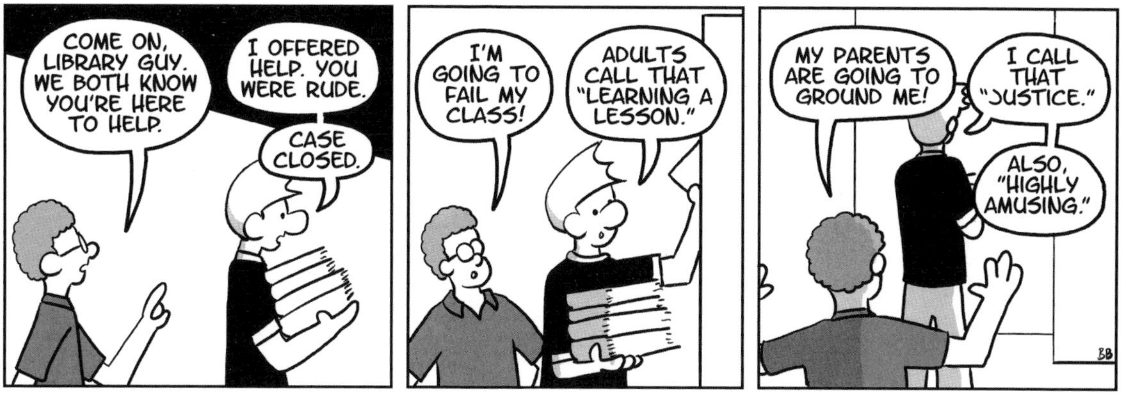
COME ON, LIBRARY GUY. WE BOTH KNOW YOU'RE HERE TO HELP.
I OFFERED HELP. YOU WERE RUDE.
CASE CLOSED.
I'M GOING TO FAIL MY CLASS!
ADULTS CALL THAT "LEARNING A LESSON."
MY PARENTS ARE GOING TO GROUND ME!
I CALL THAT "JUSTICE."
ALSO, "HIGHLY AMUSING."
BB

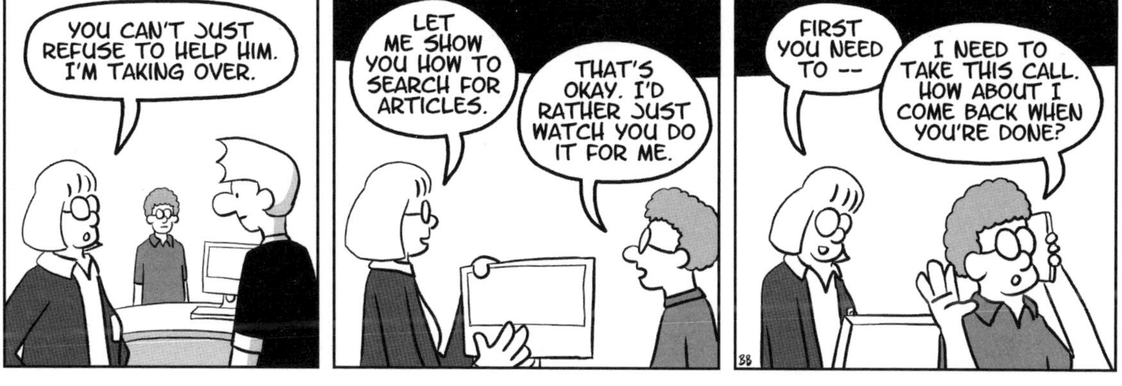
YOU CAN'T JUST REFUSE TO HELP HIM. I'M TAKING OVER.
LET ME SHOW YOU HOW TO SEARCH FOR ARTICLES.
THAT'S OKAY. I'D RATHER JUST WATCH YOU DO IT FOR ME.
FIRST YOU NEED TO --
I NEED TO TAKE THIS CALL. HOW ABOUT I COME BACK WHEN YOU'RE DONE?
BB

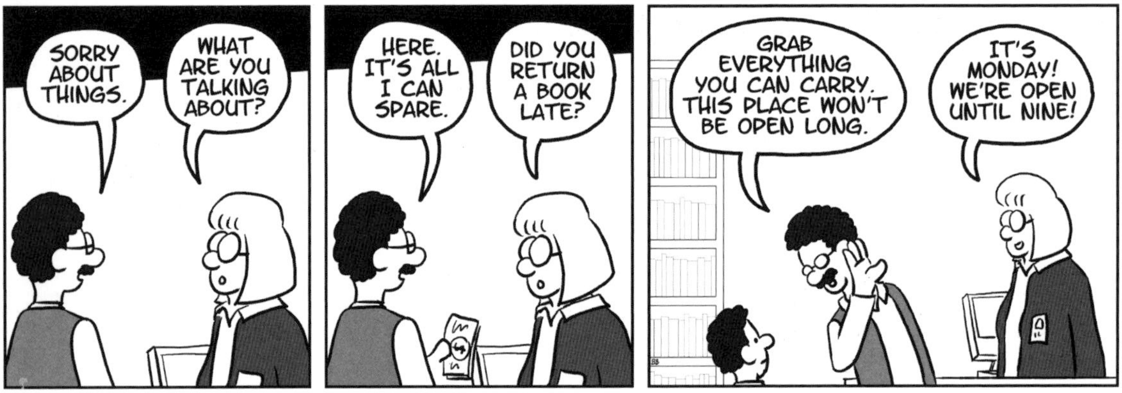
SORRY ABOUT THINGS.
WHAT ARE YOU TALKING ABOUT?
HERE. IT'S ALL I CAN SPARE.
DID YOU RETURN A BOOK LATE?
GRAB EVERYTHING YOU CAN CARRY. THIS PLACE WON'T BE OPEN LONG.
IT'S MONDAY! WE'RE OPEN UNTIL NINE!

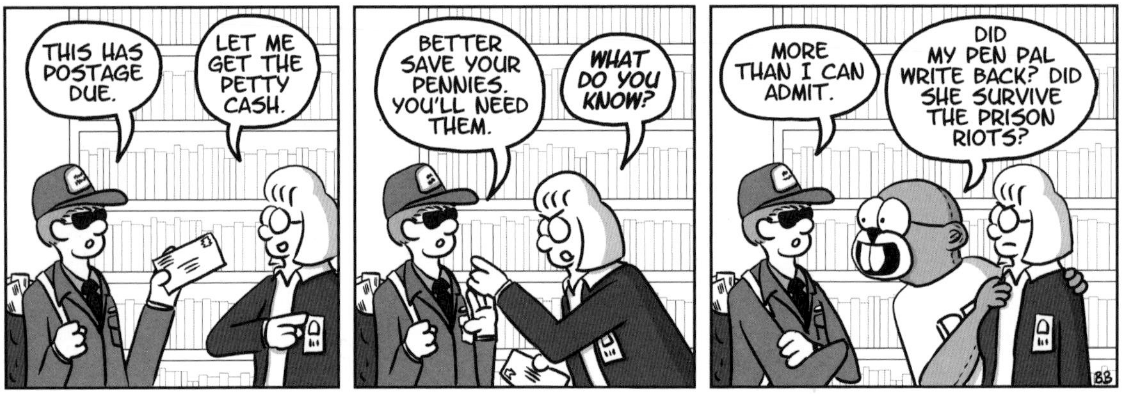
THIS HAS POSTAGE DUE.
LET ME GET THE PETTY CASH.
BETTER SAVE YOUR PENNIES. YOU'LL NEED THEM.
WHAT DO YOU KNOW?
MORE THAN I CAN ADMIT.
DID MY PEN PAL WRITE BACK? DID SHE SURVIVE THE PRISON RIOTS?

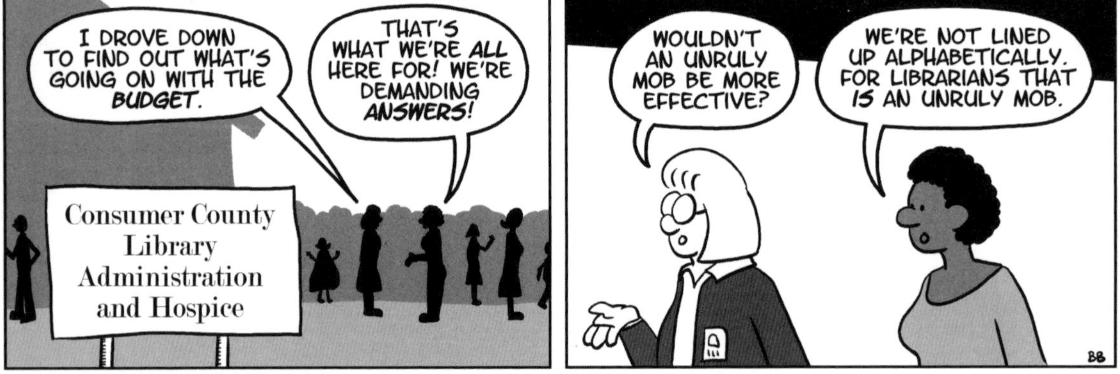
I DROVE DOWN TO FIND OUT WHAT'S GOING ON WITH THE BUDGET.
THAT'S WHAT WE'RE ALL HERE FOR! WE'RE DEMANDING ANSWERS!
Consumer County Library Administration and Hospice
WOULDN'T AN UNRULY MOB BE MORE EFFECTIVE?
WE'RE NOT LINED UP ALPHABETICALLY. FOR LIBRARIANS THAT IS AN UNRULY MOB.

Too Much Information

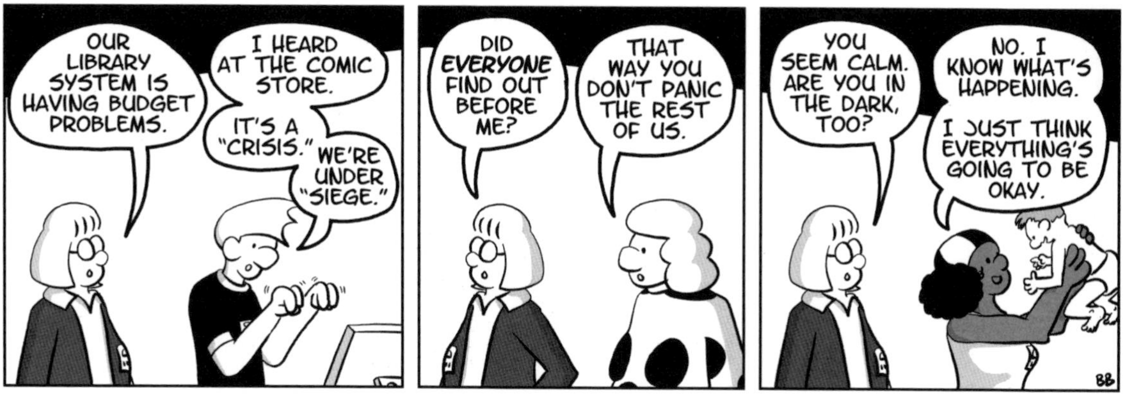

OUR LIBRARY SYSTEM IS HAVING BUDGET PROBLEMS.
I HEARD AT THE COMIC STORE.
IT'S A "CRISIS."
WE'RE UNDER "SIEGE."
DID *EVERYONE* FIND OUT BEFORE ME?
THAT WAY YOU DON'T PANIC THE REST OF US.
YOU SEEM CALM. ARE YOU IN THE DARK, TOO?
NO. I KNOW WHAT'S HAPPENING.
I JUST THINK EVERYTHING'S GOING TO BE OKAY.
BB

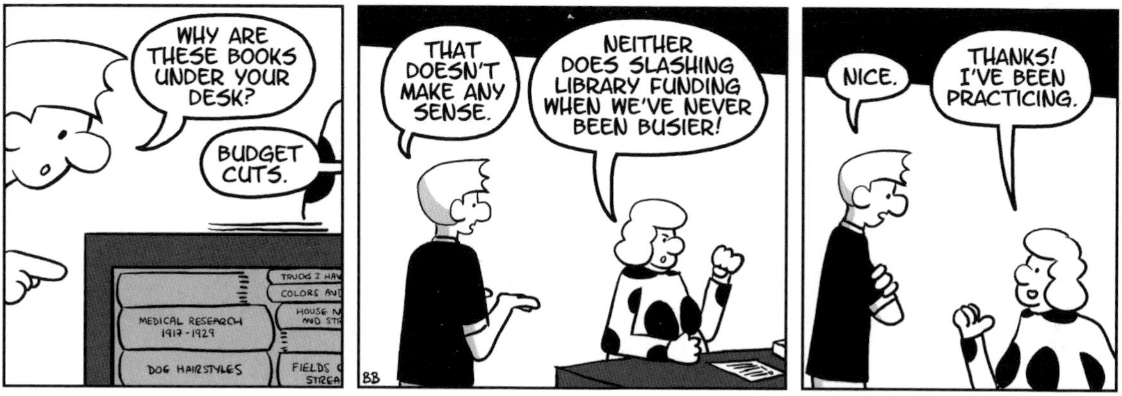

WHY ARE THESE BOOKS UNDER YOUR DESK?
BUDGET CUTS.
MEDICAL RESEARCH 1917-1929
DOG HAIRSTYLES
BB
THAT DOESN'T MAKE ANY SENSE.
NEITHER DOES SLASHING LIBRARY FUNDING WHEN WE'VE NEVER BEEN BUSIER!
NICE.
THANKS! I'VE BEEN PRACTICING.

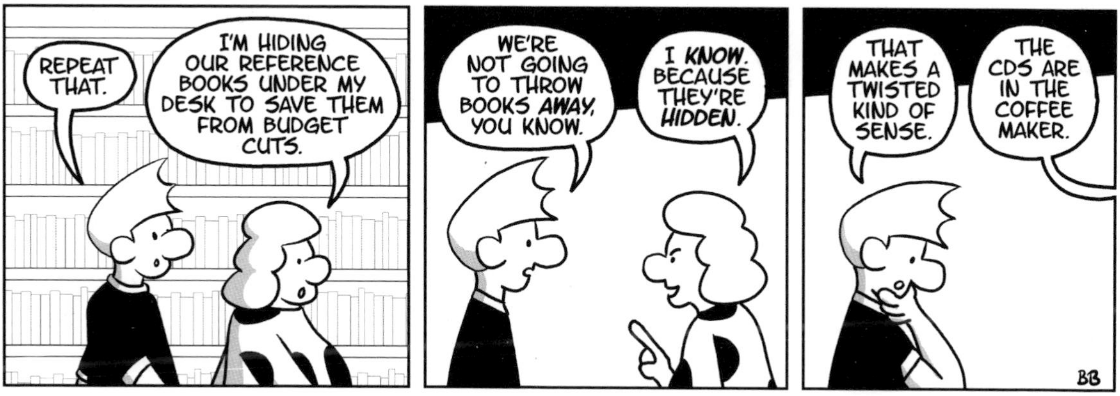

REPEAT THAT.
I'M HIDING OUR REFERENCE BOOKS UNDER MY DESK TO SAVE THEM FROM BUDGET CUTS.
WE'RE NOT GOING TO THROW BOOKS *AWAY*, YOU KNOW.
I *KNOW*. BECAUSE THEY'RE *HIDDEN*.
THAT MAKES A TWISTED KIND OF SENSE.
THE CDS ARE IN THE COFFEE MAKER.
BB

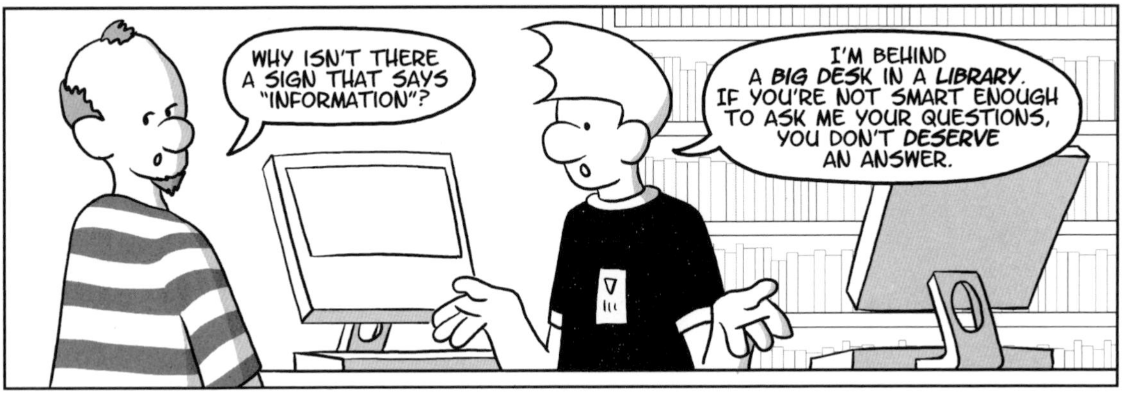
WHY ISN'T THERE A SIGN THAT SAYS "INFORMATION"?
I'M BEHIND A **BIG DESK** IN A **LIBRARY**. IF YOU'RE NOT SMART ENOUGH TO ASK ME YOUR QUESTIONS, YOU DON'T **DESERVE** AN ANSWER.

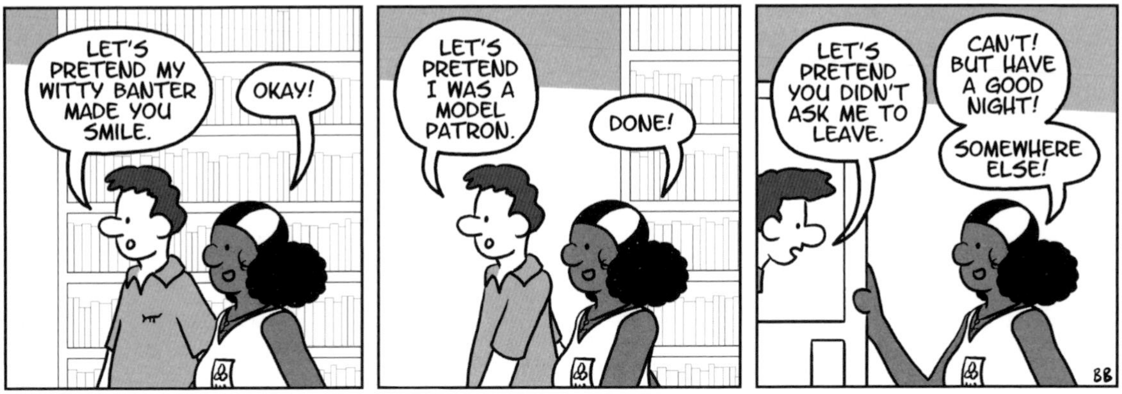
LET'S PRETEND MY WITTY BANTER MADE YOU SMILE.
OKAY!
LET'S PRETEND I WAS A MODEL PATRON.
DONE!
LET'S PRETEND YOU DIDN'T ASK ME TO LEAVE.
CAN'T! BUT HAVE A GOOD NIGHT!
SOMEWHERE ELSE!
BB

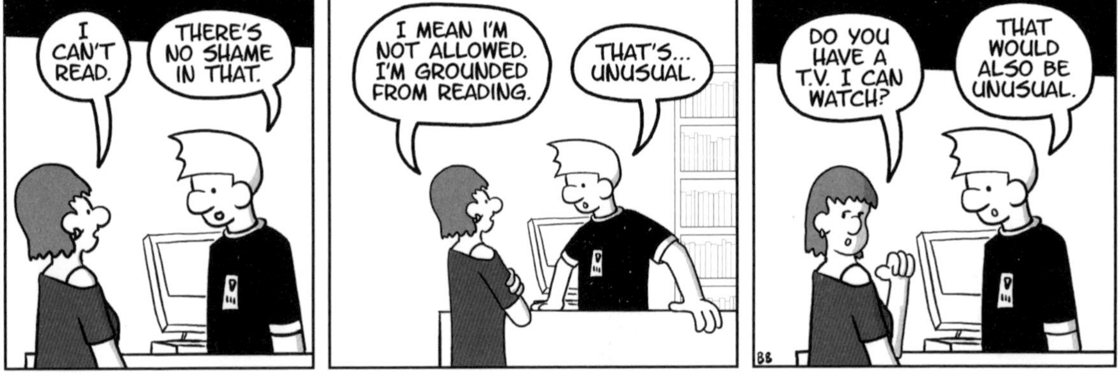
I CAN'T READ.
THERE'S NO SHAME IN THAT.
I MEAN I'M NOT ALLOWED. I'M GROUNDED FROM READING.
THAT'S... UNUSUAL.
DO YOU HAVE A T.V. I CAN WATCH?
THAT WOULD ALSO BE UNUSUAL.
BB

Too Much Information

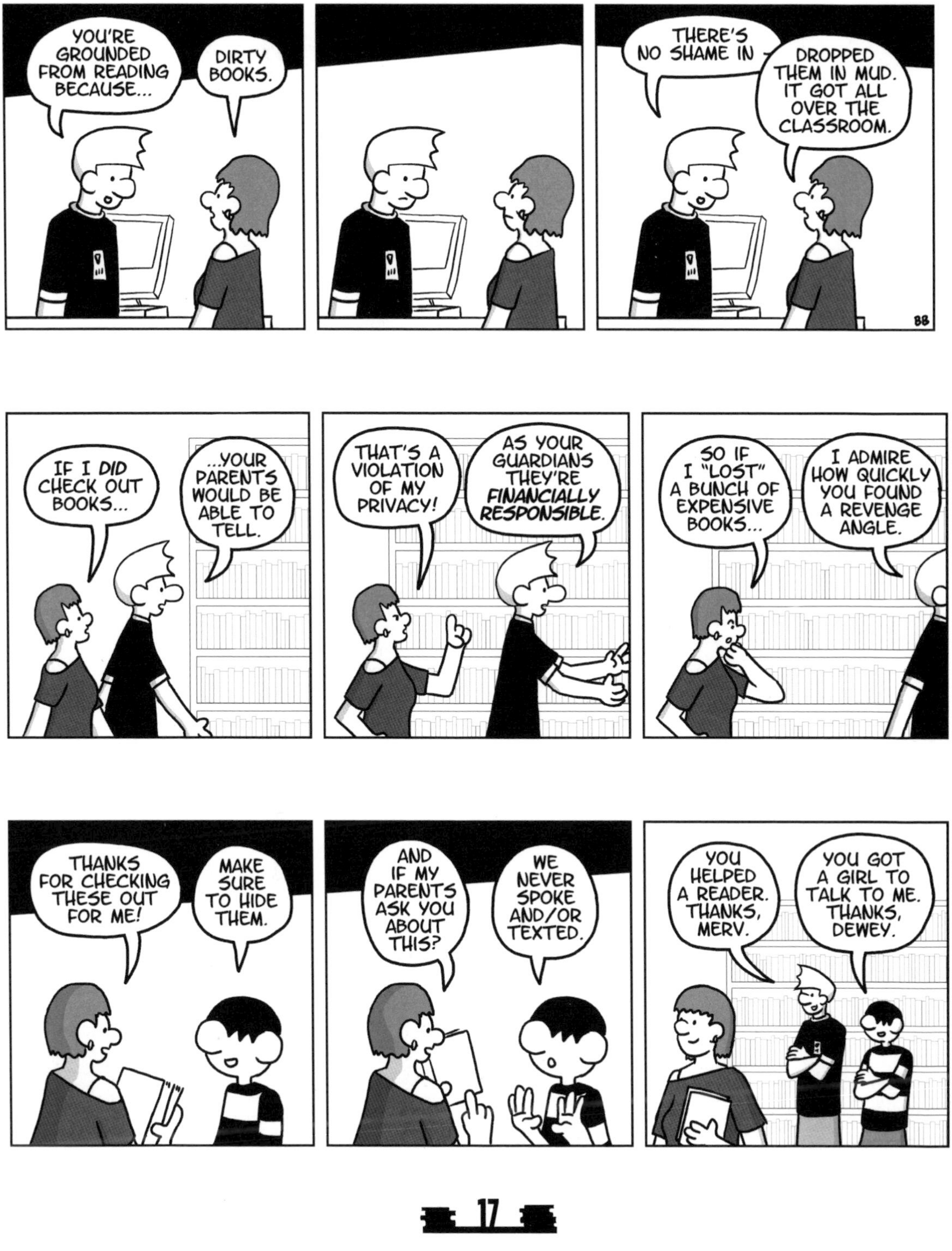

YOU'RE GROUNDED FROM READING BECAUSE...
DIRTY BOOKS.
THERE'S NO SHAME IN –
DROPPED THEM IN MUD. IT GOT ALL OVER THE CLASSROOM.
BB
IF I DID CHECK OUT BOOKS...
...YOUR PARENTS WOULD BE ABLE TO TELL.
THAT'S A VIOLATION OF MY PRIVACY!
AS YOUR GUARDIANS THEY'RE FINANCIALLY RESPONSIBLE.
SO IF I "LOST" A BUNCH OF EXPENSIVE BOOKS...
I ADMIRE HOW QUICKLY YOU FOUND A REVENGE ANGLE.
THANKS FOR CHECKING THESE OUT FOR ME!
MAKE SURE TO HIDE THEM.
AND IF MY PARENTS ASK YOU ABOUT THIS?
WE NEVER SPOKE AND/OR TEXTED.
YOU HELPED A READER. THANKS, MERV.
YOU GOT A GIRL TO TALK TO ME. THANKS, DEWEY.

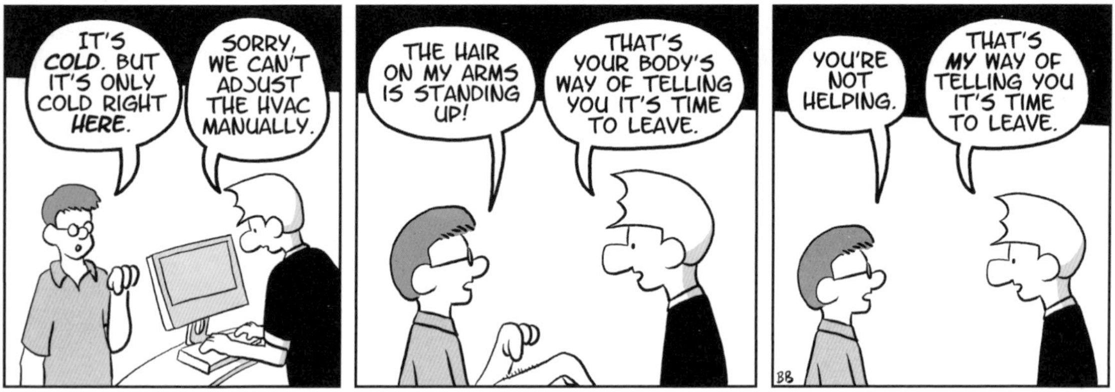
IT'S **COLD**. BUT IT'S ONLY COLD RIGHT **HERE**.
SORRY, WE CAN'T ADJUST THE HVAC MANUALLY.
THE HAIR ON MY ARMS IS STANDING UP!
THAT'S YOUR BODY'S WAY OF TELLING YOU IT'S TIME TO LEAVE.
YOU'RE NOT HELPING.
THAT'S **MY** WAY OF TELLING YOU IT'S TIME TO LEAVE.
BB

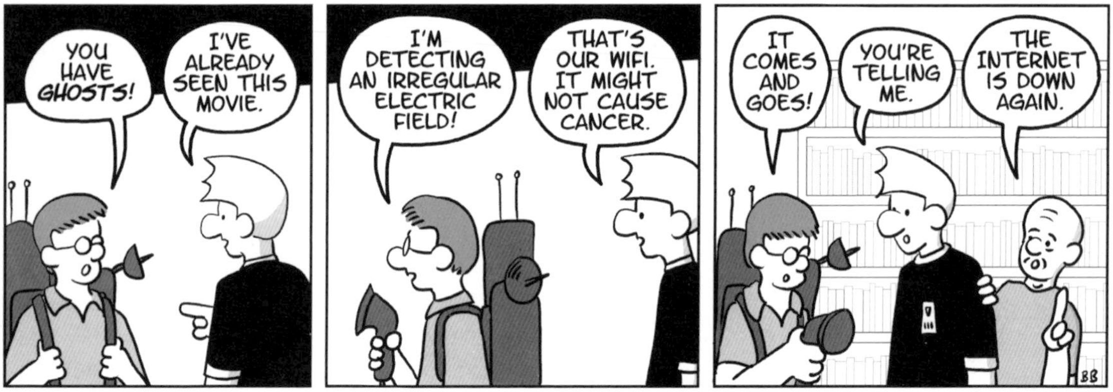
YOU HAVE **GHOSTS**!
I'VE ALREADY SEEN THIS MOVIE.
I'M DETECTING AN IRREGULAR ELECTRIC FIELD!
THAT'S OUR WIFI. IT MIGHT NOT CAUSE CANCER.
IT COMES AND GOES!
YOU'RE TELLING ME.
THE INTERNET IS DOWN AGAIN.
BB

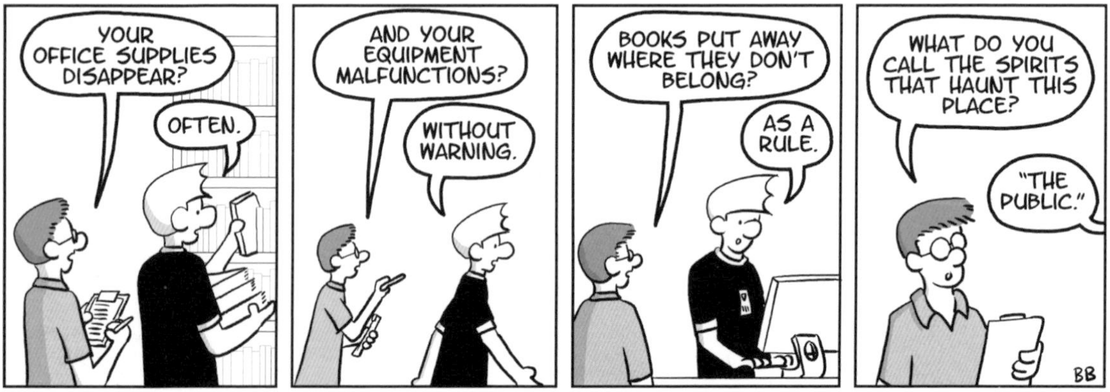
YOUR OFFICE SUPPLIES DISAPPEAR?
OFTEN.
AND YOUR EQUIPMENT MALFUNCTIONS?
WITHOUT WARNING.
BOOKS PUT AWAY WHERE THEY DON'T BELONG?
AS A RULE.
WHAT DO YOU CALL THE SPIRITS THAT HAUNT THIS PLACE?
"THE PUBLIC."
BB

Too Much Information

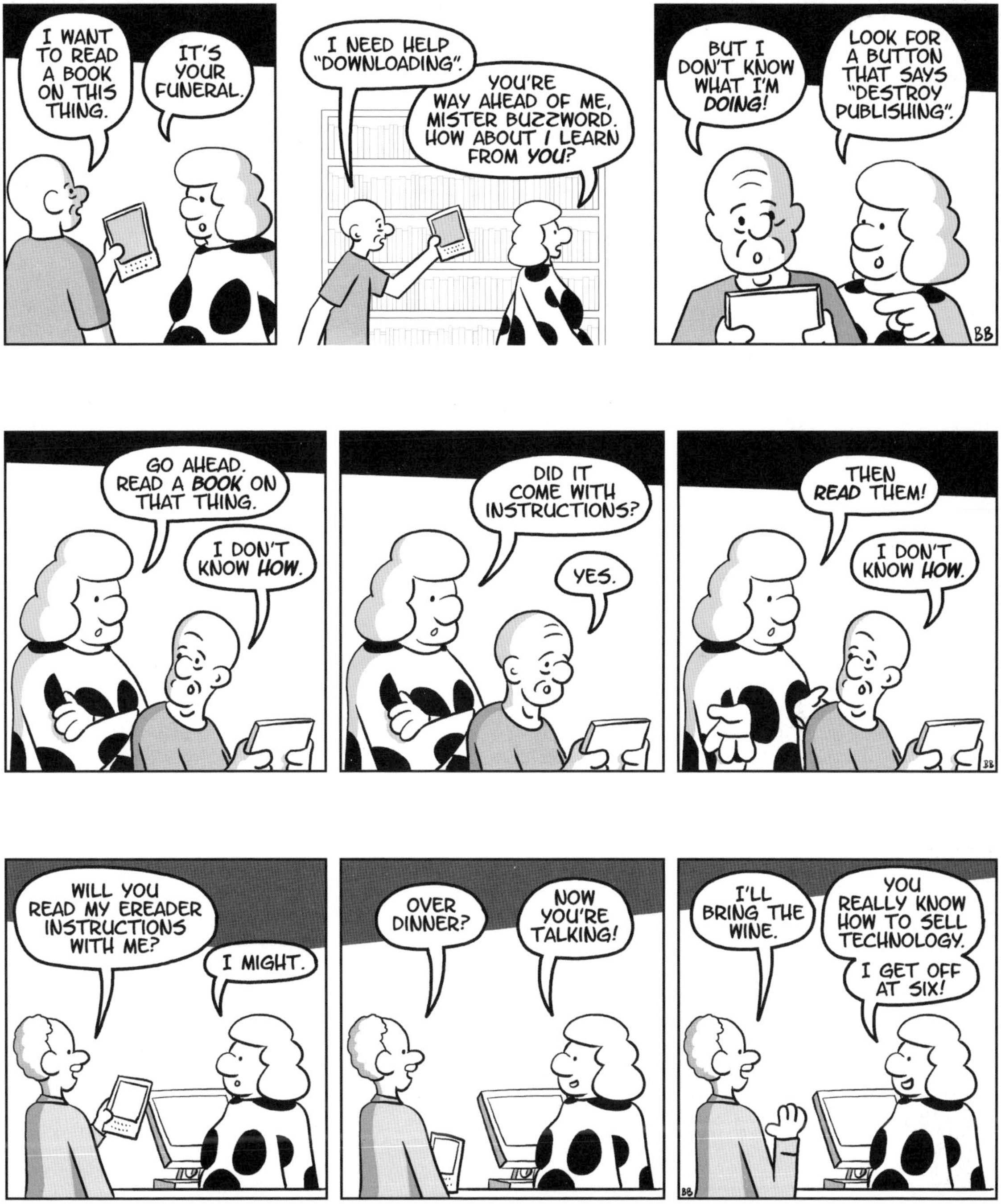
I WANT TO READ A BOOK ON THIS THING.
IT'S YOUR FUNERAL.
I NEED HELP "DOWNLOADING".
YOU'RE WAY AHEAD OF ME, MISTER BUZZWORD. HOW ABOUT *I* LEARN FROM *YOU*?
BUT I DON'T KNOW WHAT I'M *DOING*!
LOOK FOR A BUTTON THAT SAYS "DESTROY PUBLISHING".
BB
GO AHEAD. READ A *BOOK* ON THAT THING.
I DON'T KNOW *HOW*.
DID IT COME WITH INSTRUCTIONS?
YES.
THEN *READ* THEM!
I DON'T KNOW *HOW*.
BB
WILL YOU READ MY EREADER INSTRUCTIONS WITH ME?
I MIGHT.
OVER DINNER?
NOW YOU'RE TALKING!
I'LL BRING THE WINE.
YOU REALLY KNOW HOW TO SELL TECHNOLOGY.
I GET OFF AT SIX!
BB

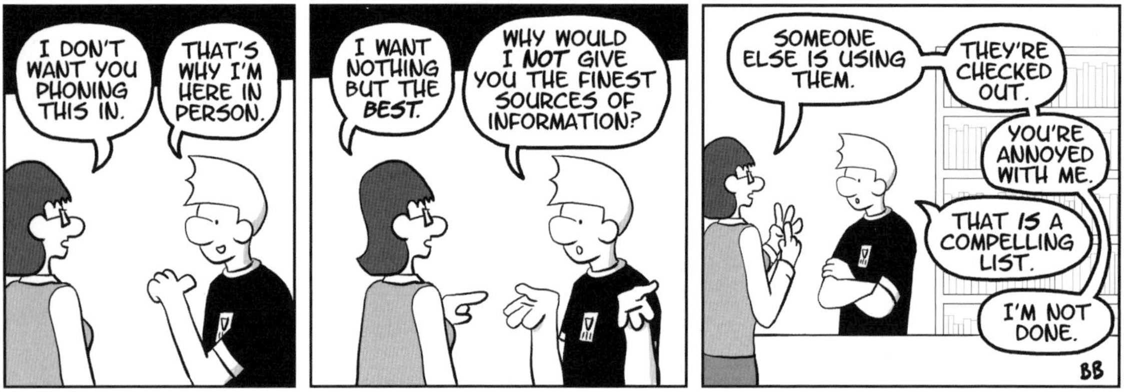
I DON'T WANT YOU PHONING THIS IN.
THAT'S WHY I'M HERE IN PERSON.
I WANT NOTHING BUT THE *BEST.*
WHY WOULD I *NOT* GIVE YOU THE FINEST SOURCES OF INFORMATION?
SOMEONE ELSE IS USING THEM.
THEY'RE CHECKED OUT.
YOU'RE ANNOYED WITH ME.
THAT *IS* A COMPELLING LIST.
I'M NOT DONE.
BB

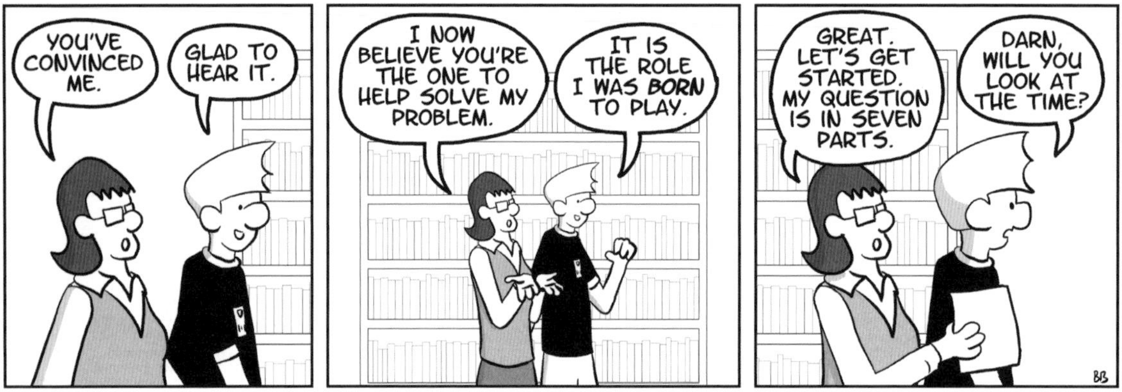
YOU'VE CONVINCED ME.
GLAD TO HEAR IT.
I NOW BELIEVE YOU'RE THE ONE TO HELP SOLVE MY PROBLEM.
IT IS THE ROLE I WAS *BORN* TO PLAY.
GREAT. LET'S GET STARTED. MY QUESTION IS IN SEVEN PARTS.
DARN, WILL YOU LOOK AT THE TIME?
BB

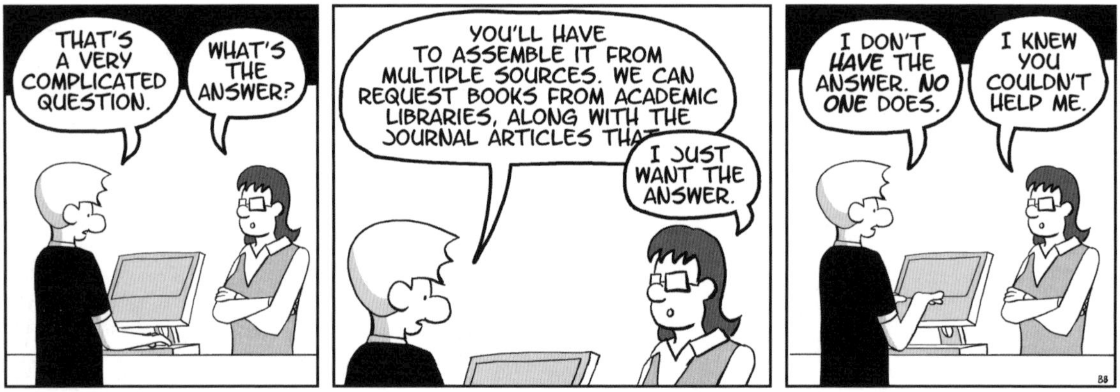
THAT'S A VERY COMPLICATED QUESTION.
WHAT'S THE ANSWER?
YOU'LL HAVE TO ASSEMBLE IT FROM MULTIPLE SOURCES. WE CAN REQUEST BOOKS FROM ACADEMIC LIBRARIES, ALONG WITH THE JOURNAL ARTICLES THAT
I JUST WANT THE ANSWER.
I DON'T *HAVE* THE ANSWER. *NO ONE* DOES.
I KNEW YOU COULDN'T HELP ME.
BB

Too Much Information

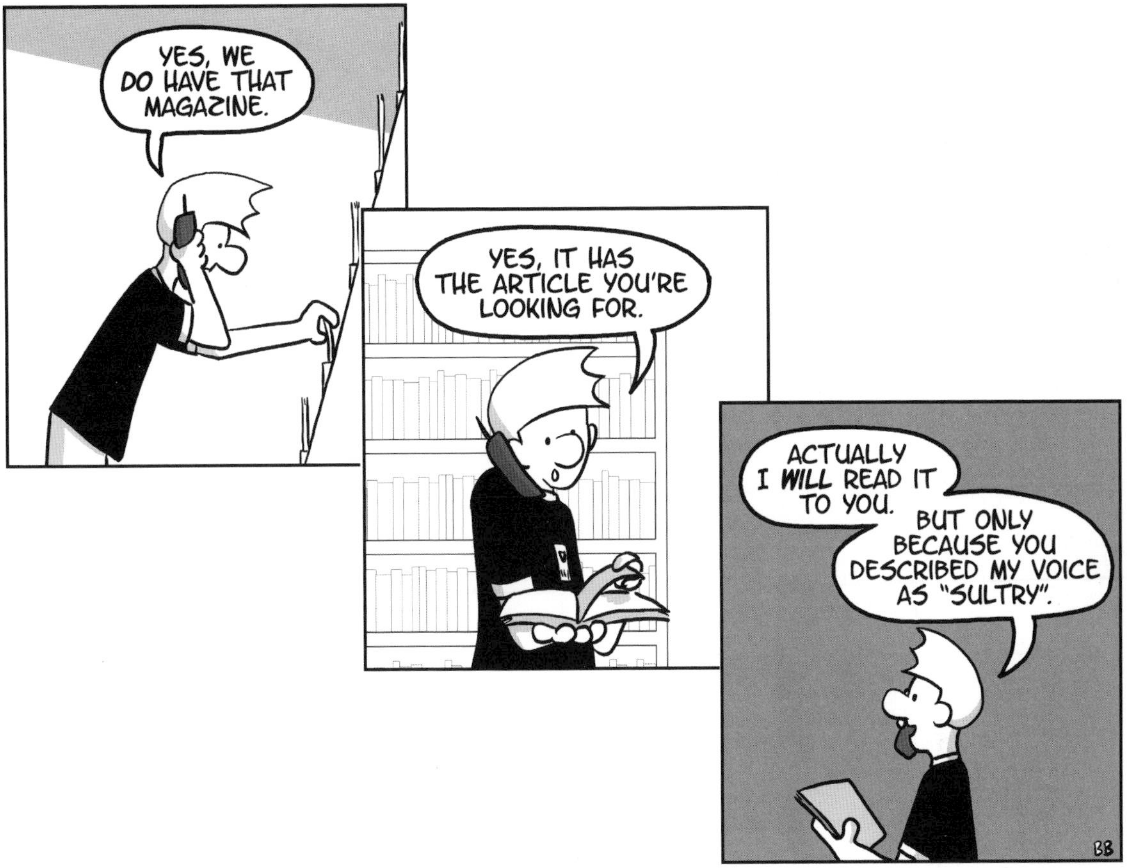

YES, WE DO HAVE THAT MAGAZINE.
YES, IT HAS THE ARTICLE YOU'RE LOOKING FOR.
ACTUALLY I WILL READ IT TO YOU.
BUT ONLY BECAUSE YOU DESCRIBED MY VOICE AS "SULTRY".
BB

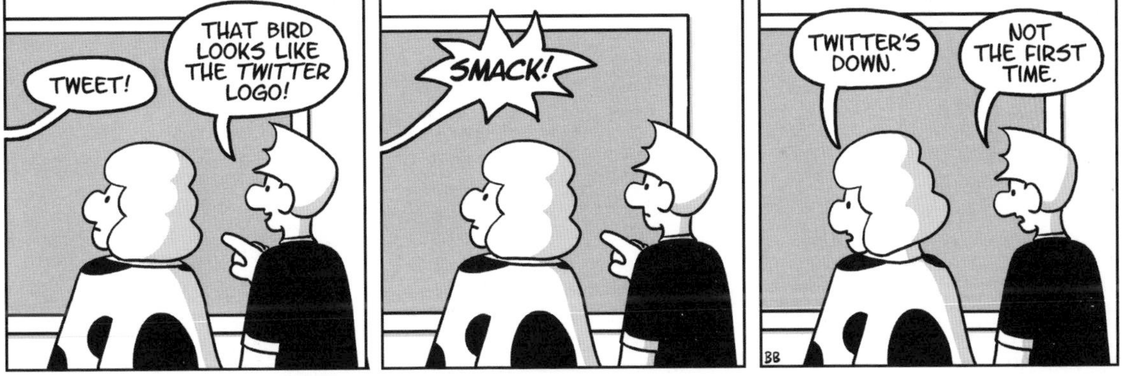

TWEET!
THAT BIRD LOOKS LIKE THE TWITTER LOGO!
SMACK!
TWITTER'S DOWN.
NOT THE FIRST TIME.
BB

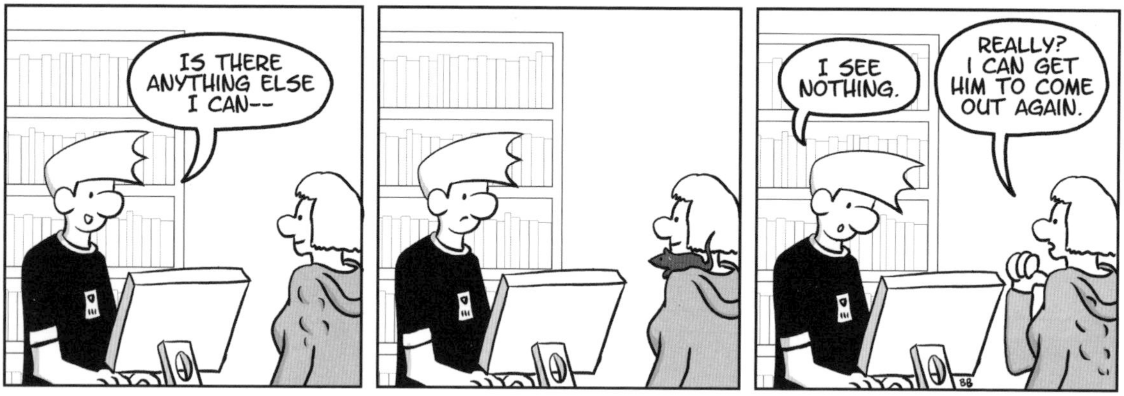
IS THERE ANYTHING ELSE I CAN--
I SEE NOTHING.
REALLY? I CAN GET HIM TO COME OUT AGAIN.
BB

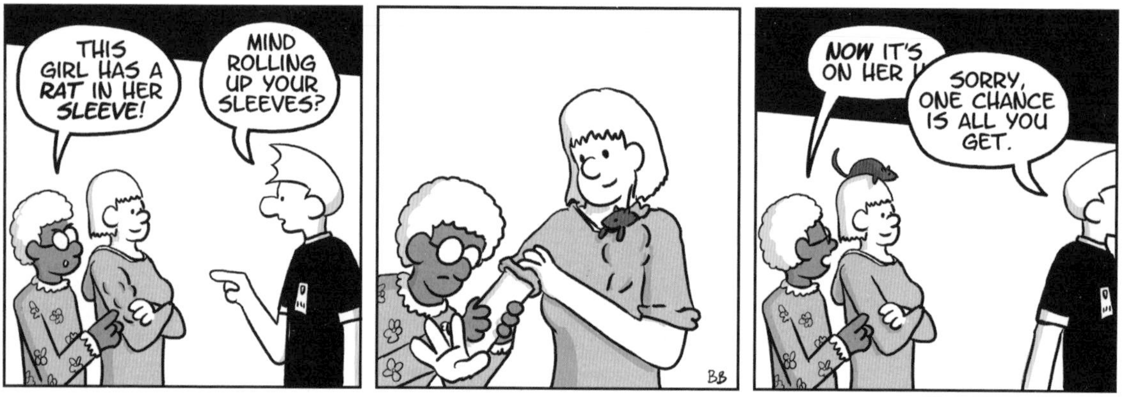
THIS GIRL HAS A **RAT** IN HER **SLEEVE**!
MIND ROLLING UP YOUR SLEEVES?
BB
NOW IT'S ON HER
SORRY, ONE CHANCE IS ALL YOU GET.

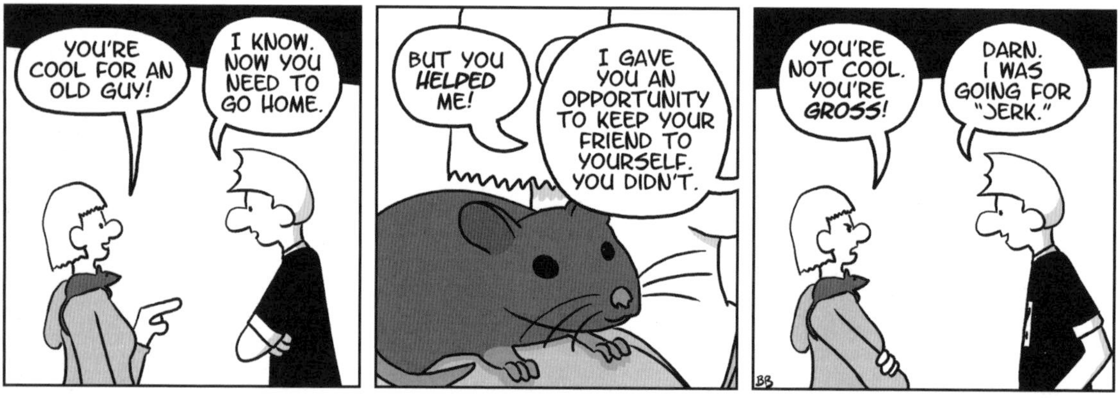
YOU'RE COOL FOR AN OLD GUY!
I KNOW. NOW YOU NEED TO GO HOME.
BUT YOU **HELPED** ME!
I GAVE YOU AN OPPORTUNITY TO KEEP YOUR FRIEND TO YOURSELF. YOU DIDN'T.
YOU'RE NOT COOL. YOU'RE **GROSS**!
DARN. I WAS GOING FOR "JERK."
BB

Too Much Information

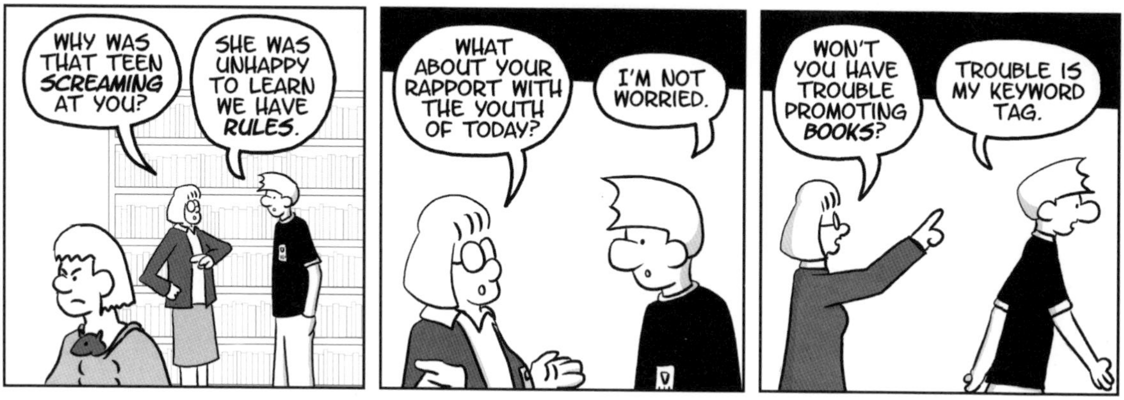

WHY WAS THAT TEEN *SCREAMING* AT YOU?
SHE WAS UNHAPPY TO LEARN WE HAVE *RULES*.
WHAT ABOUT YOUR RAPPORT WITH THE YOUTH OF TODAY?
I'M NOT WORRIED.
WON'T YOU HAVE TROUBLE PROMOTING *BOOKS*?
TROUBLE IS MY KEYWORD TAG.

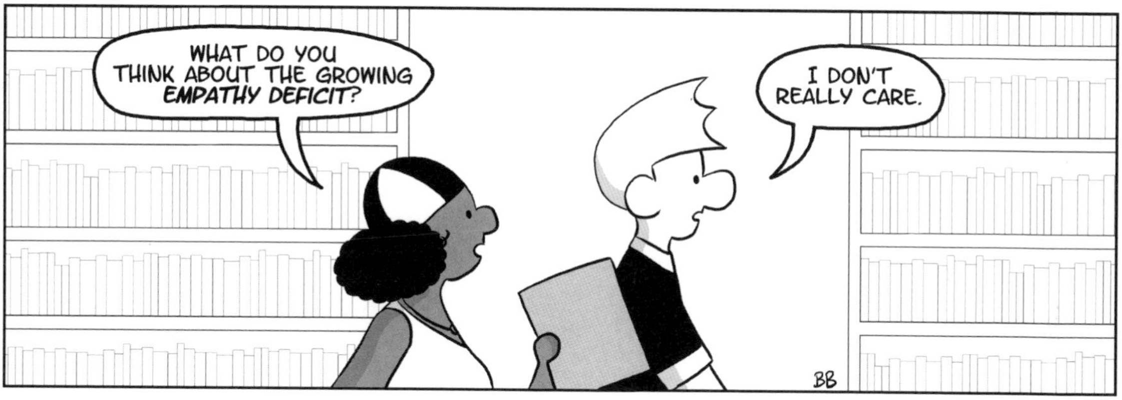

WHAT DO YOU THINK ABOUT THE GROWING *EMPATHY DEFICIT*?
I DON'T REALLY CARE.
BB

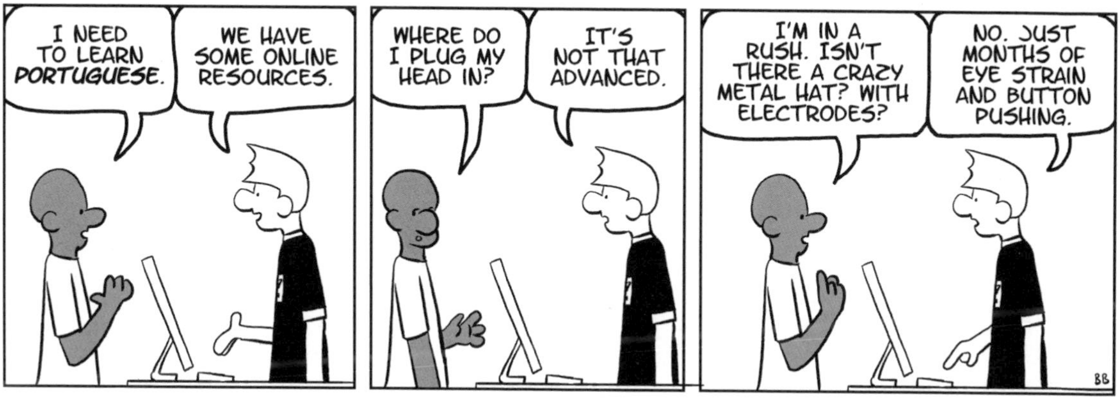

I NEED TO LEARN *PORTUGUESE*.
WE HAVE SOME ONLINE RESOURCES.
WHERE DO I PLUG MY HEAD IN?
IT'S NOT THAT ADVANCED.
I'M IN A RUSH. ISN'T THERE A CRAZY METAL HAT? WITH ELECTRODES?
NO. JUST MONTHS OF EYE STRAIN AND BUTTON PUSHING.
BB

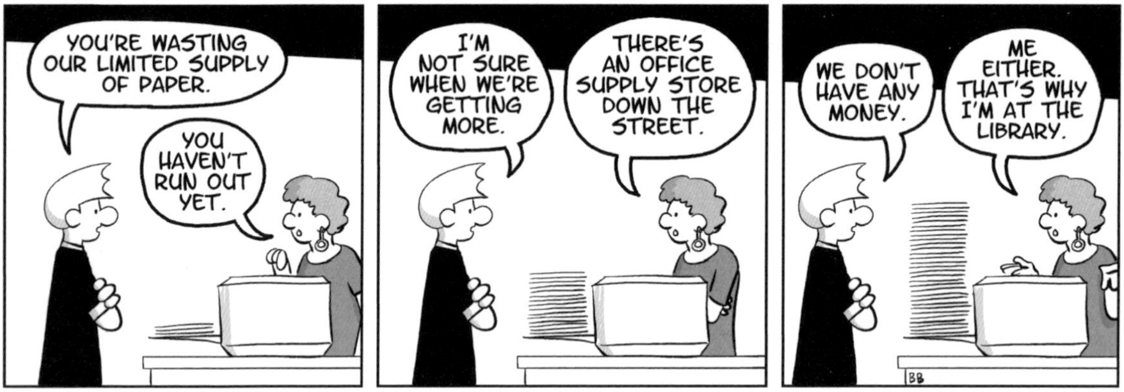
YOU'RE WASTING OUR LIMITED SUPPLY OF PAPER.
YOU HAVEN'T RUN OUT YET.
I'M NOT SURE WHEN WE'RE GETTING MORE.
THERE'S AN OFFICE SUPPLY STORE DOWN THE STREET.
WE DON'T HAVE ANY MONEY.
ME EITHER. THAT'S WHY I'M AT THE LIBRARY.
BB

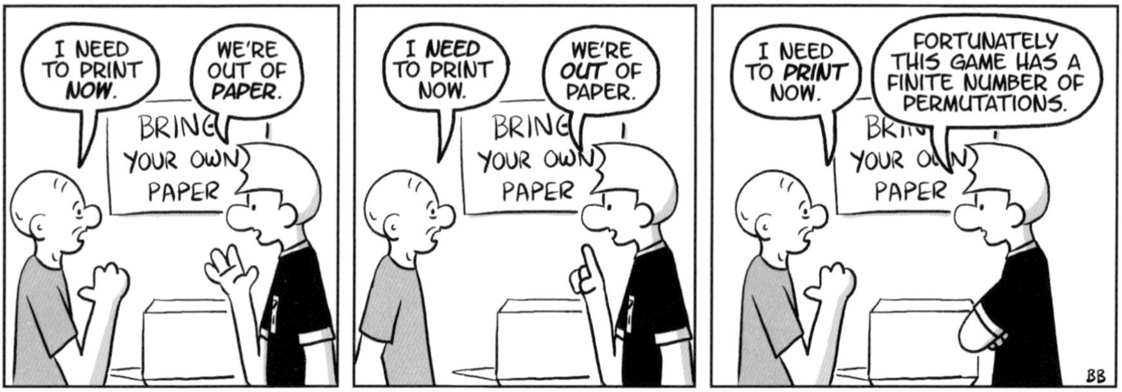
I NEED TO PRINT NOW.
WE'RE OUT OF PAPER.
BRING YOUR OWN PAPER
I NEED TO PRINT NOW.
WE'RE OUT OF PAPER.
BRING YOUR OWN PAPER
I NEED TO PRINT NOW.
FORTUNATELY THIS GAME HAS A FINITE NUMBER OF PERMUTATIONS.
PAPER
BB

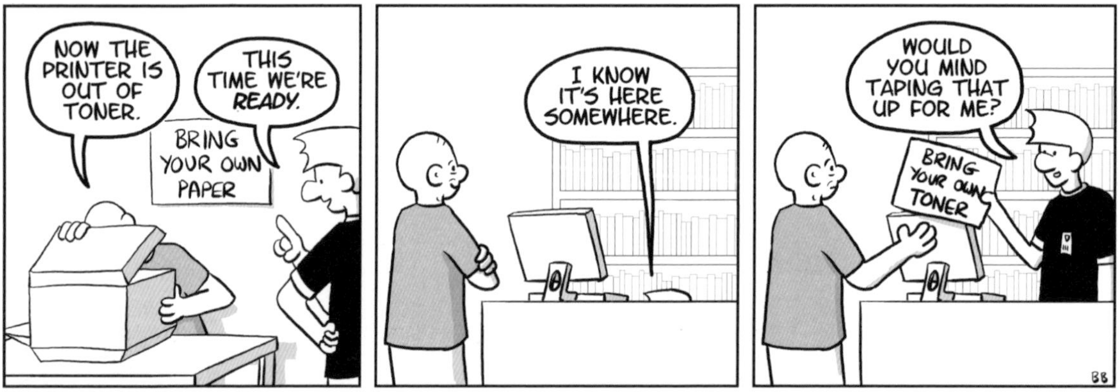
NOW THE PRINTER IS OUT OF TONER.
THIS TIME WE'RE READY.
BRING YOUR OWN PAPER
I KNOW IT'S HERE SOMEWHERE.
WOULD YOU MIND TAPING THAT UP FOR ME?
BRING YOUR OWN TONER
BB

Too Much Information

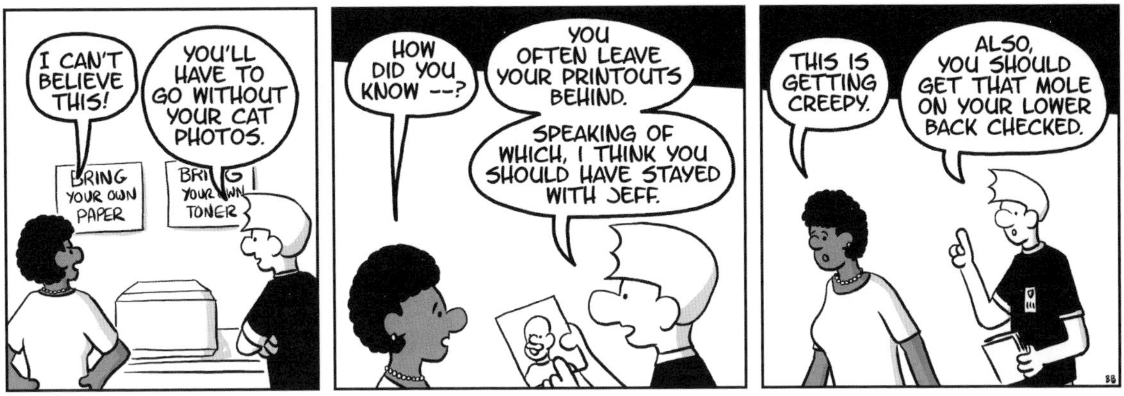
I CAN'T BELIEVE THIS!
YOU'LL HAVE TO GO WITHOUT YOUR CAT PHOTOS.
BRING YOUR OWN PAPER
BRING YOUR OWN TONER
HOW DID YOU KNOW --?
YOU OFTEN LEAVE YOUR PRINTOUTS BEHIND.
SPEAKING OF WHICH, I THINK YOU SHOULD HAVE STAYED WITH JEFF.
THIS IS GETTING CREEPY.
ALSO, YOU SHOULD GET THAT MOLE ON YOUR LOWER BACK CHECKED.
BB

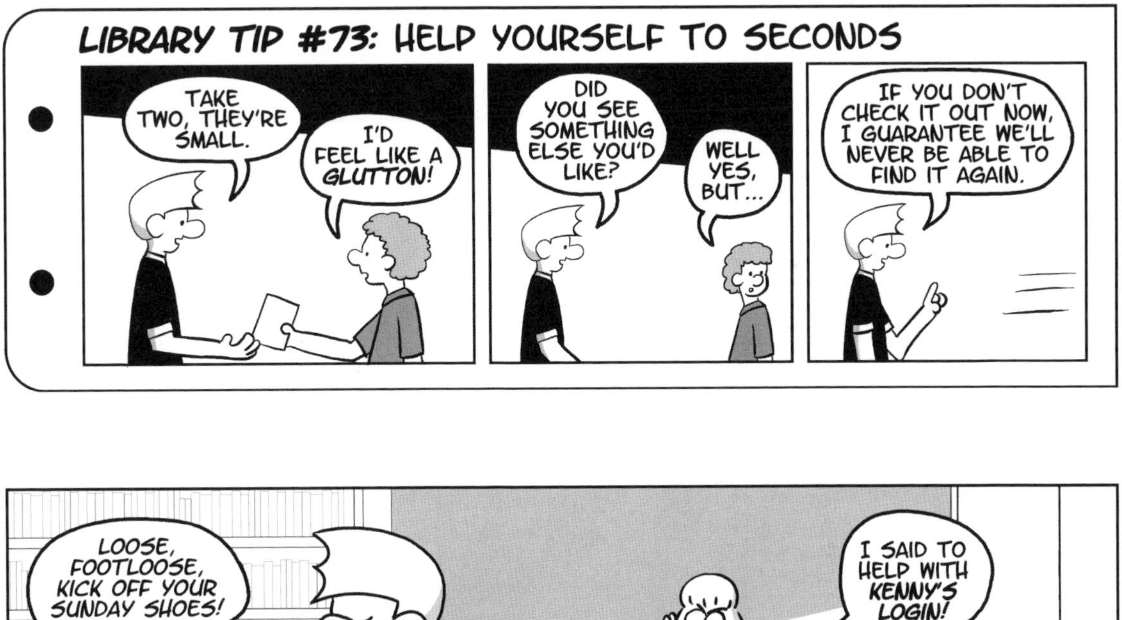
LIBRARY TIP #73: HELP YOURSELF TO SECONDS
TAKE TWO, THEY'RE SMALL.
I'D FEEL LIKE A GLUTTON!
DID YOU SEE SOMETHING ELSE YOU'D LIKE?
WELL YES, BUT...
IF YOU DON'T CHECK IT OUT NOW, I GUARANTEE WE'LL NEVER BE ABLE TO FIND IT AGAIN.

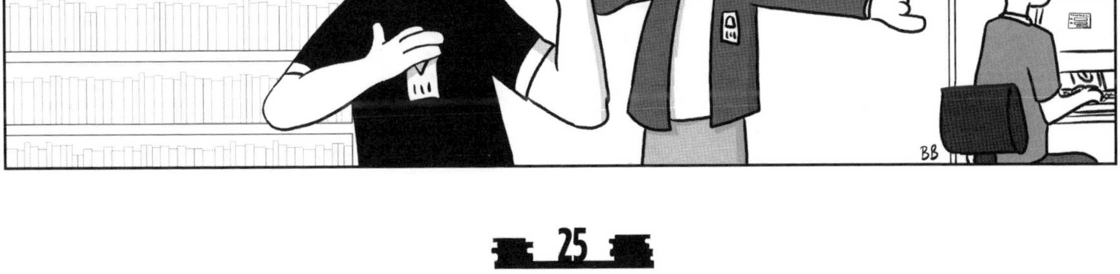
LOOSE, FOOTLOOSE, KICK OFF YOUR SUNDAY SHOES!
I SAID TO HELP WITH KENNY'S LOGIN!
BB

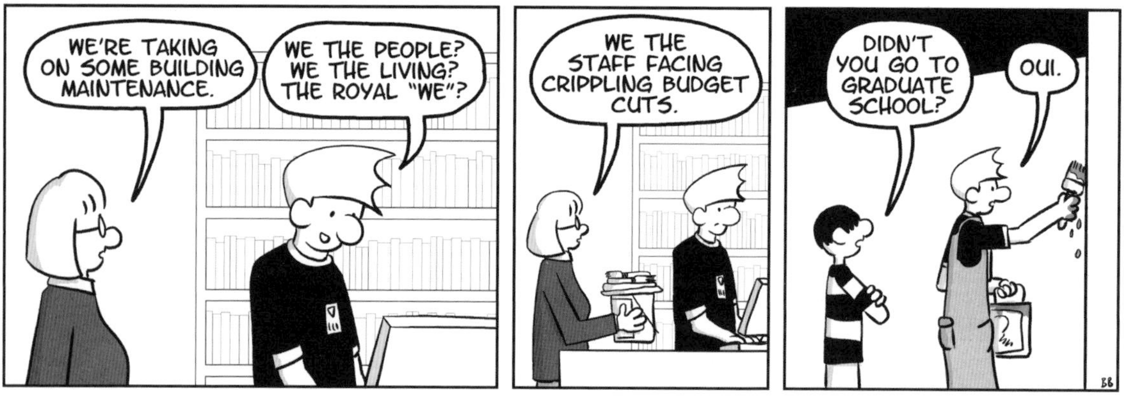
WE'RE TAKING ON SOME BUILDING MAINTENANCE.
WE THE PEOPLE? WE THE LIVING? THE ROYAL "WE"?
WE THE STAFF FACING CRIPPLING BUDGET CUTS.
DIDN'T YOU GO TO GRADUATE SCHOOL?
OUI.
BB

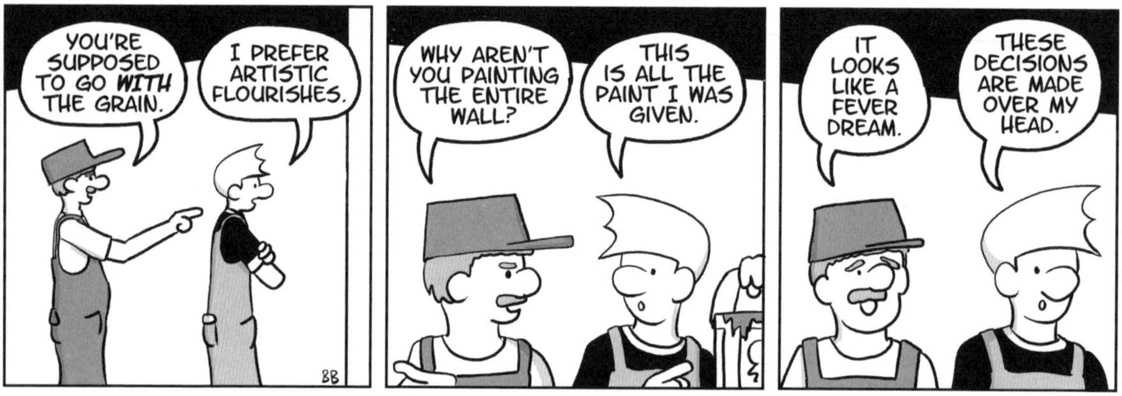
YOU'RE SUPPOSED TO GO WITH THE GRAIN.
I PREFER ARTISTIC FLOURISHES.
BB
WHY AREN'T YOU PAINTING THE ENTIRE WALL?
THIS IS ALL THE PAINT I WAS GIVEN.
IT LOOKS LIKE A FEVER DREAM.
THESE DECISIONS ARE MADE OVER MY HEAD.

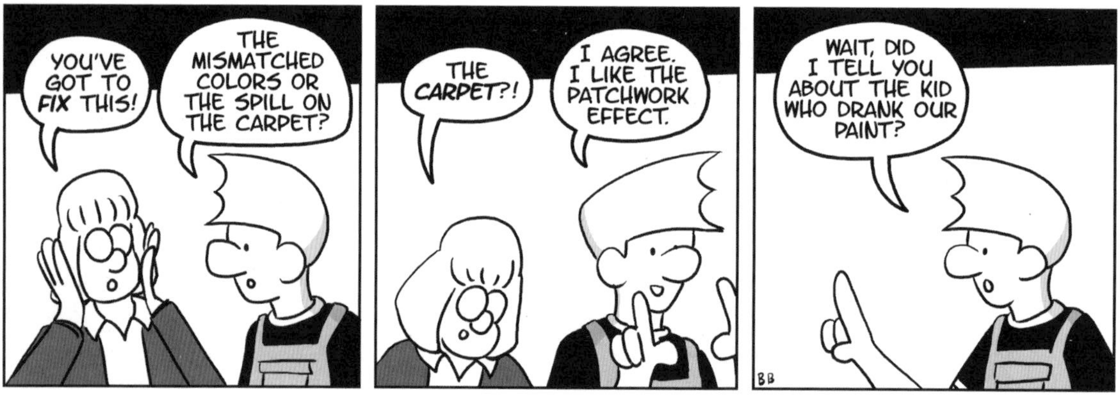
YOU'VE GOT TO FIX THIS!
THE MISMATCHED COLORS OR THE SPILL ON THE CARPET?
THE CARPET?!
I AGREE. I LIKE THE PATCHWORK EFFECT.
WAIT, DID I TELL YOU ABOUT THE KID WHO DRANK OUR PAINT?
BB

Too Much Information

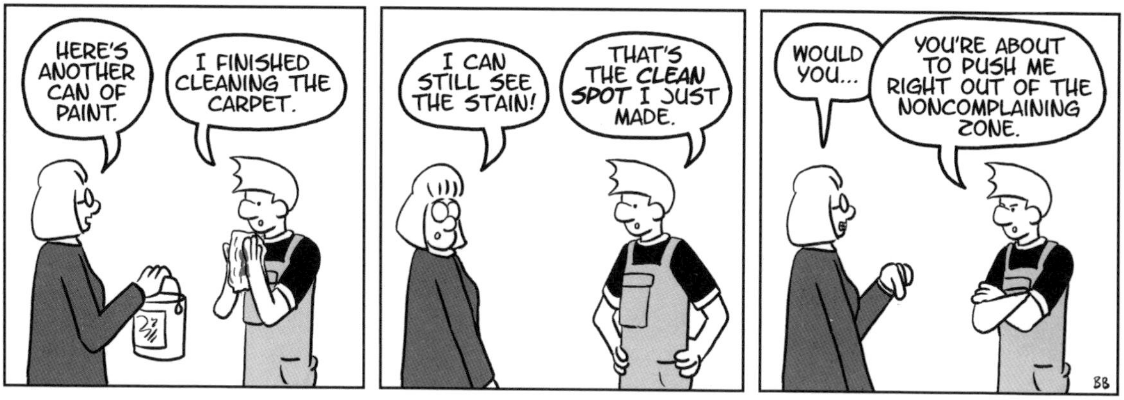
HERE'S ANOTHER CAN OF PAINT.
I FINISHED CLEANING THE CARPET.
I CAN STILL SEE THE STAIN!
THAT'S THE *CLEAN SPOT* I JUST MADE.
WOULD YOU...
YOU'RE ABOUT TO PUSH ME RIGHT OUT OF THE NONCOMPLAINING ZONE.
BB

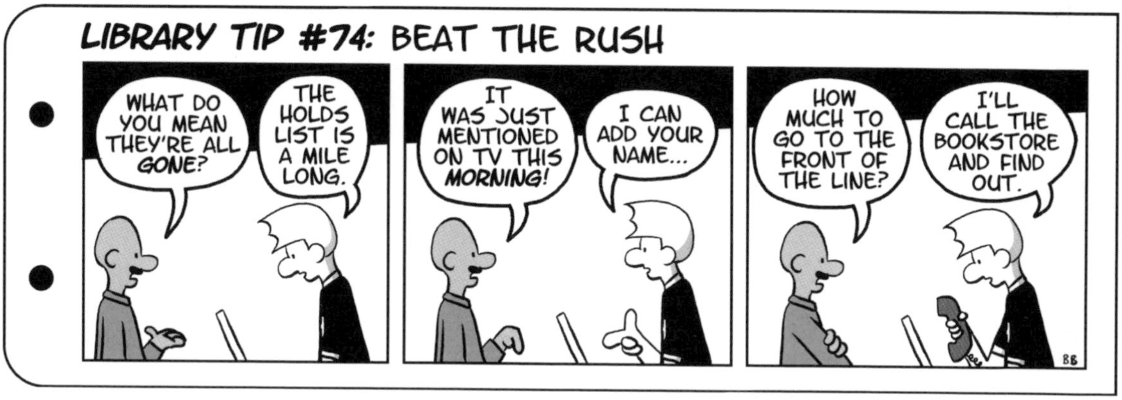
LIBRARY TIP #74: BEAT THE RUSH
WHAT DO YOU MEAN THEY'RE ALL *GONE*?
THE HOLDS LIST IS A MILE LONG.
IT WAS JUST MENTIONED ON TV THIS *MORNING*!
I CAN ADD YOUR NAME...
HOW MUCH TO GO TO THE FRONT OF THE LINE?
I'LL CALL THE BOOKSTORE AND FIND OUT.
BB

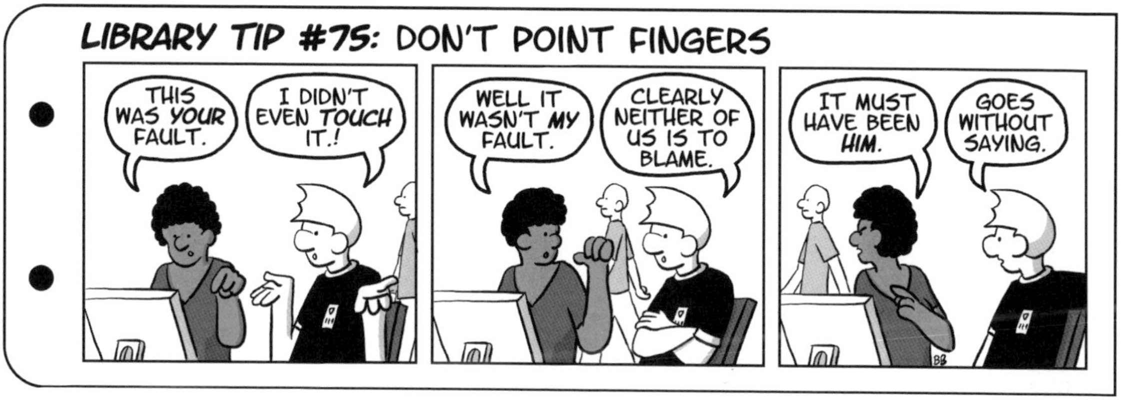
LIBRARY TIP #75: DON'T POINT FINGERS
THIS WAS *YOUR* FAULT.
I DIDN'T EVEN *TOUCH* IT.!
WELL IT WASN'T *MY* FAULT.
CLEARLY NEITHER OF US IS TO BLAME.
IT MUST HAVE BEEN *HIM*.
GOES WITHOUT SAYING.
BB

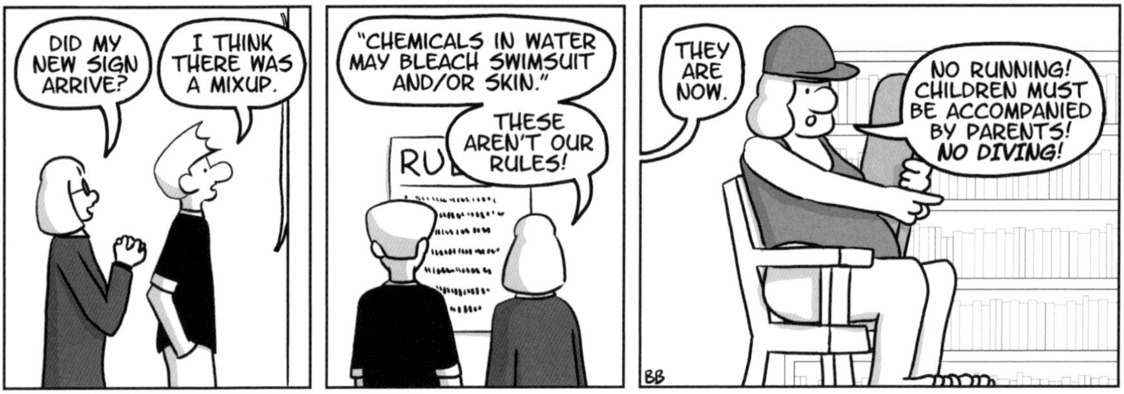
DID MY NEW SIGN ARRIVE?
I THINK THERE WAS A MIXUP.
"CHEMICALS IN WATER MAY BLEACH SWIMSUIT AND/OR SKIN."
RU
THESE AREN'T OUR RULES!
THEY ARE NOW.
NO RUNNING! CHILDREN MUST BE ACCOMPANIED BY PARENTS! NO DIVING!
BB

LIBRARY TIP #76: STAY IN THE SHALLOW END UNTIL YOU PASS THE TEST

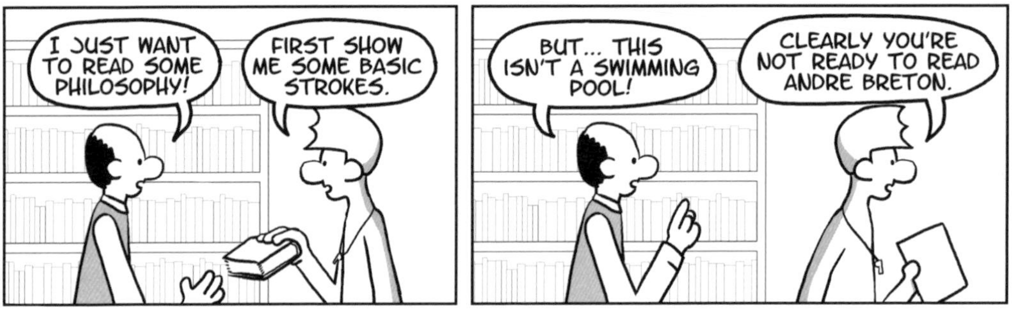
I JUST WANT TO READ SOME PHILOSOPHY!
FIRST SHOW ME SOME BASIC STROKES.
BUT... THIS ISN'T A SWIMMING POOL!
CLEARLY YOU'RE NOT READY TO READ ANDRE BRETON.

LIBRARY TIP #77: SHOWER BEFORE ENTERING

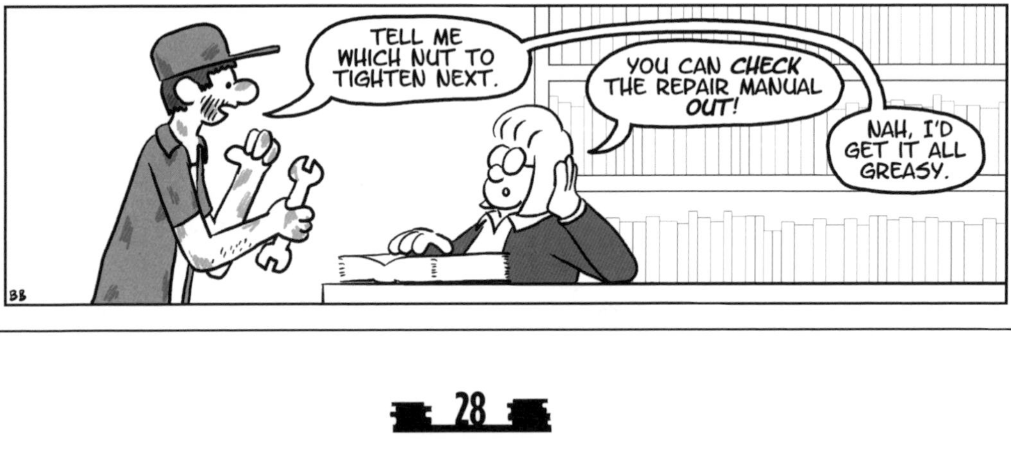
TELL ME WHICH NUT TO TIGHTEN NEXT.
YOU CAN CHECK THE REPAIR MANUAL OUT!
NAH, I'D GET IT ALL GREASY.
BB

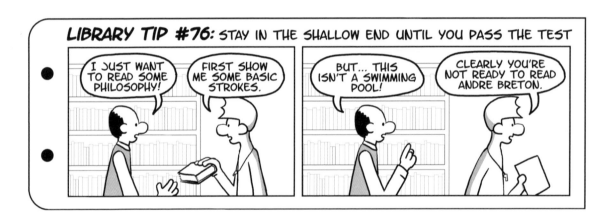

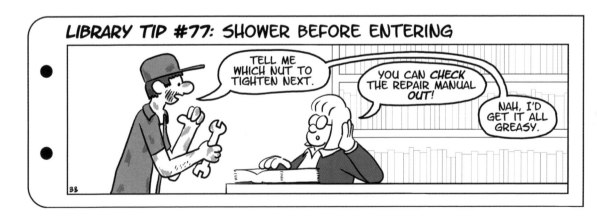

Too Much Information

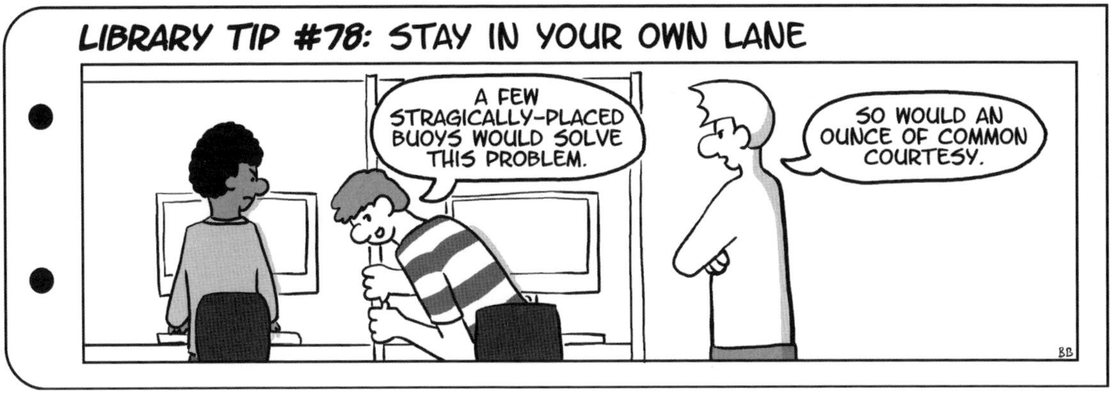
LIBRARY TIP #78: STAY IN YOUR OWN LANE
A FEW STRAGICALLY-PLACED BUOYS WOULD SOLVE THIS PROBLEM.
SO WOULD AN OUNCE OF COMMON COURTESY.
BB

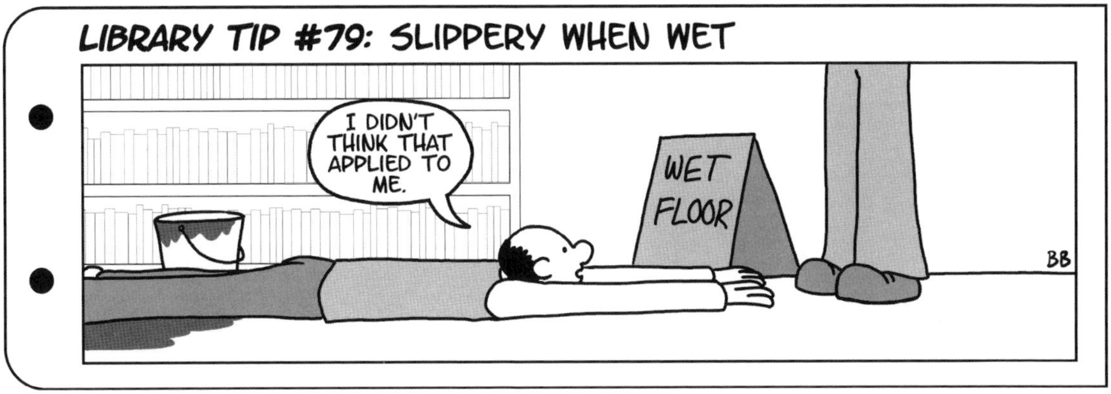
LIBRARY TIP #79: SLIPPERY WHEN WET
I DIDN'T THINK THAT APPLIED TO ME.
WET FLOOR
BB

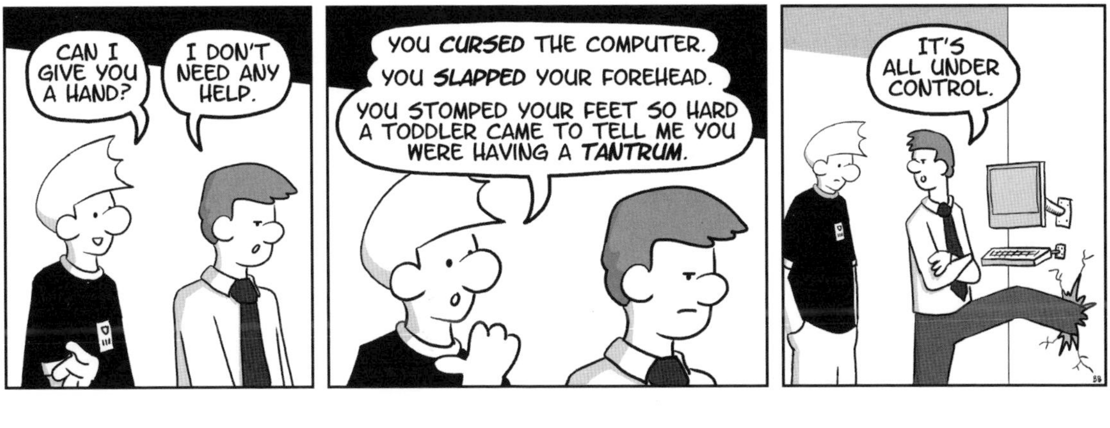
CAN I GIVE YOU A HAND?
I DON'T NEED ANY HELP.
YOU CURSED THE COMPUTER.
YOU SLAPPED YOUR FOREHEAD.
YOU STOMPED YOUR FEET SO HARD A TODDLER CAME TO TELL ME YOU WERE HAVING A TANTRUM.
IT'S ALL UNDER CONTROL.

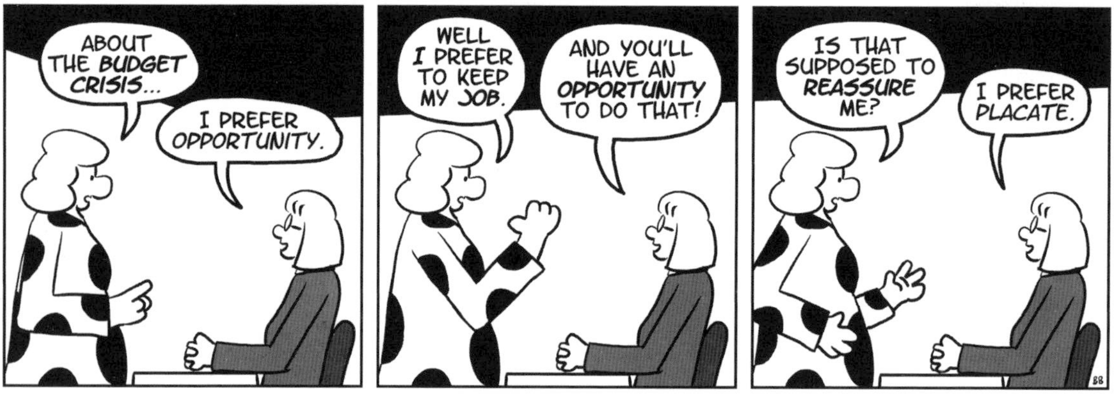
ABOUT THE BUDGET CRISIS...
I PREFER OPPORTUNITY.
WELL I PREFER TO KEEP MY JOB.
AND YOU'LL HAVE AN OPPORTUNITY TO DO THAT!
IS THAT SUPPOSED TO REASSURE ME?
I PREFER PLACATE.
BB

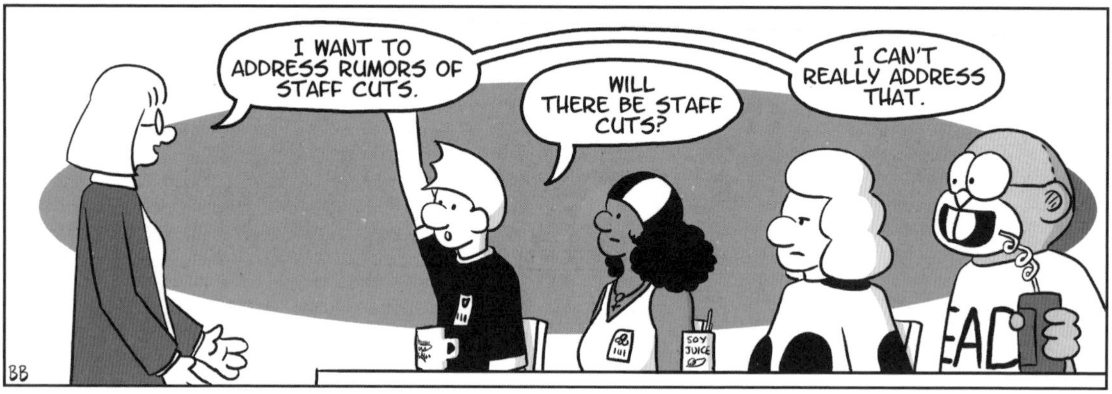
I WANT TO ADDRESS RUMORS OF STAFF CUTS.
WILL THERE BE STAFF CUTS?
I CAN'T REALLY ADDRESS THAT.
SOY JUICE
BB

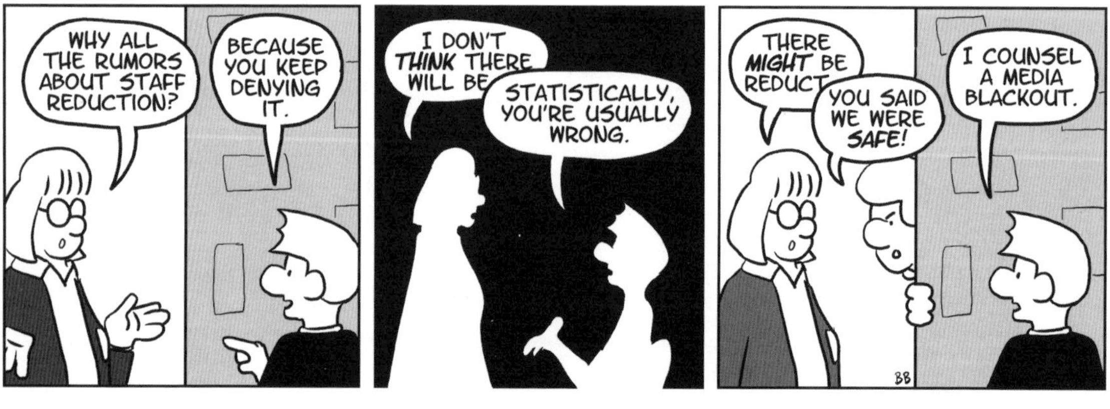
WHY ALL THE RUMORS ABOUT STAFF REDUCTION?
BECAUSE YOU KEEP DENYING IT.
I DON'T THINK THERE WILL BE
STATISTICALLY, YOU'RE USUALLY WRONG.
THERE MIGHT BE REDUCT
YOU SAID WE WERE SAFE!
I COUNSEL A MEDIA BLACKOUT.
BB

Too Much Information

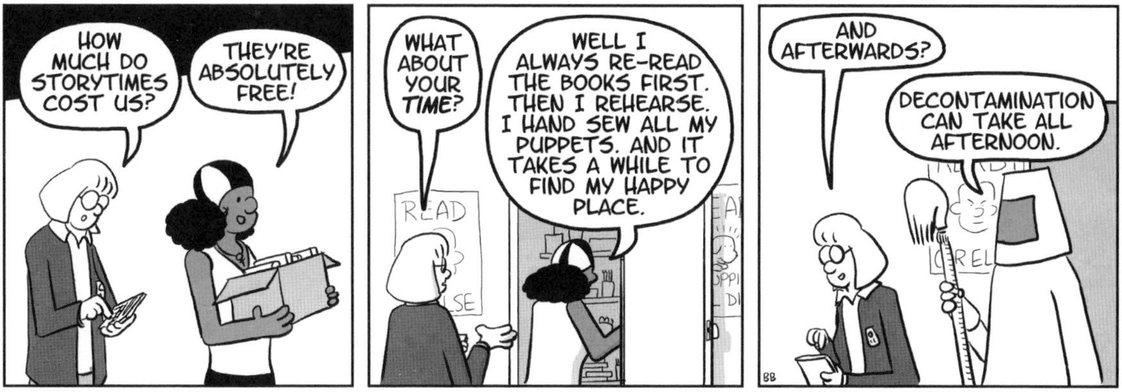
HOW MUCH DO STORYTIMES COST US?
THEY'RE ABSOLUTELY FREE!
WHAT ABOUT YOUR *TIME*?
WELL I ALWAYS RE-READ THE BOOKS FIRST. THEN I REHEARSE. I HAND SEW ALL MY PUPPETS. AND IT TAKES A WHILE TO FIND MY HAPPY PLACE.
READ
AND AFTERWARDS?
DECONTAMINATION CAN TAKE ALL AFTERNOON.
BB

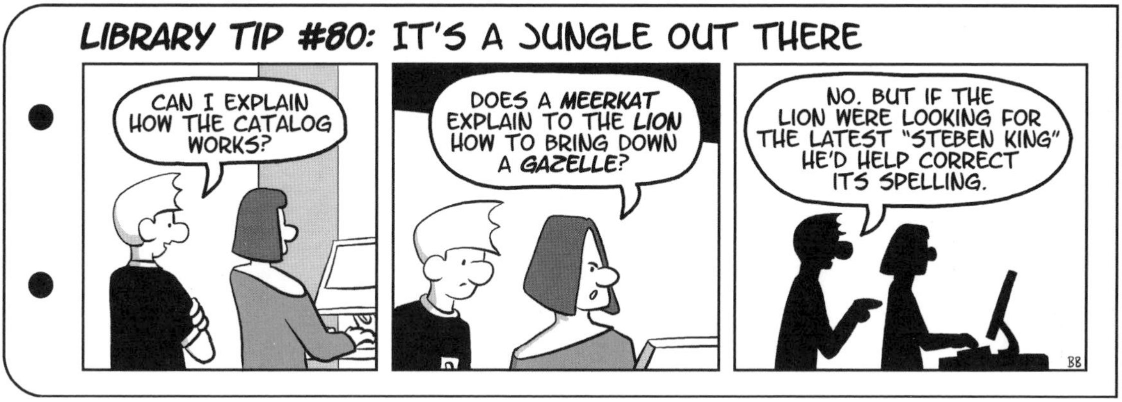
LIBRARY TIP #80: IT'S A JUNGLE OUT THERE
CAN I EXPLAIN HOW THE CATALOG WORKS?
DOES A ***MEERKAT*** EXPLAIN TO THE ***LION*** HOW TO BRING DOWN A ***GAZELLE***?
NO. BUT IF THE LION WERE LOOKING FOR THE LATEST "STEBEN KING" HE'D HELP CORRECT ITS SPELLING.
BB

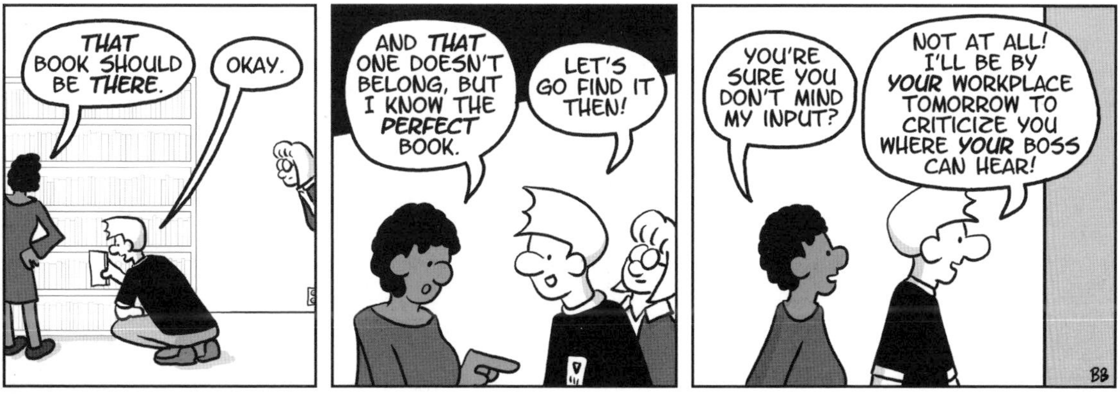
THAT BOOK SHOULD BE ***THERE***.
OKAY.
AND ***THAT*** ONE DOESN'T BELONG, BUT I KNOW THE ***PERFECT*** BOOK.
LET'S GO FIND IT THEN!
YOU'RE SURE YOU DON'T MIND MY INPUT?
NOT AT ALL! I'LL BE BY ***YOUR*** WORKPLACE TOMORROW TO CRITICIZE YOU WHERE ***YOUR*** BOSS CAN HEAR!
BB

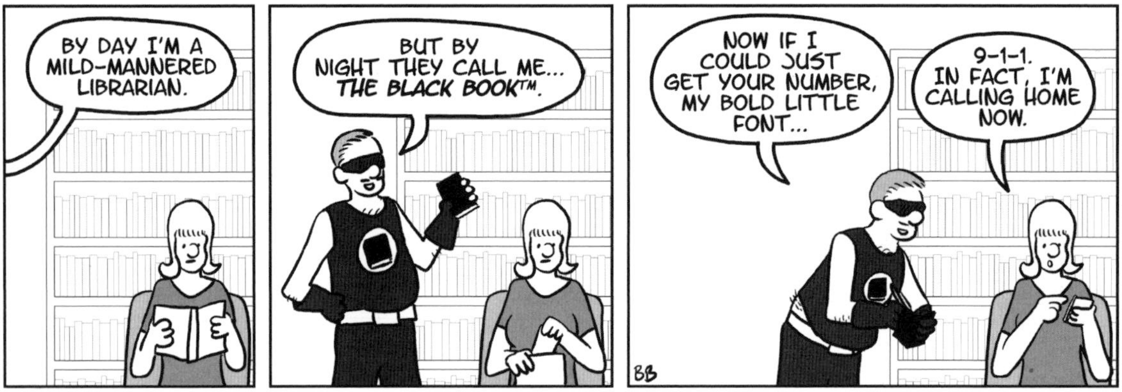
BY DAY I'M A MILD-MANNERED LIBRARIAN.
BUT BY NIGHT THEY CALL ME... *THE BLACK BOOK*™.
NOW IF I COULD JUST GET YOUR NUMBER, MY BOLD LITTLE FONT...
9-1-1. IN FACT, I'M CALLING HOME NOW.
BB

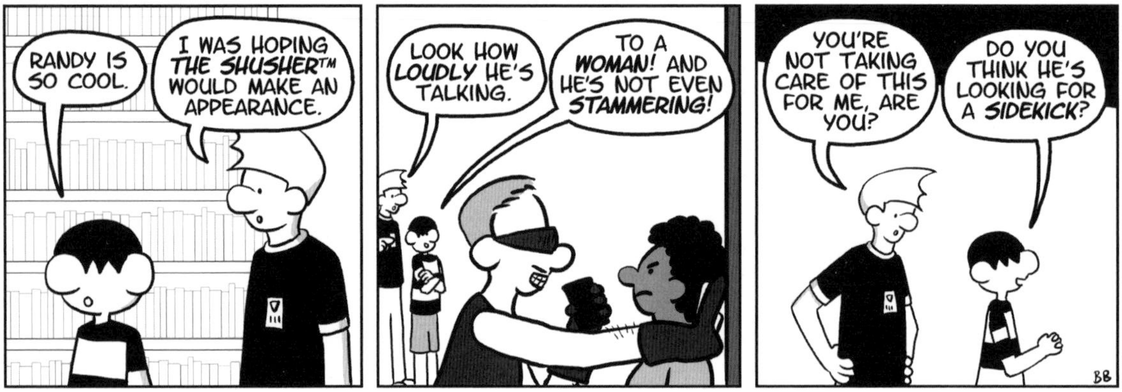
RANDY IS SO COOL.
I WAS HOPING *THE SHUSHER*™ WOULD MAKE AN APPEARANCE.
LOOK HOW *LOUDLY* HE'S TALKING.
TO A *WOMAN!* AND HE'S NOT EVEN *STAMMERING!*
YOU'RE NOT TAKING CARE OF THIS FOR ME, ARE YOU?
DO YOU THINK HE'S LOOKING FOR A *SIDEKICK?*
BB

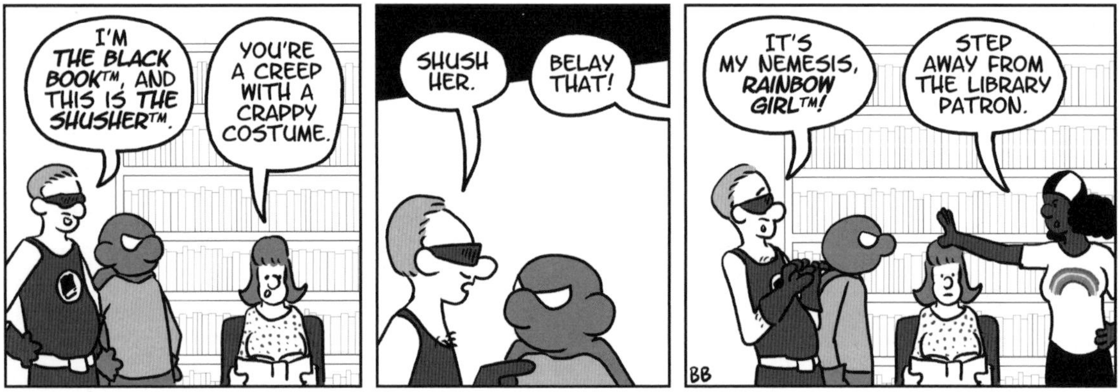
I'M *THE BLACK BOOK*™, AND THIS IS *THE SHUSHER*™.
YOU'RE A CREEP WITH A CRAPPY COSTUME.
SHUSH HER.
BELAY THAT!
IT'S MY NEMESIS, *RAINBOW GIRL*™!
STEP AWAY FROM THE LIBRARY PATRON.
BB

Too Much Information

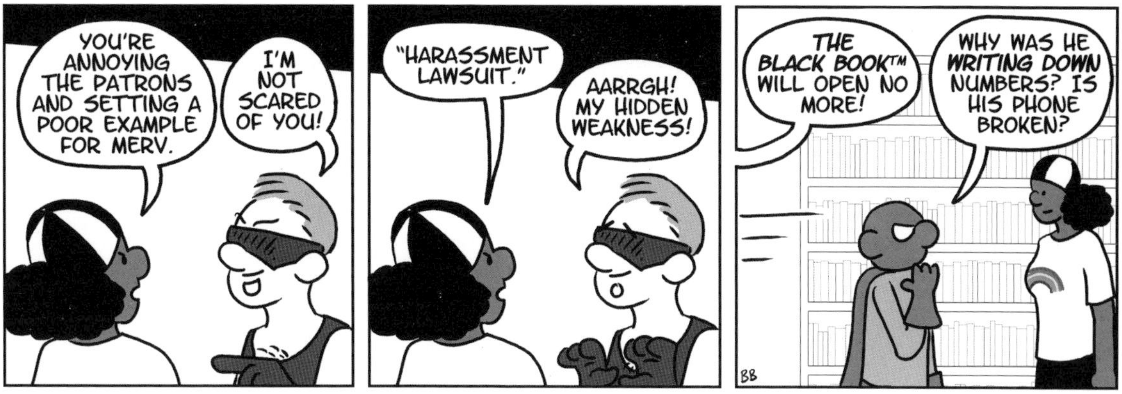

YOU'RE ANNOYING THE PATRONS AND SETTING A POOR EXAMPLE FOR MERV.
I'M NOT SCARED OF YOU!
"HARASSMENT LAWSUIT."
AARRGH! MY HIDDEN WEAKNESS!
THE BLACK BOOK™ WILL OPEN NO MORE!
WHY WAS HE WRITING DOWN NUMBERS? IS HIS PHONE BROKEN?
BB

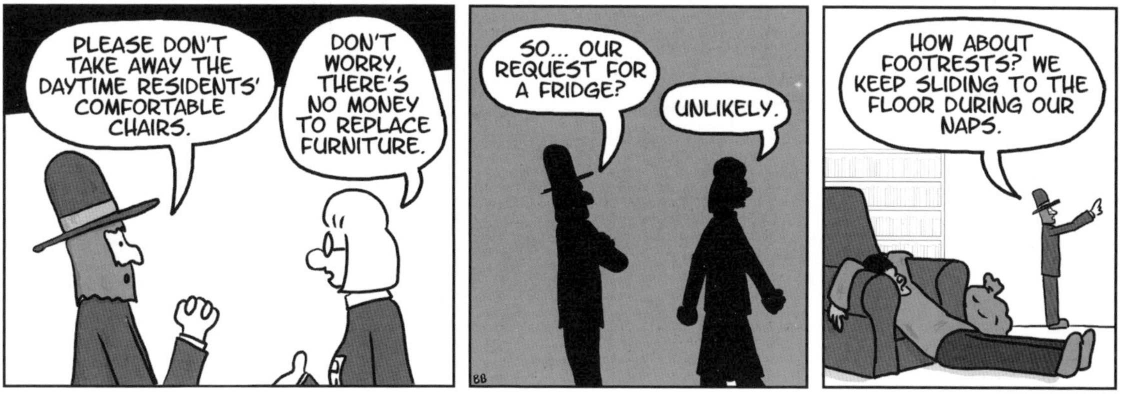

PLEASE DON'T TAKE AWAY THE DAYTIME RESIDENTS' COMFORTABLE CHAIRS.
DON'T WORRY, THERE'S NO MONEY TO REPLACE FURNITURE.
SO... OUR REQUEST FOR A FRIDGE?
UNLIKELY.
BB
HOW ABOUT FOOTRESTS? WE KEEP SLIDING TO THE FLOOR DURING OUR NAPS.

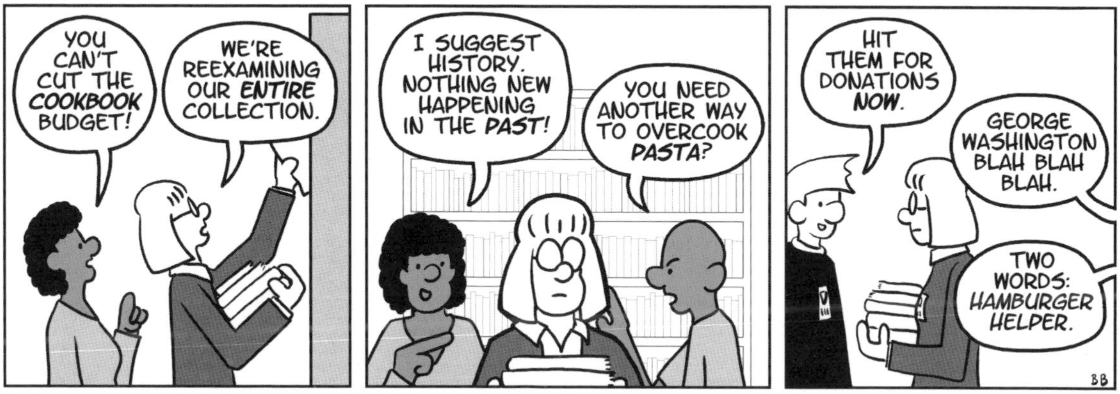

YOU CAN'T CUT THE COOKBOOK BUDGET!
WE'RE REEXAMINING OUR ENTIRE COLLECTION.
I SUGGEST HISTORY. NOTHING NEW HAPPENING IN THE PAST!
YOU NEED ANOTHER WAY TO OVERCOOK PASTA?
HIT THEM FOR DONATIONS NOW.
GEORGE WASHINGTON BLAH BLAH BLAH.
TWO WORDS: HAMBURGER HELPER.
BB

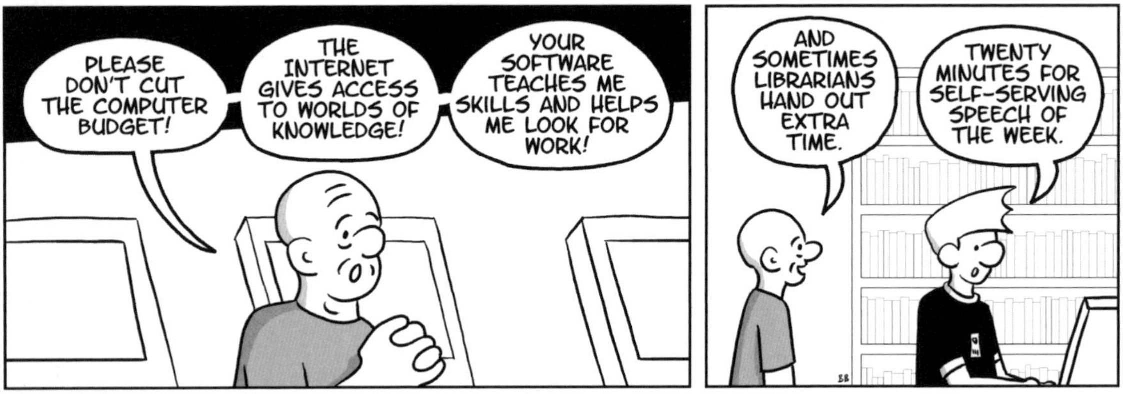
PLEASE DON'T CUT THE COMPUTER BUDGET!
THE INTERNET GIVES ACCESS TO WORLDS OF KNOWLEDGE!
YOUR SOFTWARE TEACHES ME SKILLS AND HELPS ME LOOK FOR WORK!
AND SOMETIMES LIBRARIANS HAND OUT EXTRA TIME.
TWENTY MINUTES FOR SELF-SERVING SPEECH OF THE WEEK.
BB

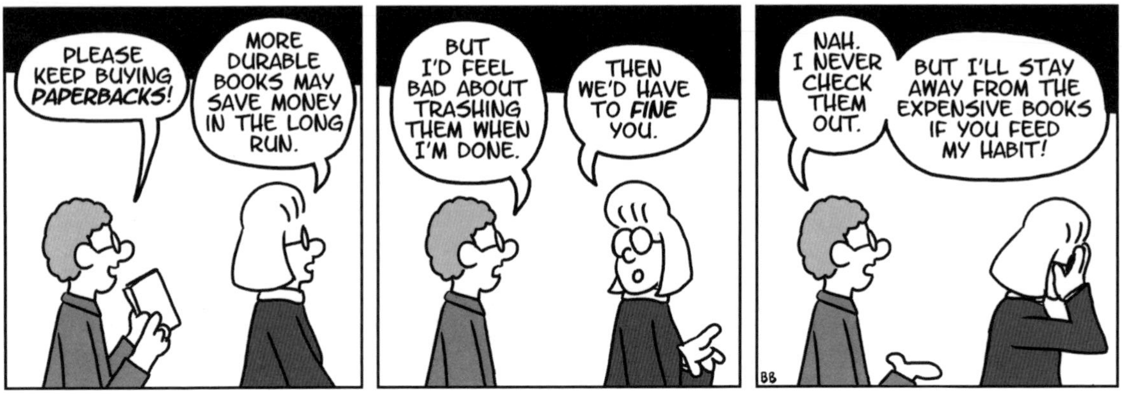
PLEASE KEEP BUYING ***PAPERBACKS***!
MORE DURABLE BOOKS MAY SAVE MONEY IN THE LONG RUN.
BUT I'D FEEL BAD ABOUT TRASHING THEM WHEN I'M DONE.
THEN WE'D HAVE TO ***FINE*** YOU.
NAH. I NEVER CHECK THEM OUT.
BUT I'LL STAY AWAY FROM THE EXPENSIVE BOOKS IF YOU FEED MY HABIT!
BB

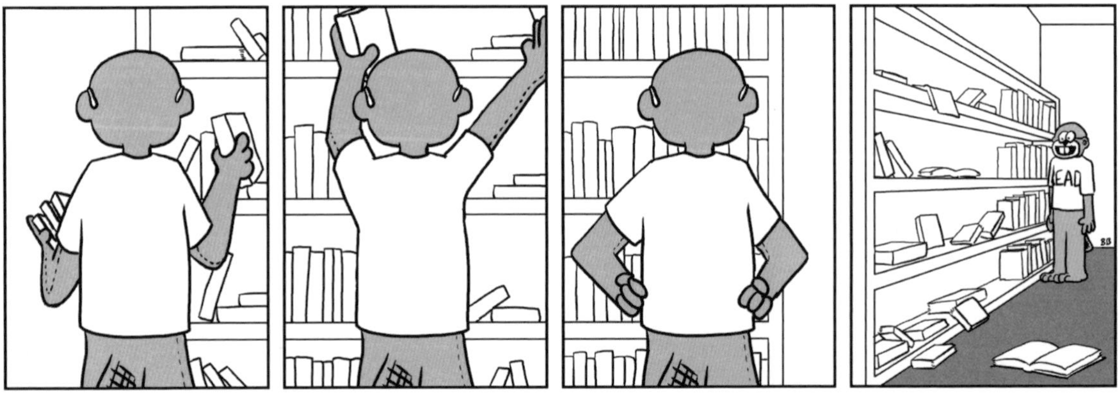
BB

Too Much Information

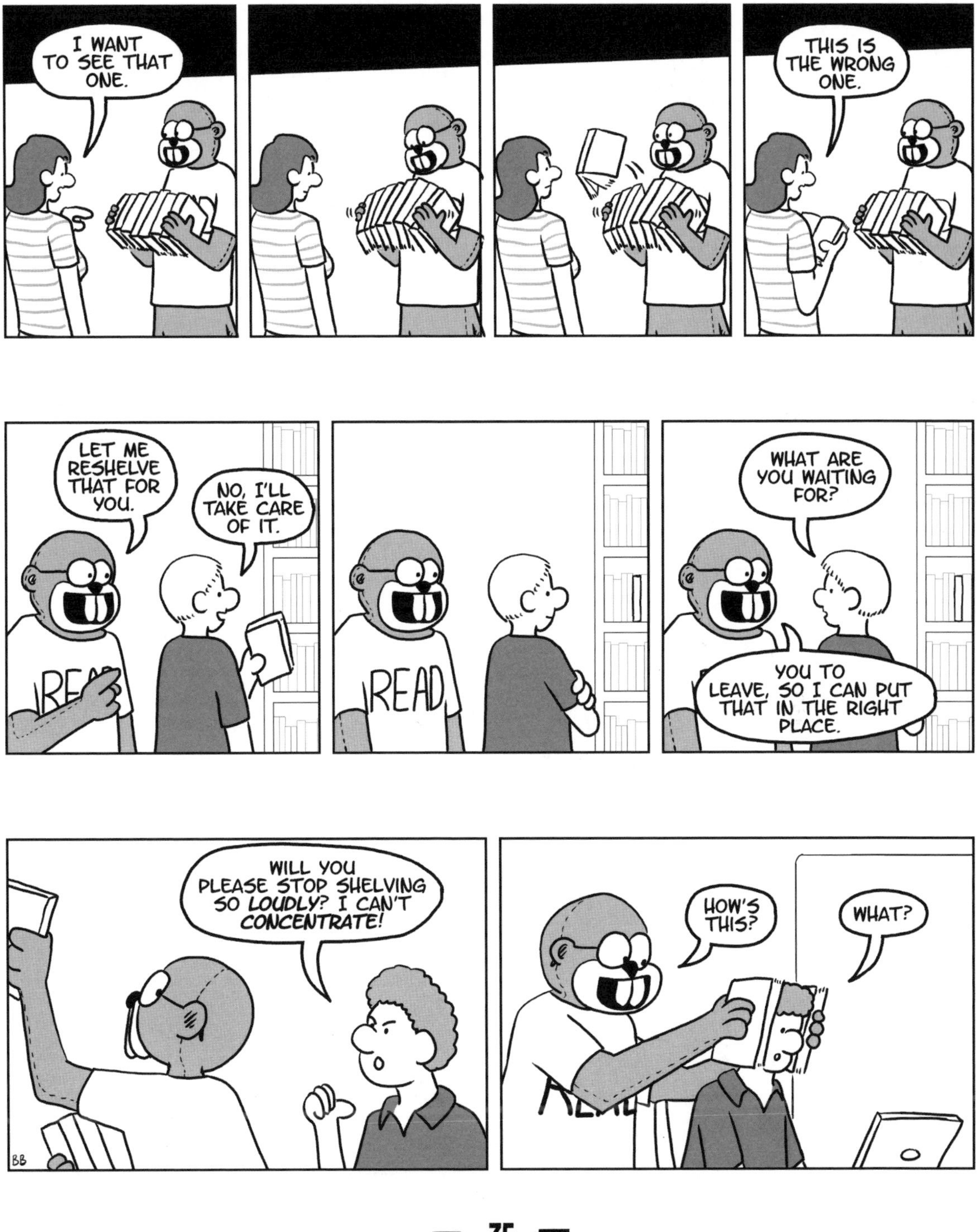
I WANT TO SEE THAT ONE.
THIS IS THE WRONG ONE.
LET ME RESHELVE THAT FOR YOU.
NO, I'LL TAKE CARE OF IT.
READ
READ
WHAT ARE YOU WAITING FOR?
YOU TO LEAVE, SO I CAN PUT THAT IN THE RIGHT PLACE.
WILL YOU PLEASE STOP SHELVING SO *LOUDLY*? I CAN'T *CONCENTRATE*!
BB
HOW'S THIS?
WHAT?

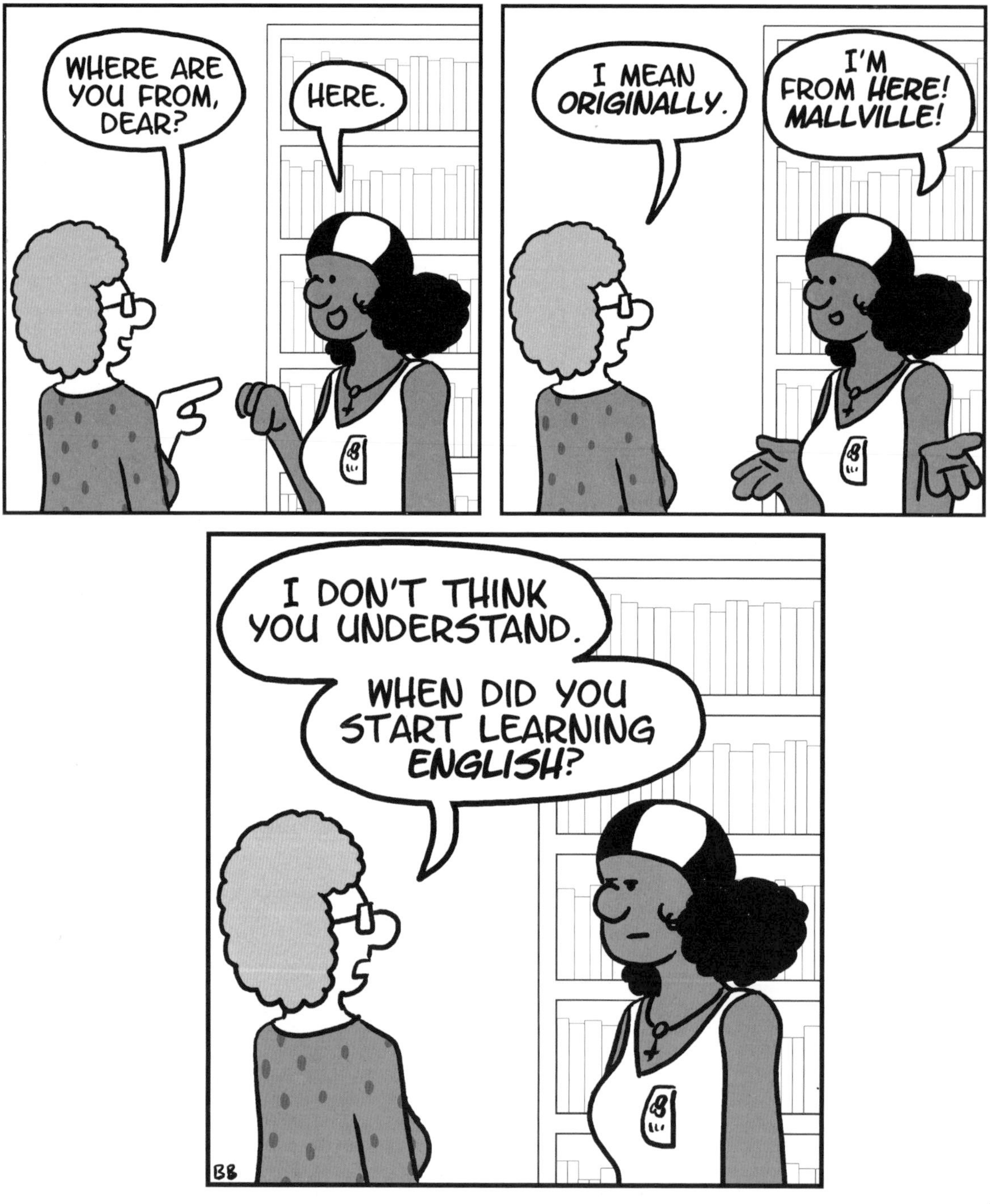
WHERE ARE YOU FROM, DEAR?
HERE.
I MEAN *ORIGINALLY*.
I'M FROM *HERE*! *MALLVILLE*!
I DON'T THINK YOU UNDERSTAND.
WHEN DID YOU START LEARNING *ENGLISH*?
BB

Too Much Information

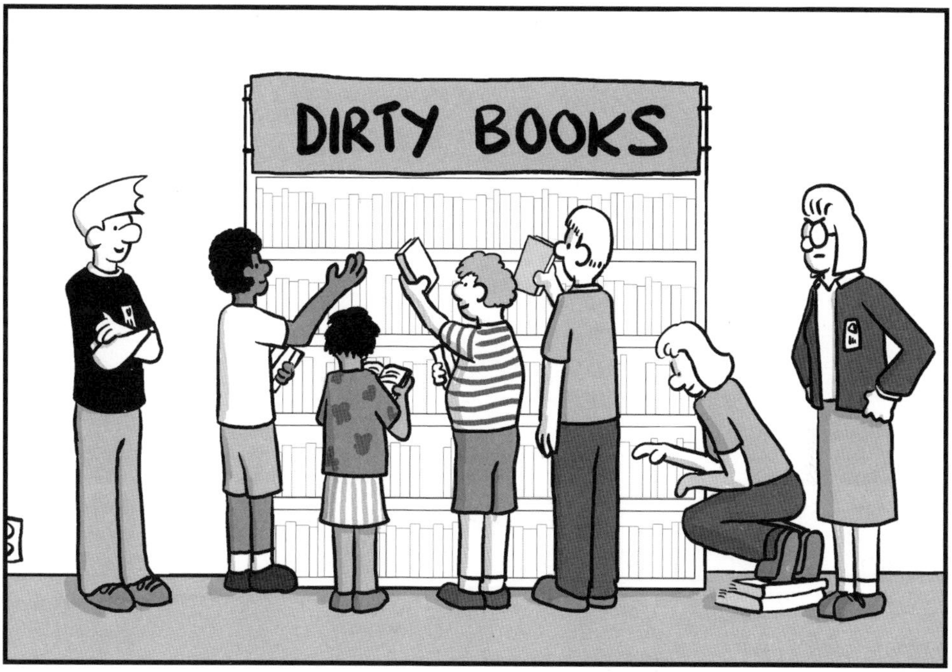
DIRTY BOOKS

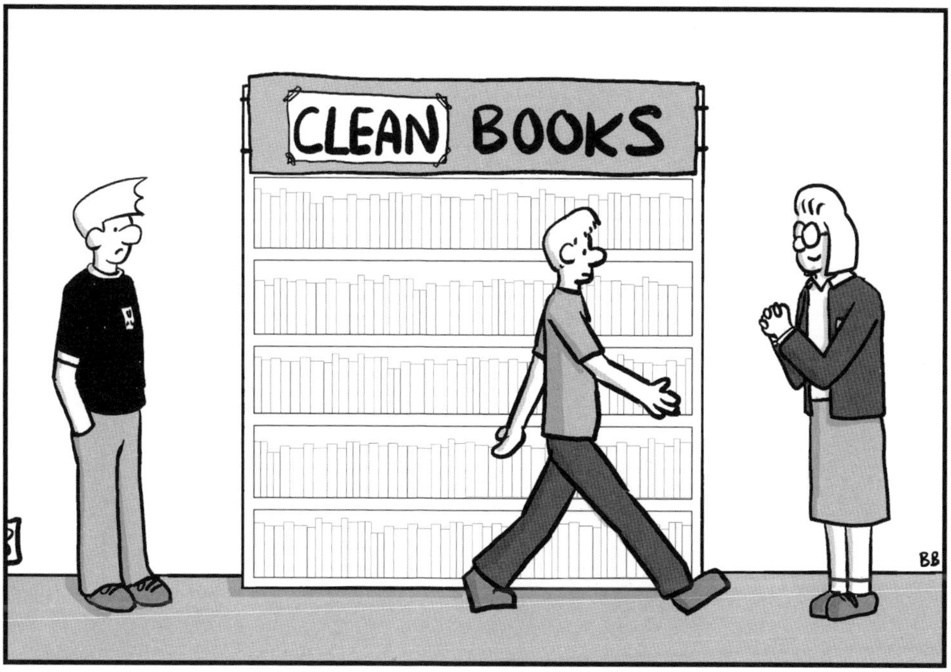
CLEAN BOOKS
BB

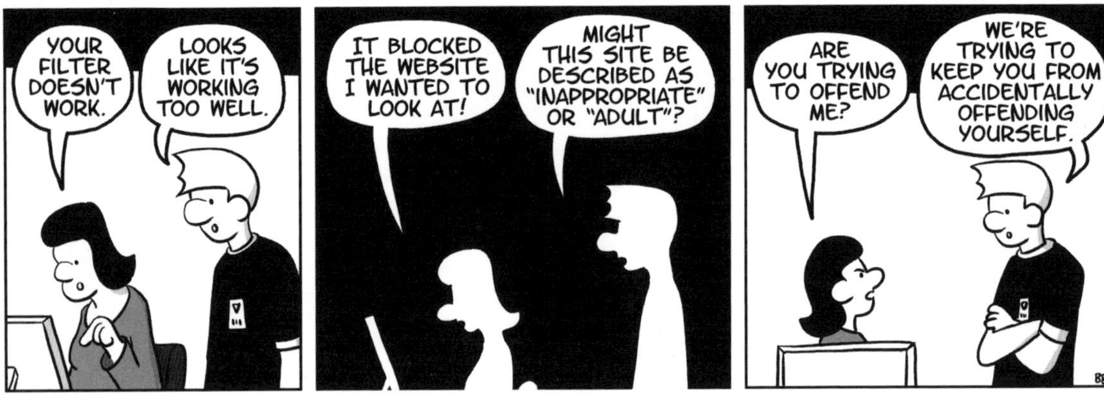
YOUR FILTER DOESN'T WORK.
LOOKS LIKE IT'S WORKING TOO WELL.
IT BLOCKED THE WEBSITE I WANTED TO LOOK AT!
MIGHT THIS SITE BE DESCRIBED AS "INAPPROPRIATE" OR "ADULT"?
ARE YOU TRYING TO OFFEND ME?
WE'RE TRYING TO KEEP YOU FROM ACCIDENTALLY OFFENDING YOURSELF.
BB

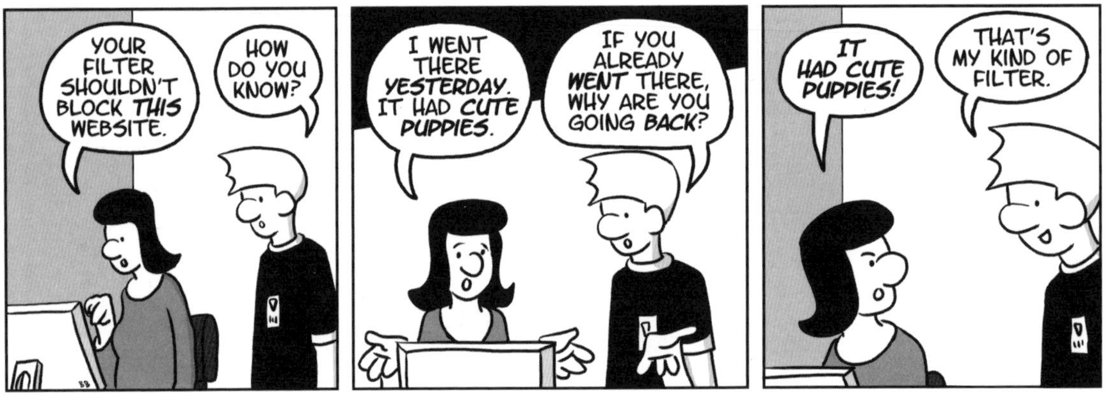
YOUR FILTER SHOULDN'T BLOCK THIS WEBSITE.
HOW DO YOU KNOW?
I WENT THERE YESTERDAY. IT HAD CUTE PUPPIES.
IF YOU ALREADY WENT THERE, WHY ARE YOU GOING BACK?
IT HAD CUTE PUPPIES!
THAT'S MY KIND OF FILTER.
BB

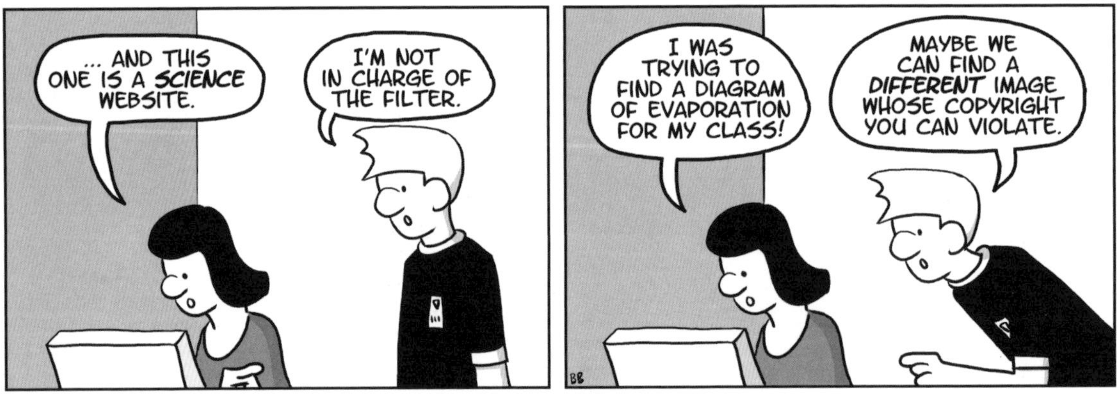
... AND THIS ONE IS A SCIENCE WEBSITE.
I'M NOT IN CHARGE OF THE FILTER.
I WAS TRYING TO FIND A DIAGRAM OF EVAPORATION FOR MY CLASS!
MAYBE WE CAN FIND A DIFFERENT IMAGE WHOSE COPYRIGHT YOU CAN VIOLATE.
BB

Too Much Information

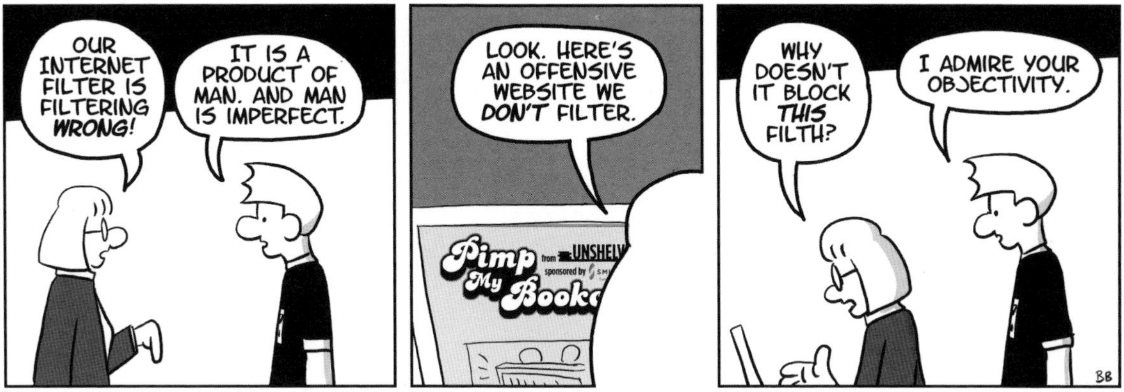
OUR INTERNET FILTER IS FILTERING WRONG!
IT IS A PRODUCT OF MAN. AND MAN IS IMPERFECT.
LOOK. HERE'S AN OFFENSIVE WEBSITE WE DON'T FILTER.
WHY DOESN'T IT BLOCK THIS FILTH?
I ADMIRE YOUR OBJECTIVITY.
BB

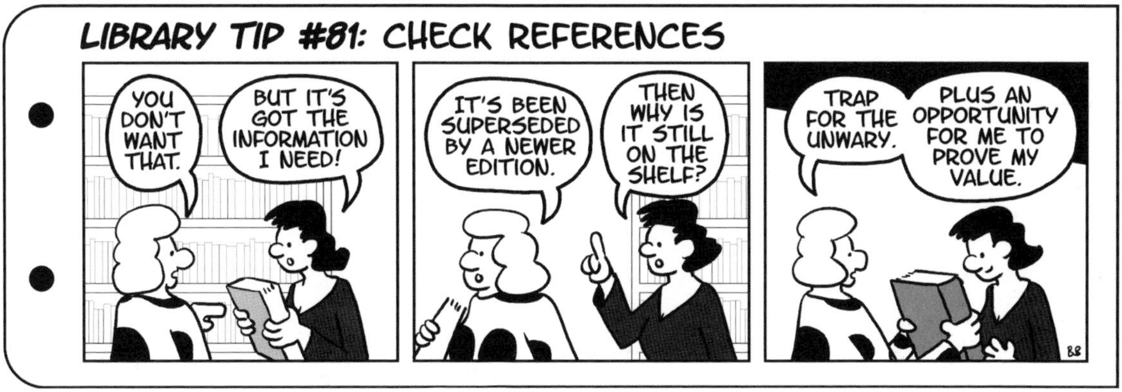
LIBRARY TIP #81: CHECK REFERENCES
YOU DON'T WANT THAT.
BUT IT'S GOT THE INFORMATION I NEED!
IT'S BEEN SUPERSEDED BY A NEWER EDITION.
THEN WHY IS IT STILL ON THE SHELF?
TRAP FOR THE UNWARY.
PLUS AN OPPORTUNITY FOR ME TO PROVE MY VALUE.
BB

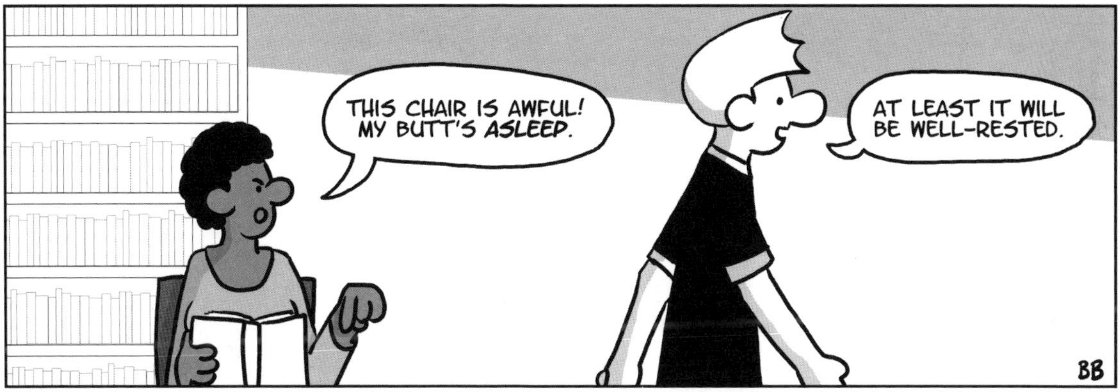
THIS CHAIR IS AWFUL! MY BUTT'S ASLEEP.
AT LEAST IT WILL BE WELL-RESTED.
BB

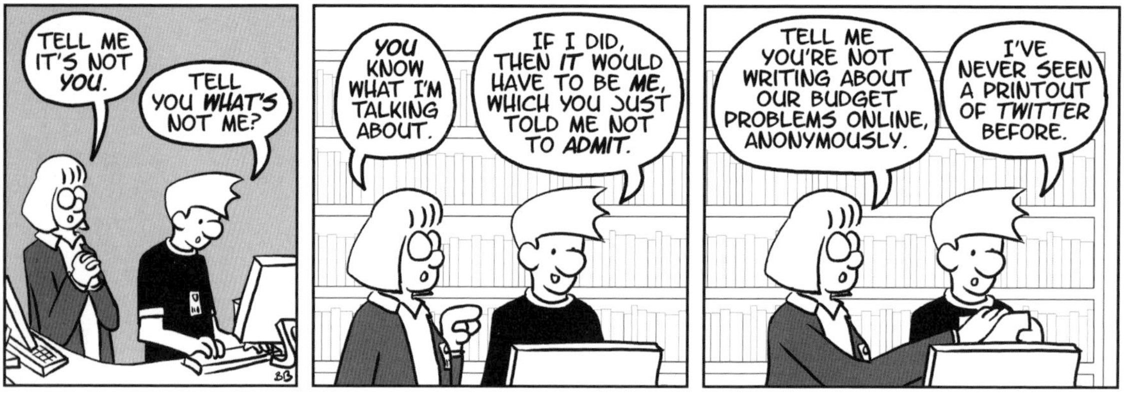
TELL ME IT'S NOT *YOU*.
TELL YOU ***WHAT'S*** NOT ME?
YOU KNOW WHAT I'M TALKING ABOUT.
IF I DID, THEN ***IT*** WOULD HAVE TO BE ***ME***, WHICH YOU JUST TOLD ME NOT TO ***ADMIT***.
TELL ME YOU'RE NOT WRITING ABOUT OUR BUDGET PROBLEMS ONLINE, ANONYMOUSLY.
I'VE NEVER SEEN A PRINTOUT OF *TWITTER* BEFORE.
BB

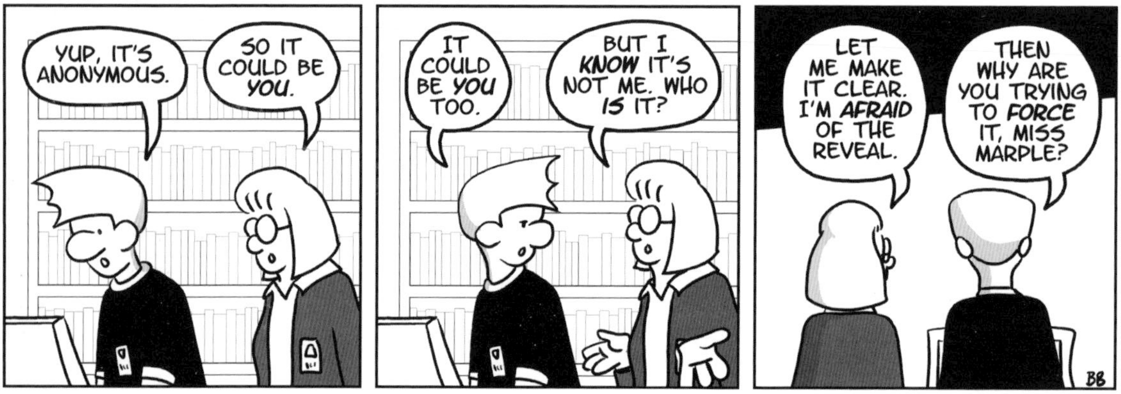
YUP, IT'S ANONYMOUS.
SO IT COULD BE ***YOU***.
IT COULD BE ***YOU*** TOO.
BUT I ***KNOW*** IT'S NOT ME. WHO ***IS*** IT?
LET ME MAKE IT CLEAR. I'M ***AFRAID*** OF THE REVEAL.
THEN WHY ARE YOU TRYING TO ***FORCE*** IT, MISS MARPLE?
BB

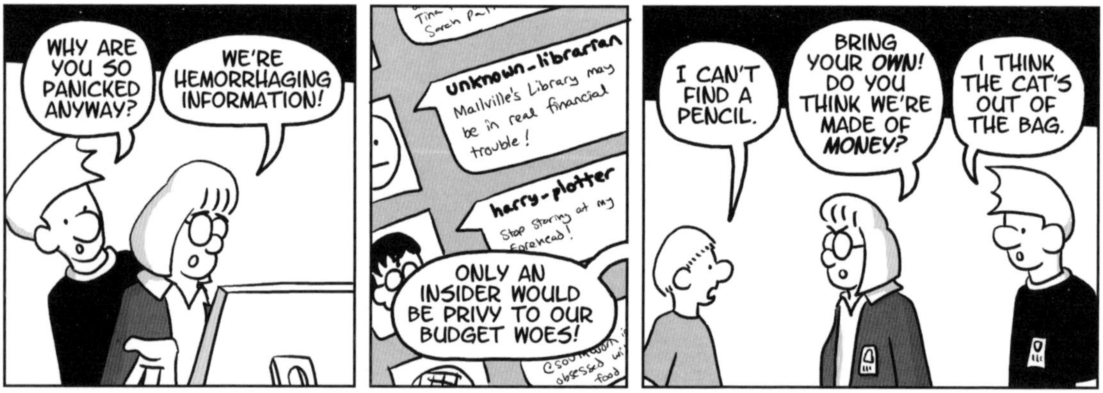
WHY ARE YOU SO PANICKED ANYWAY?
WE'RE HEMORRHAGING INFORMATION!
unknown_librarian
Mallville's Library may be in real financial trouble!
harry-plotter
Stop staring at my forehead!
ONLY AN INSIDER WOULD BE PRIVY TO OUR BUDGET WOES!
I CAN'T FIND A PENCIL.
BRING YOUR ***OWN***! DO YOU THINK WE'RE MADE OF ***MONEY?***
I THINK THE CAT'S OUT OF THE BAG.

Too Much Information

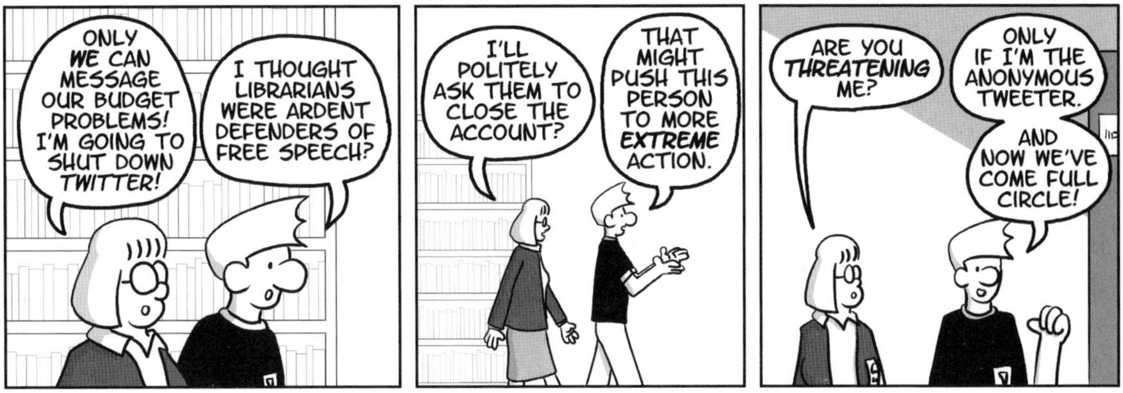
ONLY **WE** CAN MESSAGE OUR BUDGET PROBLEMS! I'M GOING TO SHUT DOWN **TWITTER**!
I THOUGHT LIBRARIANS WERE ARDENT DEFENDERS OF FREE SPEECH?
I'LL POLITELY ASK THEM TO CLOSE THE ACCOUNT?
THAT MIGHT PUSH THIS PERSON TO MORE **EXTREME** ACTION.
ARE YOU **THREATENING** ME?
ONLY IF I'M THE ANONYMOUS TWEETER.
AND NOW WE'VE COME FULL CIRCLE!

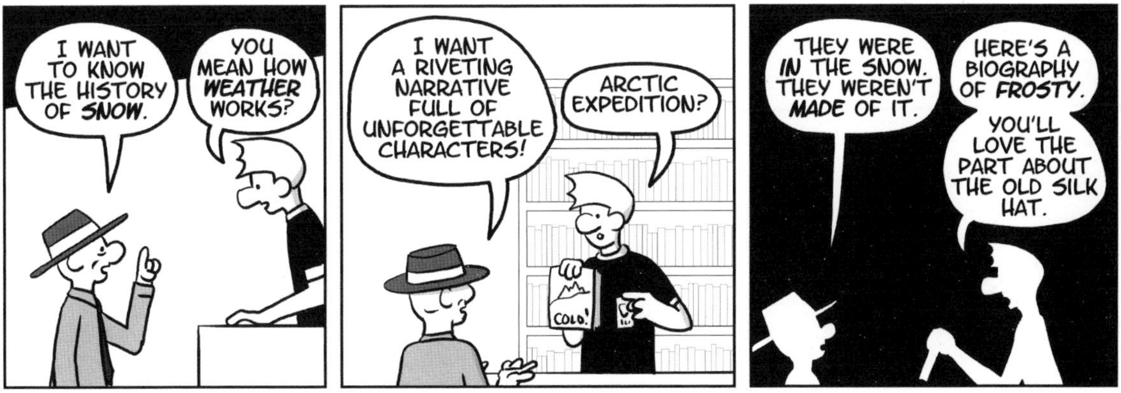
I WANT TO KNOW THE HISTORY OF **SNOW**.
YOU MEAN HOW **WEATHER** WORKS?
I WANT A RIVETING NARRATIVE FULL OF UNFORGETTABLE CHARACTERS!
ARCTIC EXPEDITION?
COLD!
THEY WERE **IN** THE SNOW. THEY WEREN'T **MADE** OF IT.
HERE'S A BIOGRAPHY OF **FROSTY**.
YOU'LL LOVE THE PART ABOUT THE OLD SILK HAT.

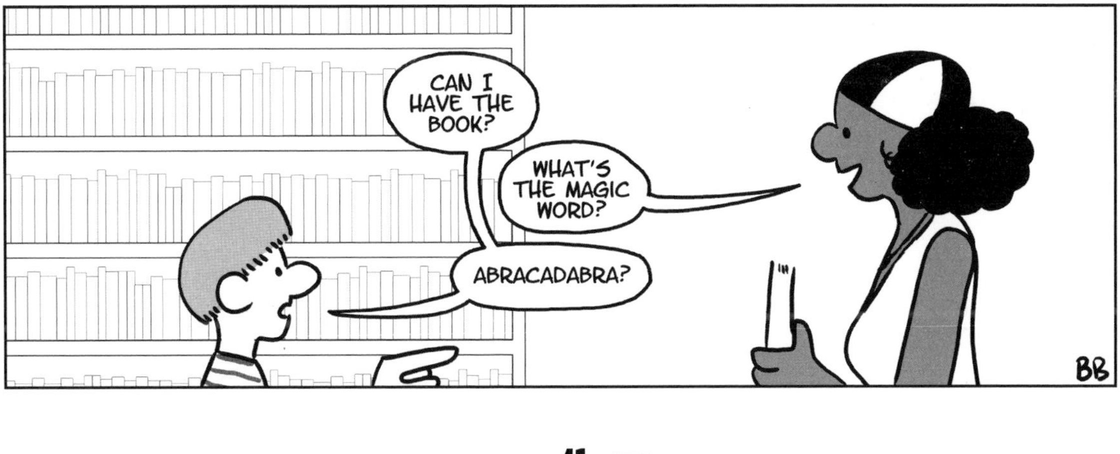
CAN I HAVE THE BOOK?
WHAT'S THE MAGIC WORD?
ABRACADABRA?
BB

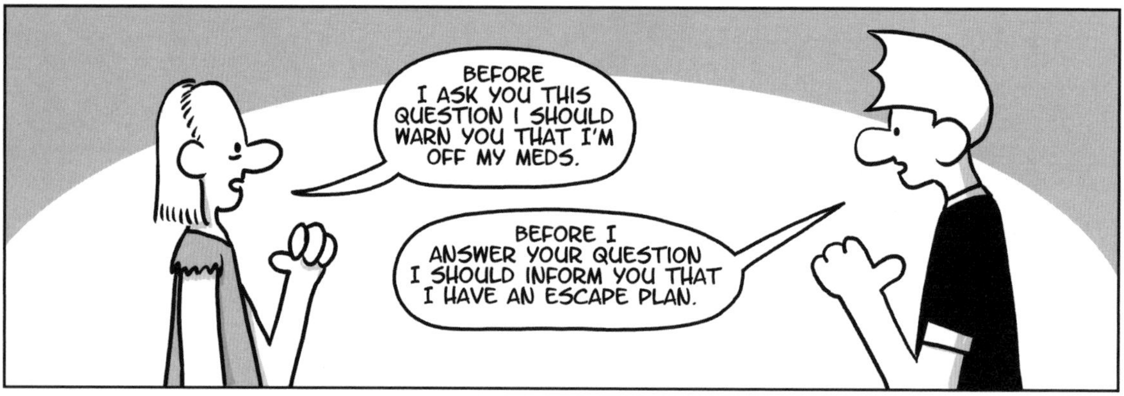
BEFORE I ASK YOU THIS QUESTION I SHOULD WARN YOU THAT I'M OFF MY MEDS.
BEFORE I ANSWER YOUR QUESTION I SHOULD INFORM YOU THAT I HAVE AN ESCAPE PLAN.

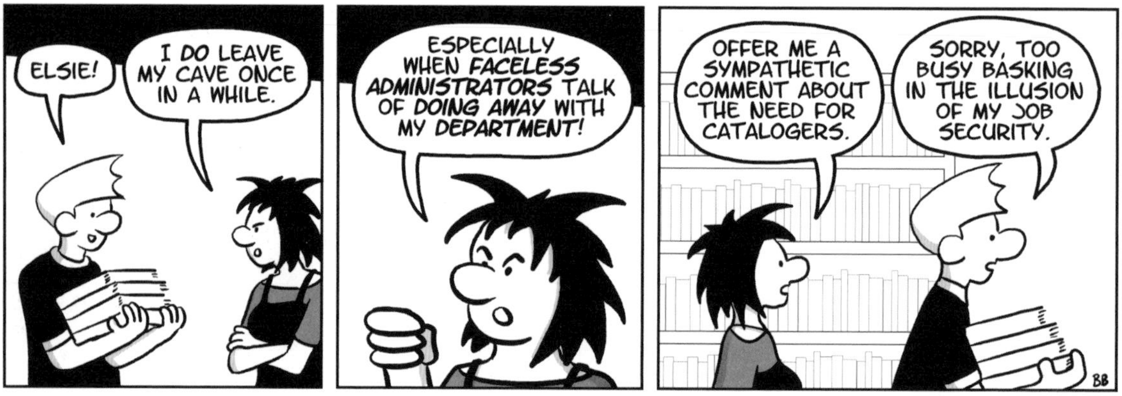
ELSIE!
I *DO* LEAVE MY CAVE ONCE IN A WHILE.
ESPECIALLY WHEN *FACELESS ADMINISTRATORS* TALK OF *DOING AWAY* WITH MY *DEPARTMENT*!
OFFER ME A SYMPATHETIC COMMENT ABOUT THE NEED FOR CATALOGERS.
SORRY, TOO BUSY BASKING IN THE ILLUSION OF MY JOB SECURITY.
BB

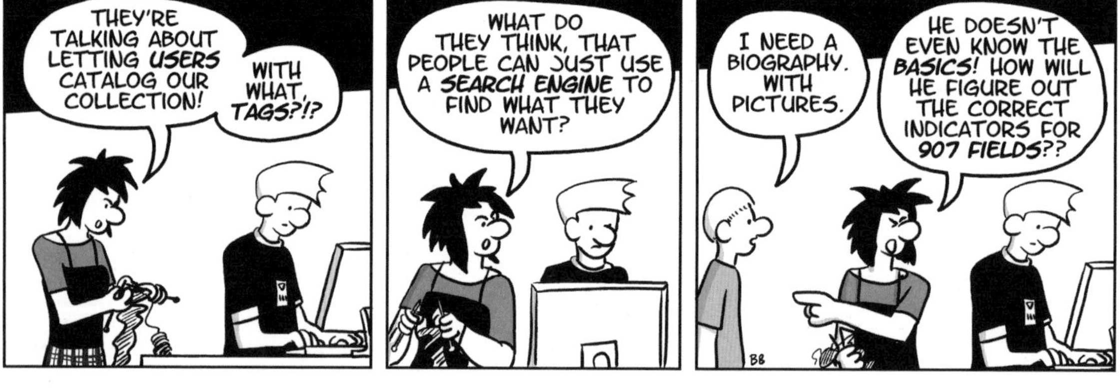
THEY'RE TALKING ABOUT LETTING *USERS* CATALOG OUR COLLECTION!
WITH WHAT, *TAGS?!?*
WHAT DO THEY THINK, THAT PEOPLE CAN JUST USE A *SEARCH ENGINE* TO FIND WHAT THEY WANT?
I NEED A BIOGRAPHY. WITH PICTURES.
HE DOESN'T EVEN KNOW THE *BASICS*! HOW WILL HE FIGURE OUT THE CORRECT INDICATORS FOR *907 FIELDS*??
BB

Too Much Information

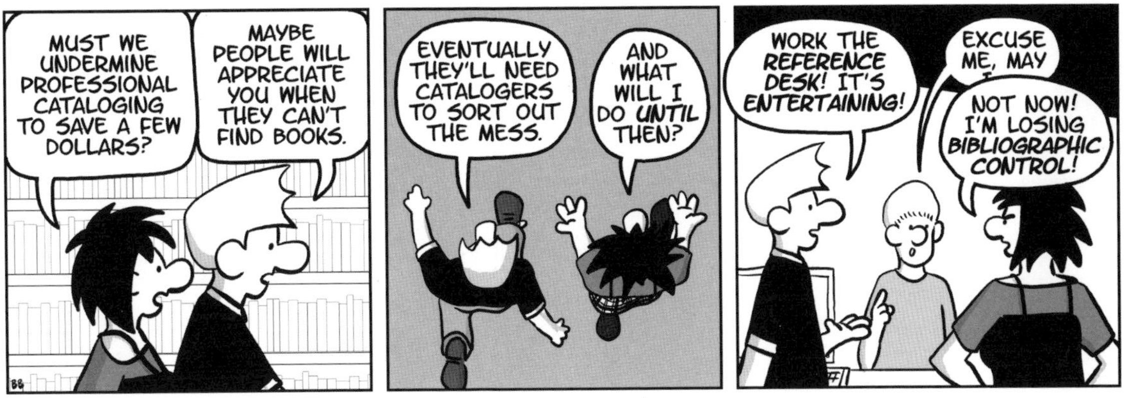

MUST WE UNDERMINE PROFESSIONAL CATALOGING TO SAVE A FEW DOLLARS?
MAYBE PEOPLE WILL APPRECIATE YOU WHEN THEY CAN'T FIND BOOKS.
EVENTUALLY THEY'LL NEED CATALOGERS TO SORT OUT THE MESS.
AND WHAT WILL I DO *UNTIL* THEN?
WORK THE *REFERENCE DESK*! IT'S *ENTERTAINING*!
EXCUSE ME, MAY
NOT NOW! I'M LOSING *BIBLIOGRAPHIC CONTROL*!

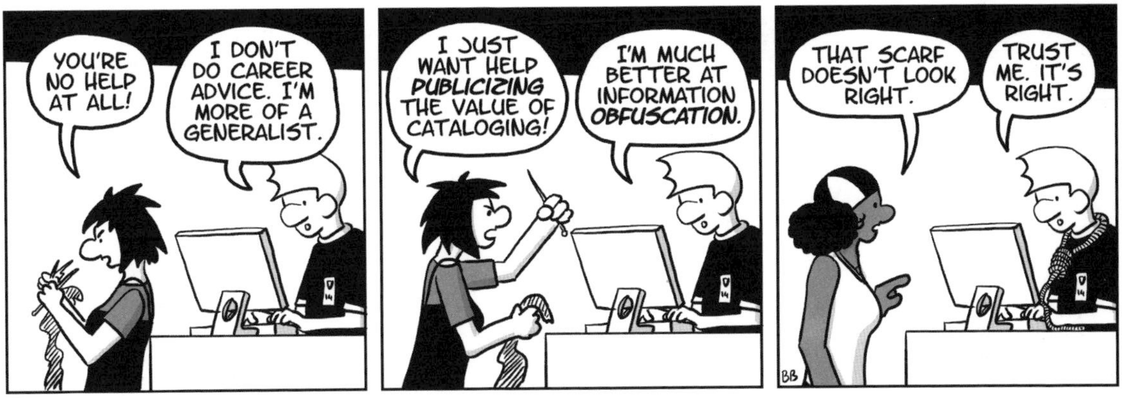

YOU'RE NO HELP AT ALL!
I DON'T DO CAREER ADVICE. I'M MORE OF A GENERALIST.
I JUST WANT HELP *PUBLICIZING* THE VALUE OF CATALOGING!
I'M MUCH BETTER AT INFORMATION *OBFUSCATION*.
THAT SCARF DOESN'T LOOK RIGHT.
TRUST ME. IT'S RIGHT.

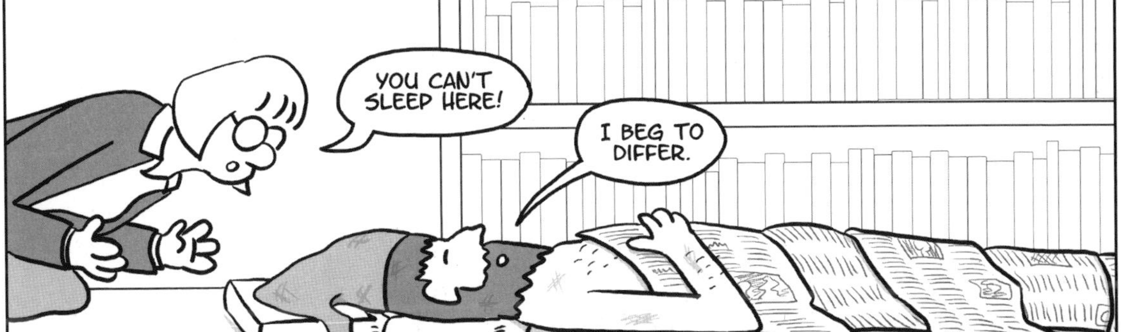

YOU CAN'T SLEEP HERE!
I BEG TO DIFFER.

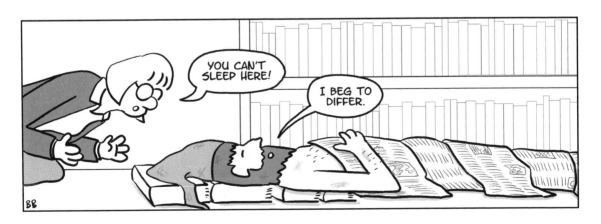

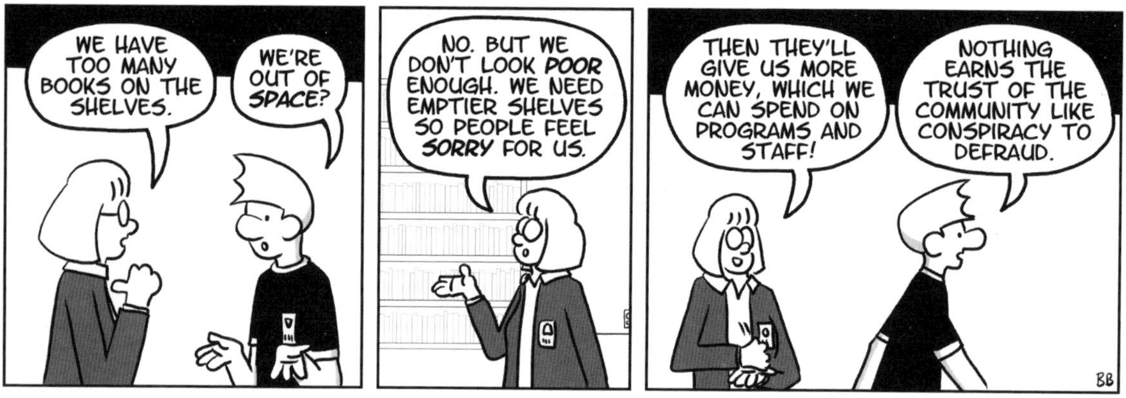
WE HAVE TOO MANY BOOKS ON THE SHELVES.
WE'RE OUT OF *SPACE*?
NO. BUT WE DON'T LOOK *POOR* ENOUGH. WE NEED EMPTIER SHELVES SO PEOPLE FEEL *SORRY* FOR US.
THEN THEY'LL GIVE US MORE MONEY, WHICH WE CAN SPEND ON PROGRAMS AND STAFF!
NOTHING EARNS THE TRUST OF THE COMMUNITY LIKE CONSPIRACY TO DEFRAUD.
BB

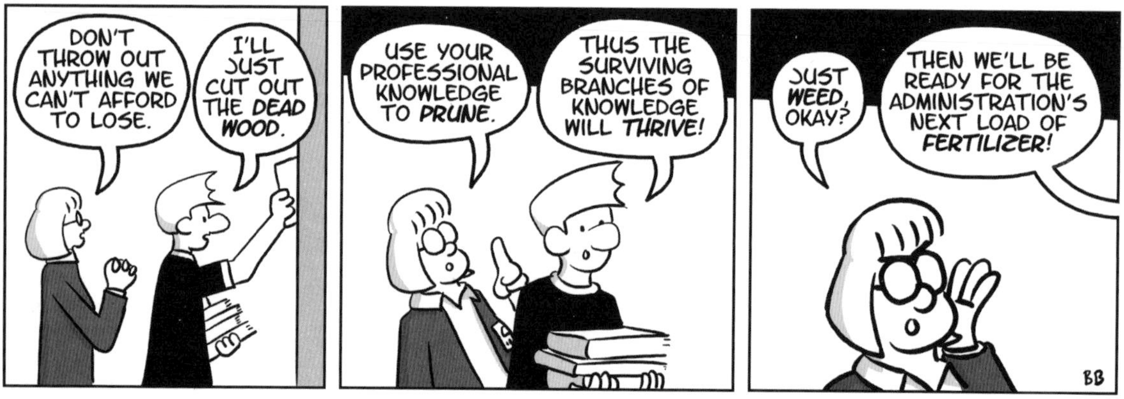
DON'T THROW OUT ANYTHING WE CAN'T AFFORD TO LOSE.
I'LL JUST CUT OUT THE *DEAD WOOD*.
USE YOUR PROFESSIONAL KNOWLEDGE TO *PRUNE*.
THUS THE SURVIVING BRANCHES OF KNOWLEDGE WILL *THRIVE*!
JUST *WEED*, OKAY?
THEN WE'LL BE READY FOR THE ADMINISTRATION'S NEXT LOAD OF *FERTILIZER*!
BB

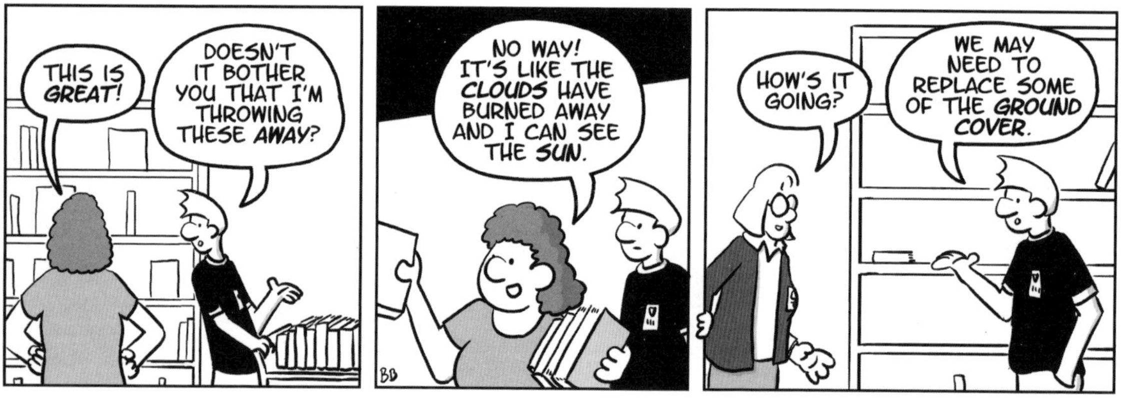
THIS IS *GREAT*!
DOESN'T IT BOTHER YOU THAT I'M THROWING THESE *AWAY*?
NO WAY! IT'S LIKE THE *CLOUDS* HAVE BURNED AWAY AND I CAN SEE THE *SUN*.
BB
HOW'S IT GOING?
WE MAY NEED TO REPLACE SOME OF THE *GROUND COVER*.

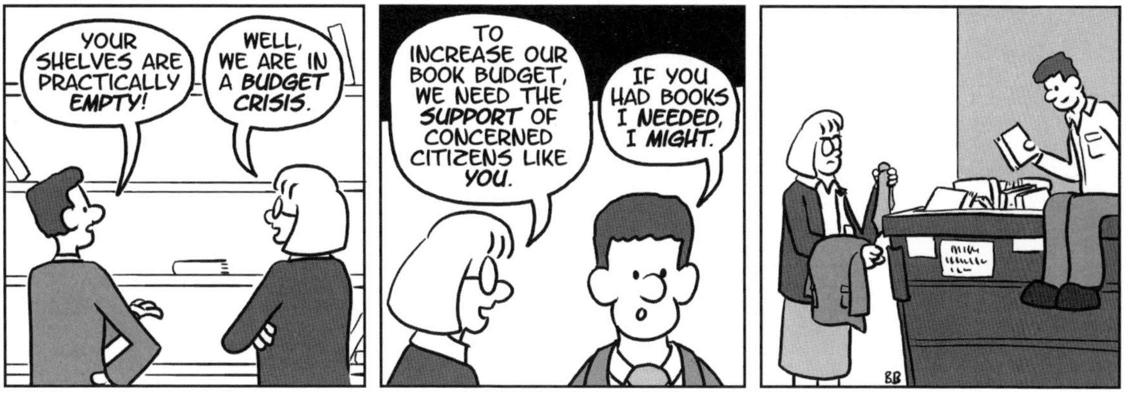
YOUR SHELVES ARE PRACTICALLY EMPTY!
WELL, WE ARE IN A BUDGET CRISIS.
TO INCREASE OUR BOOK BUDGET, WE NEED THE SUPPORT OF CONCERNED CITIZENS LIKE YOU.
IF YOU HAD BOOKS I NEEDED, I MIGHT.

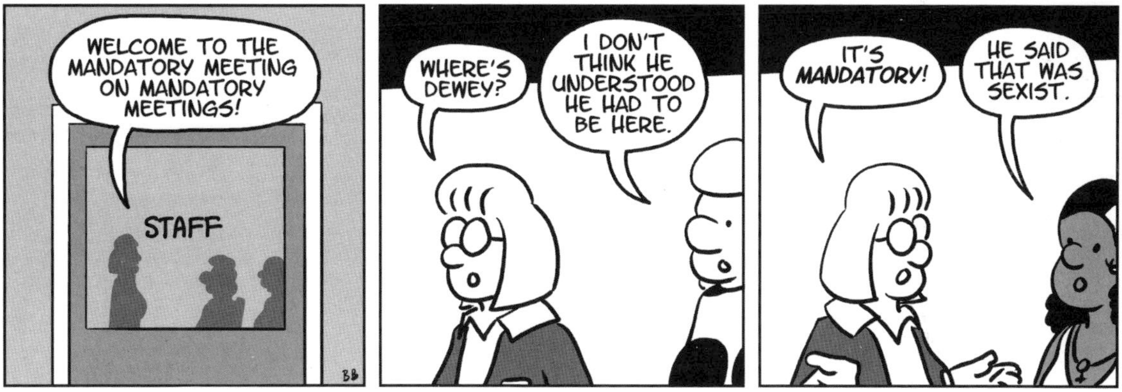
WELCOME TO THE MANDATORY MEETING ON MANDATORY MEETINGS!
STAFF
WHERE'S DEWEY?
I DON'T THINK HE UNDERSTOOD HE HAD TO BE HERE.
IT'S MANDATORY!
HE SAID THAT WAS SEXIST.

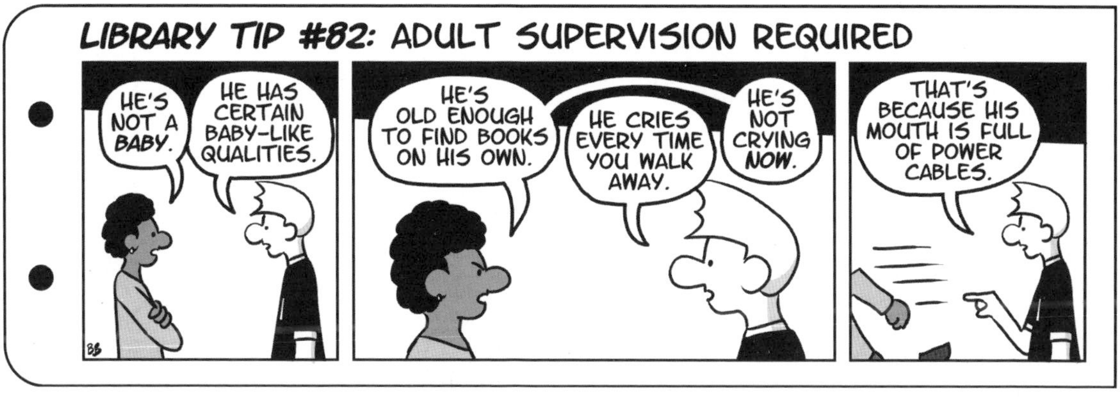
LIBRARY TIP #82: ADULT SUPERVISION REQUIRED
HE'S NOT A BABY.
HE HAS CERTAIN BABY-LIKE QUALITIES.
HE'S OLD ENOUGH TO FIND BOOKS ON HIS OWN.
HE CRIES EVERY TIME YOU WALK AWAY.
HE'S NOT CRYING NOW.
THAT'S BECAUSE HIS MOUTH IS FULL OF POWER CABLES.

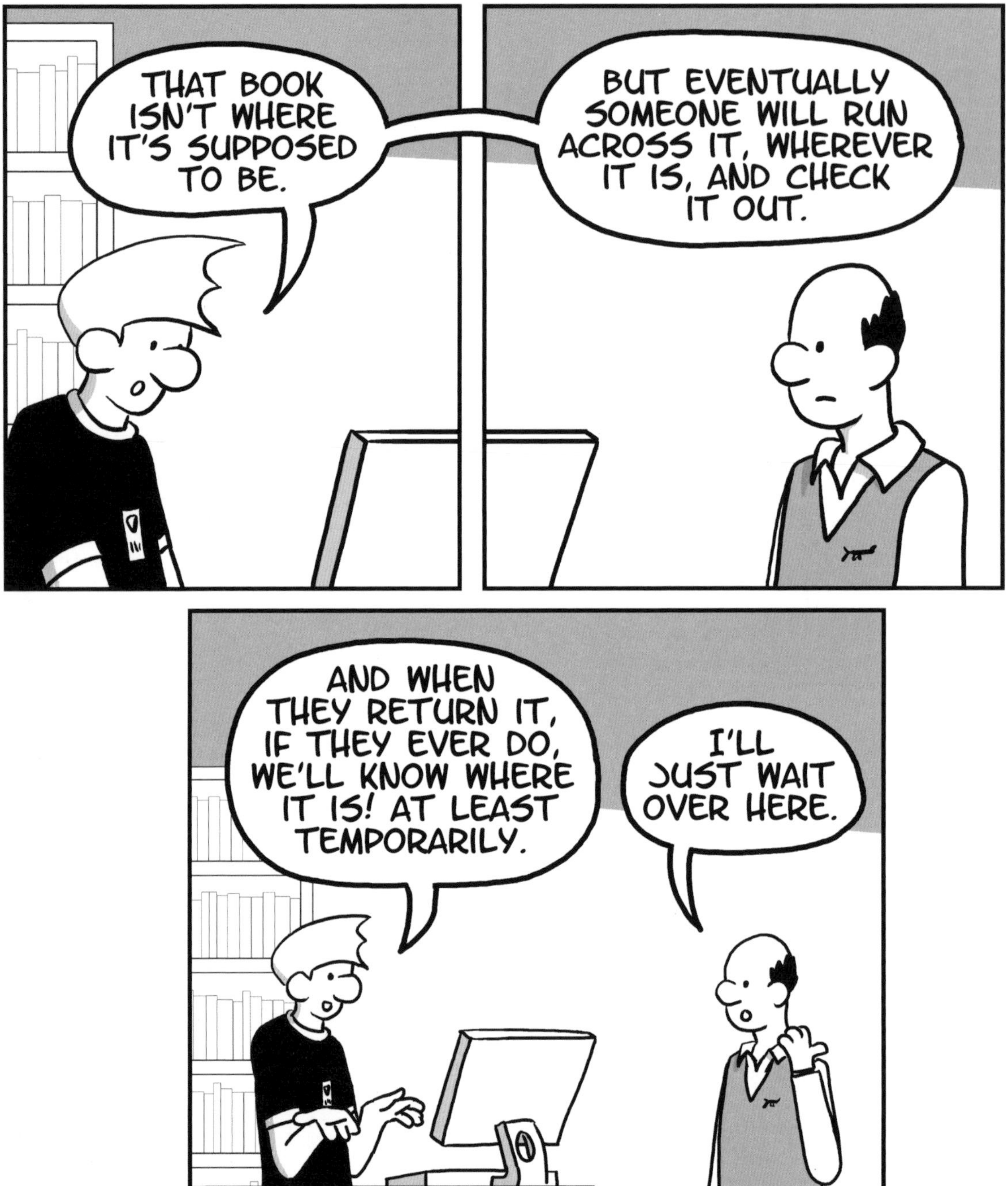
THAT BOOK ISN'T WHERE IT'S SUPPOSED TO BE.
BUT EVENTUALLY SOMEONE WILL RUN ACROSS IT, WHEREVER IT IS, AND CHECK IT OUT.
AND WHEN THEY RETURN IT, IF THEY EVER DO, WE'LL KNOW WHERE IT IS! AT LEAST TEMPORARILY.
I'LL JUST WAIT OVER HERE.

Too Much Information

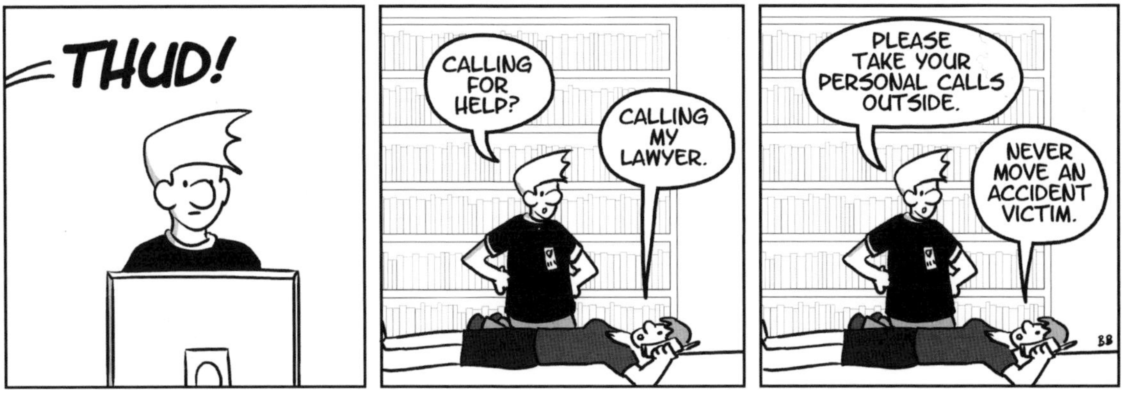
THUD!
CALLING FOR HELP?
CALLING MY LAWYER.
PLEASE TAKE YOUR PERSONAL CALLS OUTSIDE.
NEVER MOVE AN ACCIDENT VICTIM.
BB

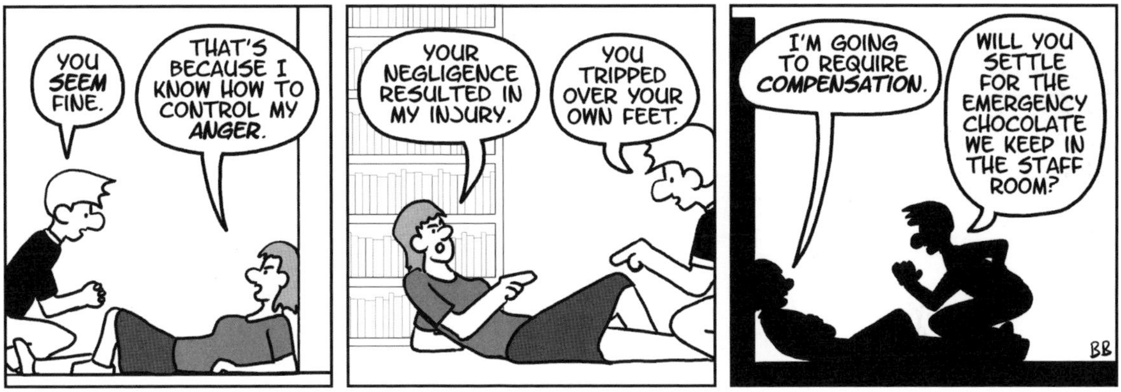
YOU SEEM FINE.
THAT'S BECAUSE I KNOW HOW TO CONTROL MY ANGER.
YOUR NEGLIGENCE RESULTED IN MY INJURY.
YOU TRIPPED OVER YOUR OWN FEET.
I'M GOING TO REQUIRE COMPENSATION.
WILL YOU SETTLE FOR THE EMERGENCY CHOCOLATE WE KEEP IN THE STAFF ROOM?
BB

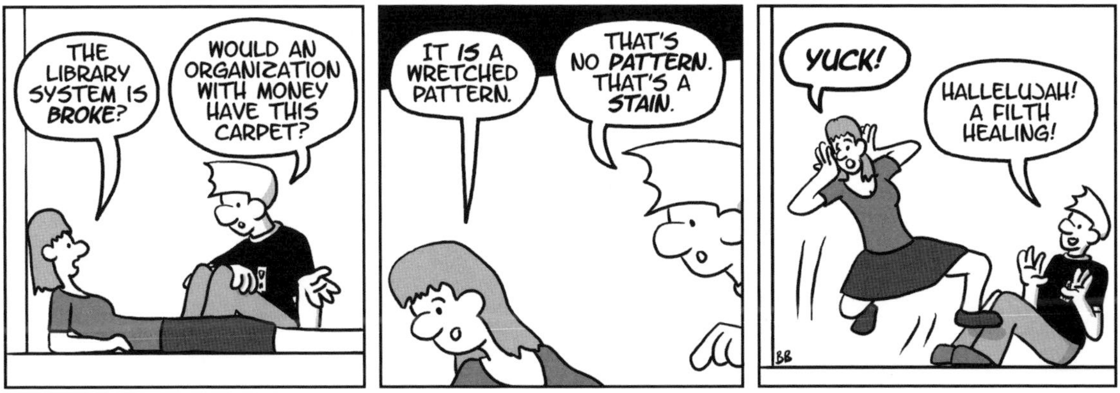
THE LIBRARY SYSTEM IS BROKE?
WOULD AN ORGANIZATION WITH MONEY HAVE THIS CARPET?
IT IS A WRETCHED PATTERN.
THAT'S NO PATTERN. THAT'S A STAIN.
YUCK!
HALLELUJAH! A FILTH HEALING!
BB

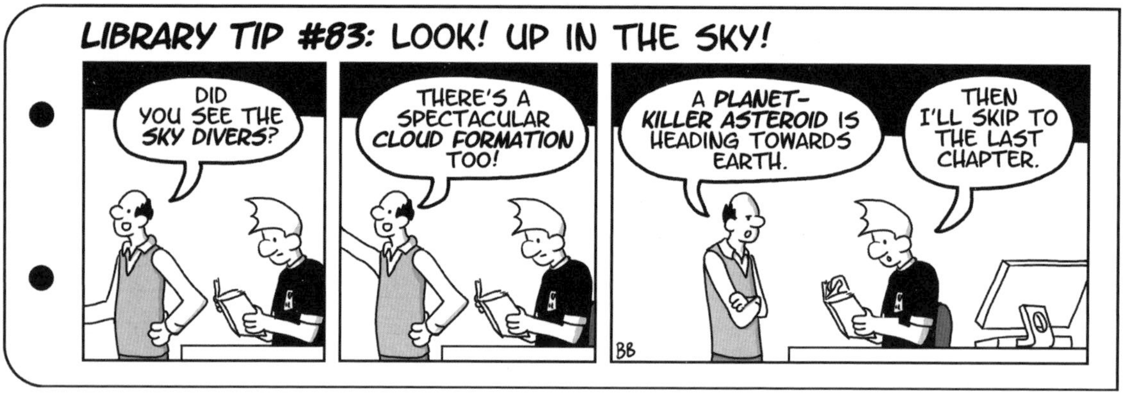
LIBRARY TIP #83: LOOK! UP IN THE SKY!
DID YOU SEE THE SKY DIVERS?
THERE'S A SPECTACULAR CLOUD FORMATION TOO!
A PLANET-KILLER ASTEROID IS HEADING TOWARDS EARTH.
THEN I'LL SKIP TO THE LAST CHAPTER.
BB

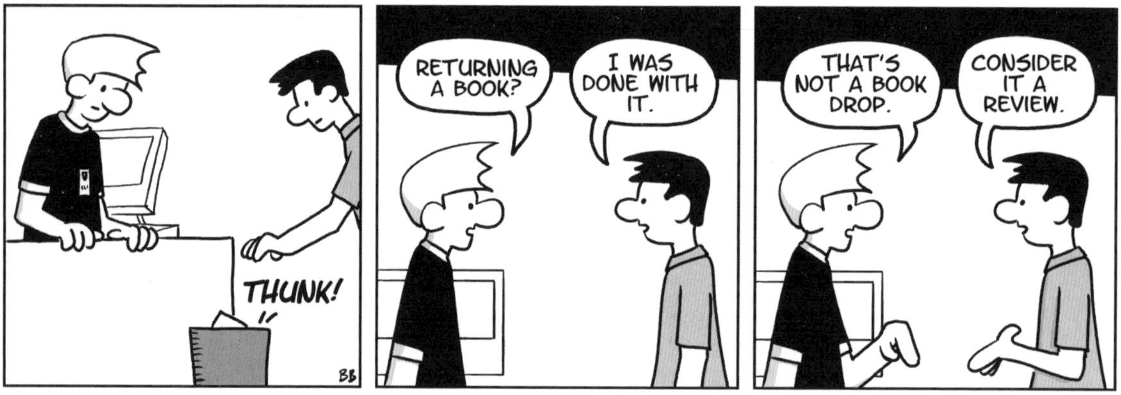
THUNK!
BB
RETURNING A BOOK?
I WAS DONE WITH IT.
THAT'S NOT A BOOK DROP.
CONSIDER IT A REVIEW.

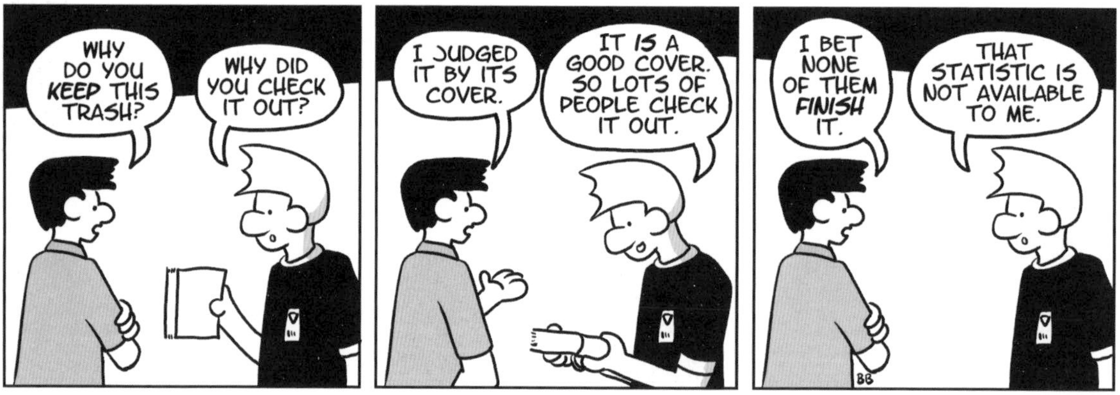
WHY DO YOU KEEP THIS TRASH?
WHY DID YOU CHECK IT OUT?
I JUDGED IT BY ITS COVER.
IT IS A GOOD COVER. SO LOTS OF PEOPLE CHECK IT OUT.
I BET NONE OF THEM FINISH IT.
THAT STATISTIC IS NOT AVAILABLE TO ME.
BB

Too Much Information

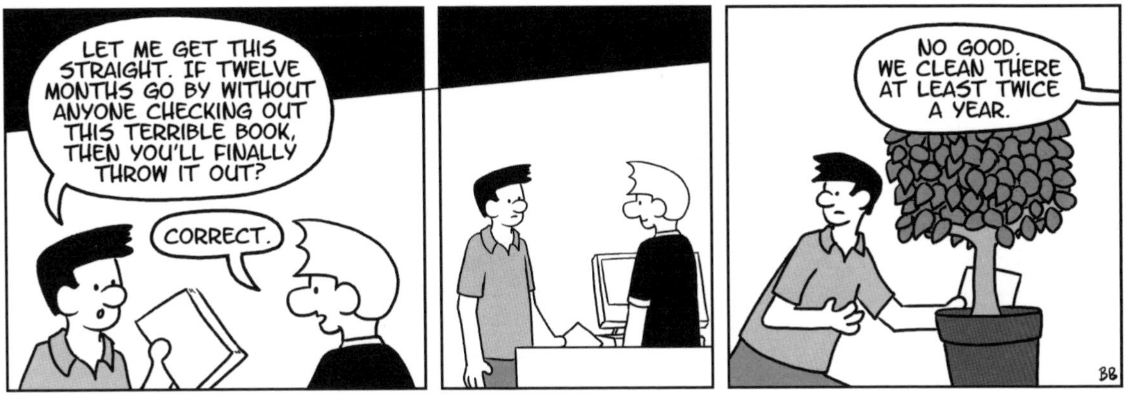
LET ME GET THIS STRAIGHT. IF TWELVE MONTHS GO BY WITHOUT ANYONE CHECKING OUT THIS TERRIBLE BOOK, THEN YOU'LL FINALLY THROW IT OUT?
CORRECT.
NO GOOD. WE CLEAN THERE AT LEAST TWICE A YEAR.
BB

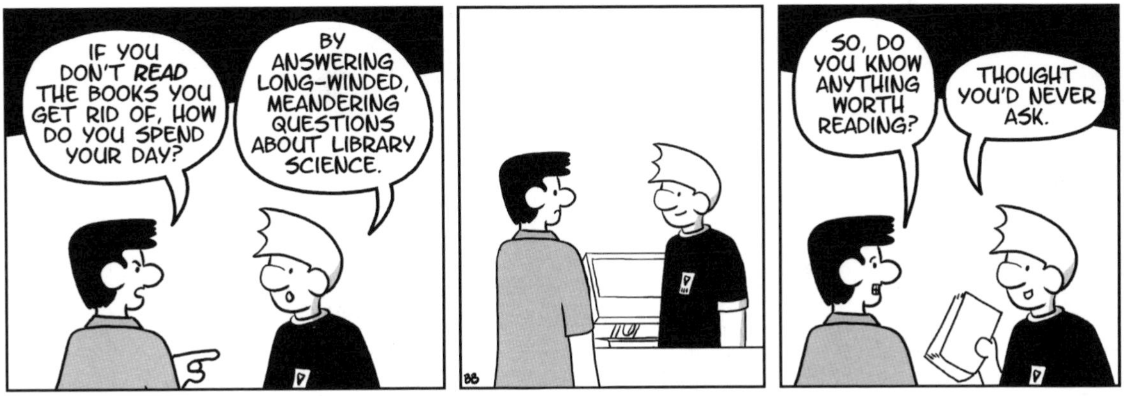
IF YOU DON'T *READ* THE BOOKS YOU GET RID OF, HOW DO YOU SPEND YOUR DAY?
BY ANSWERING LONG-WINDED, MEANDERING QUESTIONS ABOUT LIBRARY SCIENCE.
BB
SO, DO YOU KNOW ANYTHING WORTH READING?
THOUGHT YOU'D NEVER ASK.

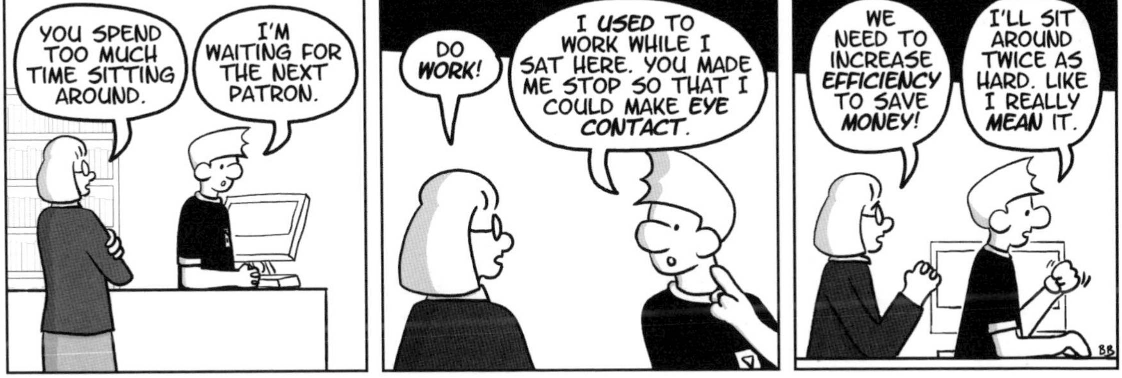
YOU SPEND TOO MUCH TIME SITTING AROUND.
I'M WAITING FOR THE NEXT PATRON.
DO *WORK!*
I *USED* TO WORK WHILE I SAT HERE. YOU MADE ME STOP SO THAT I COULD MAKE *EYE CONTACT*.
WE NEED TO INCREASE *EFFICIENCY* TO SAVE *MONEY!*
I'LL SIT AROUND TWICE AS HARD. LIKE I REALLY *MEAN* IT.
BB

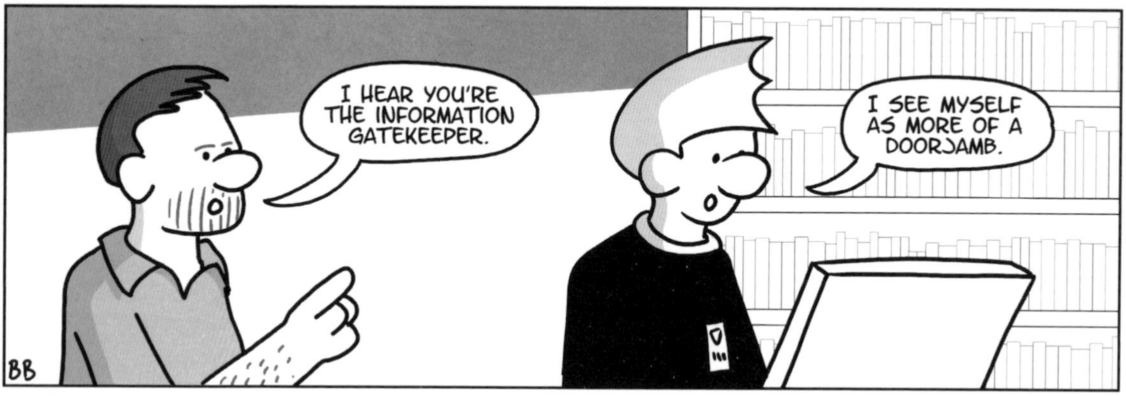
I HEAR YOU'RE THE INFORMATION GATEKEEPER.
I SEE MYSELF AS MORE OF A DOORJAMB.
BB

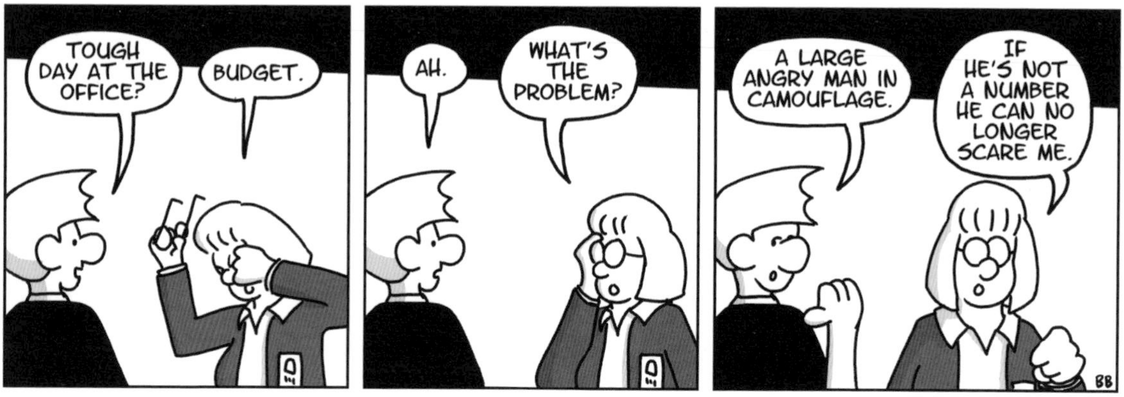
TOUGH DAY AT THE OFFICE?
BUDGET.
AH.
WHAT'S THE PROBLEM?
A LARGE ANGRY MAN IN CAMOUFLAGE.
IF HE'S NOT A NUMBER HE CAN NO LONGER SCARE ME.
BB

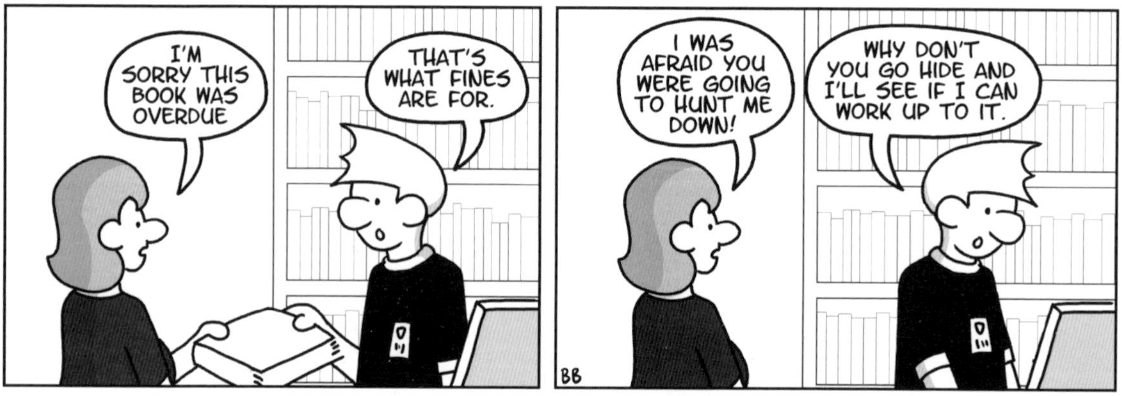
I'M SORRY THIS BOOK WAS OVERDUE
THAT'S WHAT FINES ARE FOR.
I WAS AFRAID YOU WERE GOING TO HUNT ME DOWN!
WHY DON'T YOU GO HIDE AND I'LL SEE IF I CAN WORK UP TO IT.
BB

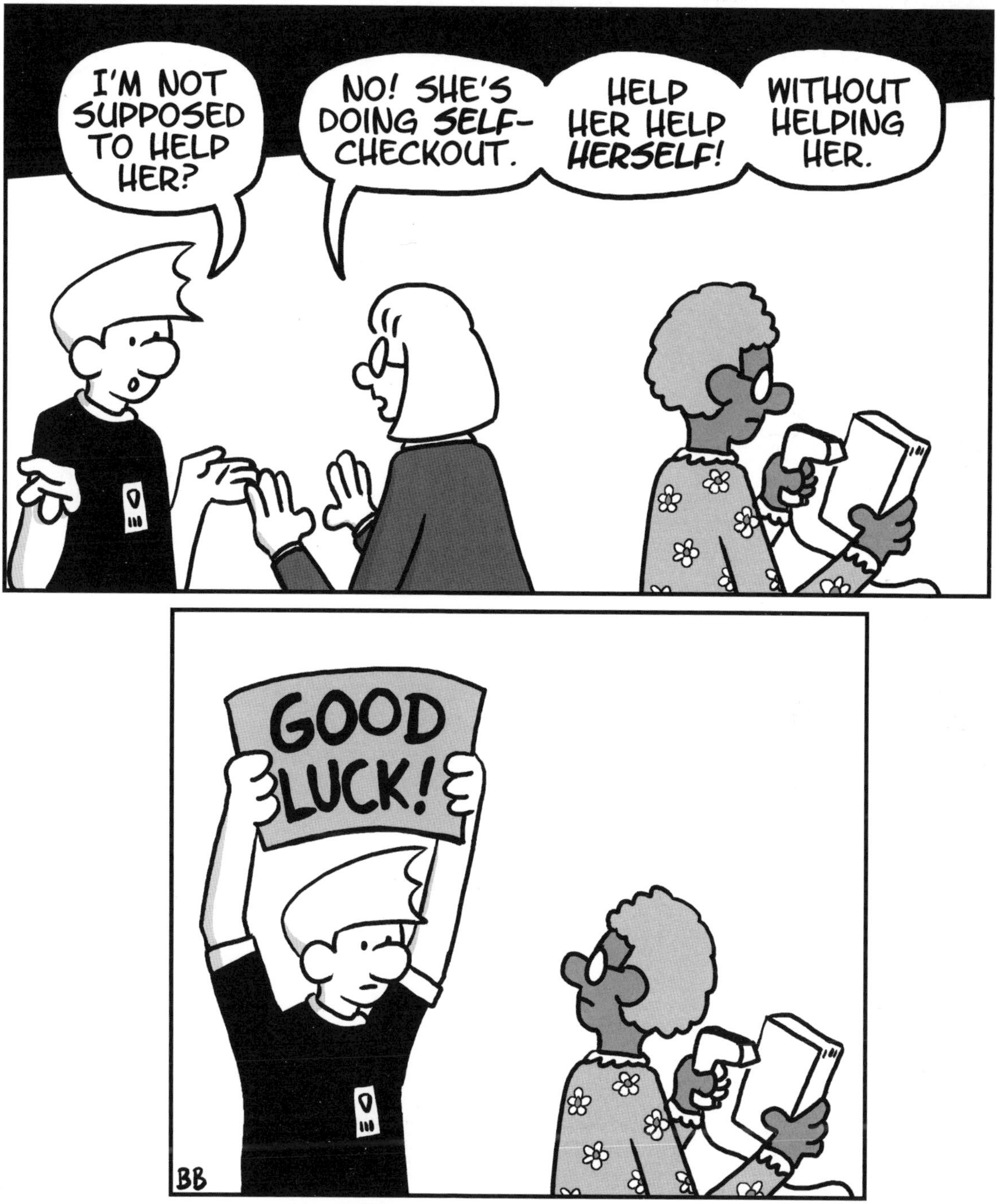
I'M NOT SUPPOSED TO HELP HER?
NO! SHE'S DOING SELF-CHECKOUT.
HELP HER HELP HERSELF!
WITHOUT HELPING HER.
GOOD LUCK!
BB

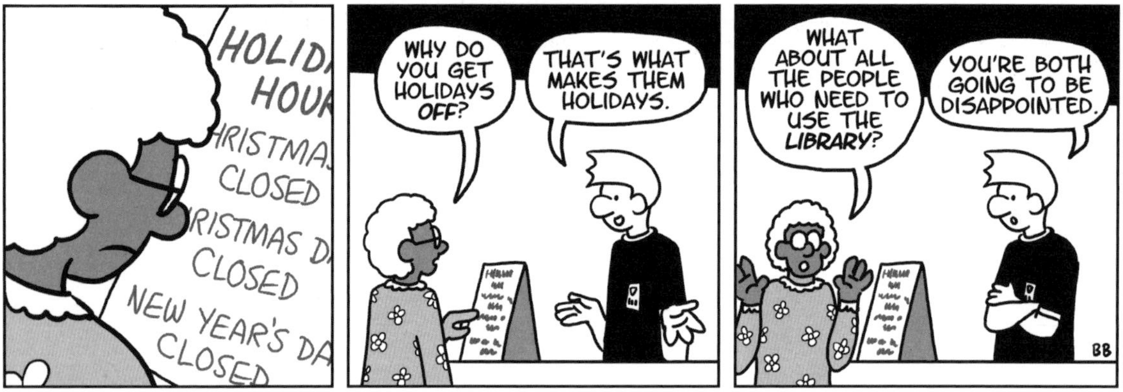
HOLID
HOUR
HRISTMAS
CLOSED
HRISTMAS D
CLOSED
NEW YEAR'S DA
CLOSED
WHY DO YOU GET HOLIDAYS *OFF*?
THAT'S WHAT MAKES THEM HOLIDAYS.
WHAT ABOUT ALL THE PEOPLE WHO NEED TO USE THE *LIBRARY*?
YOU'RE BOTH GOING TO BE DISAPPOINTED.
BB

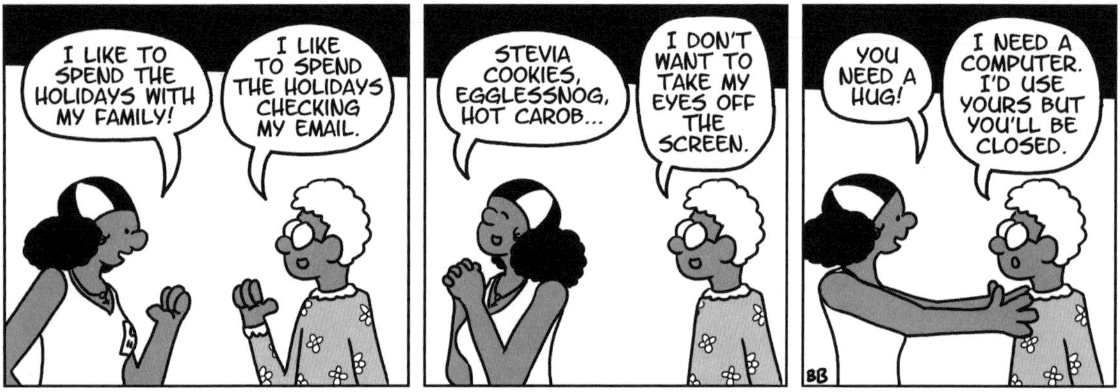
I LIKE TO SPEND THE HOLIDAYS WITH MY FAMILY!
I LIKE TO SPEND THE HOLIDAYS CHECKING MY EMAIL.
STEVIA COOKIES, EGGLESSNOG, HOT CAROB...
I DON'T WANT TO TAKE MY EYES OFF THE SCREEN.
YOU NEED A HUG!
I NEED A COMPUTER. I'D USE YOURS BUT YOU'LL BE CLOSED.
BB

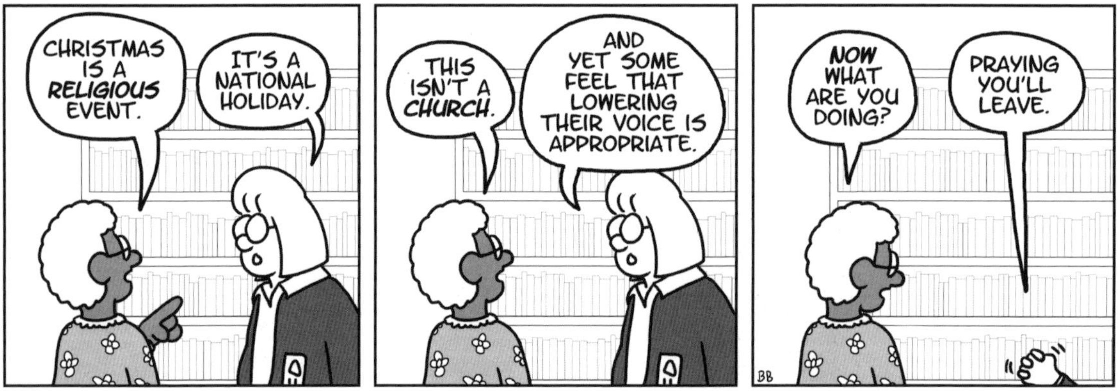
CHRISTMAS IS A **RELIGIOUS** EVENT.
IT'S A NATIONAL HOLIDAY.
THIS ISN'T A **CHURCH**.
AND YET SOME FEEL THAT LOWERING THEIR VOICE IS APPROPRIATE.
NOW WHAT ARE YOU DOING?
PRAYING YOU'LL LEAVE.
BB

Too Much Information

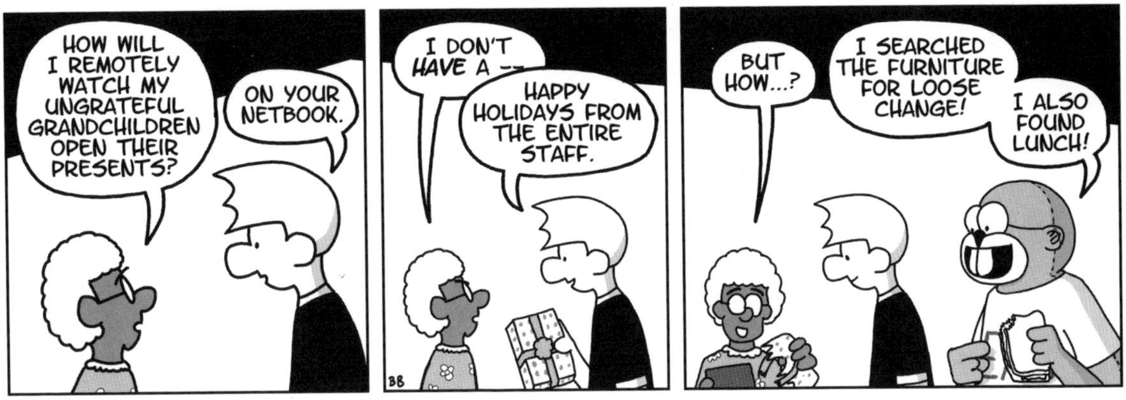

HOW WILL I REMOTELY WATCH MY UNGRATEFUL GRANDCHILDREN OPEN THEIR PRESENTS?
ON YOUR NETBOOK.
I DON'T HAVE A --
HAPPY HOLIDAYS FROM THE ENTIRE STAFF.
BB
BUT HOW...?
I SEARCHED THE FURNITURE FOR LOOSE CHANGE!
I ALSO FOUND LUNCH!

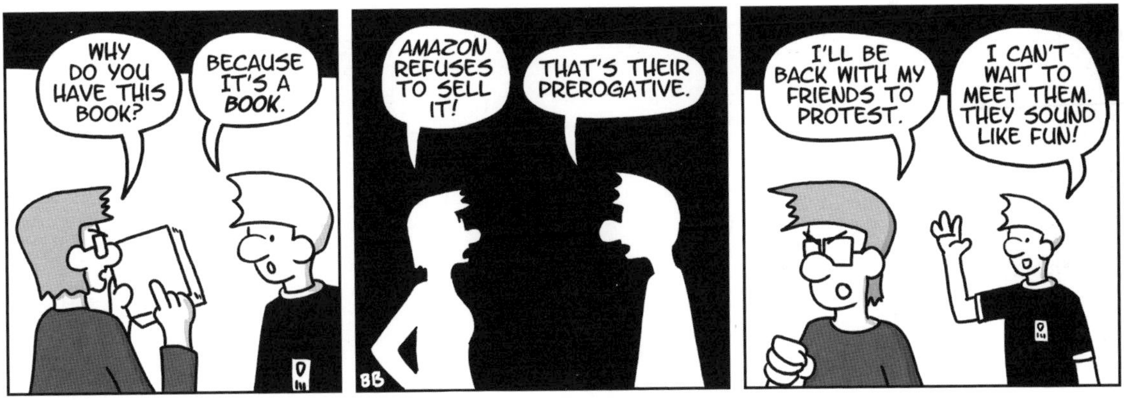

WHY DO YOU HAVE THIS BOOK?
BECAUSE IT'S A BOOK.
AMAZON REFUSES TO SELL IT!
THAT'S THEIR PREROGATIVE.
BB
I'LL BE BACK WITH MY FRIENDS TO PROTEST.
I CAN'T WAIT TO MEET THEM. THEY SOUND LIKE FUN!

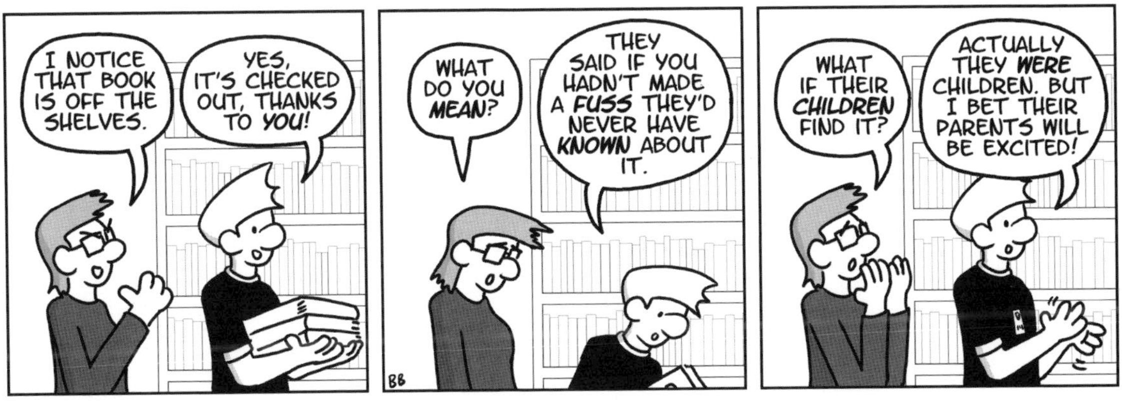

I NOTICE THAT BOOK IS OFF THE SHELVES.
YES, IT'S CHECKED OUT, THANKS TO YOU!
WHAT DO YOU MEAN?
THEY SAID IF YOU HADN'T MADE A FUSS THEY'D NEVER HAVE KNOWN ABOUT IT.
BB
WHAT IF THEIR CHILDREN FIND IT?
ACTUALLY THEY WERE CHILDREN. BUT I BET THEIR PARENTS WILL BE EXCITED!

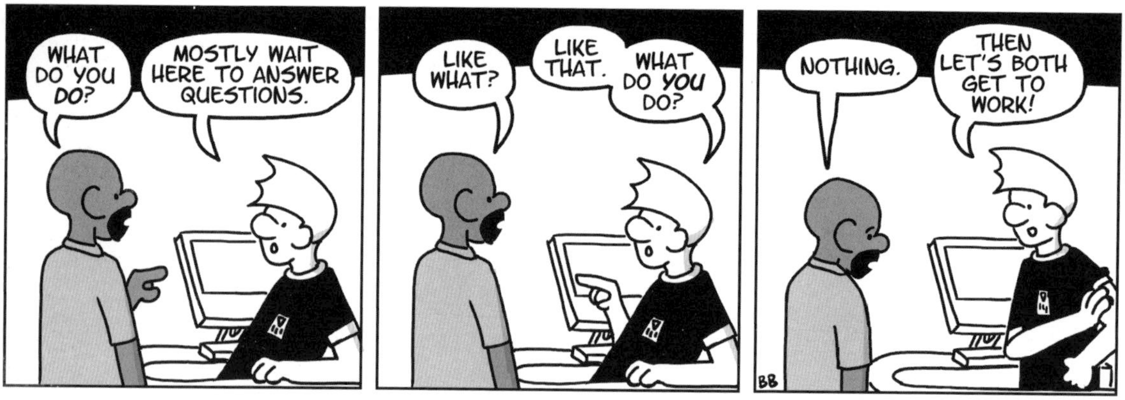
WHAT DO YOU *DO*?
MOSTLY WAIT HERE TO ANSWER QUESTIONS.
LIKE WHAT?
LIKE THAT.
WHAT DO ***YOU*** DO?
NOTHING.
THEN LET'S BOTH GET TO WORK!
BB

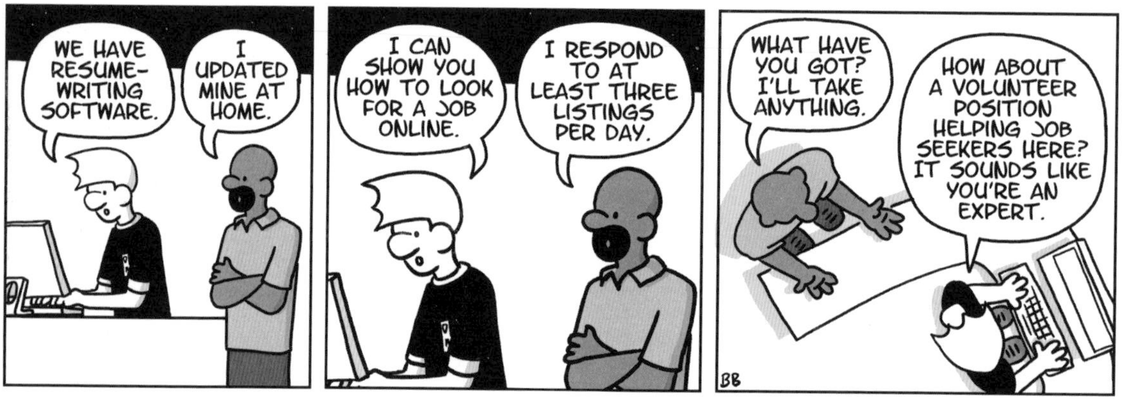
WE HAVE RESUME-WRITING SOFTWARE.
I UPDATED MINE AT HOME.
I CAN SHOW YOU HOW TO LOOK FOR A JOB ONLINE.
I RESPOND TO AT LEAST THREE LISTINGS PER DAY.
WHAT HAVE YOU GOT? I'LL TAKE ANYTHING.
HOW ABOUT A VOLUNTEER POSITION HELPING JOB SEEKERS HERE? IT SOUNDS LIKE YOU'RE AN EXPERT.
BB

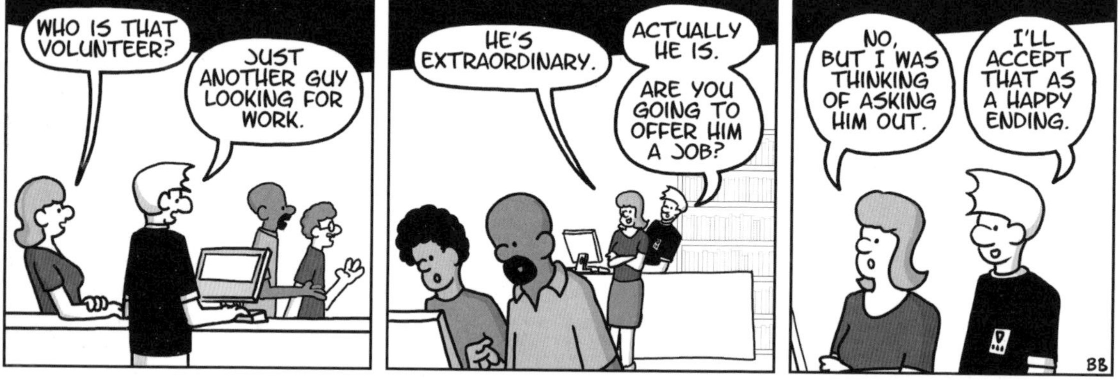
WHO IS THAT VOLUNTEER?
JUST ANOTHER GUY LOOKING FOR WORK.
HE'S EXTRAORDINARY.
ACTUALLY HE IS.
ARE YOU GOING TO OFFER HIM A JOB?
NO, BUT I WAS THINKING OF ASKING HIM OUT.
I'LL ACCEPT THAT AS A HAPPY ENDING.
BB

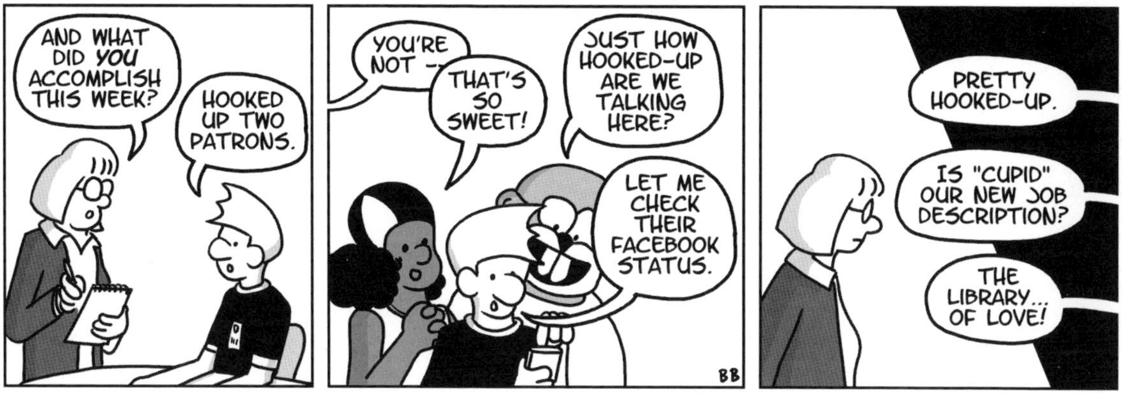
AND WHAT DID YOU ACCOMPLISH THIS WEEK?
HOOKED UP TWO PATRONS.
YOU'RE NOT --
THAT'S SO SWEET!
JUST HOW HOOKED-UP ARE WE TALKING HERE?
LET ME CHECK THEIR FACEBOOK STATUS.
BB
PRETTY HOOKED-UP.
IS "CUPID" OUR NEW JOB DESCRIPTION?
THE LIBRARY... OF LOVE!

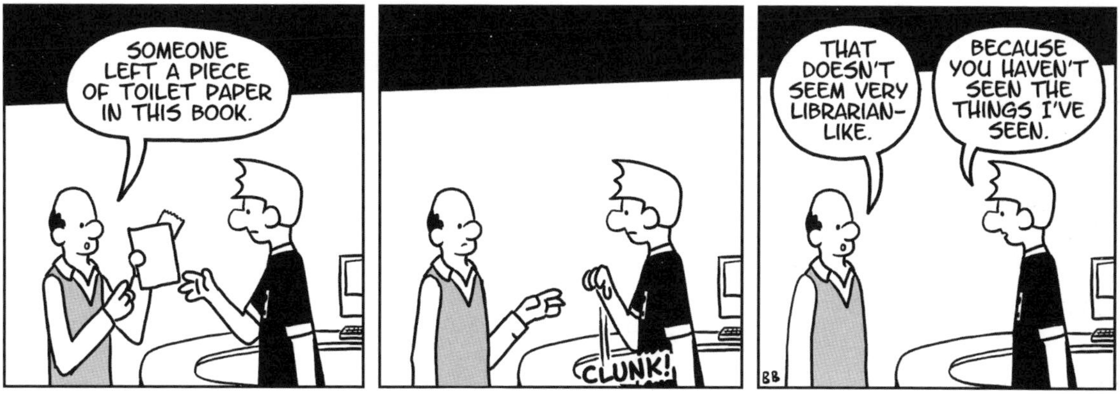
SOMEONE LEFT A PIECE OF TOILET PAPER IN THIS BOOK.
CLUNK!
THAT DOESN'T SEEM VERY LIBRARIAN-LIKE.
BECAUSE YOU HAVEN'T SEEN THE THINGS I'VE SEEN.
BB

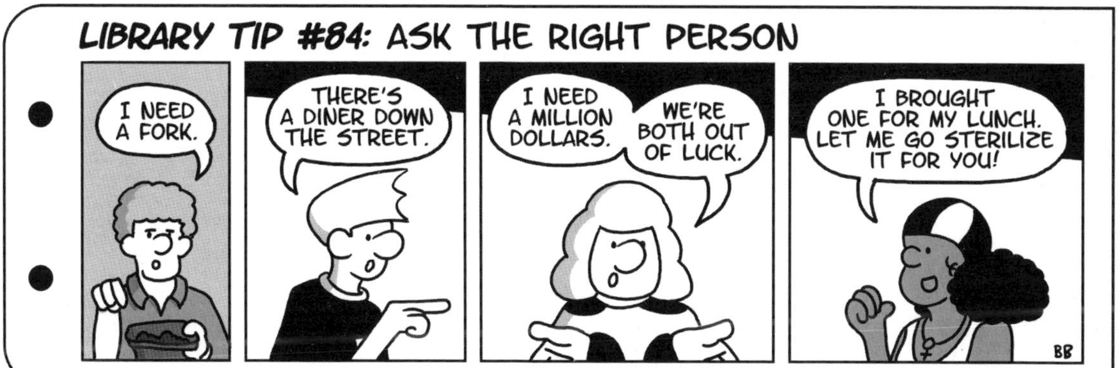
LIBRARY TIP #84: ASK THE RIGHT PERSON
I NEED A FORK.
THERE'S A DINER DOWN THE STREET.
I NEED A MILLION DOLLARS.
WE'RE BOTH OUT OF LUCK.
I BROUGHT ONE FOR MY LUNCH. LET ME GO STERILIZE IT FOR YOU!
BB

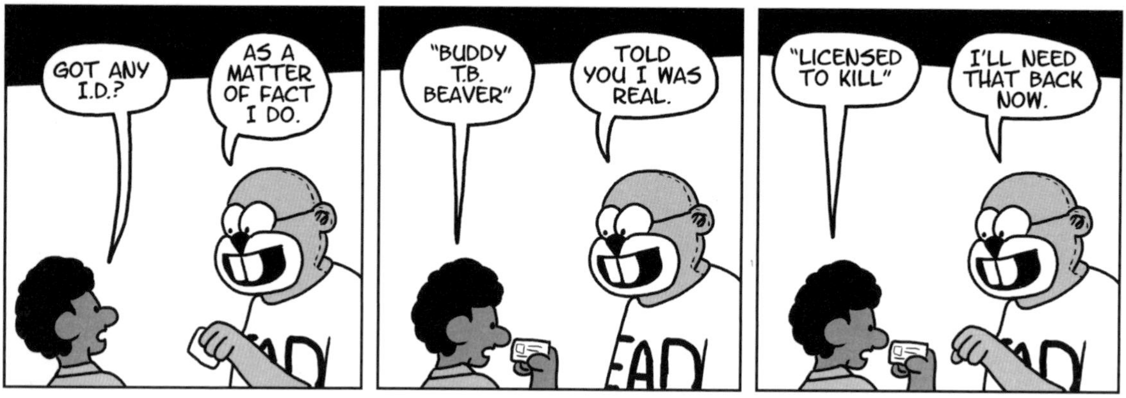
GOT ANY I.D.?
AS A MATTER OF FACT I DO.
"BUDDY T.B. BEAVER"
TOLD YOU I WAS REAL.
"LICENSED TO KILL"
I'LL NEED THAT BACK NOW.

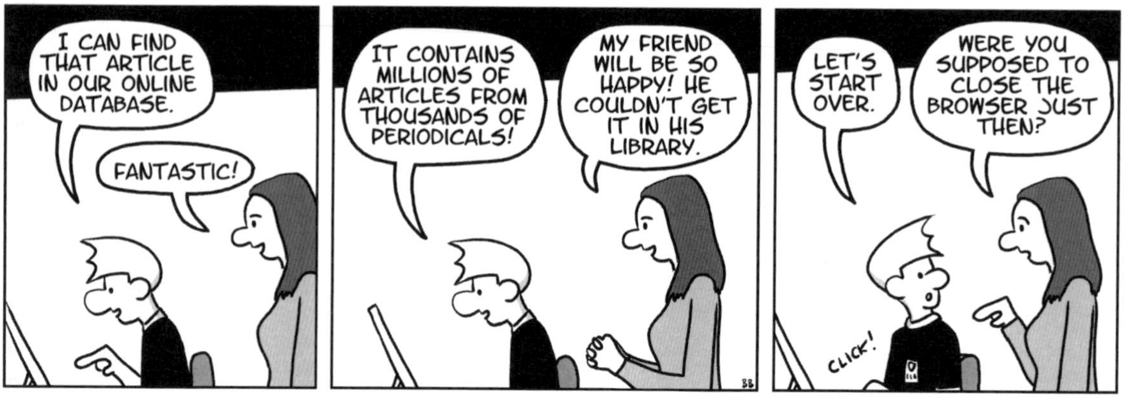
I CAN FIND THAT ARTICLE IN OUR ONLINE DATABASE.
FANTASTIC!
IT CONTAINS MILLIONS OF ARTICLES FROM THOUSANDS OF PERIODICALS!
MY FRIEND WILL BE SO HAPPY! HE COULDN'T GET IT IN HIS LIBRARY.
LET'S START OVER.
WERE YOU SUPPOSED TO CLOSE THE BROWSER JUST THEN?
CLICK!

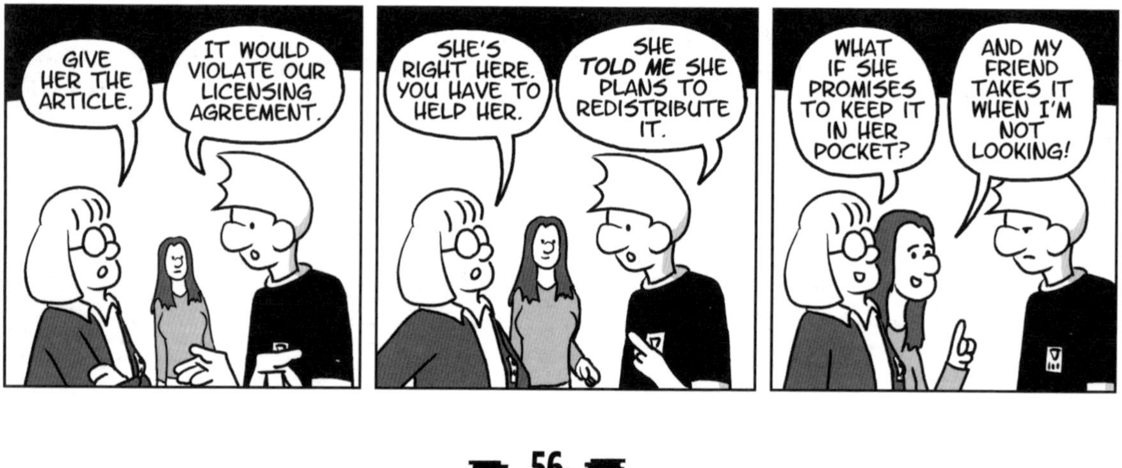
GIVE HER THE ARTICLE.
IT WOULD VIOLATE OUR LICENSING AGREEMENT.
SHE'S RIGHT HERE. YOU HAVE TO HELP HER.
SHE **TOLD ME** SHE PLANS TO REDISTRIBUTE IT.
WHAT IF SHE PROMISES TO KEEP IT IN HER POCKET?
AND MY FRIEND TAKES IT WHEN I'M NOT LOOKING!

Too Much Information

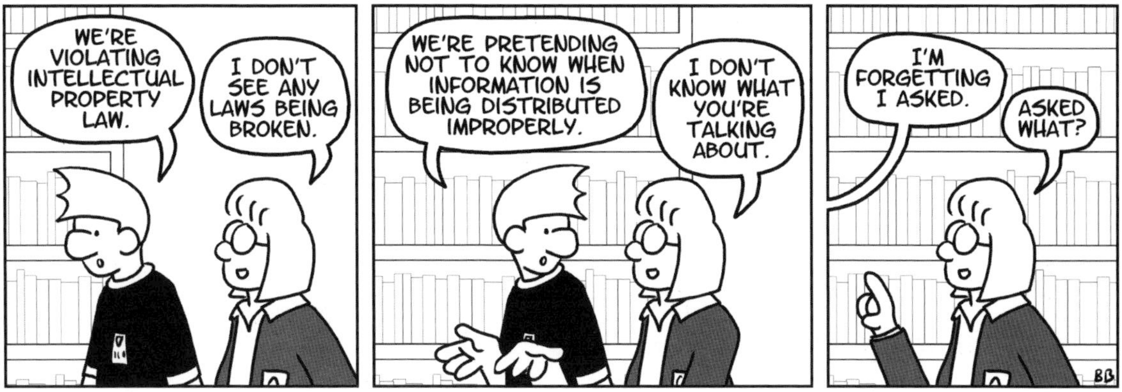

WE'RE VIOLATING INTELLECTUAL PROPERTY LAW.
I DON'T SEE ANY LAWS BEING BROKEN.
WE'RE PRETENDING NOT TO KNOW WHEN INFORMATION IS BEING DISTRIBUTED IMPROPERLY.
I DON'T KNOW WHAT YOU'RE TALKING ABOUT.
I'M FORGETTING I ASKED.
ASKED WHAT?
BB

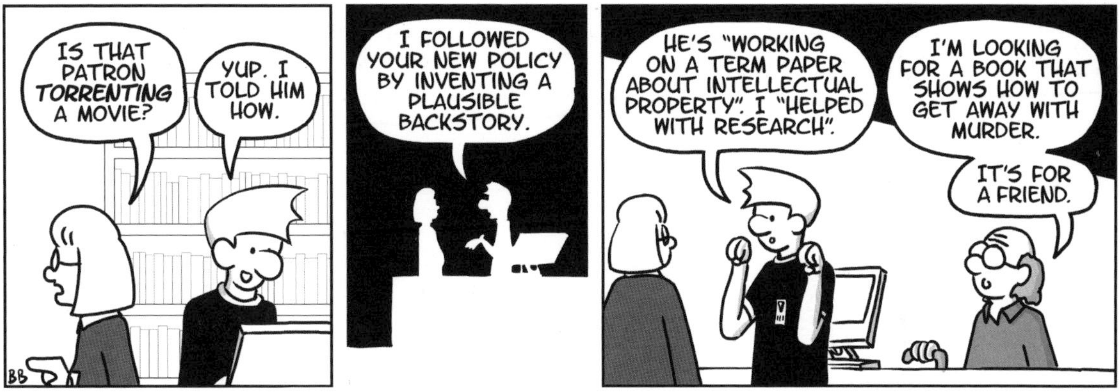

IS THAT PATRON *TORRENTING* A MOVIE?
YUP. I TOLD HIM HOW.
BB
I FOLLOWED YOUR NEW POLICY BY INVENTING A PLAUSIBLE BACKSTORY.
HE'S "WORKING ON A TERM PAPER ABOUT INTELLECTUAL PROPERTY". I "HELPED WITH RESEARCH".
I'M LOOKING FOR A BOOK THAT SHOWS HOW TO GET AWAY WITH MURDER.
IT'S FOR A FRIEND.

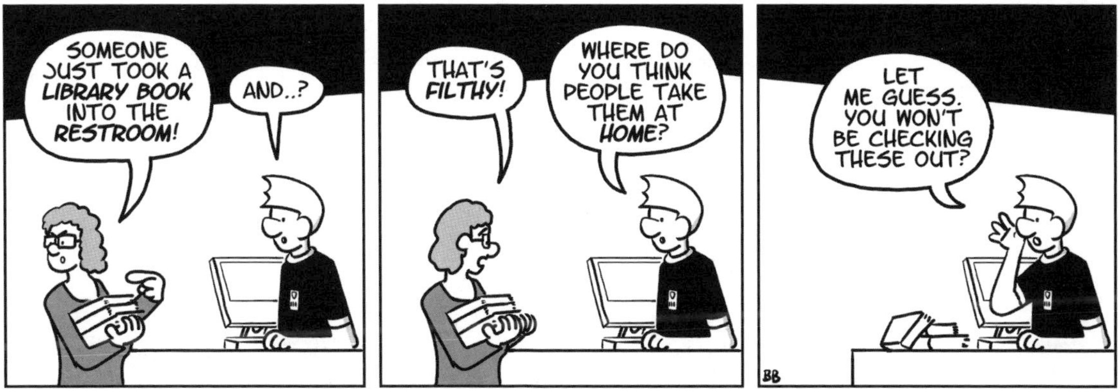

SOMEONE JUST TOOK A *LIBRARY BOOK* INTO THE *RESTROOM*!
AND..?
THAT'S *FILTHY*!
WHERE DO YOU THINK PEOPLE TAKE THEM AT *HOME*?
LET ME GUESS. YOU WON'T BE CHECKING THESE OUT?
BB

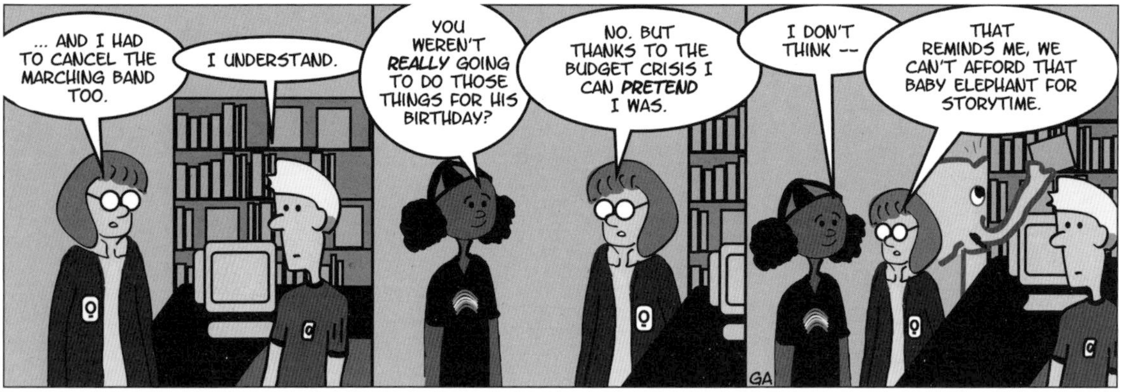
... AND I HAD TO CANCEL THE MARCHING BAND TOO.
I UNDERSTAND.
YOU WEREN'T *REALLY* GOING TO DO THOSE THINGS FOR HIS BIRTHDAY?
NO. BUT THANKS TO THE BUDGET CRISIS I CAN *PRETEND* I WAS.
I DON'T THINK --
THAT REMINDS ME, WE CAN'T AFFORD THAT BABY ELEPHANT FOR STORYTIME.
GA

Every year on Bill's birthday Gene draws the strip, and every time it's not quite what Bill had in mind. Turnabout is fair play.

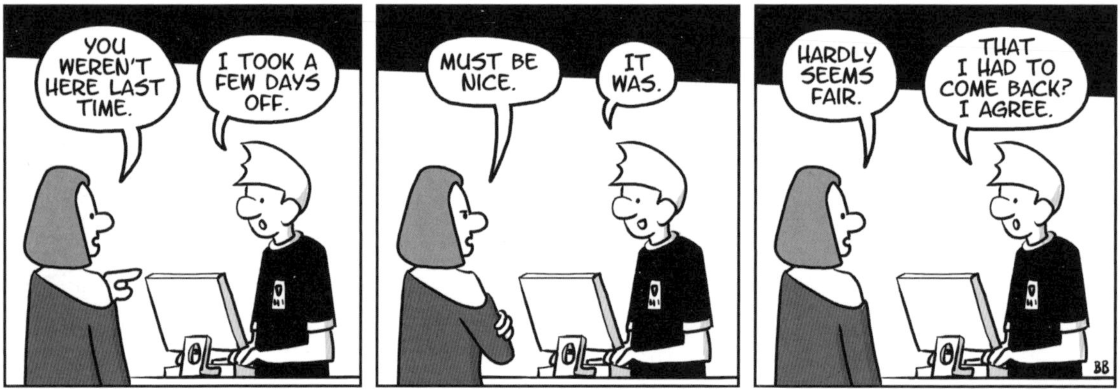
YOU WEREN'T HERE LAST TIME.
I TOOK A FEW DAYS OFF.
MUST BE NICE.
IT WAS.
HARDLY SEEMS FAIR.
THAT I HAD TO COME BACK? I AGREE.
BB

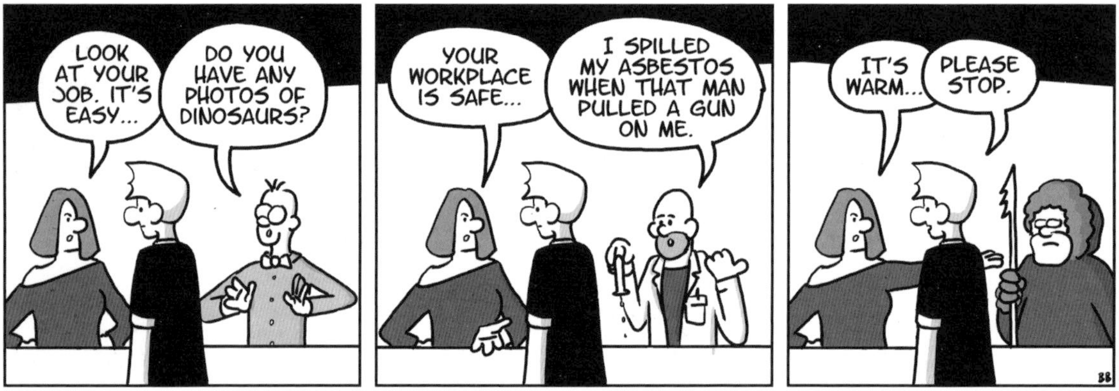
LOOK AT YOUR JOB. IT'S EASY...
DO YOU HAVE ANY PHOTOS OF DINOSAURS?
YOUR WORKPLACE IS SAFE...
I SPILLED MY ASBESTOS WHEN THAT MAN PULLED A GUN ON ME.
IT'S WARM...
PLEASE STOP.
BB

Too Much Information

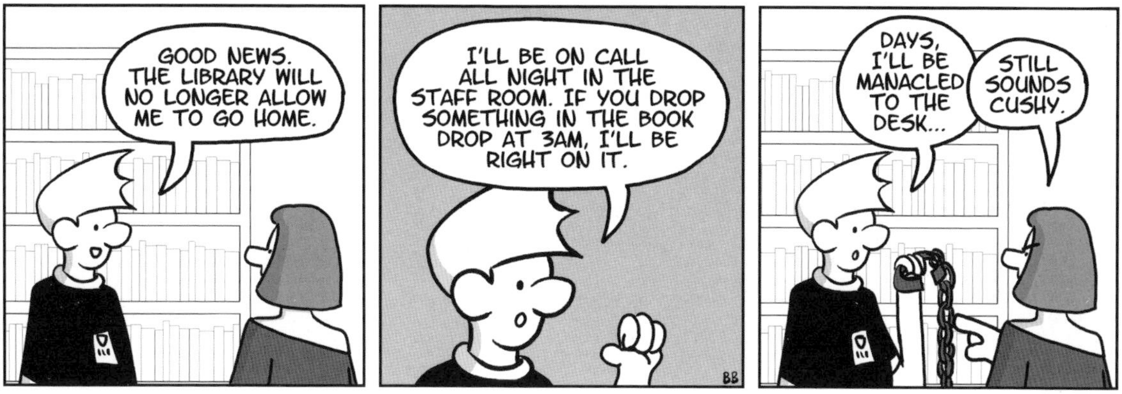
GOOD NEWS. THE LIBRARY WILL NO LONGER ALLOW ME TO GO HOME.
I'LL BE ON CALL ALL NIGHT IN THE STAFF ROOM. IF YOU DROP SOMETHING IN THE BOOK DROP AT 3AM, I'LL BE RIGHT ON IT.
BB
DAYS, I'LL BE MANACLED TO THE DESK...
STILL SOUNDS CUSHY.

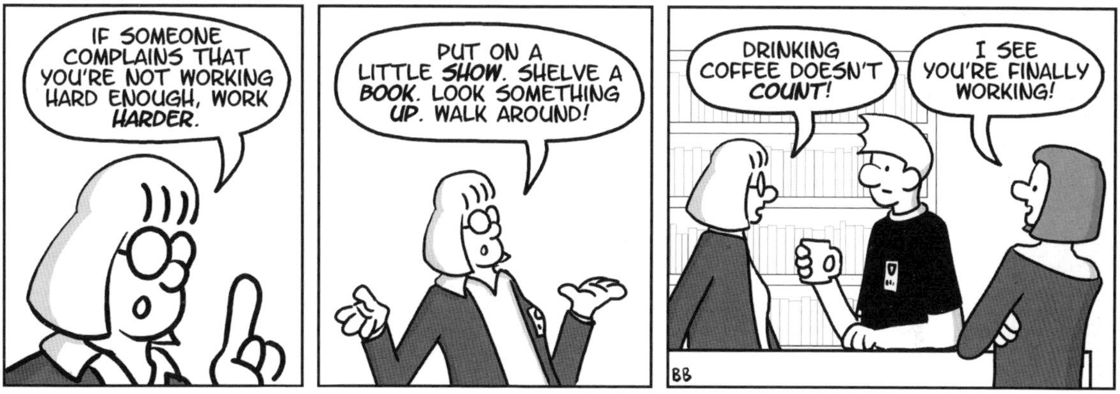
IF SOMEONE COMPLAINS THAT YOU'RE NOT WORKING HARD ENOUGH, WORK HARDER.
PUT ON A LITTLE SHOW. SHELVE A BOOK. LOOK SOMETHING UP. WALK AROUND!
DRINKING COFFEE DOESN'T COUNT!
I SEE YOU'RE FINALLY WORKING!
BB

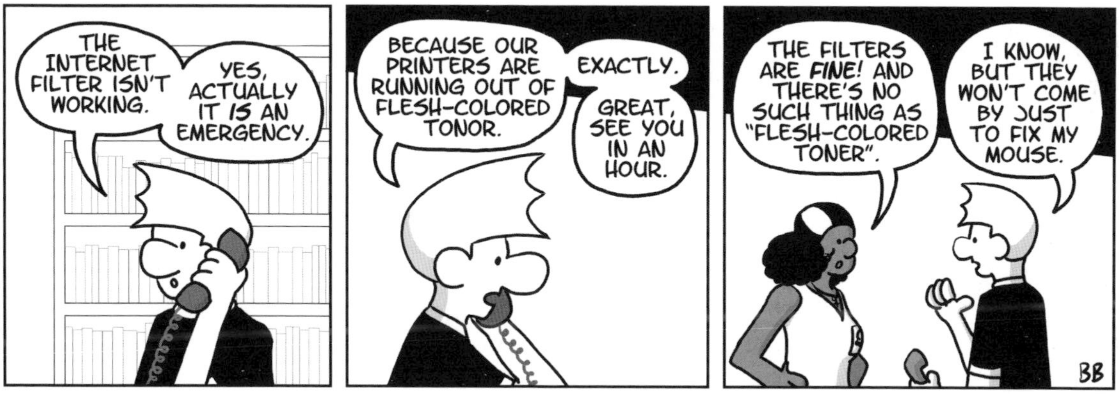
THE INTERNET FILTER ISN'T WORKING.
YES, ACTUALLY IT IS AN EMERGENCY.
BECAUSE OUR PRINTERS ARE RUNNING OUT OF FLESH-COLORED TONOR.
EXACTLY.
GREAT, SEE YOU IN AN HOUR.
THE FILTERS ARE FINE! AND THERE'S NO SUCH THING AS "FLESH-COLORED TONER".
I KNOW, BUT THEY WON'T COME BY JUST TO FIX MY MOUSE.
BB

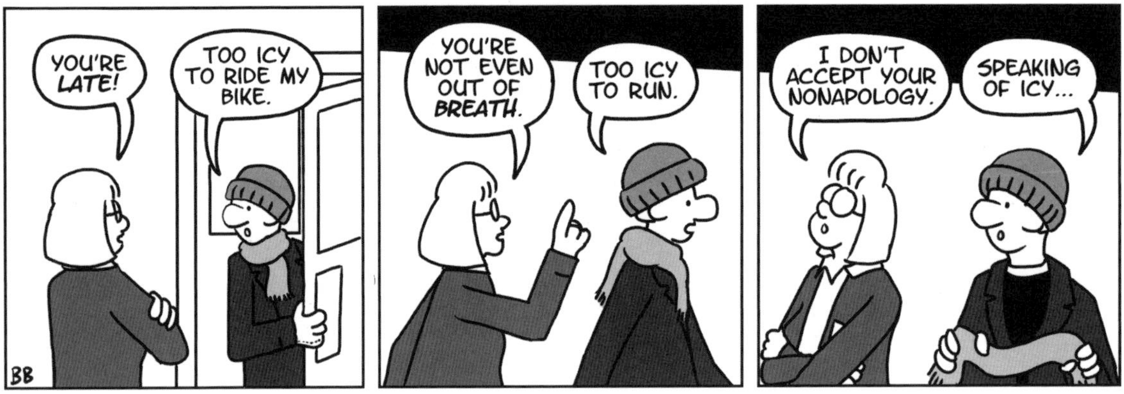
BB
YOU'RE *LATE!*
TOO ICY TO RIDE MY BIKE.
YOU'RE NOT EVEN OUT OF *BREATH*.
TOO ICY TO RUN.
I DON'T ACCEPT YOUR NONAPOLOGY.
SPEAKING OF ICY...

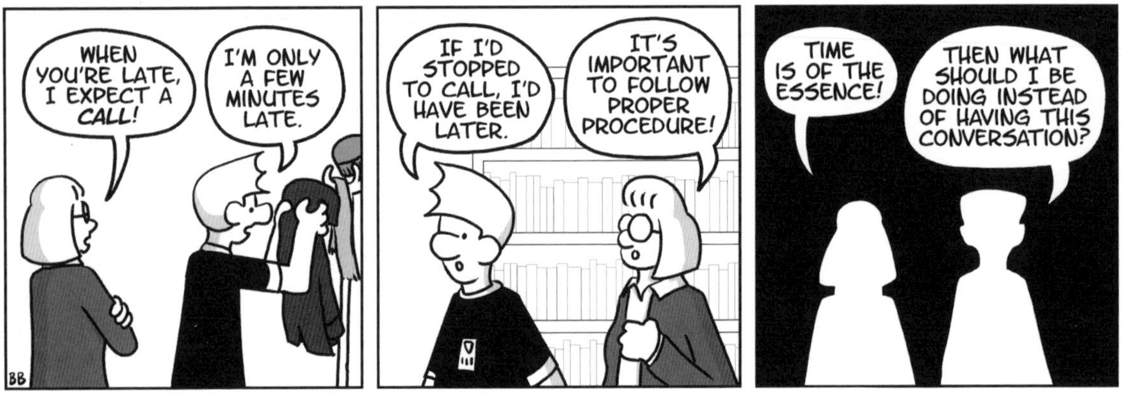
BB
WHEN YOU'RE LATE, I EXPECT A *CALL!*
I'M ONLY A FEW MINUTES LATE.
IF I'D STOPPED TO CALL, I'D HAVE BEEN LATER.
IT'S IMPORTANT TO FOLLOW PROPER PROCEDURE!
TIME IS OF THE ESSENCE!
THEN WHAT SHOULD I BE DOING INSTEAD OF HAVING THIS CONVERSATION?

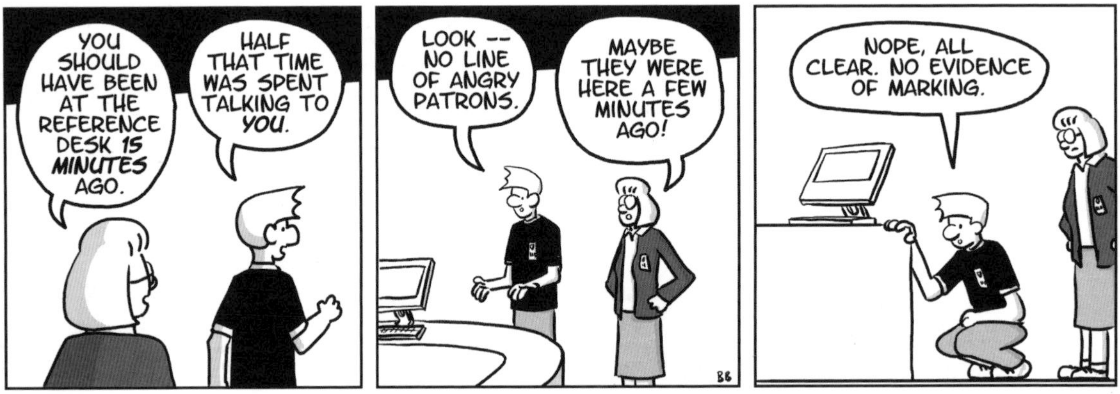
YOU SHOULD HAVE BEEN AT THE REFERENCE DESK **15 MINUTES** AGO.
HALF THAT TIME WAS SPENT TALKING TO *YOU*.
LOOK -- NO LINE OF ANGRY PATRONS.
MAYBE THEY WERE HERE A FEW MINUTES AGO!
BB
NOPE, ALL CLEAR. NO EVIDENCE OF MARKING.

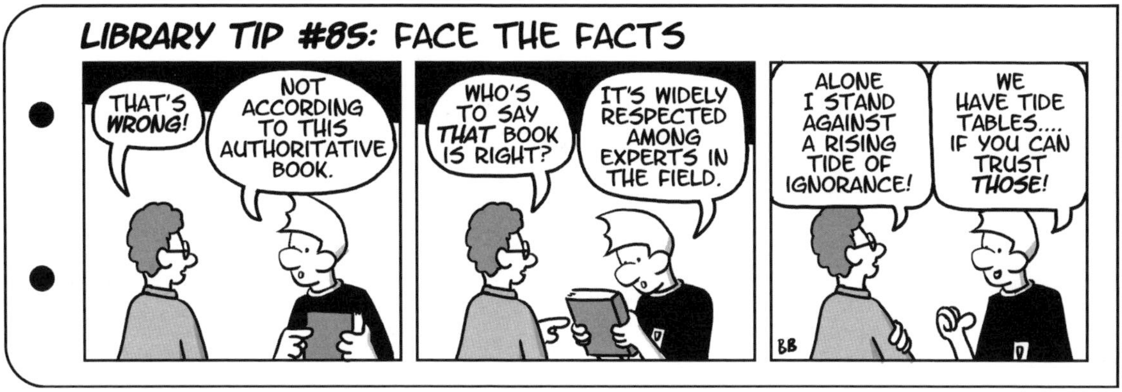
LIBRARY TIP #85: FACE THE FACTS
THAT'S WRONG!
NOT ACCORDING TO THIS AUTHORITATIVE BOOK.
WHO'S TO SAY THAT BOOK IS RIGHT?
IT'S WIDELY RESPECTED AMONG EXPERTS IN THE FIELD.
ALONE I STAND AGAINST A RISING TIDE OF IGNORANCE!
WE HAVE TIDE TABLES.... IF YOU CAN TRUST THOSE!
BB

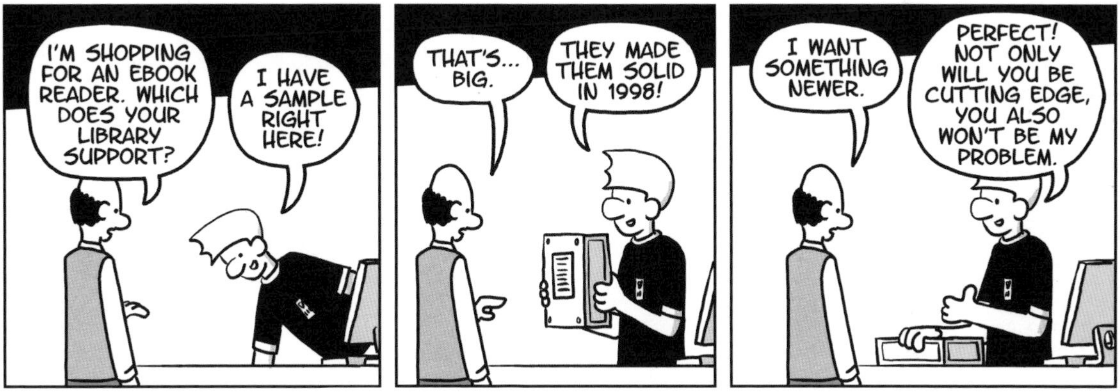
I'M SHOPPING FOR AN EBOOK READER. WHICH DOES YOUR LIBRARY SUPPORT?
I HAVE A SAMPLE RIGHT HERE!
THAT'S... BIG.
THEY MADE THEM SOLID IN 1998!
I WANT SOMETHING NEWER.
PERFECT! NOT ONLY WILL YOU BE CUTTING EDGE, YOU ALSO WON'T BE MY PROBLEM.

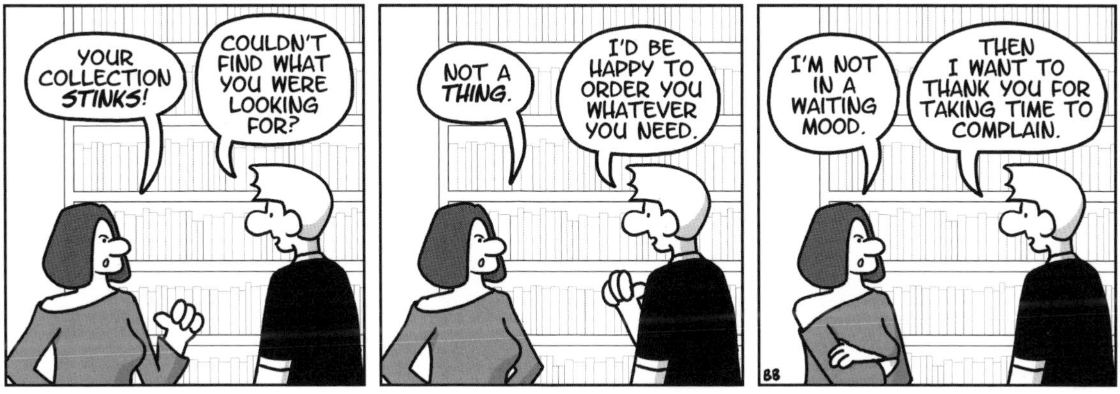
YOUR COLLECTION STINKS!
COULDN'T FIND WHAT YOU WERE LOOKING FOR?
NOT A THING.
I'D BE HAPPY TO ORDER YOU WHATEVER YOU NEED.
I'M NOT IN A WAITING MOOD.
THEN I WANT TO THANK YOU FOR TAKING TIME TO COMPLAIN.
BB

The Book Not Taken

with heartfelt apologies to Robert Frost

Two books converged on a yellowed shelf,
And sorry I could not read both And be one reader, long I stood
And looked up long as I could
And to where others the lower shelf outgreweth;
BB

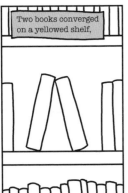

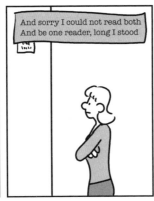

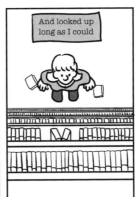

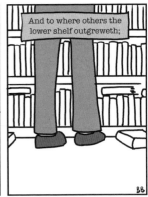

Then took the one, just as fair,
And having perhaps the better cover, Because it looked sassy and showed bare;
TRUE CONFESSIONS OF A NANNY
TRUE CONFESSIONS OF A NANNY
Though as for that, the young au-pair Didn't need me; she had a lover,
BB

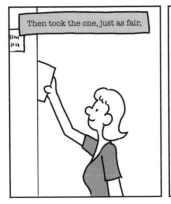

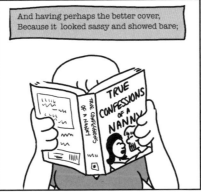

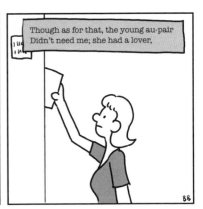

Too Much Information

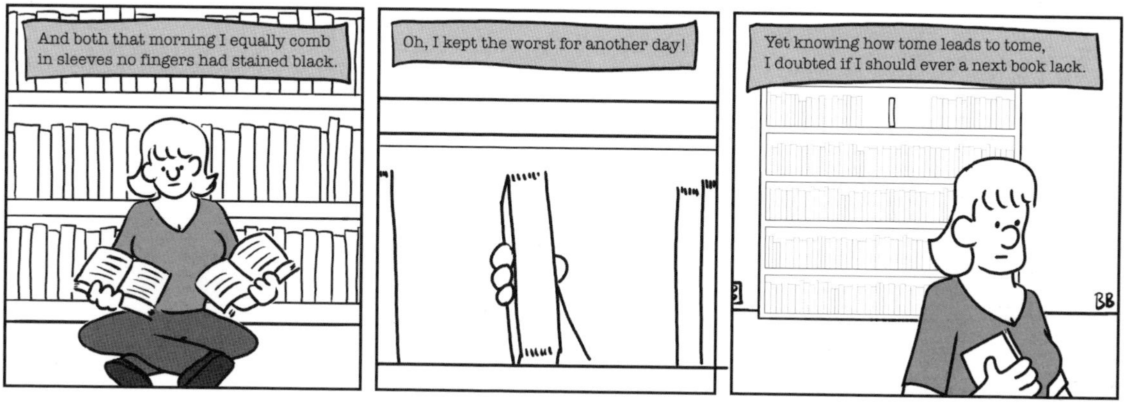
And both that morning I equally comb
in sleeves no fingers had stained black.
Oh, I kept the worst for another day!
Yet knowing how tome leads to tome,
I doubted if I should ever a next book lack.
BB

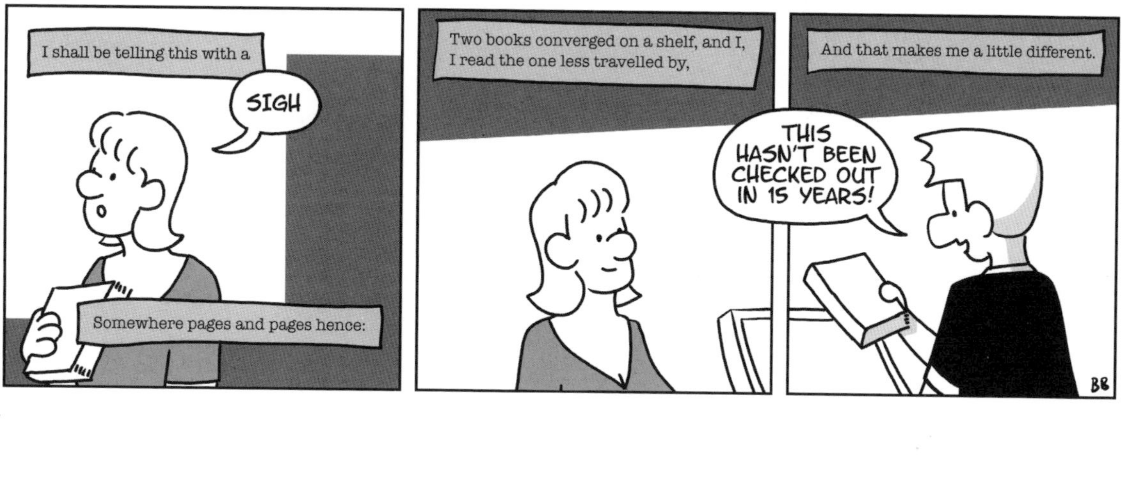
I shall be telling this with a
SIGH
Somewhere pages and pages hence:
Two books converged on a shelf, and I,
I read the one less travelled by,
And that makes me a little different.
THIS HASN'T BEEN CHECKED OUT IN 15 YEARS!
BB

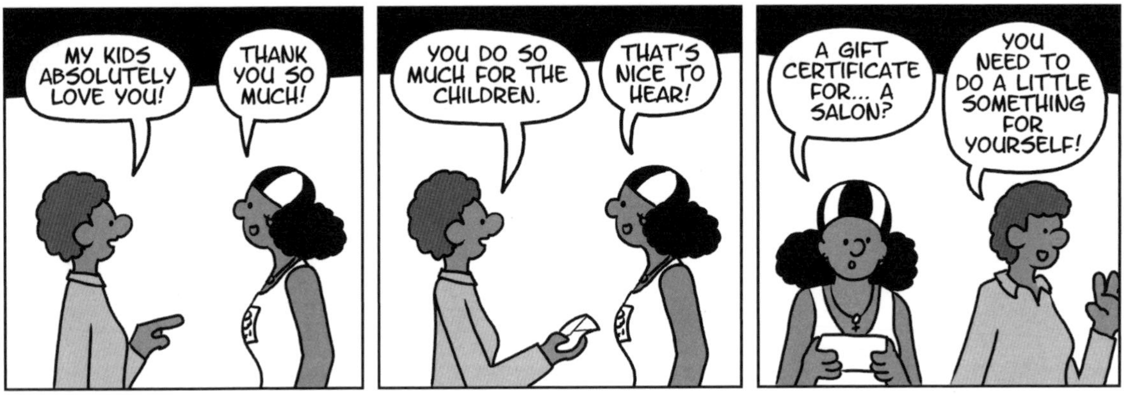
MY KIDS ABSOLUTELY LOVE YOU!
THANK YOU SO MUCH!
YOU DO SO MUCH FOR THE CHILDREN.
THAT'S NICE TO HEAR!
A GIFT CERTIFICATE FOR... A SALON?
YOU NEED TO DO A LITTLE SOMETHING FOR YOURSELF!

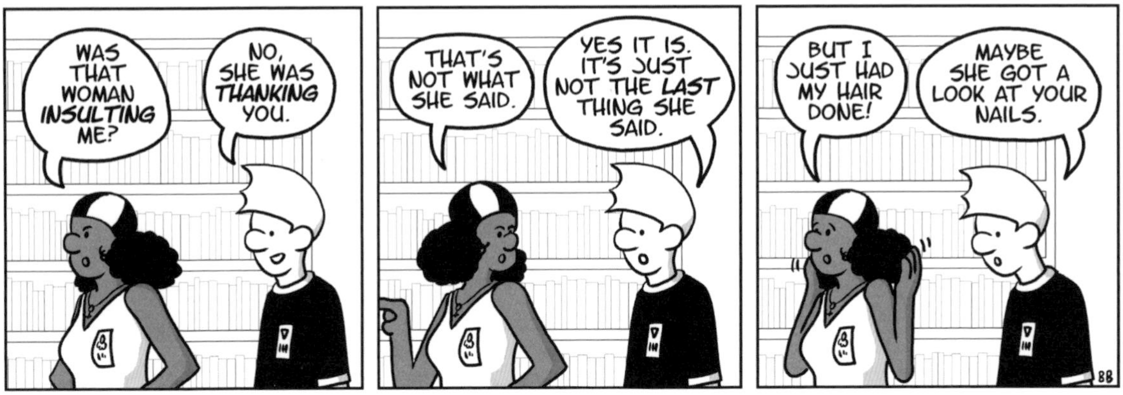
WAS THAT WOMAN *INSULTING* ME?
NO, SHE WAS *THANKING* YOU.
THAT'S NOT WHAT SHE SAID.
YES IT IS. IT'S JUST NOT THE *LAST* THING SHE SAID.
BUT I JUST HAD MY HAIR DONE!
MAYBE SHE GOT A LOOK AT YOUR NAILS.

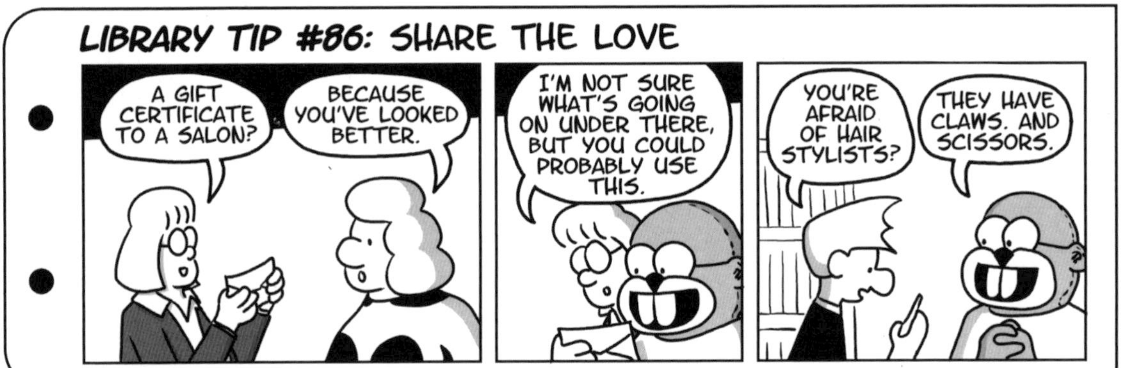
LIBRARY TIP #86: SHARE THE LOVE
A GIFT CERTIFICATE TO A SALON?
BECAUSE YOU'VE LOOKED BETTER.
I'M NOT SURE WHAT'S GOING ON UNDER THERE, BUT YOU COULD PROBABLY USE THIS.
YOU'RE AFRAID OF HAIR STYLISTS?
THEY HAVE CLAWS. AND SCISSORS.

Too Much Information

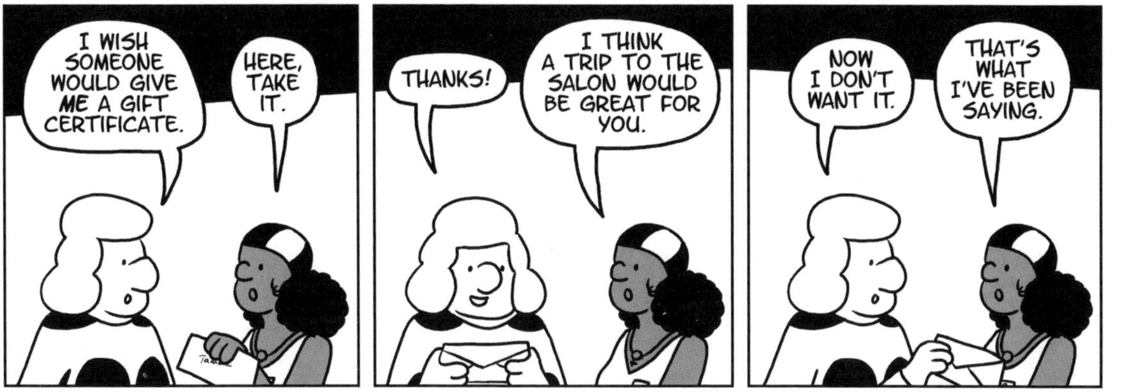
I WISH SOMEONE WOULD GIVE *ME* A GIFT CERTIFICATE.
HERE, TAKE IT.
THANKS!
I THINK A TRIP TO THE SALON WOULD BE GREAT FOR YOU.
NOW I DON'T WANT IT.
THAT'S WHAT I'VE BEEN SAYING.

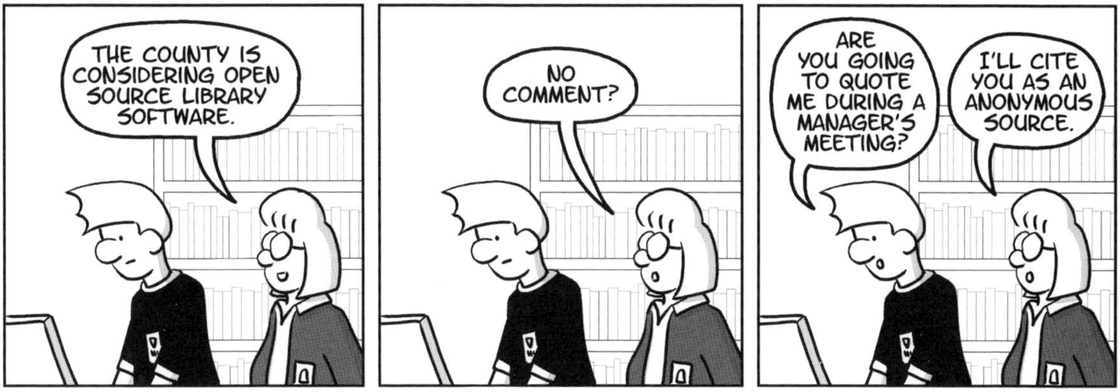
THE COUNTY IS CONSIDERING OPEN SOURCE LIBRARY SOFTWARE.
NO COMMENT?
ARE YOU GOING TO QUOTE ME DURING A MANAGER'S MEETING?
I'LL CITE YOU AS AN ANONYMOUS SOURCE.

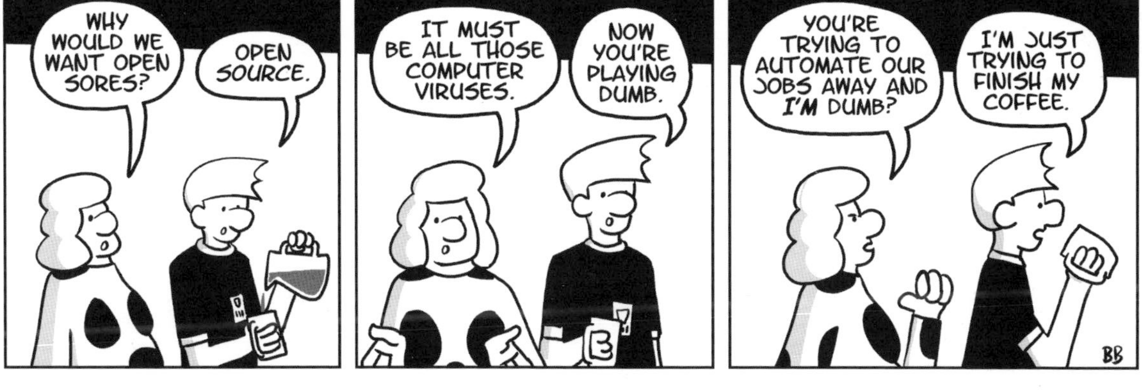
WHY WOULD WE WANT OPEN SORES?
OPEN SOURCE.
IT MUST BE ALL THOSE COMPUTER VIRUSES.
NOW YOU'RE PLAYING DUMB.
YOU'RE TRYING TO AUTOMATE OUR JOBS AWAY AND *I'M* DUMB?
I'M JUST TRYING TO FINISH MY COFFEE.
BB

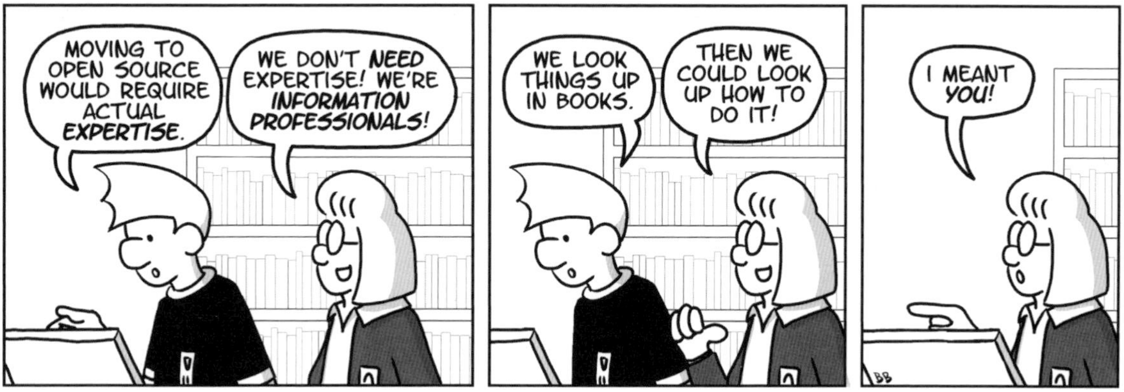
MOVING TO OPEN SOURCE WOULD REQUIRE ACTUAL **EXPERTISE**.
WE DON'T **NEED** EXPERTISE! WE'RE ***INFORMATION PROFESSIONALS***!
WE LOOK THINGS UP IN BOOKS.
THEN WE COULD LOOK UP HOW TO DO IT!
I MEANT ***YOU***!
BB

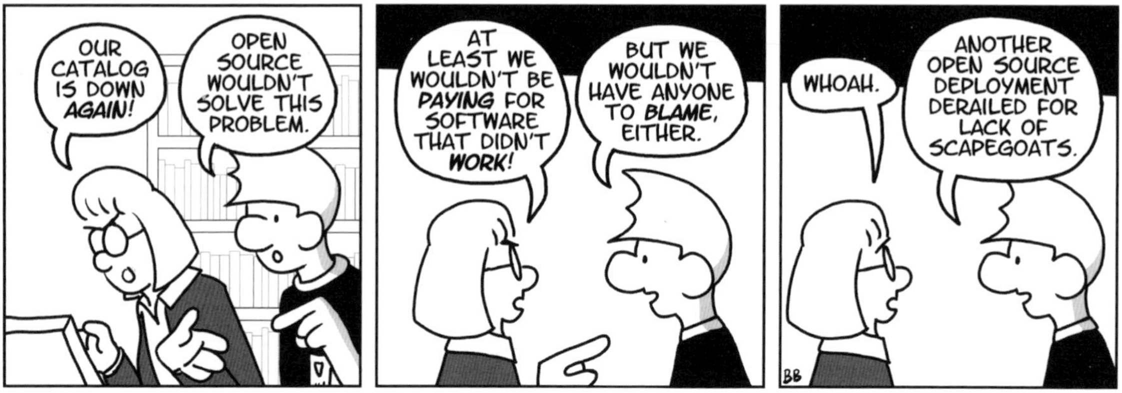
OUR CATALOG IS DOWN ***AGAIN***!
OPEN SOURCE WOULDN'T SOLVE THIS PROBLEM.
AT LEAST WE WOULDN'T BE ***PAYING*** FOR SOFTWARE THAT DIDN'T ***WORK***!
BUT WE WOULDN'T HAVE ANYONE TO ***BLAME***, EITHER.
WHOAH.
ANOTHER OPEN SOURCE DEPLOYMENT DERAILED FOR LACK OF SCAPEGOATS.
BB

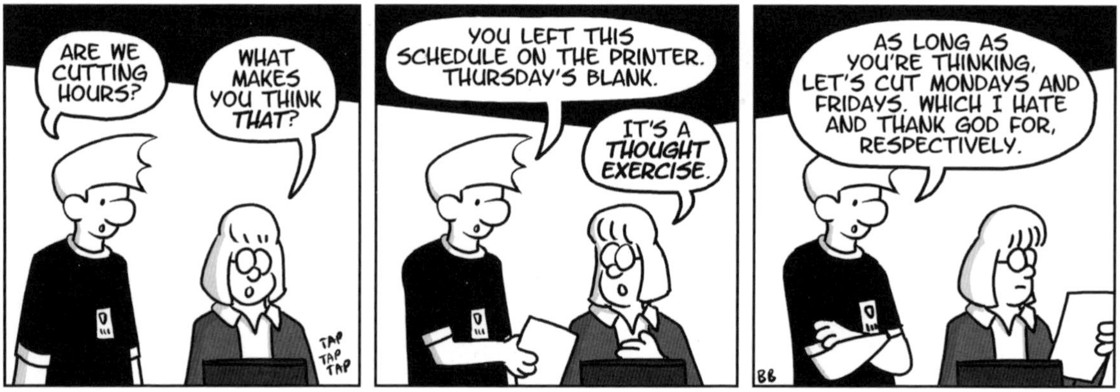
ARE WE CUTTING HOURS?
WHAT MAKES YOU THINK ***THAT***?
TAP TAP TAP
YOU LEFT THIS SCHEDULE ON THE PRINTER. THURSDAY'S BLANK.
IT'S A ***THOUGHT EXERCISE***.
AS LONG AS YOU'RE THINKING, LET'S CUT MONDAYS AND FRIDAYS. WHICH I HATE AND THANK GOD FOR, RESPECTIVELY.
BB

Too Much Information

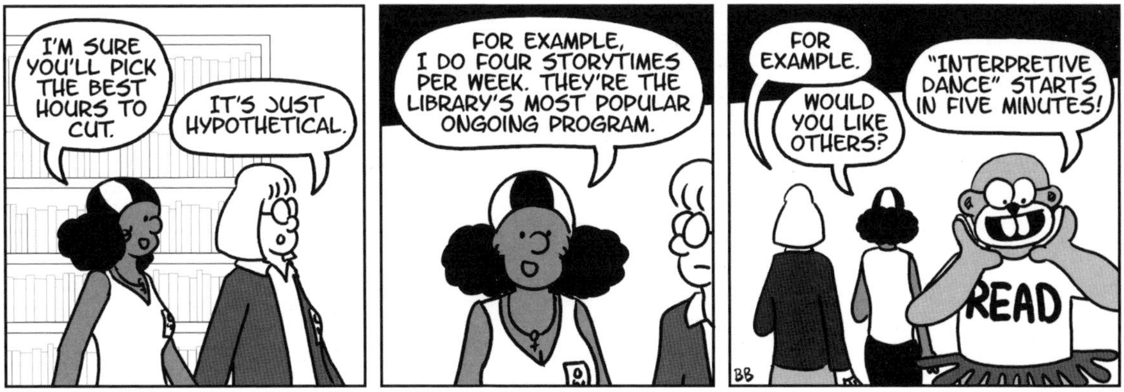

I'M SURE YOU'LL PICK THE BEST HOURS TO CUT.
IT'S JUST HYPOTHETICAL.
FOR EXAMPLE, I DO FOUR STORYTIMES PER WEEK. THEY'RE THE LIBRARY'S MOST POPULAR ONGOING PROGRAM.
FOR EXAMPLE.
WOULD YOU LIKE OTHERS?
"INTERPRETIVE DANCE" STARTS IN FIVE MINUTES!
READ
BB

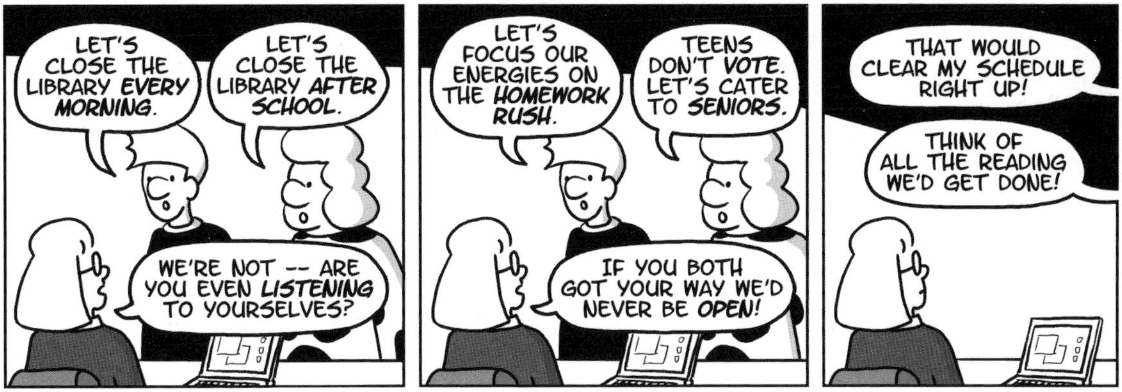

LET'S CLOSE THE LIBRARY **EVERY MORNING**.
LET'S CLOSE THE LIBRARY **AFTER SCHOOL**.
WE'RE NOT -- ARE YOU EVEN **LISTENING** TO YOURSELVES?
LET'S FOCUS OUR ENERGIES ON THE **HOMEWORK RUSH**.
TEENS DON'T **VOTE**. LET'S CATER TO **SENIORS**.
IF YOU BOTH GOT YOUR WAY WE'D NEVER BE **OPEN**!
THAT WOULD CLEAR MY SCHEDULE RIGHT UP!
THINK OF ALL THE READING WE'D GET DONE!

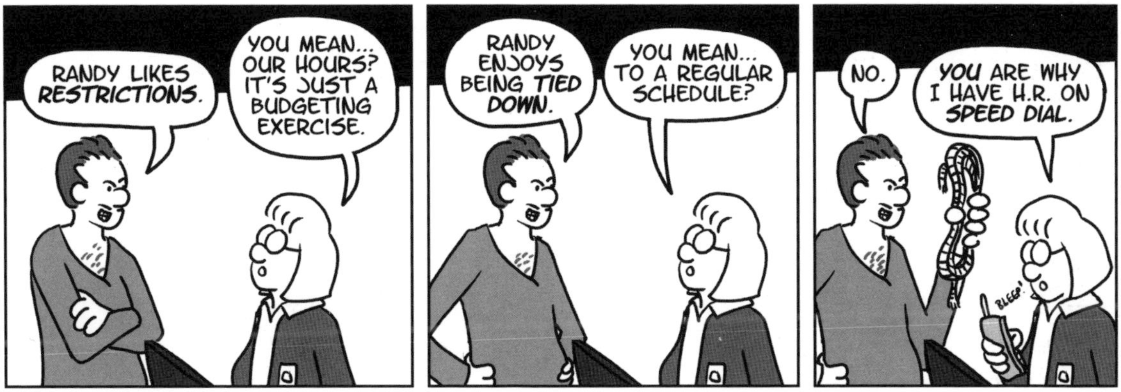

RANDY LIKES **RESTRICTIONS**.
YOU MEAN... OUR HOURS? IT'S JUST A BUDGETING EXERCISE.
RANDY ENJOYS BEING **TIED DOWN**.
YOU MEAN... TO A REGULAR SCHEDULE?
NO.
YOU ARE WHY I HAVE H.R. ON ***SPEED DIAL***.
BLEEP!

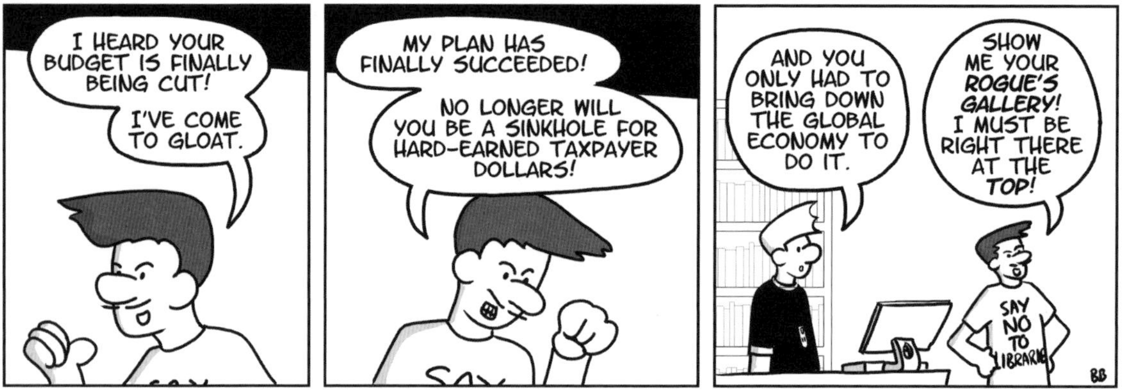
I HEARD YOUR BUDGET IS FINALLY BEING CUT!
I'VE COME TO GLOAT.
MY PLAN HAS FINALLY SUCCEEDED!
NO LONGER WILL YOU BE A SINKHOLE FOR HARD-EARNED TAXPAYER DOLLARS!
AND YOU ONLY HAD TO BRING DOWN THE GLOBAL ECONOMY TO DO IT.
SHOW ME YOUR ROGUE'S GALLERY! I MUST BE RIGHT THERE AT THE TOP!
SAY NO TO
BB

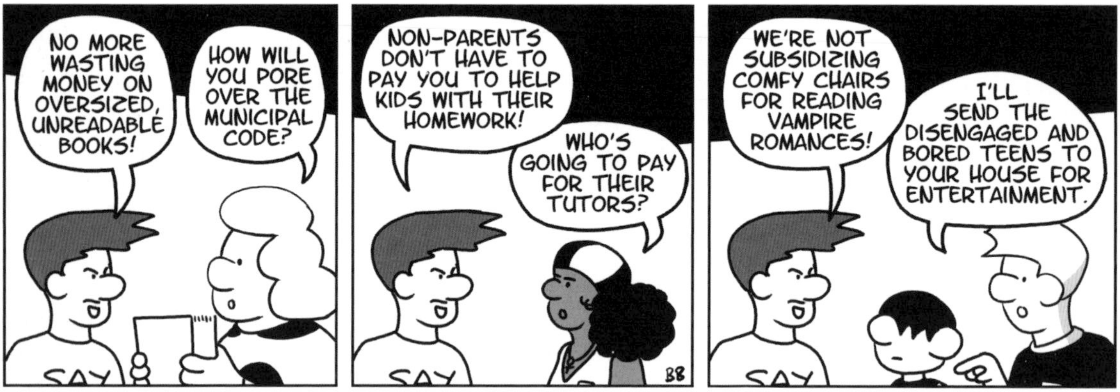
NO MORE WASTING MONEY ON OVERSIZED, UNREADABLE BOOKS!
HOW WILL YOU PORE OVER THE MUNICIPAL CODE?
NON-PARENTS DON'T HAVE TO PAY YOU TO HELP KIDS WITH THEIR HOMEWORK!
WHO'S GOING TO PAY FOR THEIR TUTORS?
BB
WE'RE NOT SUBSIDIZING COMFY CHAIRS FOR READING VAMPIRE ROMANCES!
I'LL SEND THE DISENGAGED AND BORED TEENS TO YOUR HOUSE FOR ENTERTAINMENT.

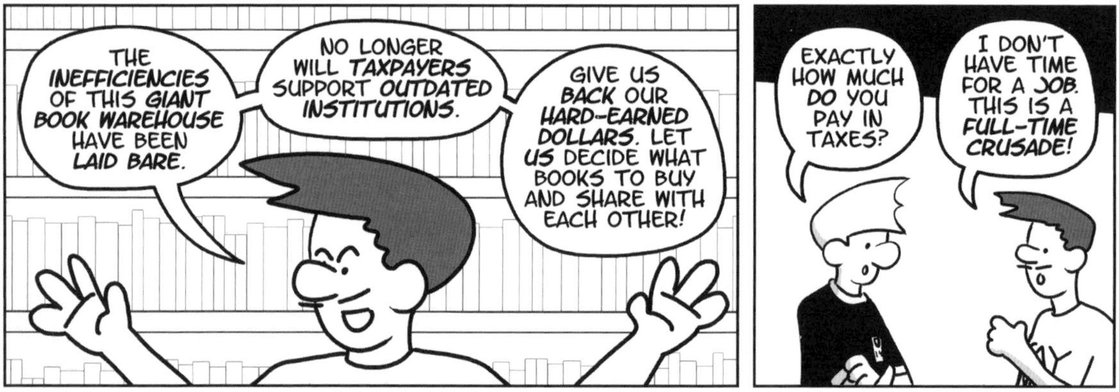
THE INEFFICIENCIES OF THIS GIANT BOOK WAREHOUSE HAVE BEEN LAID BARE.
NO LONGER WILL TAXPAYERS SUPPORT OUTDATED INSTITUTIONS.
GIVE US BACK OUR HARD-EARNED DOLLARS. LET US DECIDE WHAT BOOKS TO BUY AND SHARE WITH EACH OTHER!
EXACTLY HOW MUCH DO YOU PAY IN TAXES?
I DON'T HAVE TIME FOR A JOB. THIS IS A FULL-TIME CRUSADE!

Too Much Information

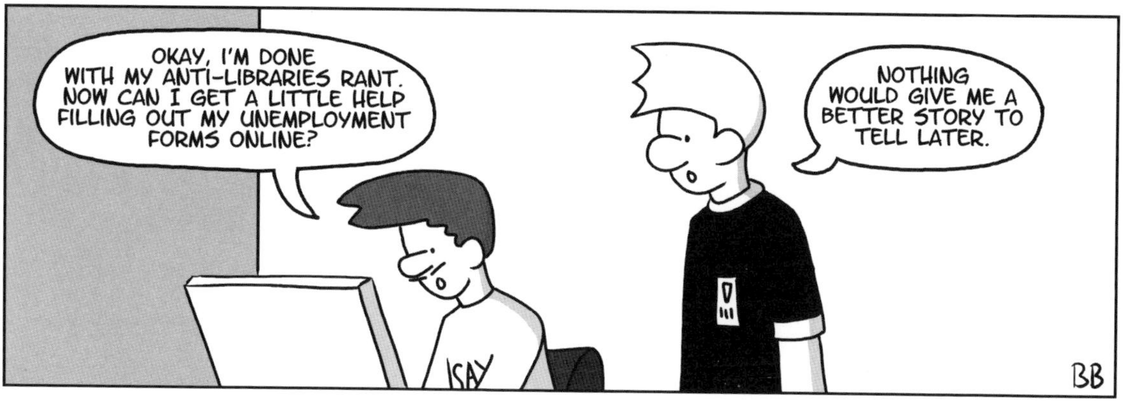
OKAY, I'M DONE WITH MY ANTI-LIBRARIES RANT. NOW CAN I GET A LITTLE HELP FILLING OUT MY UNEMPLOYMENT FORMS ONLINE?
NOTHING WOULD GIVE ME A BETTER STORY TO TELL LATER.
BB

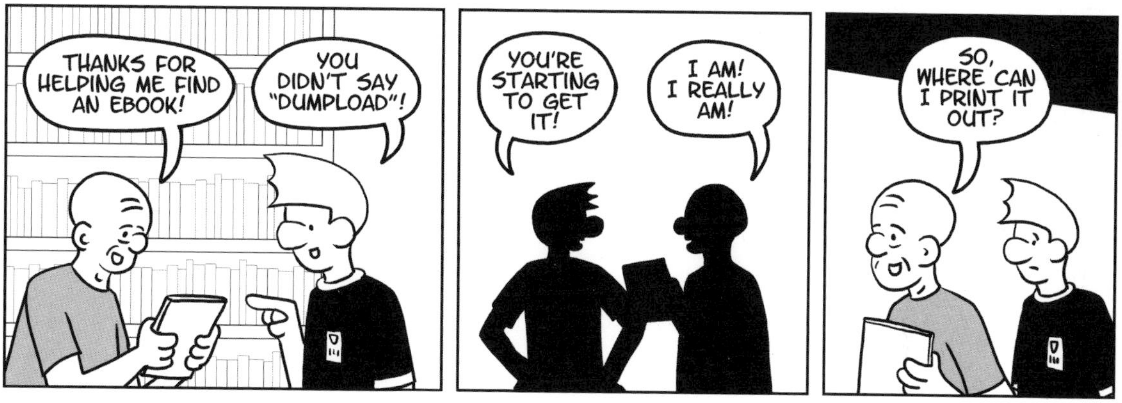
THANKS FOR HELPING ME FIND AN EBOOK!
YOU DIDN'T SAY "DUMPLOAD"!
YOU'RE STARTING TO GET IT!
I AM! I REALLY AM!
SO, WHERE CAN I PRINT IT OUT?

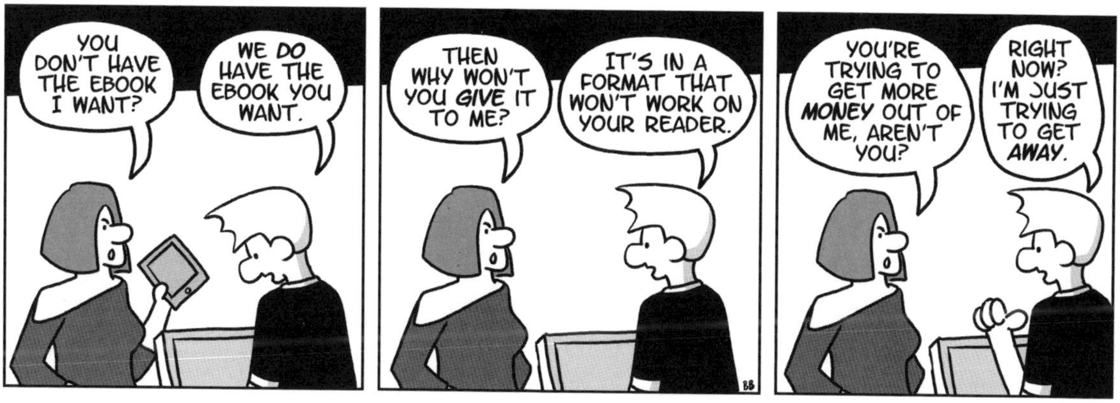
YOU DON'T HAVE THE EBOOK I WANT?
WE *DO* HAVE THE EBOOK YOU WANT.
THEN WHY WON'T YOU *GIVE* IT TO ME?
IT'S IN A FORMAT THAT WON'T WORK ON YOUR READER.
YOU'RE TRYING TO GET MORE **MONEY** OUT OF ME, AREN'T YOU?
RIGHT NOW? I'M JUST TRYING TO GET *AWAY*.
BB

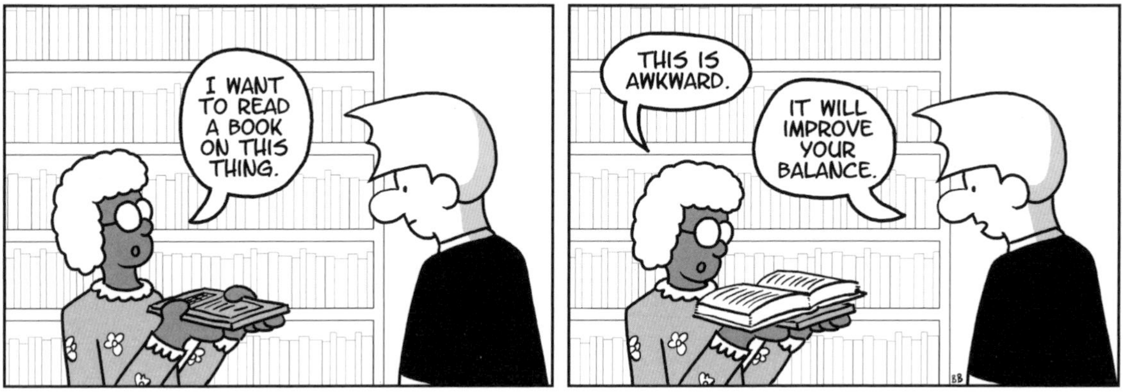
I WANT TO READ A BOOK ON THIS THING.
THIS IS AWKWARD.
IT WILL IMPROVE YOUR BALANCE.
BB

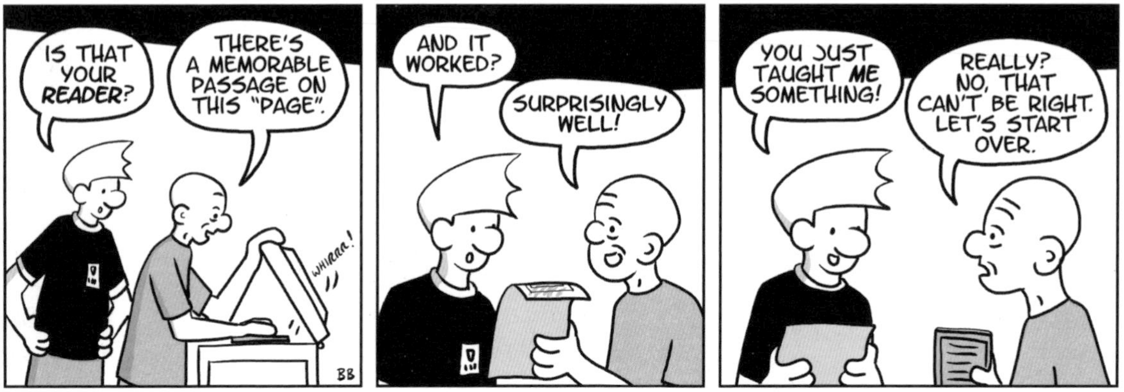
IS THAT YOUR READER?
THERE'S A MEMORABLE PASSAGE ON THIS "PAGE".
WHIRRR!
BB
AND IT WORKED?
SURPRISINGLY WELL!
YOU JUST TAUGHT ME SOMETHING!
REALLY? NO, THAT CAN'T BE RIGHT. LET'S START OVER.

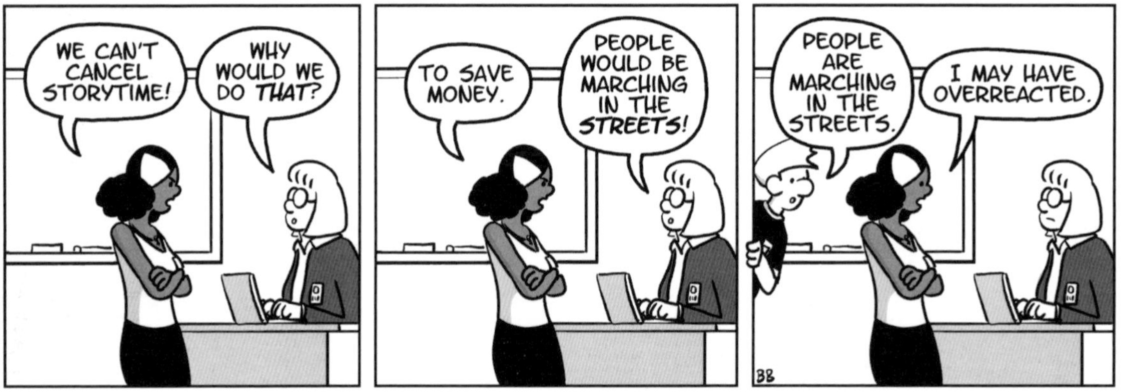
WE CAN'T CANCEL STORYTIME!
WHY WOULD WE DO THAT?
TO SAVE MONEY.
PEOPLE WOULD BE MARCHING IN THE STREETS!
PEOPLE ARE MARCHING IN THE STREETS.
I MAY HAVE OVERREACTED.
BB

Too Much Information

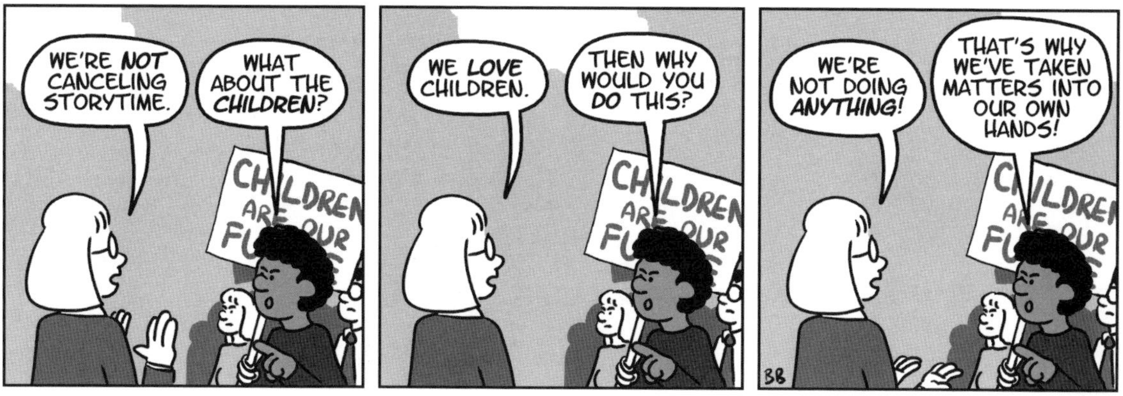

WE'RE NOT CANCELING STORYTIME.
WHAT ABOUT THE CHILDREN?
WE LOVE CHILDREN.
THEN WHY WOULD YOU DO THIS?
WE'RE NOT DOING ANYTHING!
THAT'S WHY WE'VE TAKEN MATTERS INTO OUR OWN HANDS!
BB

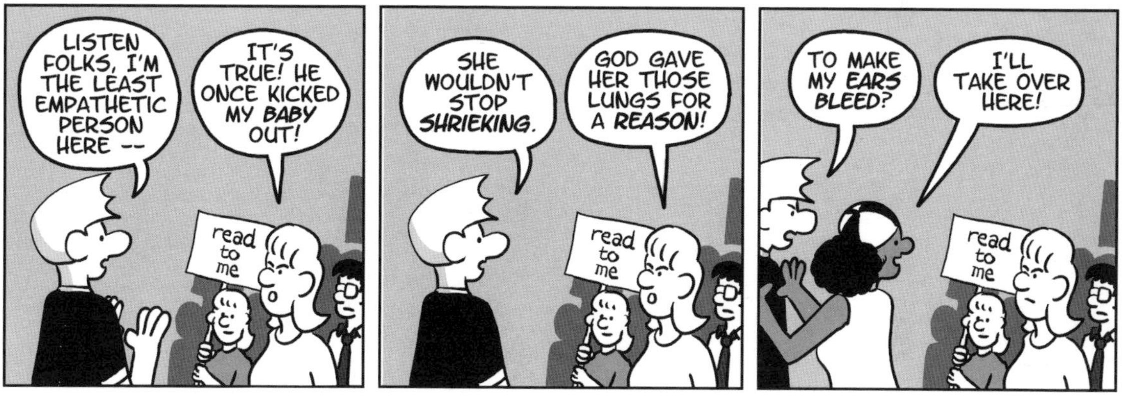

LISTEN FOLKS, I'M THE LEAST EMPATHETIC PERSON HERE --
IT'S TRUE! HE ONCE KICKED MY BABY OUT!
read to me
SHE WOULDN'T STOP SHRIEKING.
GOD GAVE HER THOSE LUNGS FOR A REASON!
read to me
TO MAKE MY EARS BLEED?
I'LL TAKE OVER HERE!
read to me

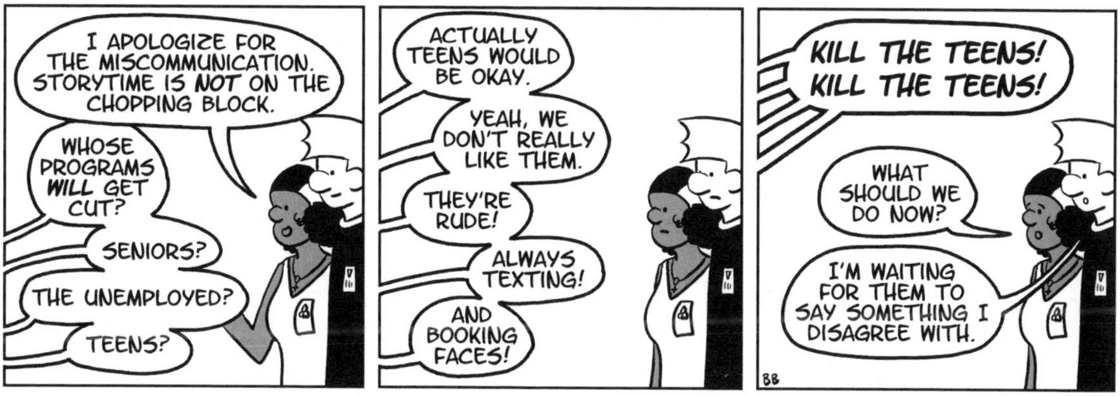

I APOLOGIZE FOR THE MISCOMMUNICATION. STORYTIME IS NOT ON THE CHOPPING BLOCK.
WHOSE PROGRAMS WILL GET CUT?
SENIORS?
THE UNEMPLOYED?
TEENS?
ACTUALLY TEENS WOULD BE OKAY.
YEAH, WE DON'T REALLY LIKE THEM.
THEY'RE RUDE!
ALWAYS TEXTING!
AND BOOKING FACES!
KILL THE TEENS! KILL THE TEENS!
WHAT SHOULD WE DO NOW?
I'M WAITING FOR THEM TO SAY SOMETHING I DISAGREE WITH.
BB

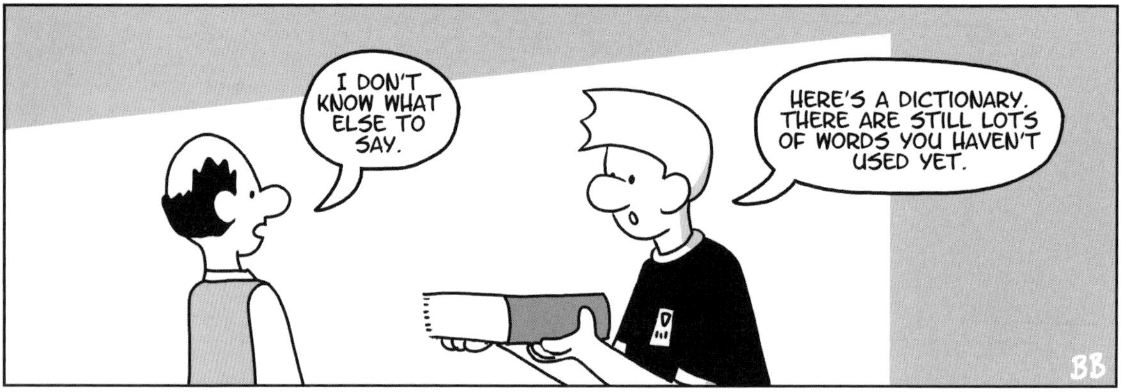
I DON'T KNOW WHAT ELSE TO SAY.
HERE'S A DICTIONARY. THERE ARE STILL LOTS OF WORDS YOU HAVEN'T USED YET.

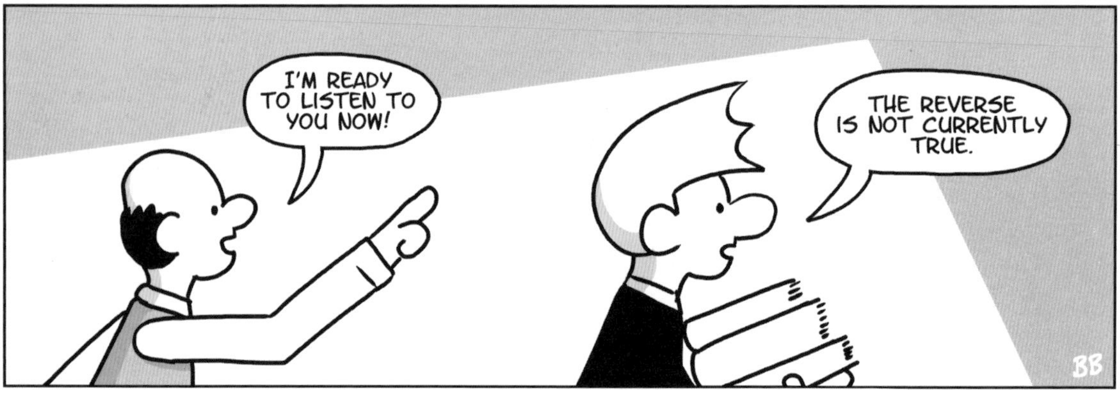
I'M READY TO LISTEN TO YOU NOW!
THE REVERSE IS NOT CURRENTLY TRUE.

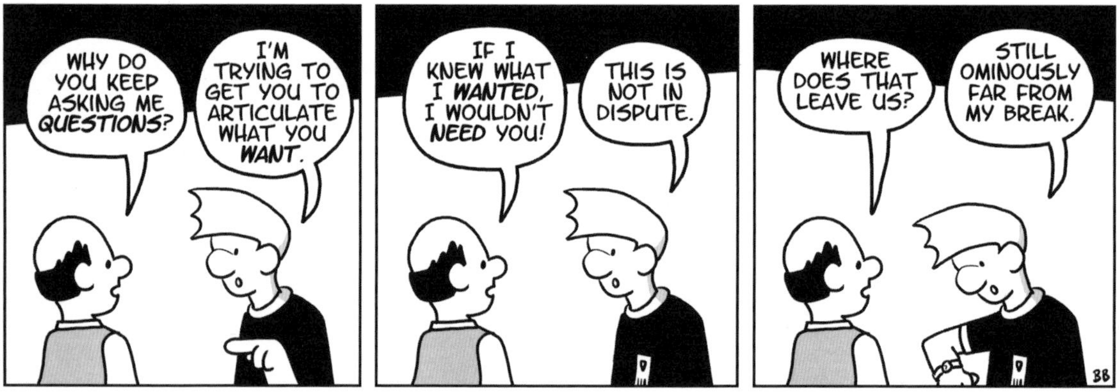
WHY DO YOU KEEP ASKING ME *QUESTIONS*?
I'M TRYING TO GET YOU TO ARTICULATE WHAT YOU *WANT*.
IF I KNEW WHAT I *WANTED*, I WOULDN'T *NEED* YOU!
THIS IS NOT IN DISPUTE.
WHERE DOES THAT LEAVE US?
STILL OMINOUSLY FAR FROM MY BREAK.

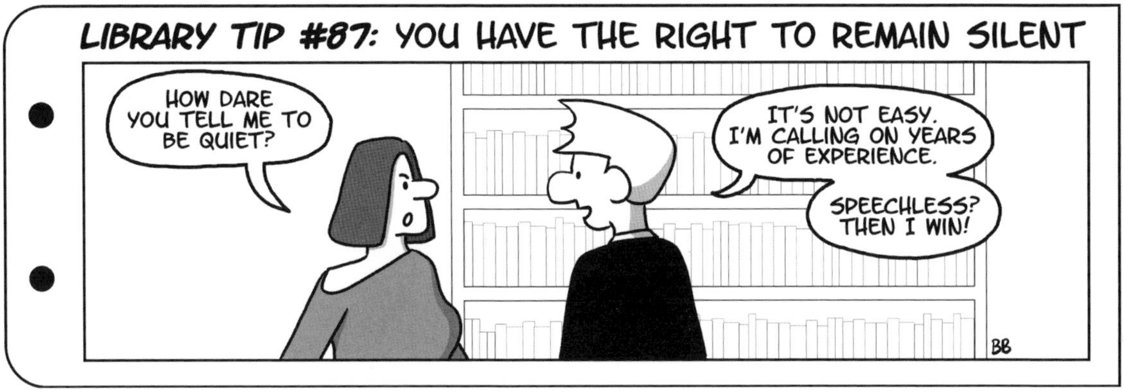
LIBRARY TIP #87: YOU HAVE THE RIGHT TO REMAIN SILENT
HOW DARE YOU TELL ME TO BE QUIET?
IT'S NOT EASY. I'M CALLING ON YEARS OF EXPERIENCE.
SPEECHLESS? THEN I WIN!
BB

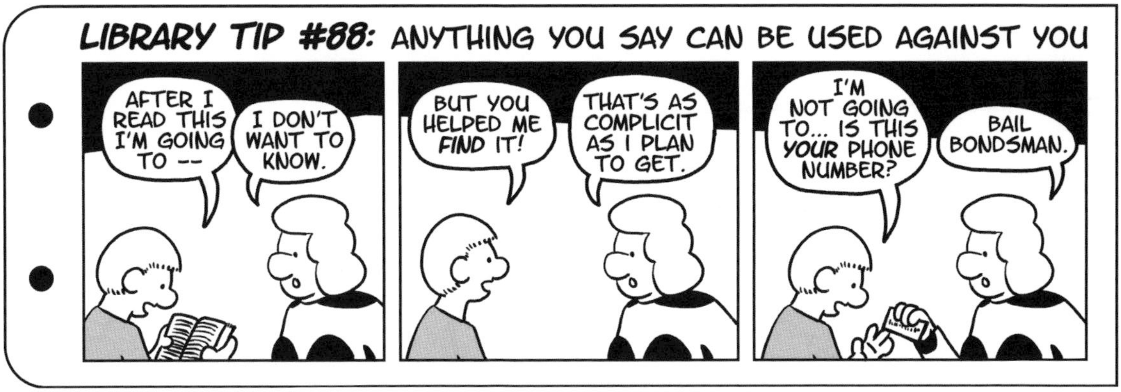
LIBRARY TIP #88: ANYTHING YOU SAY CAN BE USED AGAINST YOU
AFTER I READ THIS I'M GOING TO --
I DON'T WANT TO KNOW.
BUT YOU HELPED ME *FIND* IT!
THAT'S AS COMPLICIT AS I PLAN TO GET.
I'M NOT GOING TO... IS THIS *YOUR* PHONE NUMBER?
BAIL BONDSMAN.

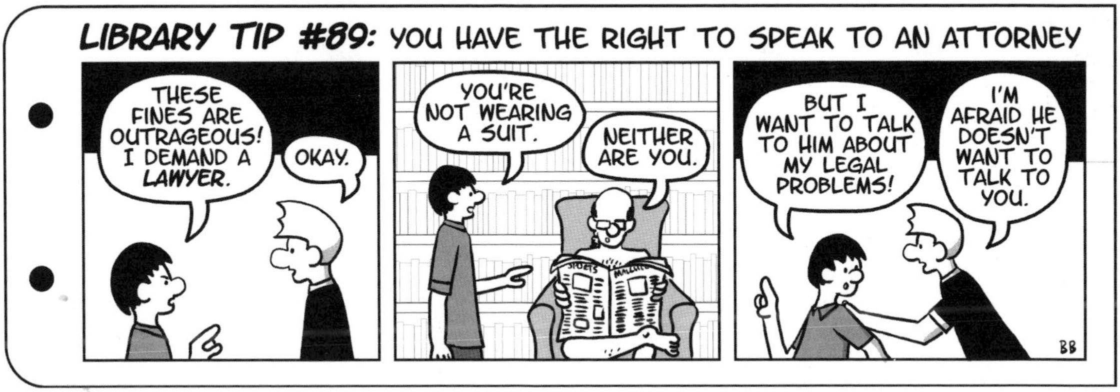
LIBRARY TIP #89: YOU HAVE THE RIGHT TO SPEAK TO AN ATTORNEY
THESE FINES ARE OUTRAGEOUS! I DEMAND A *LAWYER*.
OKAY.
YOU'RE NOT WEARING A SUIT.
NEITHER ARE YOU.
BUT I WANT TO TALK TO HIM ABOUT MY LEGAL PROBLEMS!
I'M AFRAID HE DOESN'T WANT TO TALK TO YOU.
BB

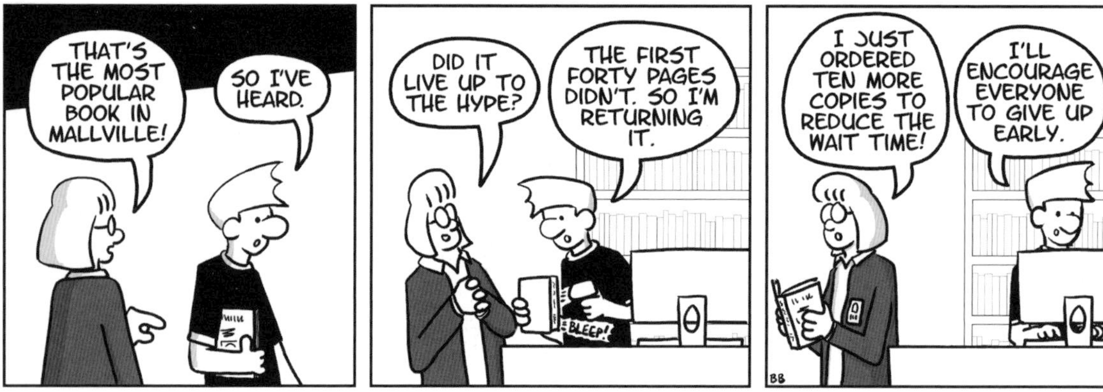
THAT'S THE MOST POPULAR BOOK IN MALLVILLE!
SO I'VE HEARD.
DID IT LIVE UP TO THE HYPE?
THE FIRST FORTY PAGES DIDN'T. SO I'M RETURNING IT.
BLEEP!
I JUST ORDERED TEN MORE COPIES TO REDUCE THE WAIT TIME!
I'LL ENCOURAGE EVERYONE TO GIVE UP EARLY.
BB

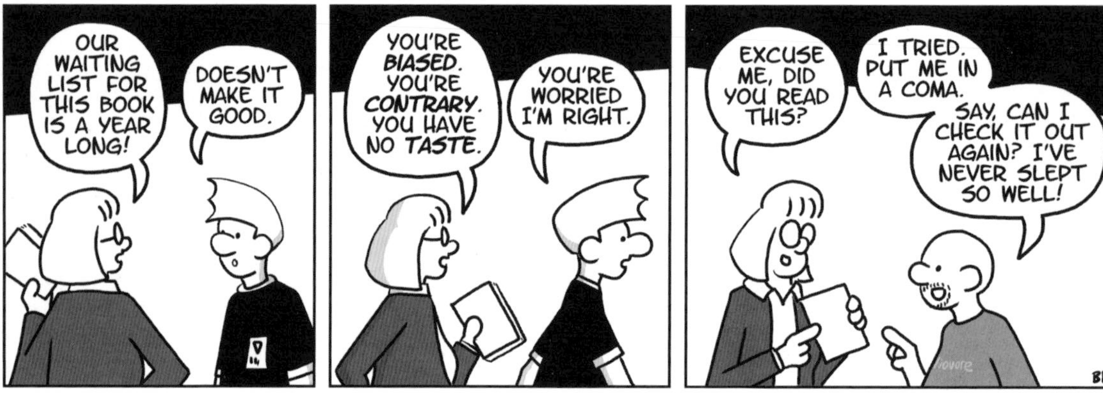
OUR WAITING LIST FOR THIS BOOK IS A YEAR LONG!
DOESN'T MAKE IT GOOD.
YOU'RE BIASED. YOU'RE CONTRARY. YOU HAVE NO TASTE.
YOU'RE WORRIED I'M RIGHT.
EXCUSE ME, DID YOU READ THIS?
I TRIED. PUT ME IN A COMA.
SAY, CAN I CHECK IT OUT AGAIN? I'VE NEVER SLEPT SO WELL!
BB

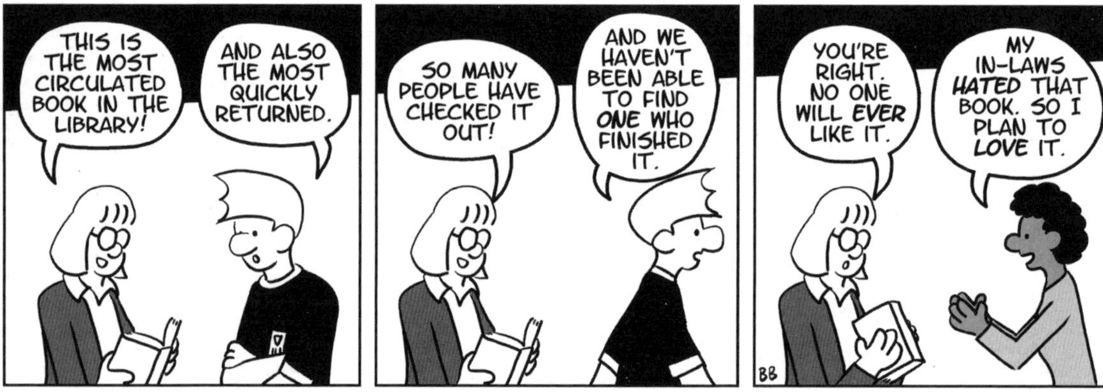
THIS IS THE MOST CIRCULATED BOOK IN THE LIBRARY!
AND ALSO THE MOST QUICKLY RETURNED.
SO MANY PEOPLE HAVE CHECKED IT OUT!
AND WE HAVEN'T BEEN ABLE TO FIND ONE WHO FINISHED IT.
YOU'RE RIGHT. NO ONE WILL EVER LIKE IT.
MY IN-LAWS HATED THAT BOOK. SO I PLAN TO LOVE IT.
BB

Too Much Information

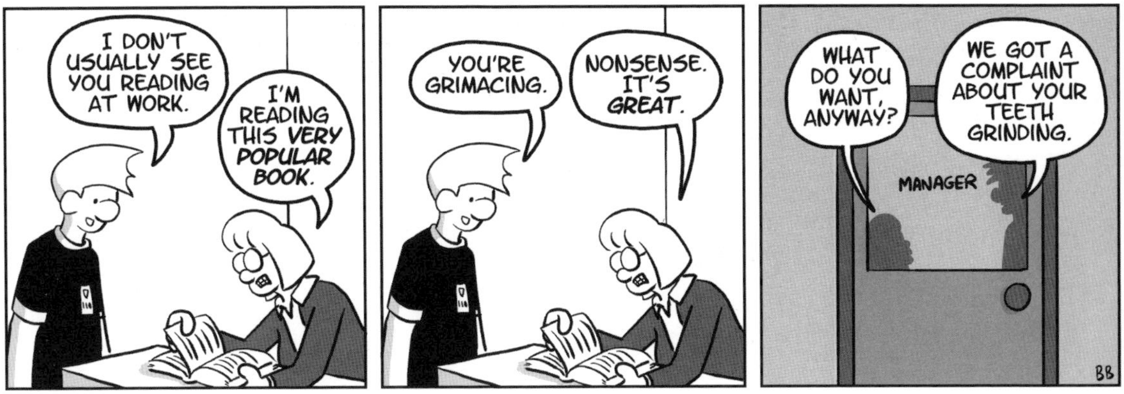
I DON'T USUALLY SEE YOU READING AT WORK.
I'M READING THIS VERY POPULAR BOOK.
YOU'RE GRIMACING.
NONSENSE. IT'S GREAT.
MANAGER
WHAT DO YOU WANT, ANYWAY?
WE GOT A COMPLAINT ABOUT YOUR TEETH GRINDING.
BB

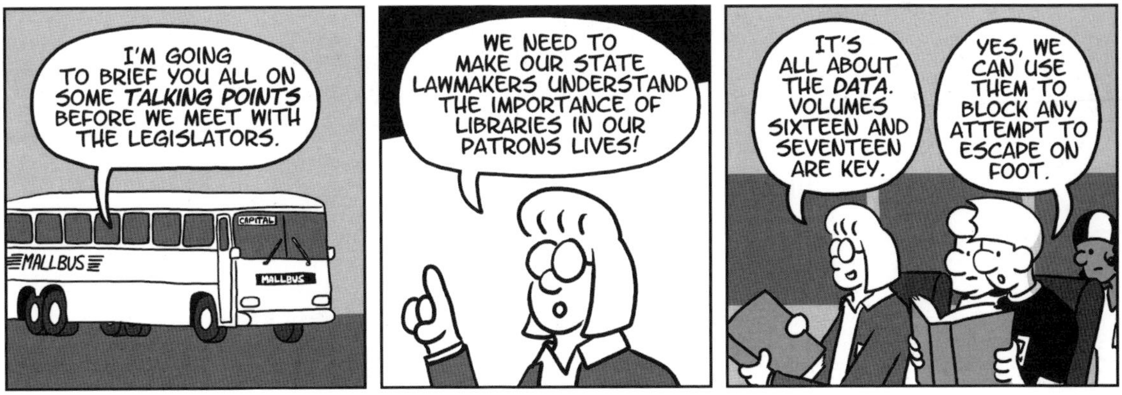
I'M GOING TO BRIEF YOU ALL ON SOME TALKING POINTS BEFORE WE MEET WITH THE LEGISLATORS.
CAPITAL
MALLBUS
MALLBUS
WE NEED TO MAKE OUR STATE LAWMAKERS UNDERSTAND THE IMPORTANCE OF LIBRARIES IN OUR PATRONS LIVES!
IT'S ALL ABOUT THE DATA. VOLUMES SIXTEEN AND SEVENTEEN ARE KEY.
YES, WE CAN USE THEM TO BLOCK ANY ATTEMPT TO ESCAPE ON FOOT.

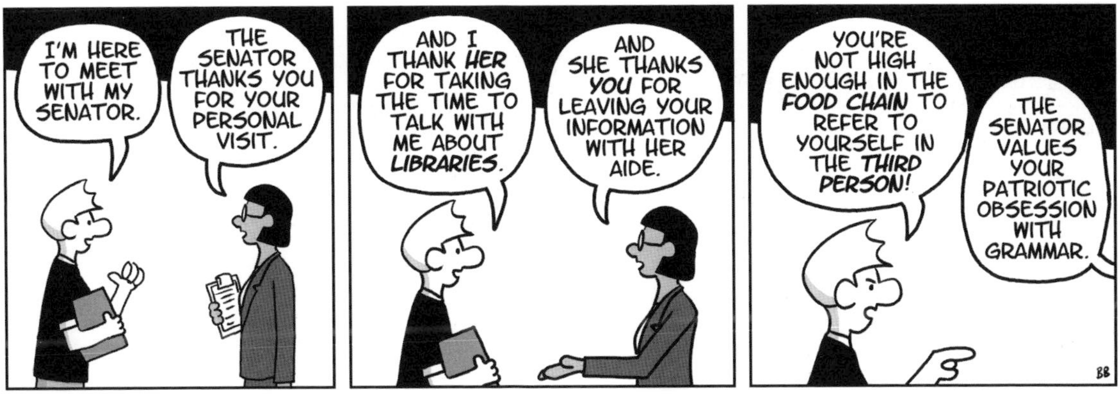
I'M HERE TO MEET WITH MY SENATOR.
THE SENATOR THANKS YOU FOR YOUR PERSONAL VISIT.
AND I THANK HER FOR TAKING THE TIME TO TALK WITH ME ABOUT LIBRARIES.
AND SHE THANKS YOU FOR LEAVING YOUR INFORMATION WITH HER AIDE.
YOU'RE NOT HIGH ENOUGH IN THE FOOD CHAIN TO REFER TO YOURSELF IN THE THIRD PERSON!
THE SENATOR VALUES YOUR PATRIOTIC OBSESSION WITH GRAMMAR.
BB

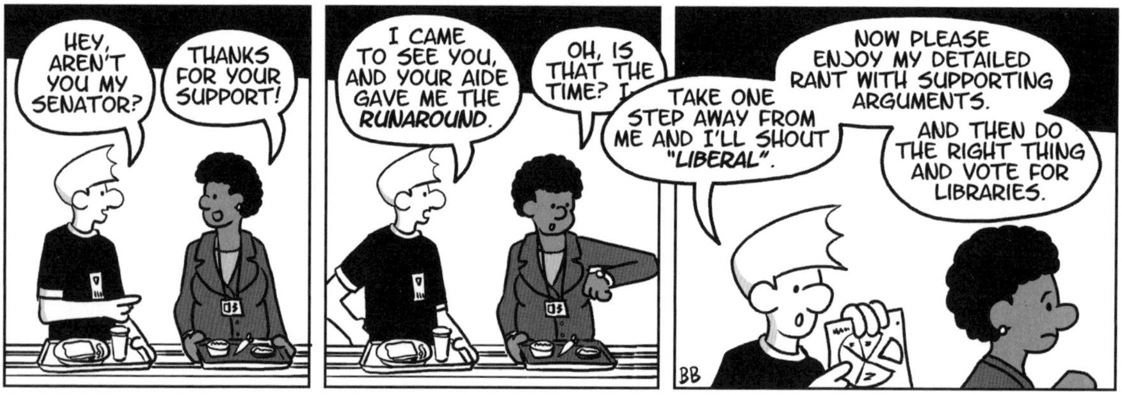
HEY, AREN'T YOU MY SENATOR?
THANKS FOR YOUR SUPPORT!
I CAME TO SEE YOU, AND YOUR AIDE GAVE ME THE *RUNAROUND*.
OH, IS THAT THE TIME? I
TAKE ONE STEP AWAY FROM ME AND I'LL SHOUT *"LIBERAL"*.
NOW PLEASE ENJOY MY DETAILED RANT WITH SUPPORTING ARGUMENTS.
AND THEN DO THE RIGHT THING AND VOTE FOR LIBRARIES.

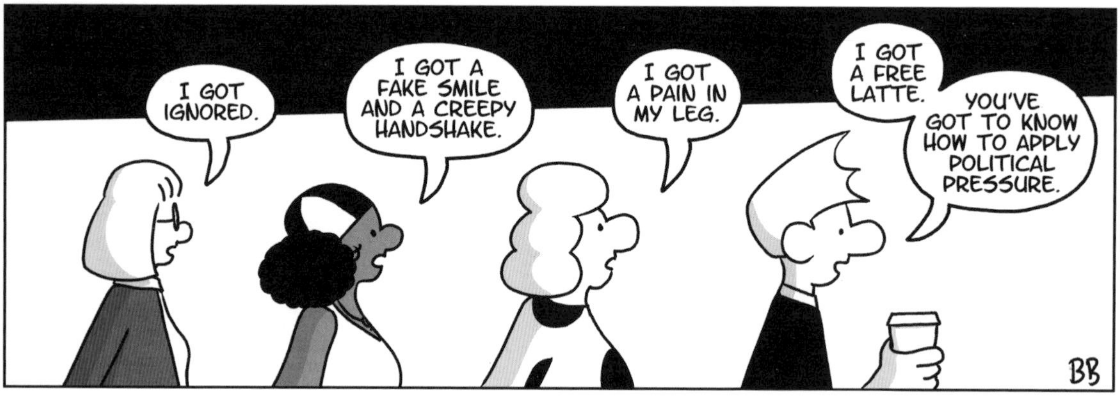
I GOT IGNORED.
I GOT A FAKE SMILE AND A CREEPY HANDSHAKE.
I GOT A PAIN IN MY LEG.
I GOT A FREE LATTE.
YOU'VE GOT TO KNOW HOW TO APPLY POLITICAL PRESSURE.

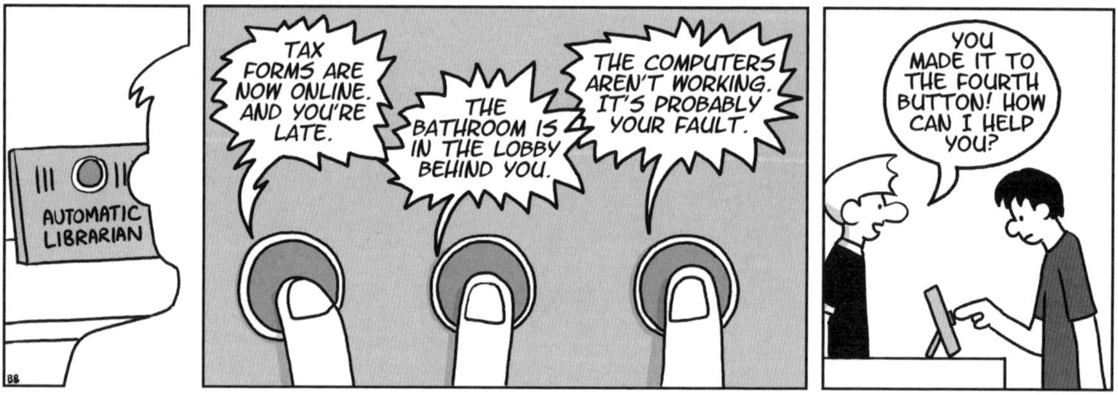
AUTOMATIC LIBRARIAN
TAX FORMS ARE NOW ONLINE. AND YOU'RE LATE.
THE BATHROOM IS IN THE LOBBY BEHIND YOU.
THE COMPUTERS AREN'T WORKING. IT'S PROBABLY YOUR FAULT.
YOU MADE IT TO THE FOURTH BUTTON! HOW CAN I HELP YOU?

Too Much Information

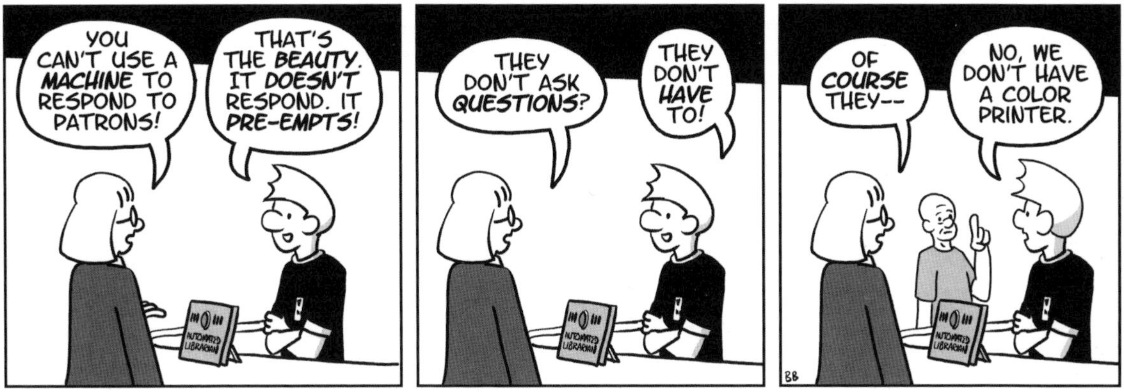
YOU CAN'T USE A MACHINE TO RESPOND TO PATRONS!
THAT'S THE BEAUTY. IT DOESN'T RESPOND. IT PRE-EMPTS!
THEY DON'T ASK QUESTIONS?
THEY DON'T HAVE TO!
OF COURSE THEY--
NO, WE DON'T HAVE A COLOR PRINTER.
AUTOMATED LIBRARIAN
BB

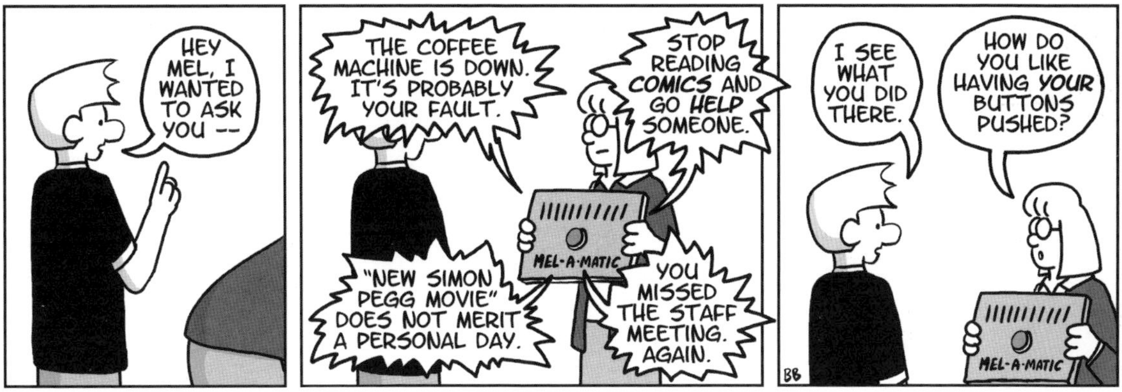
HEY MEL, I WANTED TO ASK YOU --
THE COFFEE MACHINE IS DOWN. IT'S PROBABLY YOUR FAULT.
STOP READING COMICS AND GO HELP SOMEONE.
"NEW SIMON PEGG MOVIE" DOES NOT MERIT A PERSONAL DAY.
YOU MISSED THE STAFF MEETING. AGAIN.
MEL-A-MATIC
I SEE WHAT YOU DID THERE.
HOW DO YOU LIKE HAVING YOUR BUTTONS PUSHED?
MEL-A-MATIC
BB

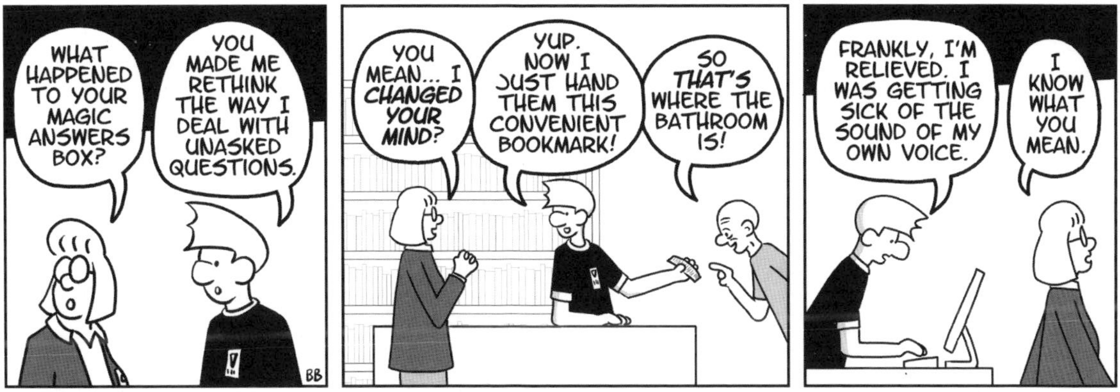
WHAT HAPPENED TO YOUR MAGIC ANSWERS BOX?
YOU MADE ME RETHINK THE WAY I DEAL WITH UNASKED QUESTIONS.
BB
YOU MEAN... I CHANGED YOUR MIND?
YUP. NOW I JUST HAND THEM THIS CONVENIENT BOOKMARK!
SO THAT'S WHERE THE BATHROOM IS!
FRANKLY, I'M RELIEVED. I WAS GETTING SICK OF THE SOUND OF MY OWN VOICE.
I KNOW WHAT YOU MEAN.

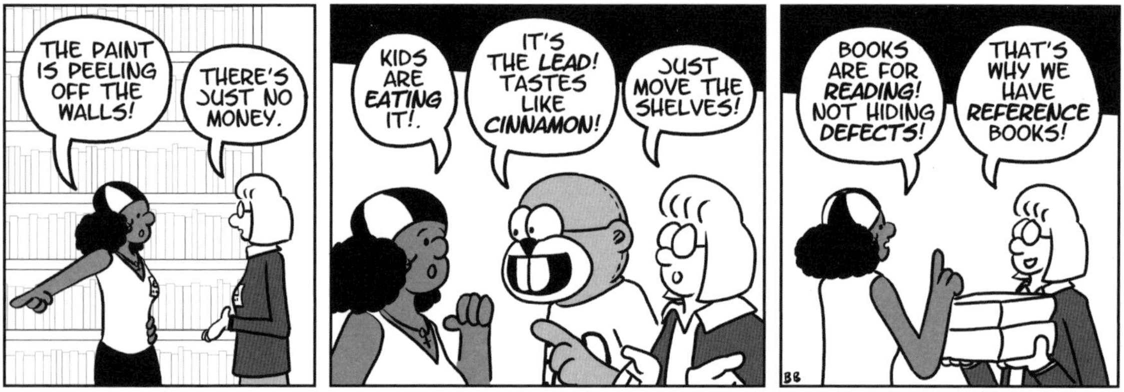
THE PAINT IS PEELING OFF THE WALLS!
THERE'S JUST NO MONEY.
KIDS ARE *EATING* IT!.
IT'S THE *LEAD!* TASTES LIKE *CINNAMON!*
JUST MOVE THE SHELVES!
BOOKS ARE FOR *READING!* NOT HIDING *DEFECTS!*
THAT'S WHY WE HAVE ***REFERENCE*** BOOKS!
BB

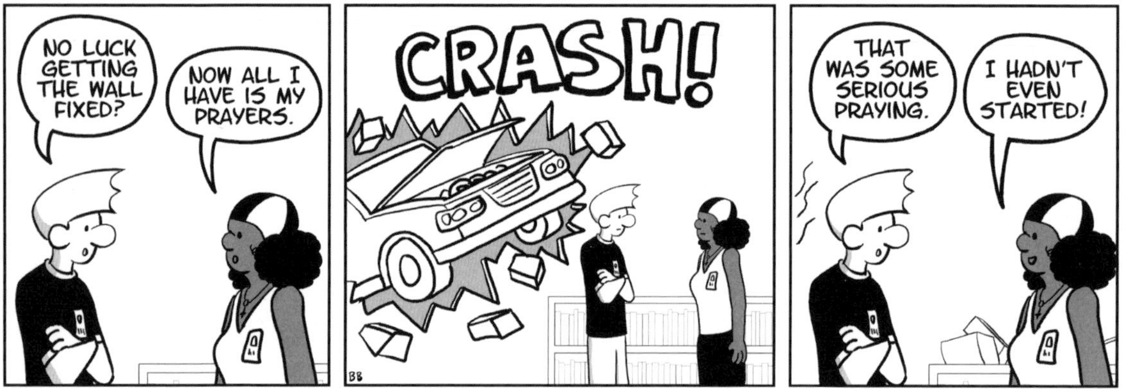
NO LUCK GETTING THE WALL FIXED?
NOW ALL I HAVE IS MY PRAYERS.
CRASH!
BB
THAT WAS SOME SERIOUS PRAYING.
I HADN'T EVEN STARTED!

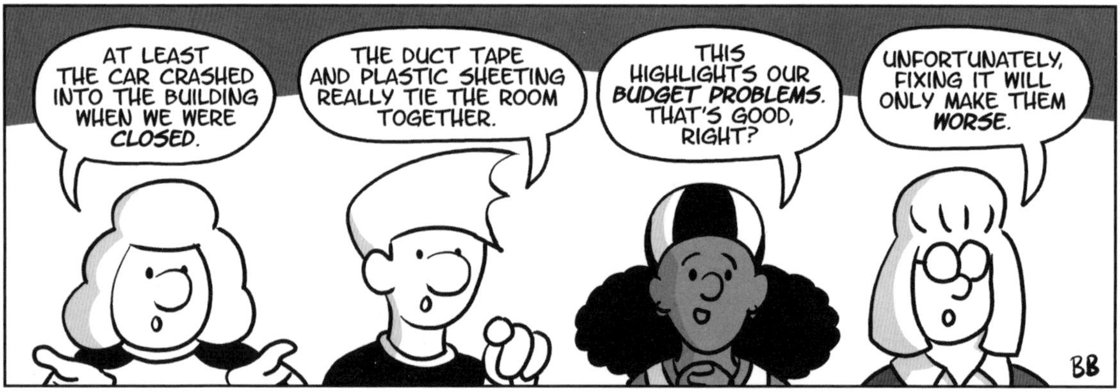
AT LEAST THE CAR CRASHED INTO THE BUILDING WHEN WE WERE *CLOSED*.
THE DUCT TAPE AND PLASTIC SHEETING REALLY TIE THE ROOM TOGETHER.
THIS HIGHLIGHTS OUR *BUDGET PROBLEMS*. THAT'S GOOD, RIGHT?
UNFORTUNATELY, FIXING IT WILL ONLY MAKE THEM *WORSE*.
BB

Too Much Information

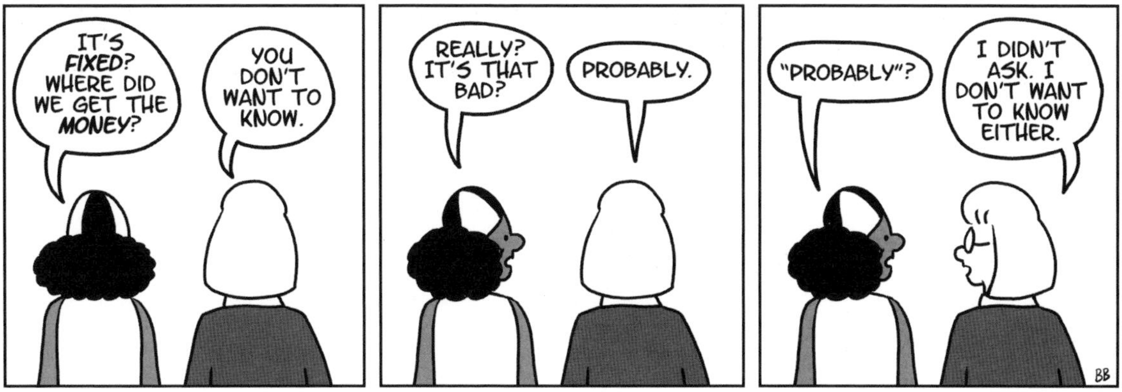
IT'S *FIXED*? WHERE DID WE GET THE *MONEY*?
YOU DON'T WANT TO KNOW.
REALLY? IT'S THAT BAD?
PROBABLY.
"PROBABLY"?
I DIDN'T ASK. I DON'T WANT TO KNOW EITHER.
BB

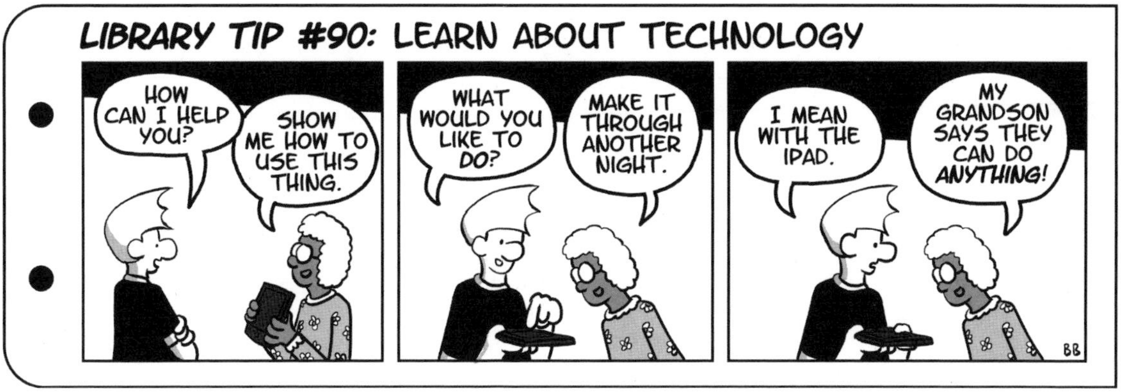
LIBRARY TIP #90: LEARN ABOUT TECHNOLOGY
HOW CAN I HELP YOU?
SHOW ME HOW TO USE THIS THING.
WHAT WOULD YOU LIKE TO *DO*?
MAKE IT THROUGH ANOTHER NIGHT.
I MEAN WITH THE IPAD.
MY GRANDSON SAYS THEY CAN DO *ANYTHING*!
BB

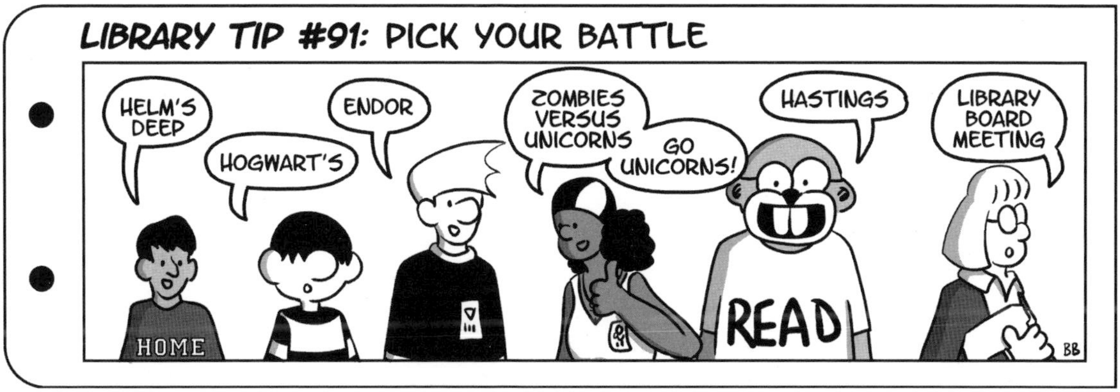
LIBRARY TIP #91: PICK YOUR BATTLE
HELM'S DEEP
HOGWART'S
ENDOR
ZOMBIES VERSUS UNICORNS
GO UNICORNS!
HASTINGS
LIBRARY BOARD MEETING
HOME
READ
BB

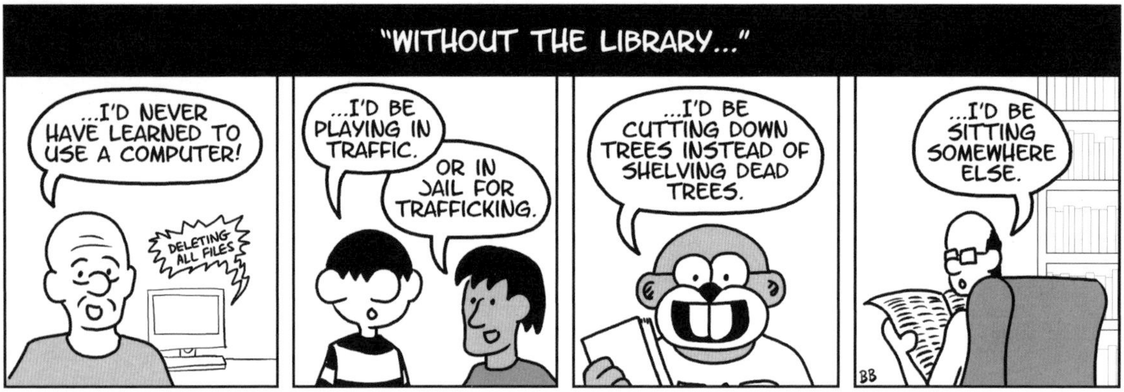
"WITHOUT THE LIBRARY..."
...I'D NEVER HAVE LEARNED TO USE A COMPUTER!
DELETING ALL FILES
...I'D BE PLAYING IN TRAFFIC.
OR IN JAIL FOR TRAFFICKING.
...I'D BE CUTTING DOWN TREES INSTEAD OF SHELVING DEAD TREES.
...I'D BE SITTING SOMEWHERE ELSE.
BB

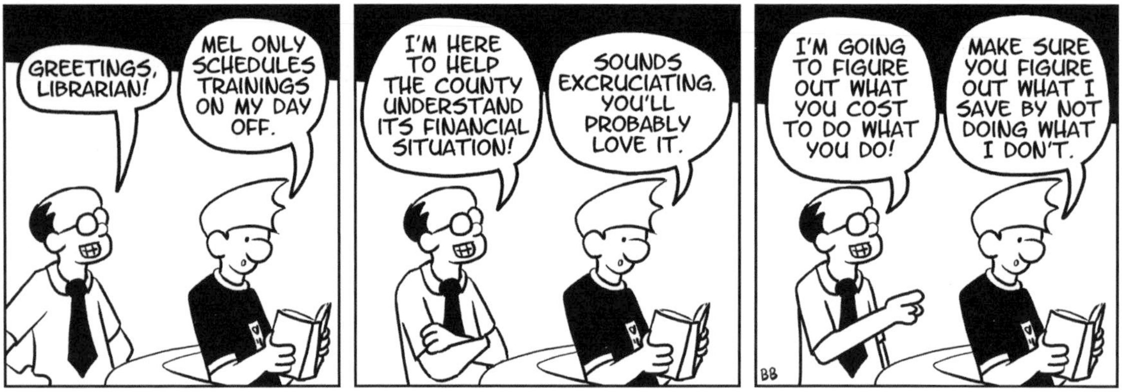
GREETINGS, LIBRARIAN!
MEL ONLY SCHEDULES TRAININGS ON MY DAY OFF.
I'M HERE TO HELP THE COUNTY UNDERSTAND ITS FINANCIAL SITUATION!
SOUNDS EXCRUCIATING. YOU'LL PROBABLY LOVE IT.
I'M GOING TO FIGURE OUT WHAT YOU COST TO DO WHAT YOU DO!
MAKE SURE YOU FIGURE OUT WHAT I SAVE BY NOT DOING WHAT I DON'T.
BB

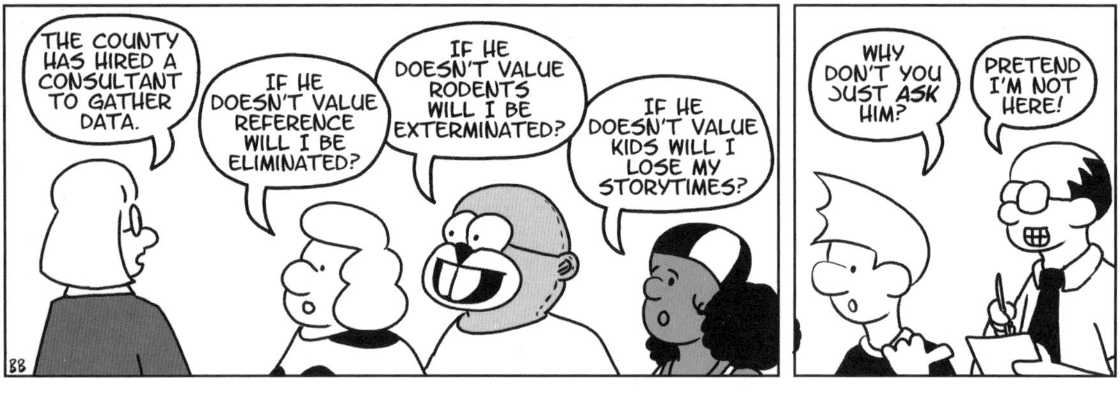
THE COUNTY HAS HIRED A CONSULTANT TO GATHER DATA.
IF HE DOESN'T VALUE REFERENCE WILL I BE ELIMINATED?
IF HE DOESN'T VALUE RODENTS WILL I BE EXTERMINATED?
IF HE DOESN'T VALUE KIDS WILL I LOSE MY STORYTIMES?
WHY DON'T YOU JUST ASK HIM?
PRETEND I'M NOT HERE!
BB

Too Much Information

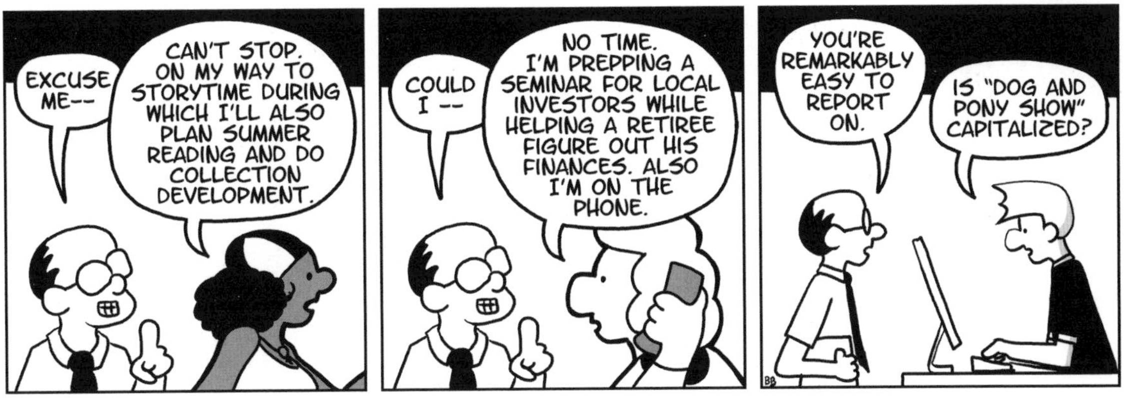
EXCUSE ME--
CAN'T STOP. ON MY WAY TO STORYTIME DURING WHICH I'LL ALSO PLAN SUMMER READING AND DO COLLECTION DEVELOPMENT.
COULD I --
NO TIME. I'M PREPPING A SEMINAR FOR LOCAL INVESTORS WHILE HELPING A RETIREE FIGURE OUT HIS FINANCES. ALSO I'M ON THE PHONE.
YOU'RE REMARKABLY EASY TO REPORT ON.
IS "DOG AND PONY SHOW" CAPITALIZED?
BB

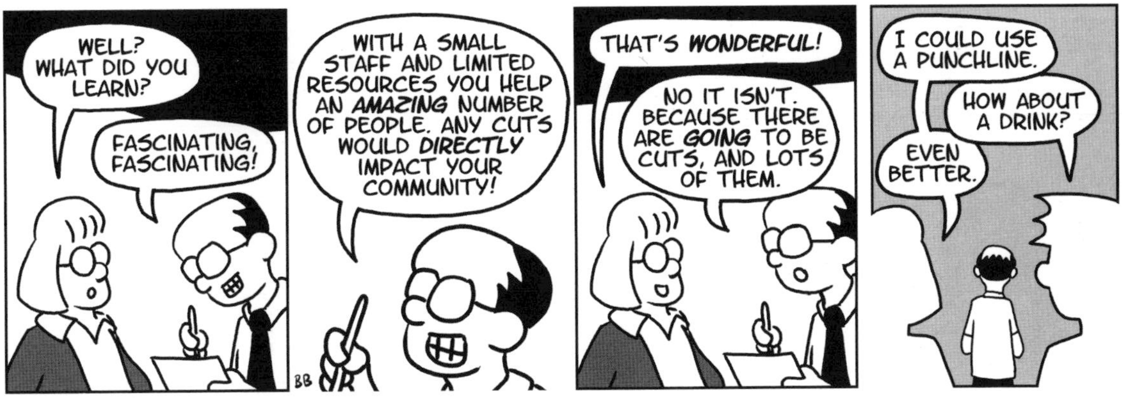
WELL? WHAT DID YOU LEARN?
FASCINATING, FASCINATING!
BB
WITH A SMALL STAFF AND LIMITED RESOURCES YOU HELP AN AMAZING NUMBER OF PEOPLE. ANY CUTS WOULD DIRECTLY IMPACT YOUR COMMUNITY!
THAT'S WONDERFUL!
NO IT ISN'T. BECAUSE THERE ARE GOING TO BE CUTS, AND LOTS OF THEM.
I COULD USE A PUNCHLINE.
HOW ABOUT A DRINK?
EVEN BETTER.

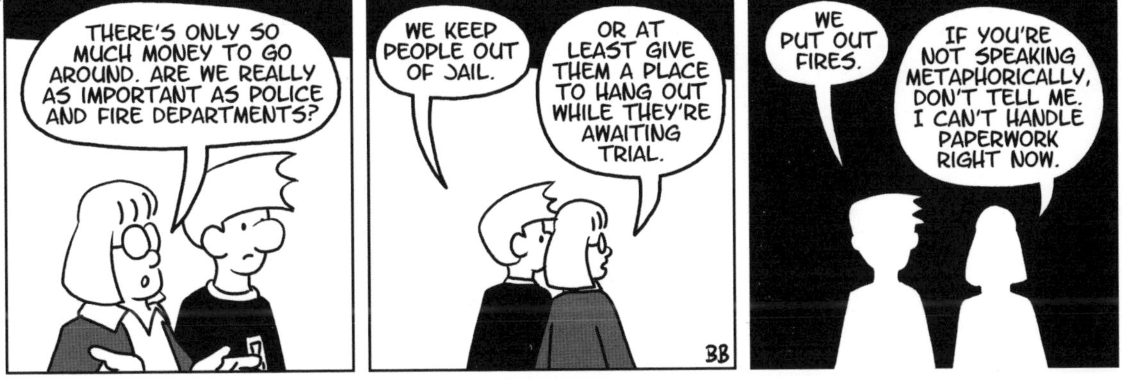
THERE'S ONLY SO MUCH MONEY TO GO AROUND. ARE WE REALLY AS IMPORTANT AS POLICE AND FIRE DEPARTMENTS?
WE KEEP PEOPLE OUT OF JAIL.
OR AT LEAST GIVE THEM A PLACE TO HANG OUT WHILE THEY'RE AWAITING TRIAL.
BB
WE PUT OUT FIRES.
IF YOU'RE NOT SPEAKING METAPHORICALLY, DON'T TELL ME. I CAN'T HANDLE PAPERWORK RIGHT NOW.

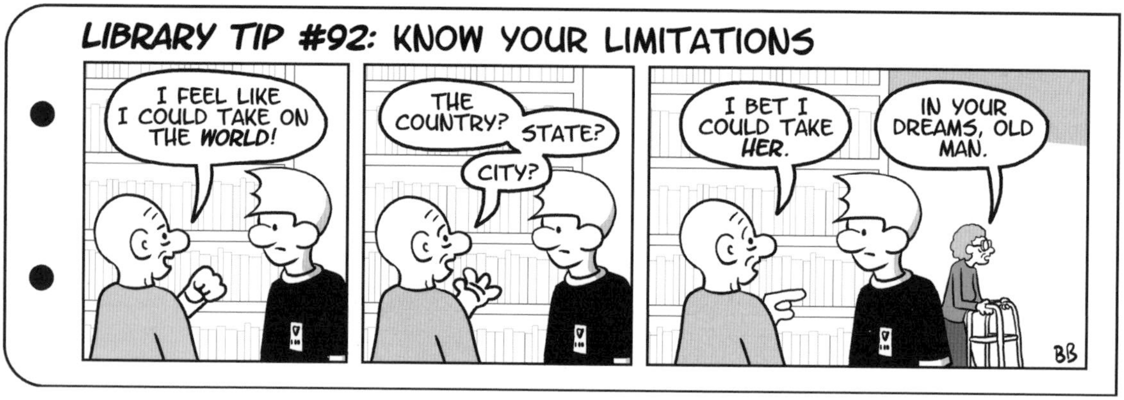
LIBRARY TIP #92: KNOW YOUR LIMITATIONS
I FEEL LIKE I COULD TAKE ON THE WORLD!
THE COUNTRY?
STATE?
CITY?
I BET I COULD TAKE HER.
IN YOUR DREAMS, OLD MAN.
BB

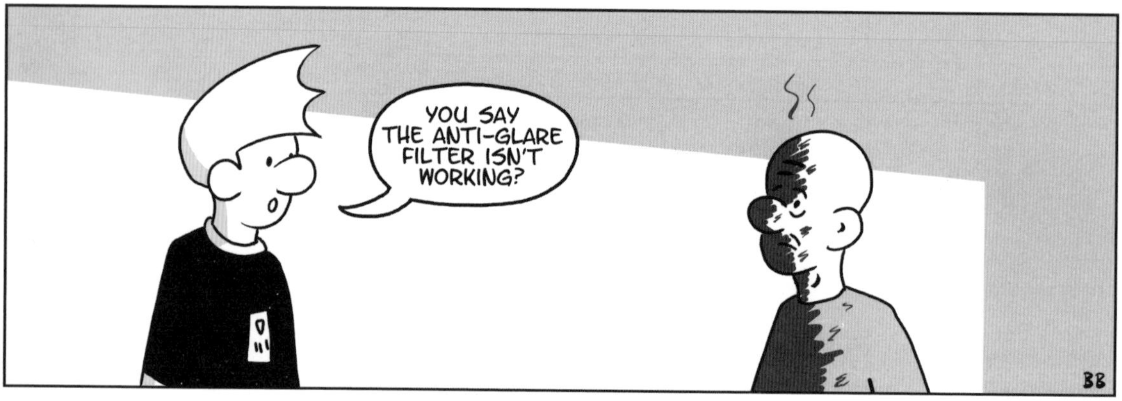
YOU SAY THE ANTI-GLARE FILTER ISN'T WORKING?
BB

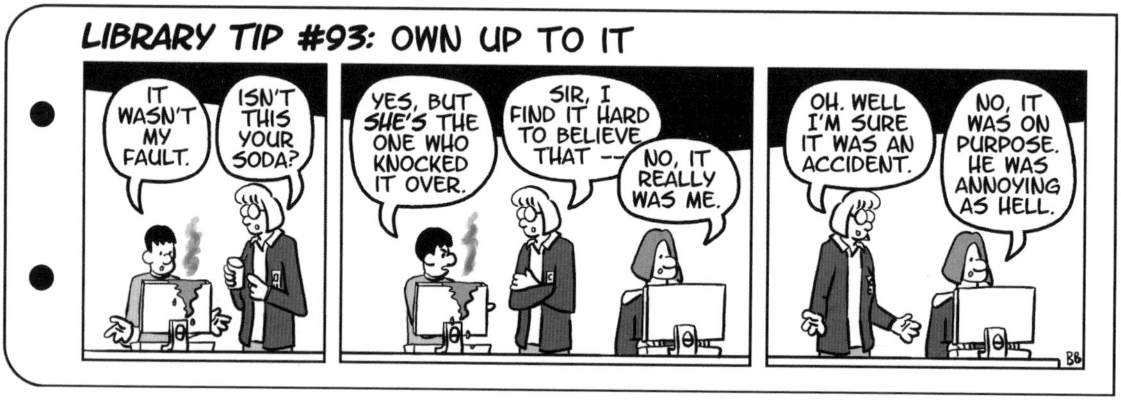
LIBRARY TIP #93: OWN UP TO IT
IT WASN'T MY FAULT.
ISN'T THIS YOUR SODA?
YES, BUT SHE'S THE ONE WHO KNOCKED IT OVER.
SIR, I FIND IT HARD TO BELIEVE THAT --
NO, IT REALLY WAS ME.
OH. WELL I'M SURE IT WAS AN ACCIDENT.
NO, IT WAS ON PURPOSE. HE WAS ANNOYING AS HELL.
BB

Too Much Information

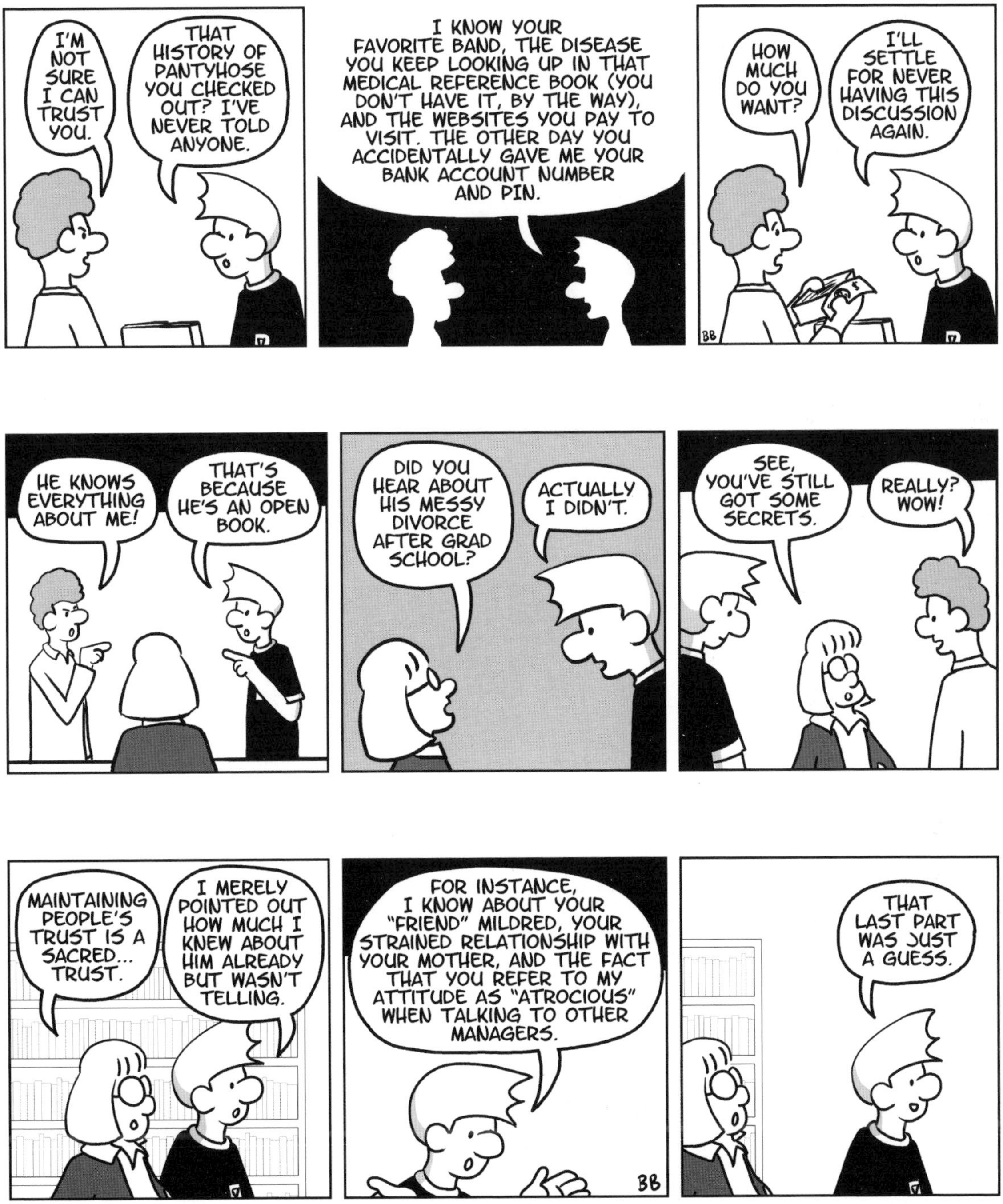

I'M NOT SURE I CAN TRUST YOU.
THAT HISTORY OF PANTYHOSE YOU CHECKED OUT? I'VE NEVER TOLD ANYONE.
I KNOW YOUR FAVORITE BAND, THE DISEASE YOU KEEP LOOKING UP IN THAT MEDICAL REFERENCE BOOK (YOU DON'T HAVE IT, BY THE WAY), AND THE WEBSITES YOU PAY TO VISIT. THE OTHER DAY YOU ACCIDENTALLY GAVE ME YOUR BANK ACCOUNT NUMBER AND PIN.
HOW MUCH DO YOU WANT?
I'LL SETTLE FOR NEVER HAVING THIS DISCUSSION AGAIN.
BB
HE KNOWS EVERYTHING ABOUT ME!
THAT'S BECAUSE HE'S AN OPEN BOOK.
DID YOU HEAR ABOUT HIS MESSY DIVORCE AFTER GRAD SCHOOL?
ACTUALLY I DIDN'T.
SEE, YOU'VE STILL GOT SOME SECRETS.
REALLY? WOW!
MAINTAINING PEOPLE'S TRUST IS A SACRED... TRUST.
I MERELY POINTED OUT HOW MUCH I KNEW ABOUT HIM ALREADY BUT WASN'T TELLING.
FOR INSTANCE, I KNOW ABOUT YOUR "FRIEND" MILDRED, YOUR STRAINED RELATIONSHIP WITH YOUR MOTHER, AND THE FACT THAT YOU REFER TO MY ATTITUDE AS "ATROCIOUS" WHEN TALKING TO OTHER MANAGERS.
BB
THAT LAST PART WAS JUST A GUESS.

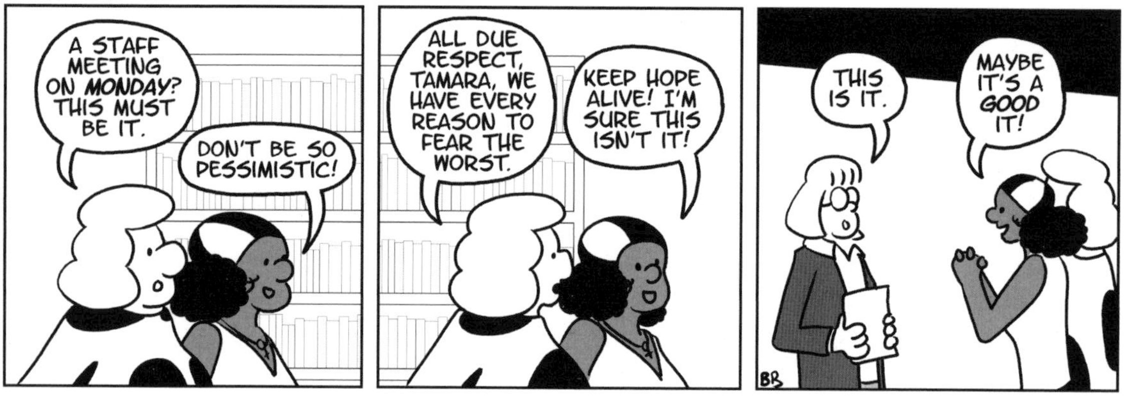
A STAFF MEETING ON MONDAY? THIS MUST BE IT.
DON'T BE SO PESSIMISTIC!
ALL DUE RESPECT, TAMARA, WE HAVE EVERY REASON TO FEAR THE WORST.
KEEP HOPE ALIVE! I'M SURE THIS ISN'T IT!
THIS IS IT.
MAYBE IT'S A GOOD IT!
BB

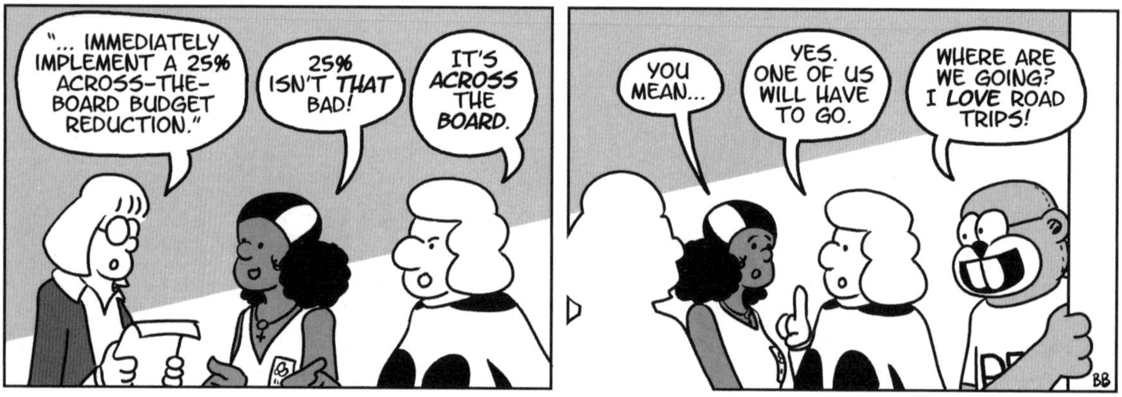
"... IMMEDIATELY IMPLEMENT A 25% ACROSS-THE-BOARD BUDGET REDUCTION."
25% ISN'T THAT BAD!
IT'S ACROSS THE BOARD.
YOU MEAN...
YES. ONE OF US WILL HAVE TO GO.
WHERE ARE WE GOING? I LOVE ROAD TRIPS!
BB

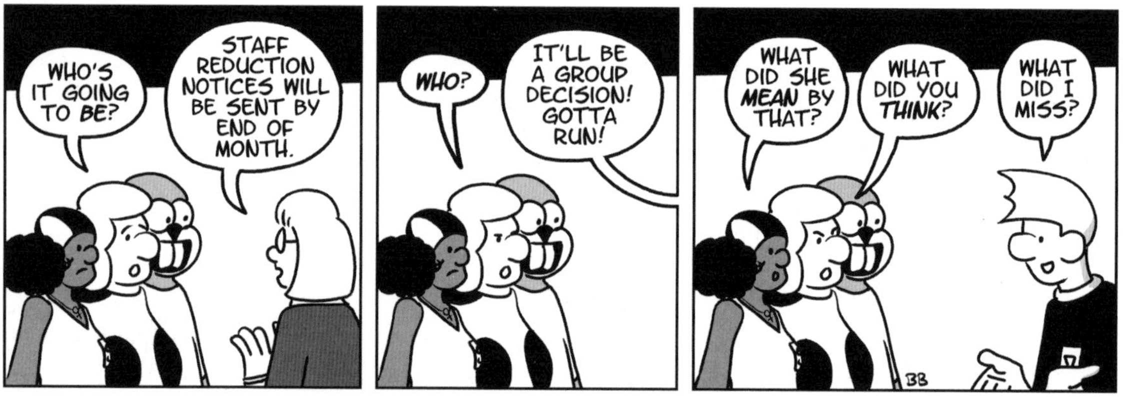
WHO'S IT GOING TO BE?
STAFF REDUCTION NOTICES WILL BE SENT BY END OF MONTH.
WHO?
IT'LL BE A GROUP DECISION! GOTTA RUN!
WHAT DID SHE MEAN BY THAT?
WHAT DID YOU THINK?
WHAT DID I MISS?
BB

Too Much Information

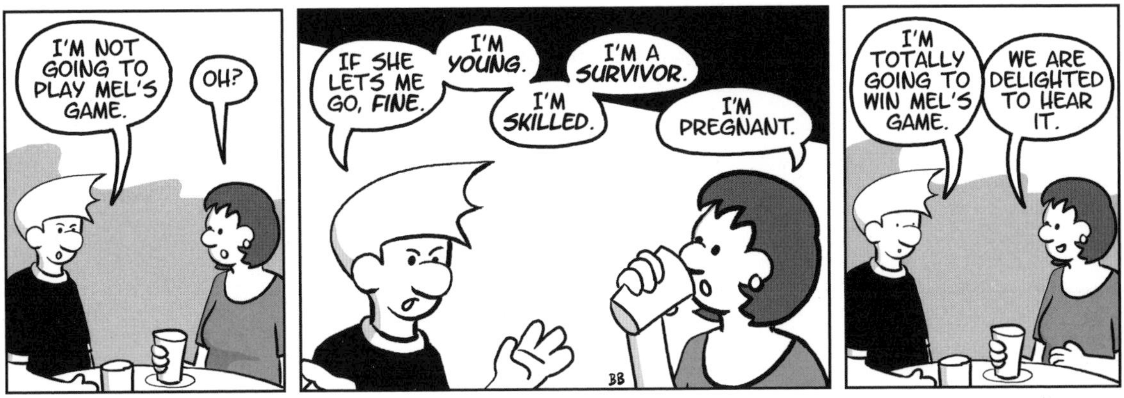

I'M NOT GOING TO PLAY MEL'S GAME.
OH?
IF SHE LETS ME GO, **FINE**.
I'M **YOUNG**.
I'M **SKILLED**.
I'M A **SURVIVOR**.
I'M PREGNANT.
I'M TOTALLY GOING TO WIN MEL'S GAME.
WE ARE DELIGHTED TO HEAR IT.
BB

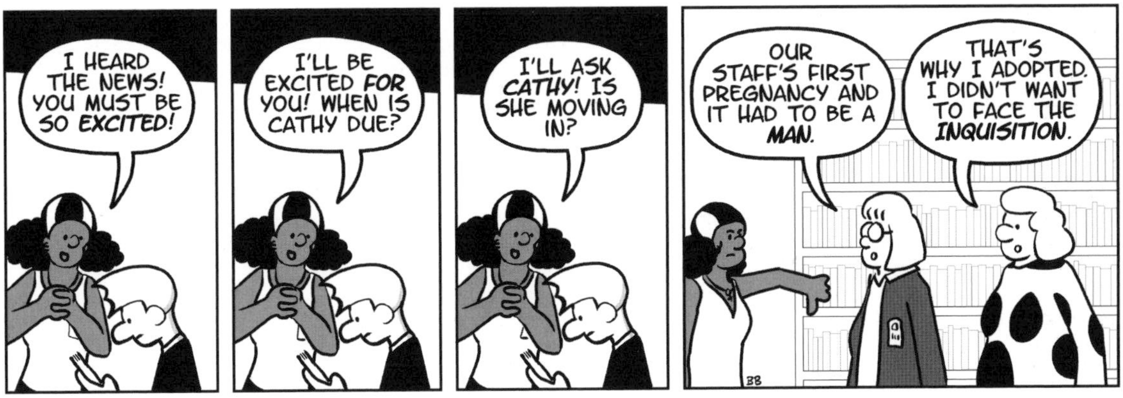

I HEARD THE NEWS! YOU MUST BE SO **EXCITED**!
I'LL BE EXCITED **FOR** YOU! WHEN IS CATHY DUE?
I'LL ASK **CATHY**! IS SHE MOVING IN?
OUR STAFF'S FIRST PREGNANCY AND IT HAD TO BE A **MAN**.
THAT'S WHY I ADOPTED. I DIDN'T WANT TO FACE THE **INQUISITION**.
BB

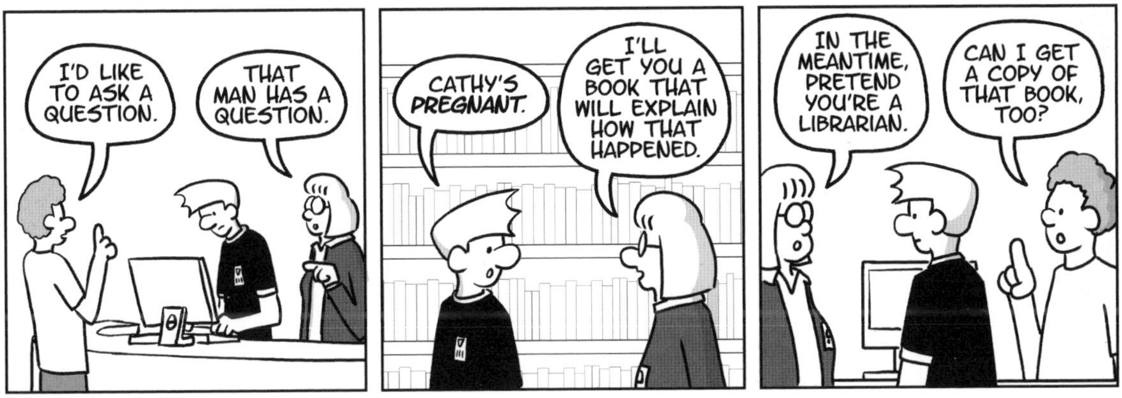

I'D LIKE TO ASK A QUESTION.
THAT MAN HAS A QUESTION.
CATHY'S **PREGNANT**.
I'LL GET YOU A BOOK THAT WILL EXPLAIN HOW THAT HAPPENED.
IN THE MEANTIME, PRETEND YOU'RE A LIBRARIAN.
CAN I GET A COPY OF THAT BOOK, TOO?

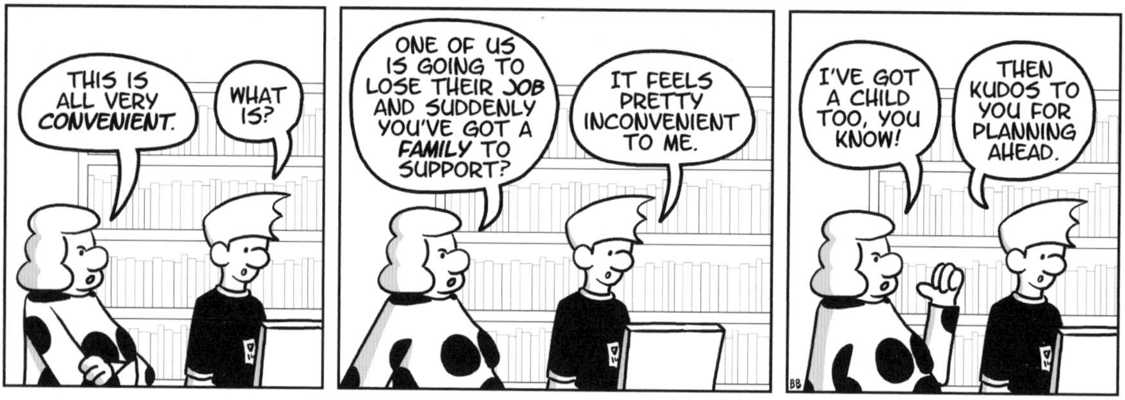
THIS IS ALL VERY **CONVENIENT**.
WHAT IS?
ONE OF US IS GOING TO LOSE THEIR **JOB** AND SUDDENLY YOU'VE GOT A **FAMILY** TO SUPPORT?
IT FEELS PRETTY INCONVENIENT TO ME.
I'VE GOT A CHILD TOO, YOU KNOW!
THEN KUDOS TO YOU FOR PLANNING AHEAD.
BB

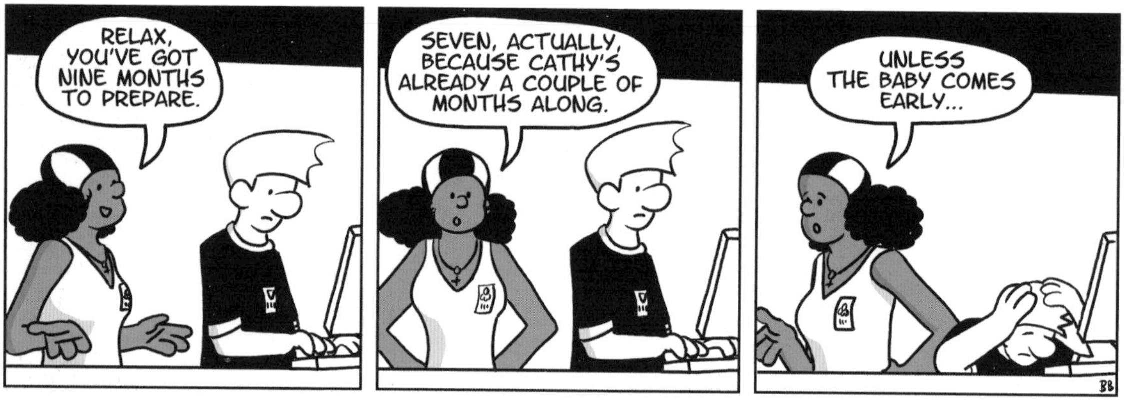
RELAX, YOU'VE GOT NINE MONTHS TO PREPARE.
SEVEN, ACTUALLY, BECAUSE CATHY'S ALREADY A COUPLE OF MONTHS ALONG.
UNLESS THE BABY COMES EARLY...
BB

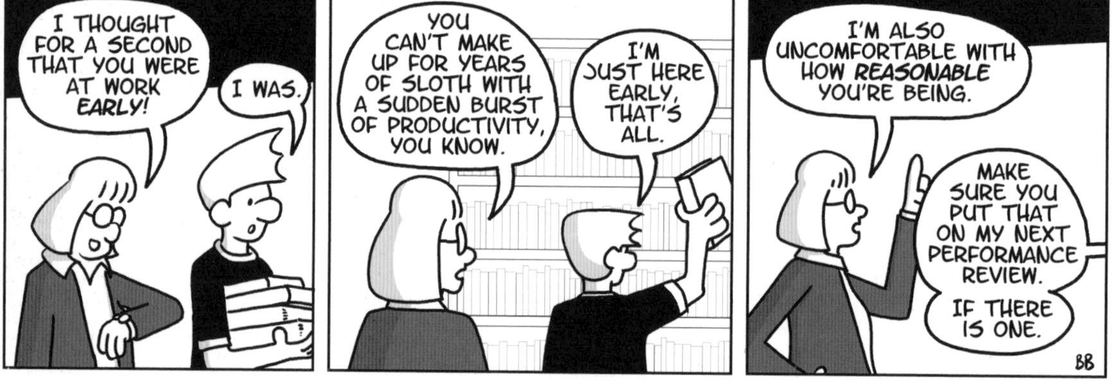
I THOUGHT FOR A SECOND THAT YOU WERE AT WORK **EARLY**!
I WAS.
YOU CAN'T MAKE UP FOR YEARS OF SLOTH WITH A SUDDEN BURST OF PRODUCTIVITY, YOU KNOW.
I'M JUST HERE EARLY, THAT'S ALL.
I'M ALSO UNCOMFORTABLE WITH HOW **REASONABLE** YOU'RE BEING.
MAKE SURE YOU PUT THAT ON MY NEXT PERFORMANCE REVIEW.
IF THERE IS ONE.
BB

Too Much Information

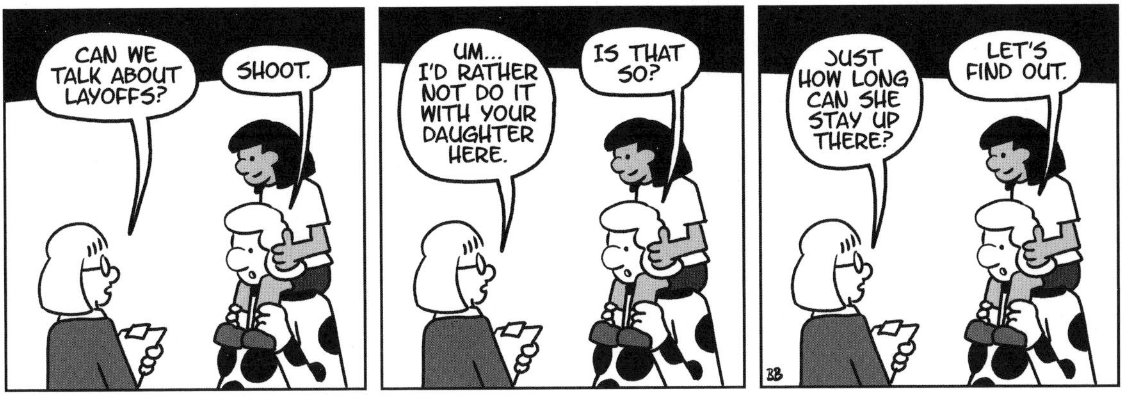
CAN WE TALK ABOUT LAYOFFS?
SHOOT.
UM... I'D RATHER NOT DO IT WITH YOUR DAUGHTER HERE.
IS THAT SO?
JUST HOW LONG CAN SHE STAY UP THERE?
LET'S FIND OUT.
BB

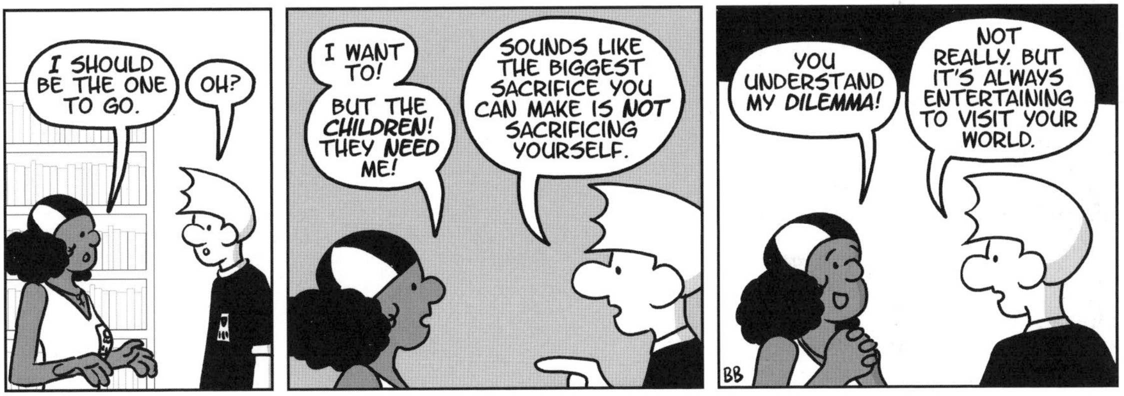
I SHOULD BE THE ONE TO GO.
OH?
I WANT TO!
BUT THE CHILDREN! THEY NEED ME!
SOUNDS LIKE THE BIGGEST SACRIFICE YOU CAN MAKE IS NOT SACRIFICING YOURSELF.
YOU UNDERSTAND MY DILEMMA!
NOT REALLY. BUT IT'S ALWAYS ENTERTAINING TO VISIT YOUR WORLD.
BB

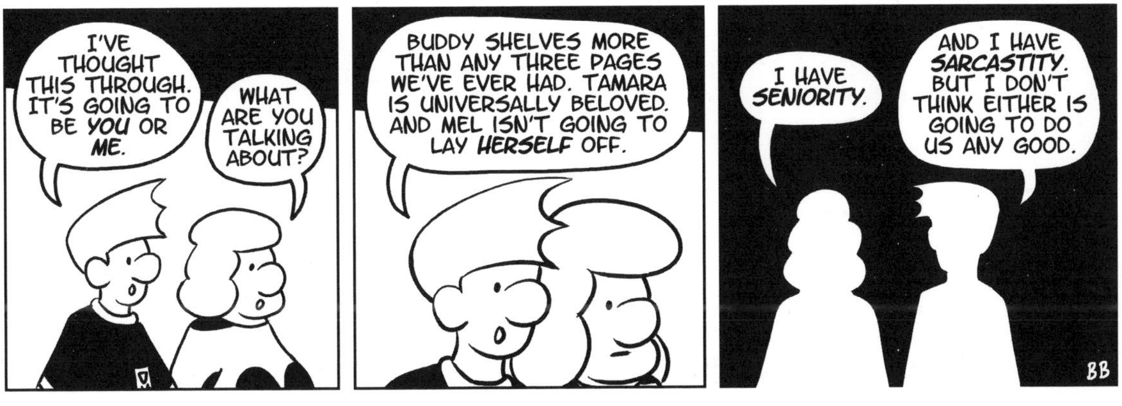
I'VE THOUGHT THIS THROUGH. IT'S GOING TO BE YOU OR ME.
WHAT ARE YOU TALKING ABOUT?
BUDDY SHELVES MORE THAN ANY THREE PAGES WE'VE EVER HAD. TAMARA IS UNIVERSALLY BELOVED. AND MEL ISN'T GOING TO LAY HERSELF OFF.
I HAVE SENIORITY.
AND I HAVE SARCASTITY. BUT I DON'T THINK EITHER IS GOING TO DO US ANY GOOD.
BB

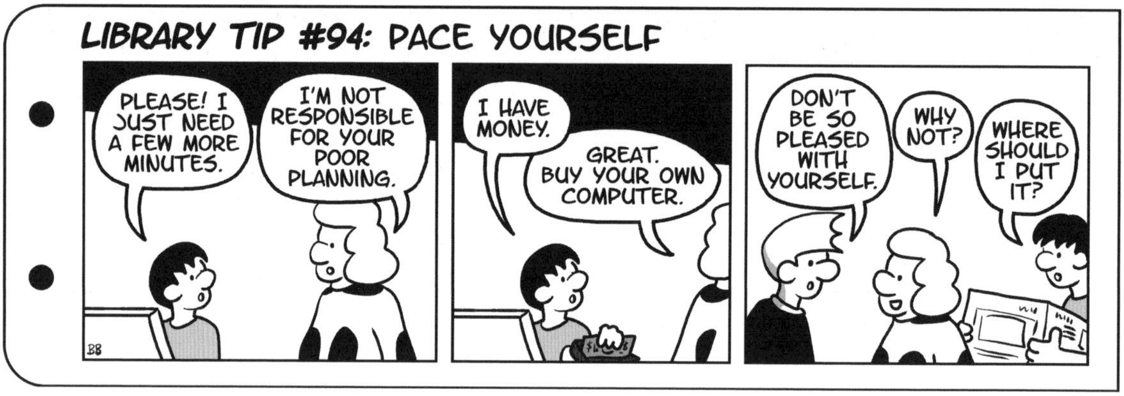
LIBRARY TIP #94: PACE YOURSELF
PLEASE! I JUST NEED A FEW MORE MINUTES.
I'M NOT RESPONSIBLE FOR YOUR POOR PLANNING.
I HAVE MONEY.
GREAT. BUY YOUR OWN COMPUTER.
DON'T BE SO PLEASED WITH YOURSELF.
WHY NOT?
WHERE SHOULD I PUT IT?
BB

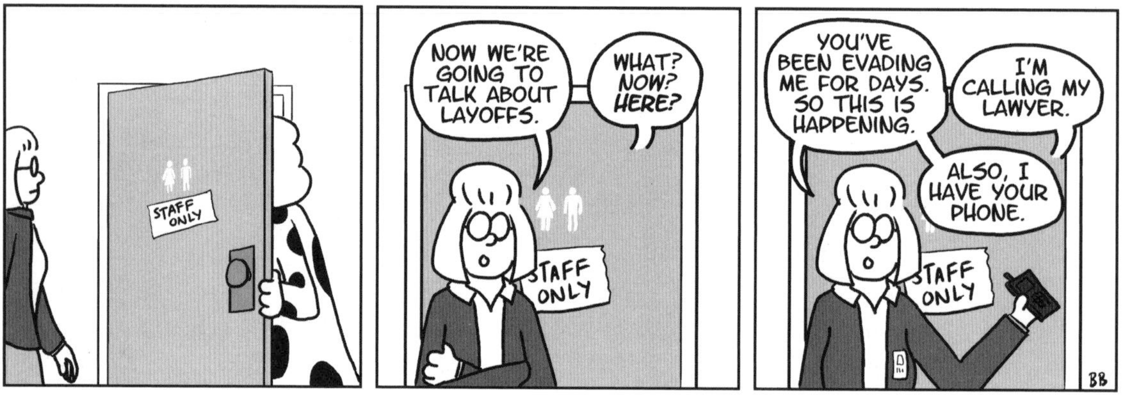
STAFF ONLY
NOW WE'RE GOING TO TALK ABOUT LAYOFFS.
WHAT? *NOW? HERE?*
YOU'VE BEEN EVADING ME FOR DAYS. SO THIS IS HAPPENING.
I'M CALLING MY LAWYER.
ALSO, I HAVE YOUR PHONE.
BB

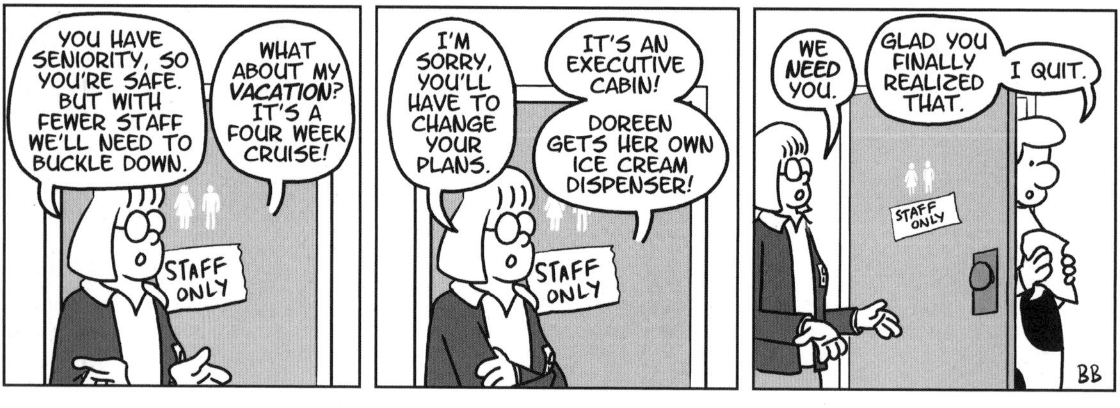
YOU HAVE SENIORITY, SO YOU'RE SAFE. BUT WITH FEWER STAFF WE'LL NEED TO BUCKLE DOWN.
WHAT ABOUT MY *VACATION*? IT'S A FOUR WEEK CRUISE!
I'M SORRY, YOU'LL HAVE TO CHANGE YOUR PLANS.
IT'S AN EXECUTIVE CABIN!
DOREEN GETS HER OWN ICE CREAM DISPENSER!
WE *NEED* YOU.
GLAD YOU FINALLY REALIZED THAT.
I QUIT.
BB

Too Much Information

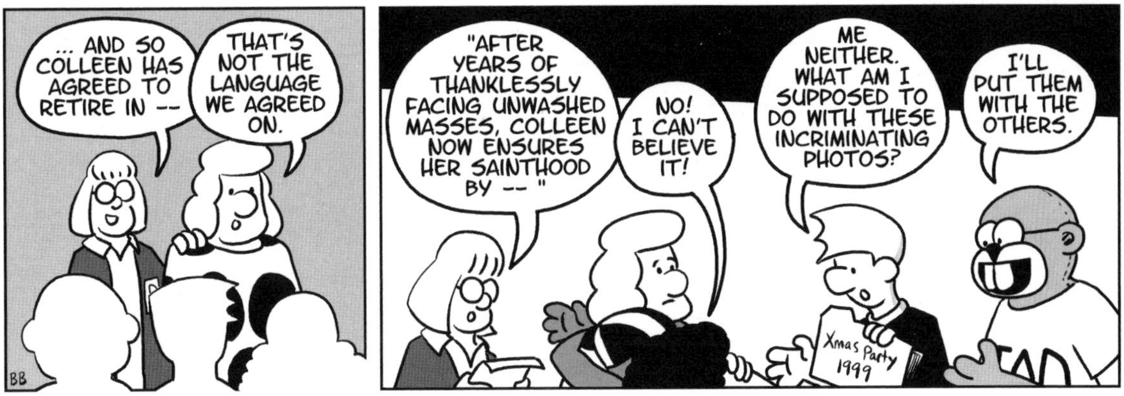

... AND SO COLLEEN HAS AGREED TO RETIRE IN --
THAT'S NOT THE LANGUAGE WE AGREED ON.
"AFTER YEARS OF THANKLESSLY FACING UNWASHED MASSES, COLLEEN NOW ENSURES HER SAINTHOOD BY -- "
NO! I CAN'T BELIEVE IT!
ME NEITHER. WHAT AM I SUPPOSED TO DO WITH THESE INCRIMINATING PHOTOS?
Xmas Party 1999
I'LL PUT THEM WITH THE OTHERS.

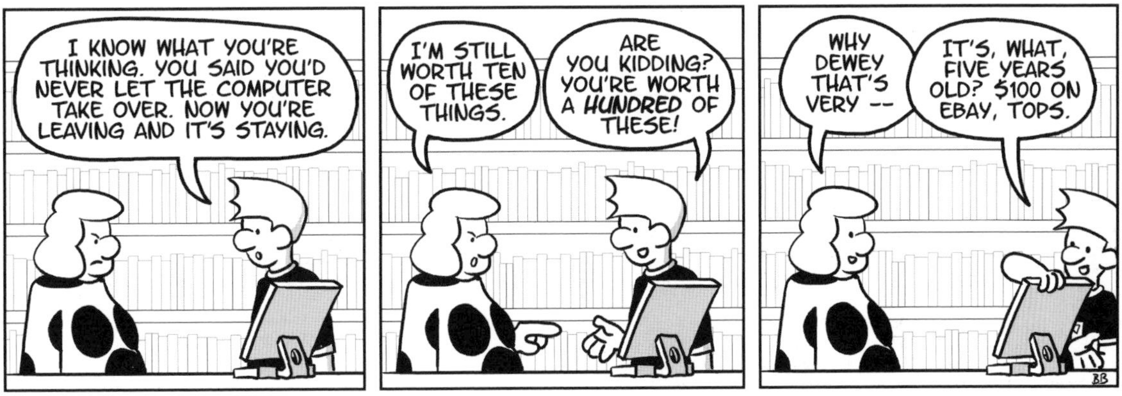

I KNOW WHAT YOU'RE THINKING. YOU SAID YOU'D NEVER LET THE COMPUTER TAKE OVER. NOW YOU'RE LEAVING AND IT'S STAYING.
I'M STILL WORTH TEN OF THESE THINGS.
ARE YOU KIDDING? YOU'RE WORTH A HUNDRED OF THESE!
WHY DEWEY THAT'S VERY --
IT'S, WHAT, FIVE YEARS OLD? $100 ON EBAY, TOPS.

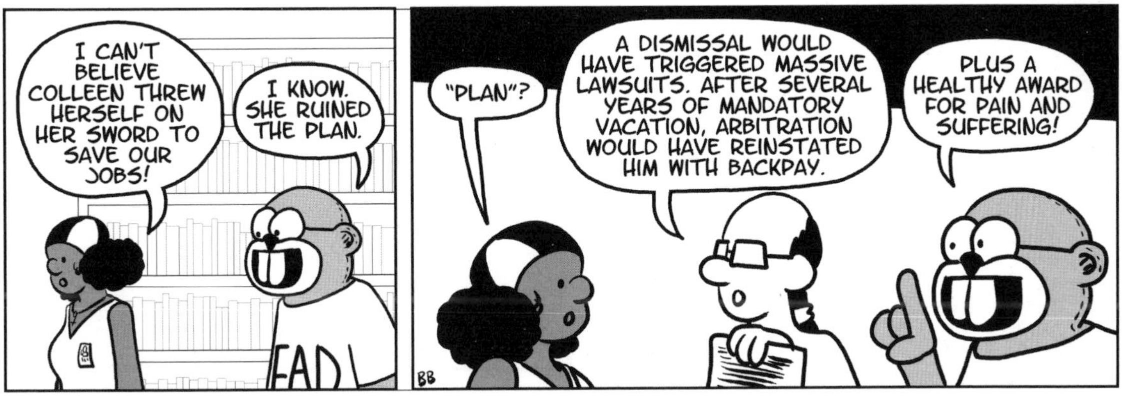

I CAN'T BELIEVE COLLEEN THREW HERSELF ON HER SWORD TO SAVE OUR JOBS!
I KNOW. SHE RUINED THE PLAN.
"PLAN"?
A DISMISSAL WOULD HAVE TRIGGERED MASSIVE LAWSUITS. AFTER SEVERAL YEARS OF MANDATORY VACATION, ARBITRATION WOULD HAVE REINSTATED HIM WITH BACKPAY.
PLUS A HEALTHY AWARD FOR PAIN AND SUFFERING!

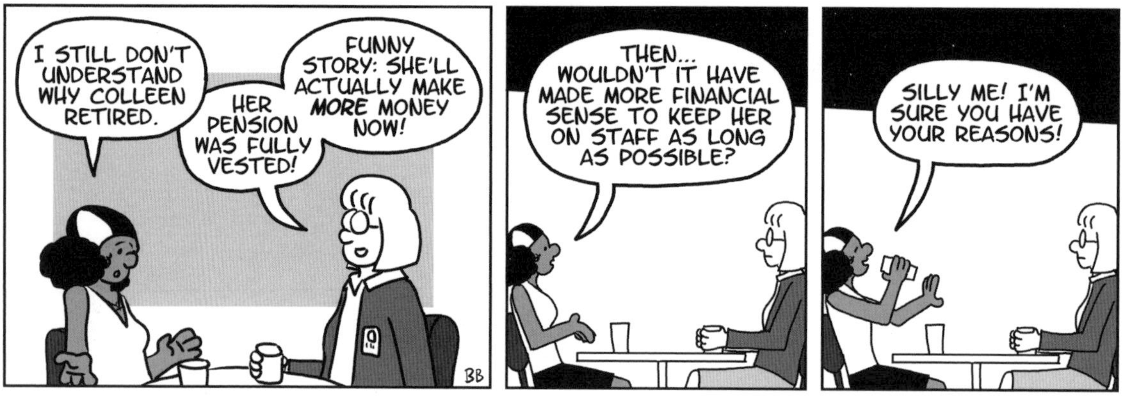
I STILL DON'T UNDERSTAND WHY COLLEEN RETIRED.
HER PENSION WAS FULLY VESTED!
FUNNY STORY: SHE'LL ACTUALLY MAKE **MORE** MONEY NOW!
THEN... WOULDN'T IT HAVE MADE MORE FINANCIAL SENSE TO KEEP HER ON STAFF AS LONG AS POSSIBLE?
SILLY ME! I'M SURE YOU HAVE YOUR REASONS!
BB

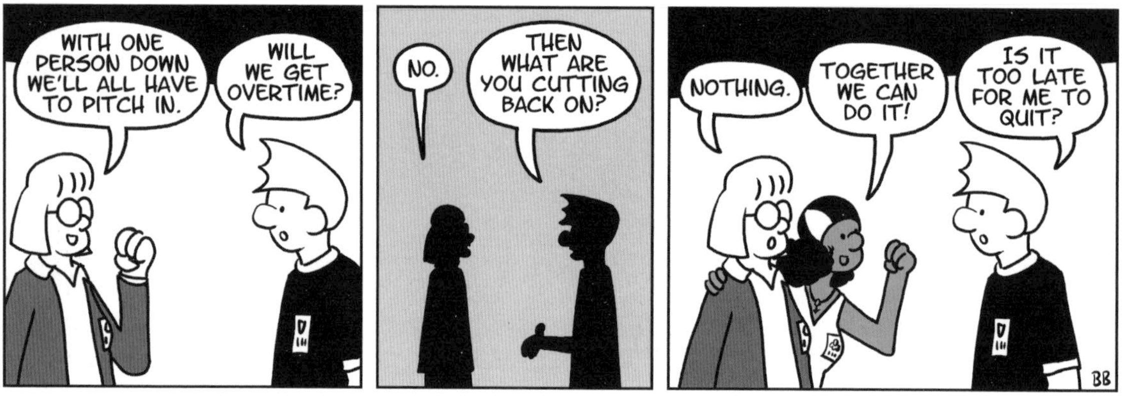
WITH ONE PERSON DOWN WE'LL ALL HAVE TO PITCH IN.
WILL WE GET OVERTIME?
NO.
THEN WHAT ARE YOU CUTTING BACK ON?
NOTHING.
TOGETHER WE CAN DO IT!
IS IT TOO LATE FOR ME TO QUIT?
BB

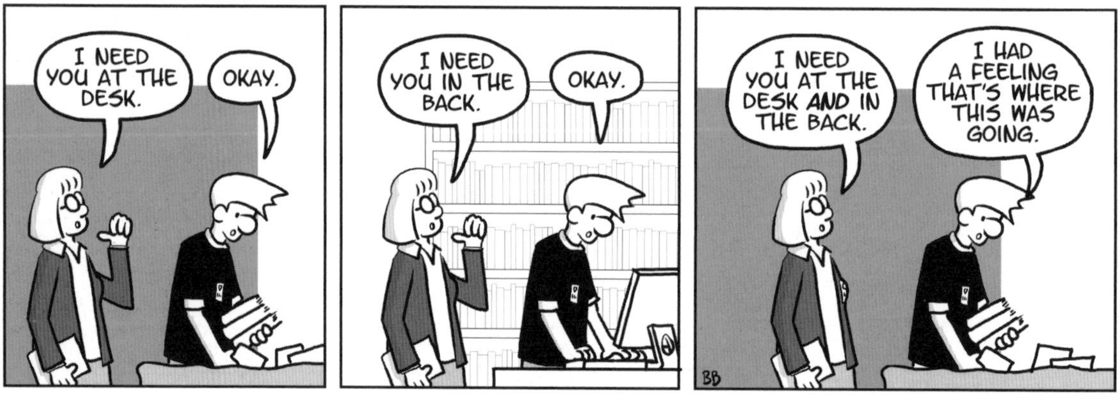
I NEED YOU AT THE DESK.
OKAY.
I NEED YOU IN THE BACK.
OKAY.
I NEED YOU AT THE DESK **AND** IN THE BACK.
I HAD A FEELING THAT'S WHERE THIS WAS GOING.
BB

Too Much Information

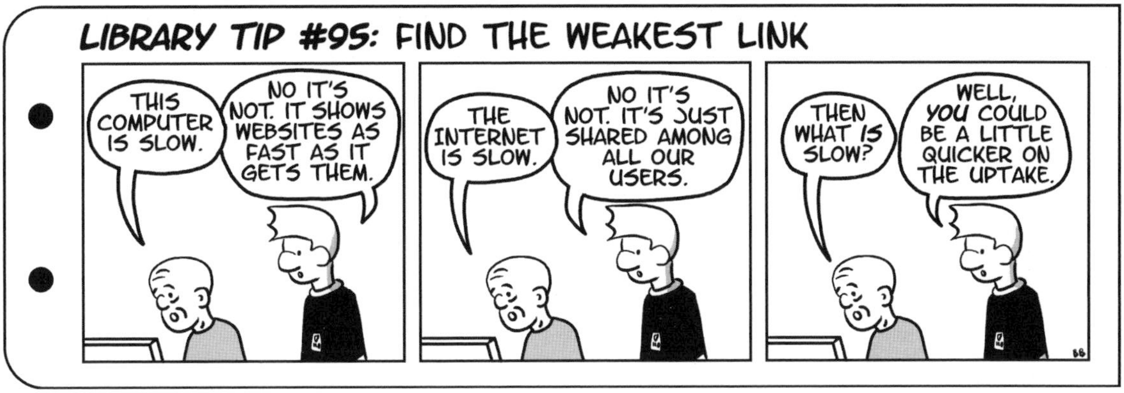
LIBRARY TIP #95: FIND THE WEAKEST LINK
THIS COMPUTER IS SLOW.
NO IT'S NOT. IT SHOWS WEBSITES AS FAST AS IT GETS THEM.
THE INTERNET IS SLOW.
NO IT'S NOT. IT'S JUST SHARED AMONG ALL OUR USERS.
THEN WHAT *IS* SLOW?
WELL, *YOU* COULD BE A LITTLE QUICKER ON THE UPTAKE.
BB

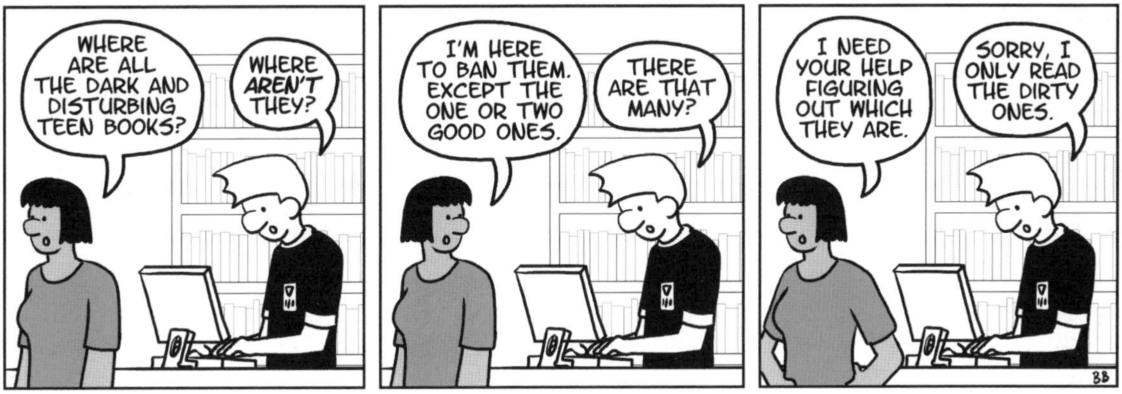
WHERE ARE ALL THE DARK AND DISTURBING TEEN BOOKS?
WHERE *AREN'T* THEY?
I'M HERE TO BAN THEM. EXCEPT THE ONE OR TWO GOOD ONES.
THERE ARE THAT MANY?
I NEED YOUR HELP FIGURING OUT WHICH THEY ARE.
SORRY, I ONLY READ THE DIRTY ONES.
BB

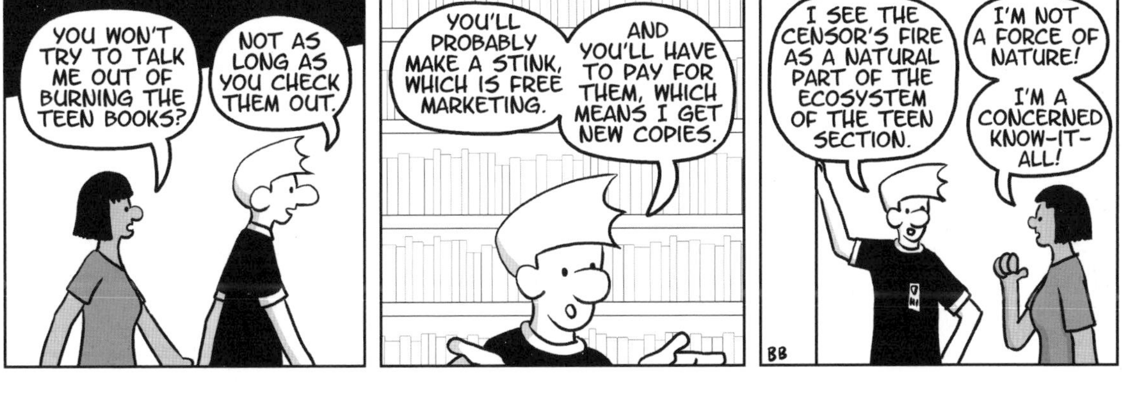
YOU WON'T TRY TO TALK ME OUT OF BURNING THE TEEN BOOKS?
NOT AS LONG AS YOU CHECK THEM OUT.
YOU'LL PROBABLY MAKE A STINK, WHICH IS FREE MARKETING.
AND YOU'LL HAVE TO PAY FOR THEM, WHICH MEANS I GET NEW COPIES.
I SEE THE CENSOR'S FIRE AS A NATURAL PART OF THE ECOSYSTEM OF THE TEEN SECTION.
I'M NOT A FORCE OF NATURE!
I'M A CONCERNED KNOW-IT-ALL!
BB

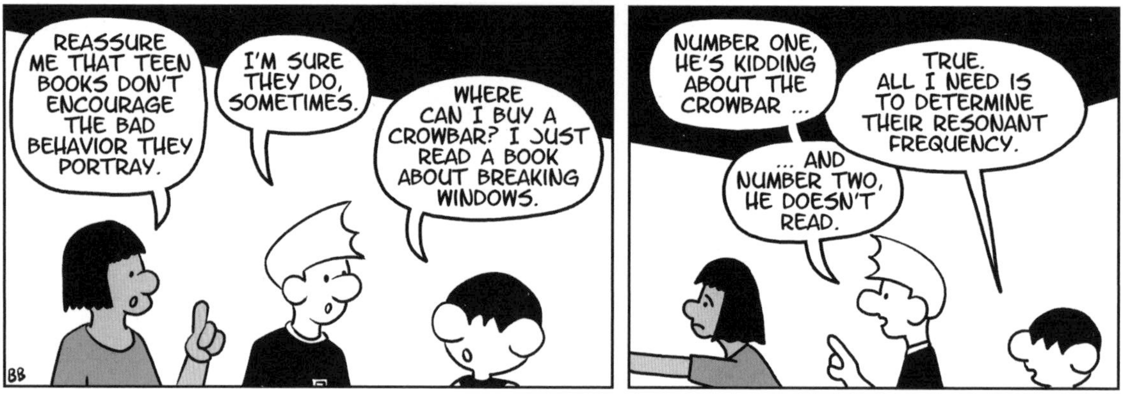
REASSURE ME THAT TEEN BOOKS DON'T ENCOURAGE THE BAD BEHAVIOR THEY PORTRAY.
I'M SURE THEY DO, SOMETIMES.
WHERE CAN I BUY A CROWBAR? I JUST READ A BOOK ABOUT BREAKING WINDOWS.
NUMBER ONE, HE'S KIDDING ABOUT THE CROWBAR ...
... AND NUMBER TWO, HE DOESN'T READ.
TRUE. ALL I NEED IS TO DETERMINE THEIR RESONANT FREQUENCY.
BB

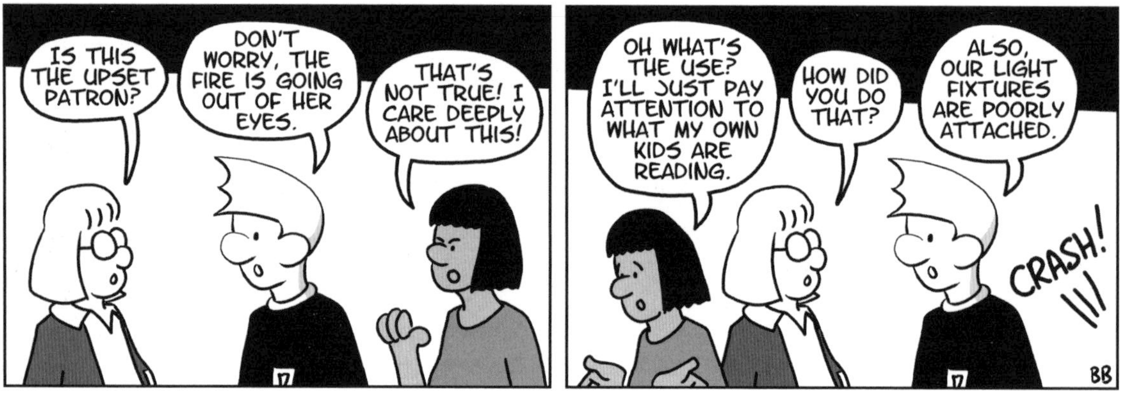
IS THIS THE UPSET PATRON?
DON'T WORRY, THE FIRE IS GOING OUT OF HER EYES.
THAT'S NOT TRUE! I CARE DEEPLY ABOUT THIS!
OH WHAT'S THE USE? I'LL JUST PAY ATTENTION TO WHAT MY OWN KIDS ARE READING.
HOW DID YOU DO THAT?
ALSO, OUR LIGHT FIXTURES ARE POORLY ATTACHED.
CRASH!
BB

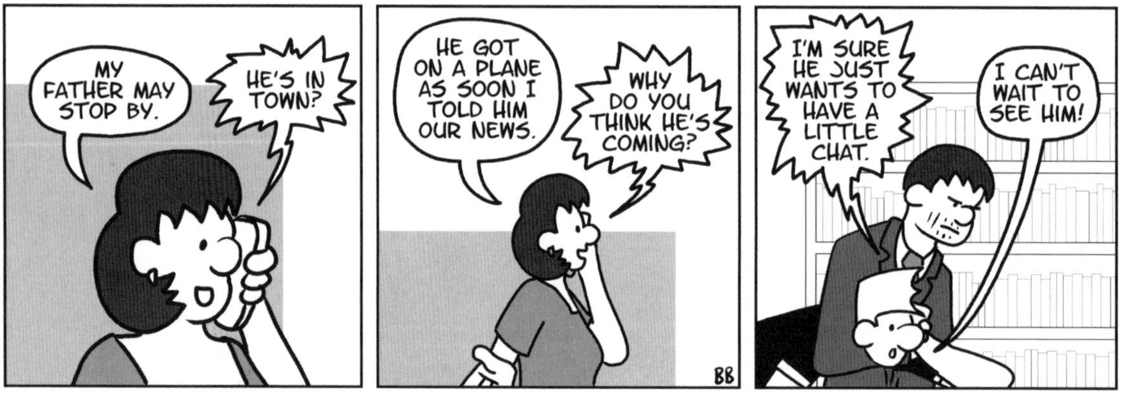
MY FATHER MAY STOP BY.
HE'S IN TOWN?
HE GOT ON A PLANE AS SOON I TOLD HIM OUR NEWS.
WHY DO YOU THINK HE'S COMING?
BB
I'M SURE HE JUST WANTS TO HAVE A LITTLE CHAT.
I CAN'T WAIT TO SEE HIM!

Too Much Information

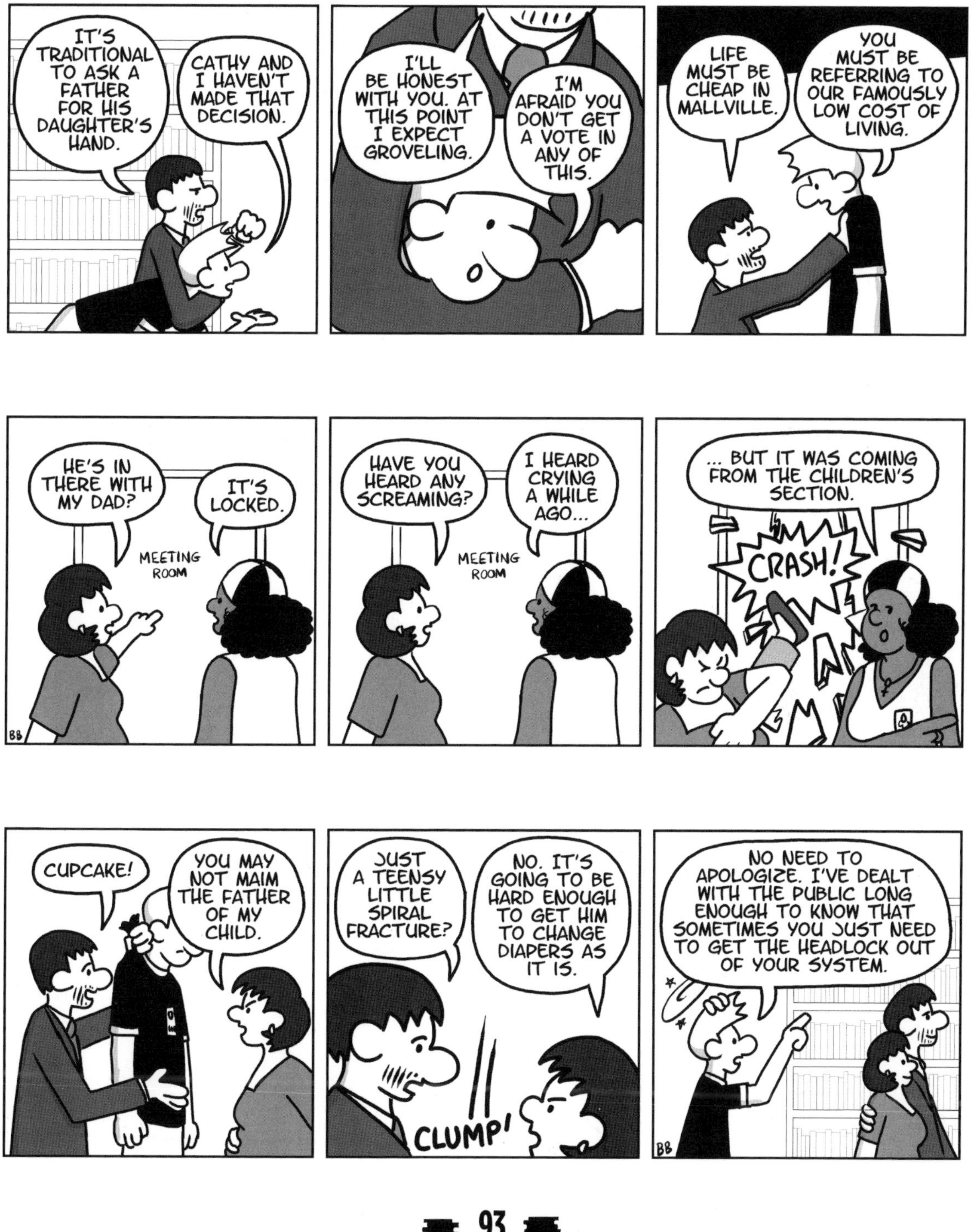
IT'S TRADITIONAL TO ASK A FATHER FOR HIS DAUGHTER'S HAND.
CATHY AND I HAVEN'T MADE THAT DECISION.
I'LL BE HONEST WITH YOU. AT THIS POINT I EXPECT GROVELING.
I'M AFRAID YOU DON'T GET A VOTE IN ANY OF THIS.
LIFE MUST BE CHEAP IN MALLVILLE.
YOU MUST BE REFERRING TO OUR FAMOUSLY LOW COST OF LIVING.
HE'S IN THERE WITH MY DAD?
IT'S LOCKED.
MEETING ROOM
BB
HAVE YOU HEARD ANY SCREAMING?
I HEARD CRYING A WHILE AGO...
MEETING ROOM
... BUT IT WAS COMING FROM THE CHILDREN'S SECTION.
CRASH!
CUPCAKE!
YOU MAY NOT MAIM THE FATHER OF MY CHILD.
JUST A TEENSY LITTLE SPIRAL FRACTURE?
NO. IT'S GOING TO BE HARD ENOUGH TO GET HIM TO CHANGE DIAPERS AS IT IS.
CLUMP!
NO NEED TO APOLOGIZE. I'VE DEALT WITH THE PUBLIC LONG ENOUGH TO KNOW THAT SOMETIMES YOU JUST NEED TO GET THE HEADLOCK OUT OF YOUR SYSTEM.
BB

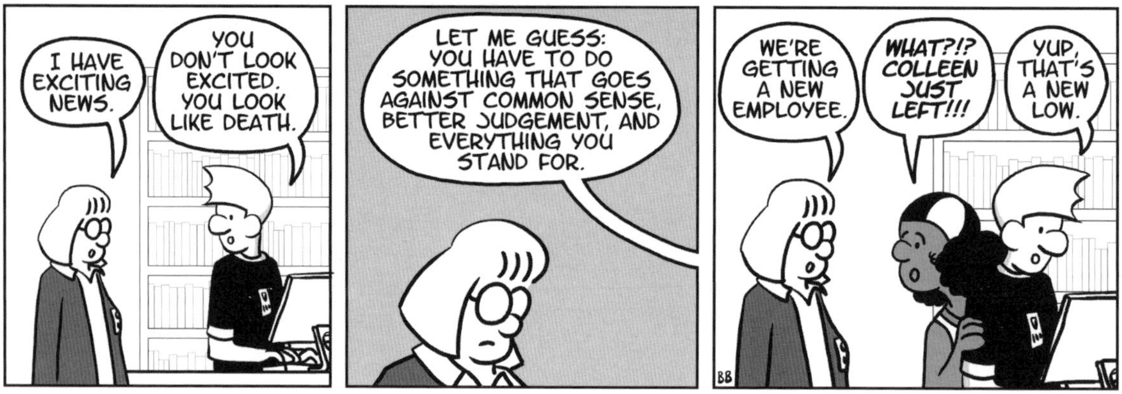
I HAVE EXCITING NEWS.
YOU DON'T LOOK EXCITED. YOU LOOK LIKE DEATH.
LET ME GUESS: YOU HAVE TO DO SOMETHING THAT GOES AGAINST COMMON SENSE, BETTER JUDGEMENT, AND EVERYTHING YOU STAND FOR.
WE'RE GETTING A NEW EMPLOYEE.
WHAT?!? COLLEEN JUST LEFT!!!
YUP, THAT'S A NEW LOW.
BB

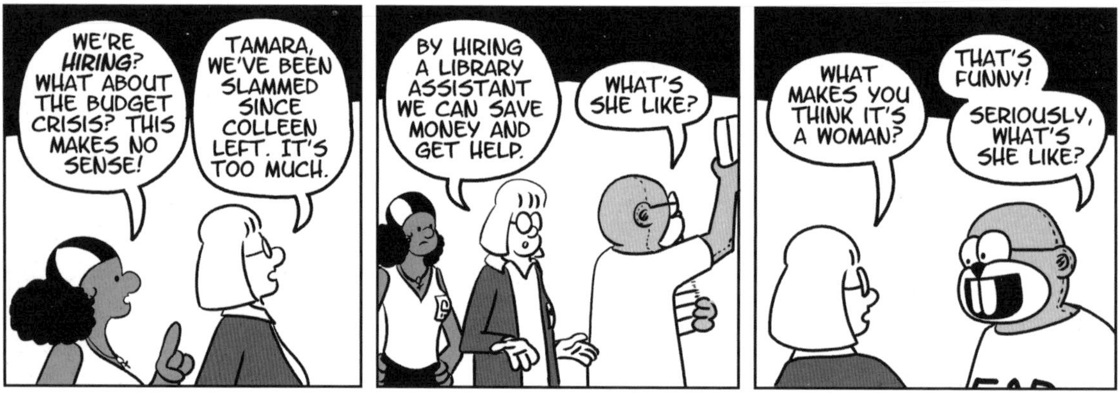
WE'RE HIRING? WHAT ABOUT THE BUDGET CRISIS? THIS MAKES NO SENSE!
TAMARA, WE'VE BEEN SLAMMED SINCE COLLEEN LEFT. IT'S TOO MUCH.
BY HIRING A LIBRARY ASSISTANT WE CAN SAVE MONEY AND GET HELP.
WHAT'S SHE LIKE?
WHAT MAKES YOU THINK IT'S A WOMAN?
THAT'S FUNNY!
SERIOUSLY, WHAT'S SHE LIKE?

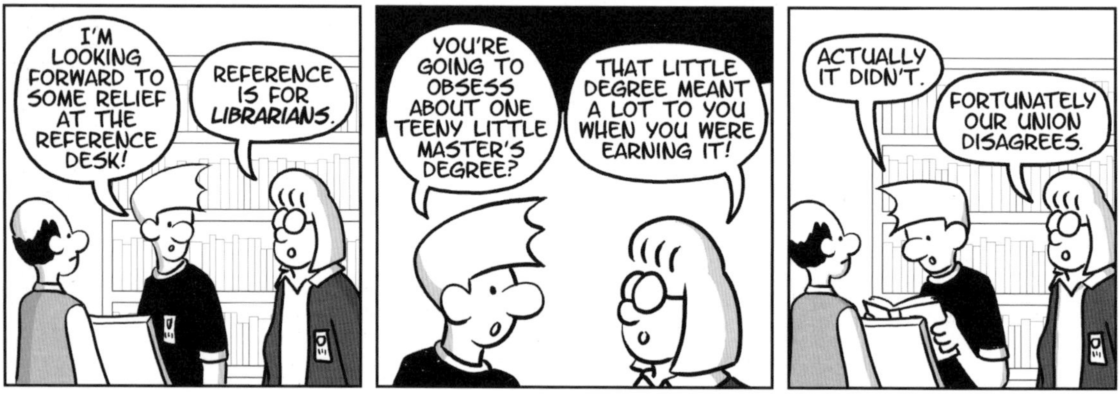
I'M LOOKING FORWARD TO SOME RELIEF AT THE REFERENCE DESK!
REFERENCE IS FOR LIBRARIANS.
YOU'RE GOING TO OBSESS ABOUT ONE TEENY LITTLE MASTER'S DEGREE?
THAT LITTLE DEGREE MEANT A LOT TO YOU WHEN YOU WERE EARNING IT!
ACTUALLY IT DIDN'T.
FORTUNATELY OUR UNION DISAGREES.

Too Much Information

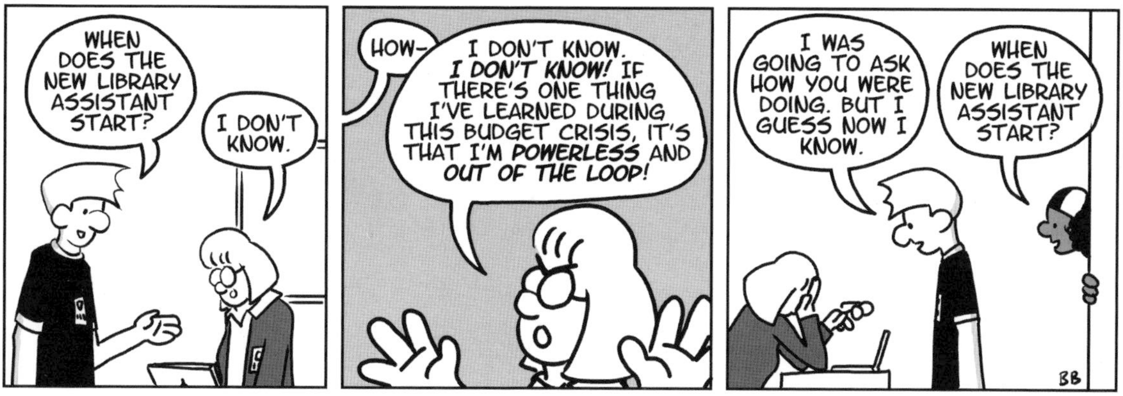
WHEN DOES THE NEW LIBRARY ASSISTANT START?
I DON'T KNOW.
HOW-
I DON'T KNOW. *I DON'T KNOW!* IF THERE'S ONE THING I'VE LEARNED DURING THIS BUDGET CRISIS, IT'S THAT I'M *POWERLESS* AND *OUT OF THE LOOP!*
I WAS GOING TO ASK HOW YOU WERE DOING. BUT I GUESS NOW I KNOW.
WHEN DOES THE NEW LIBRARY ASSISTANT START?
BB

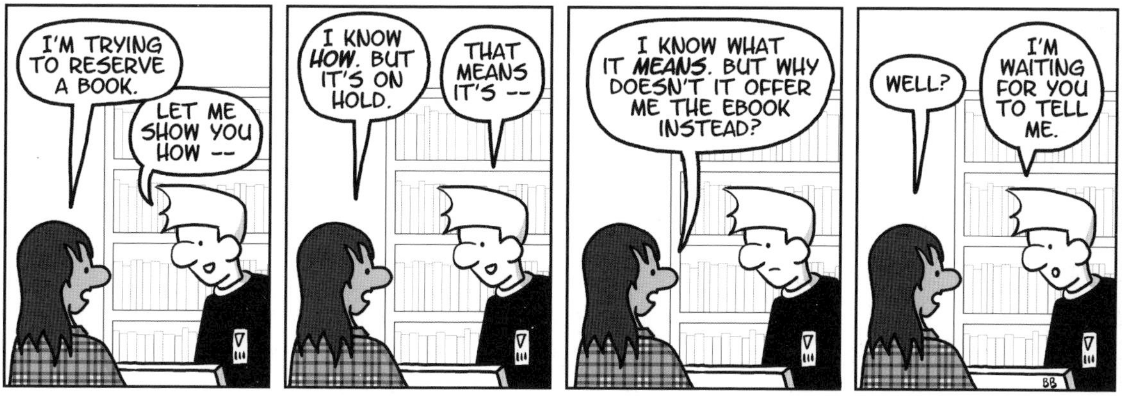
I'M TRYING TO RESERVE A BOOK.
LET ME SHOW YOU HOW --
I KNOW *HOW*. BUT IT'S ON HOLD.
THAT MEANS IT'S --
I KNOW WHAT IT *MEANS*. BUT WHY DOESN'T IT OFFER ME THE EBOOK INSTEAD?
WELL?
I'M WAITING FOR YOU TO TELL ME.
BB

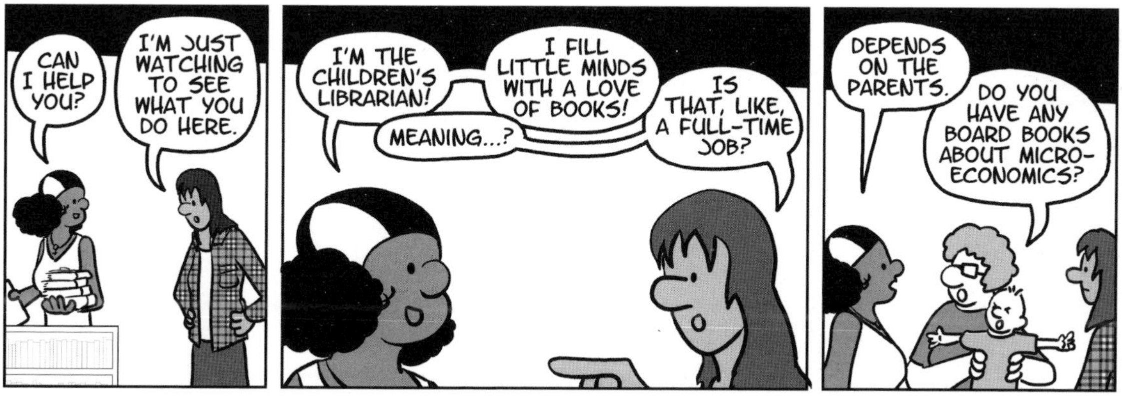
CAN I HELP YOU?
I'M JUST WATCHING TO SEE WHAT YOU DO HERE.
I'M THE CHILDREN'S LIBRARIAN!
MEANING...?
I FILL LITTLE MINDS WITH A LOVE OF BOOKS!
IS THAT, LIKE, A FULL-TIME JOB?
DEPENDS ON THE PARENTS.
DO YOU HAVE ANY BOARD BOOKS ABOUT MICRO-ECONOMICS?

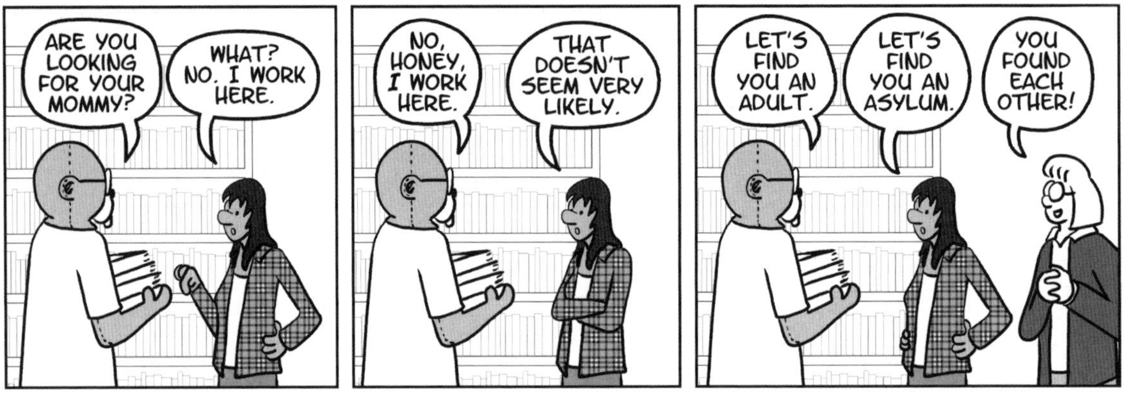
ARE YOU LOOKING FOR YOUR MOMMY?
WHAT? NO. I WORK HERE.
NO, HONEY, I WORK HERE.
THAT DOESN'T SEEM VERY LIKELY.
LET'S FIND YOU AN ADULT.
LET'S FIND YOU AN ASYLUM.
YOU FOUND EACH OTHER!

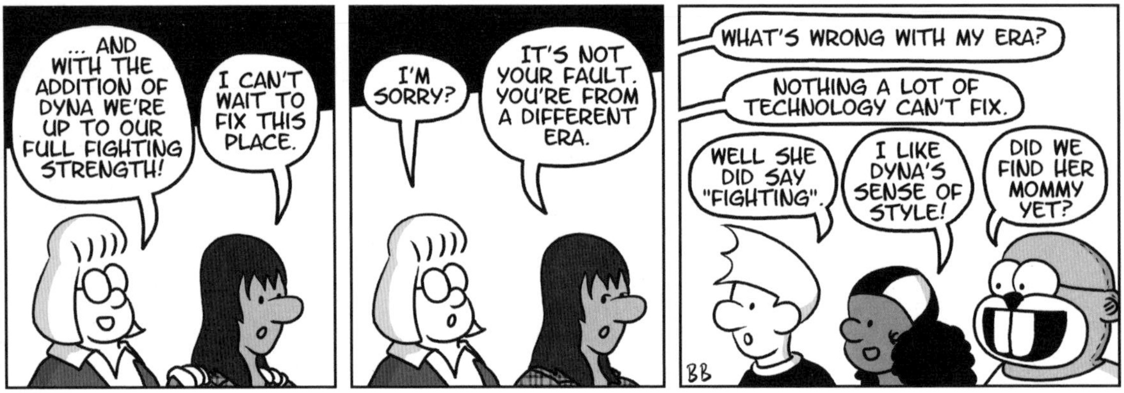
... AND WITH THE ADDITION OF DYNA WE'RE UP TO OUR FULL FIGHTING STRENGTH!
I CAN'T WAIT TO FIX THIS PLACE.
I'M SORRY?
IT'S NOT YOUR FAULT. YOU'RE FROM A DIFFERENT ERA.
WHAT'S WRONG WITH MY ERA?
NOTHING A LOT OF TECHNOLOGY CAN'T FIX.
WELL SHE DID SAY "FIGHTING".
I LIKE DYNA'S SENSE OF STYLE!
DID WE FIND HER MOMMY YET?
BB

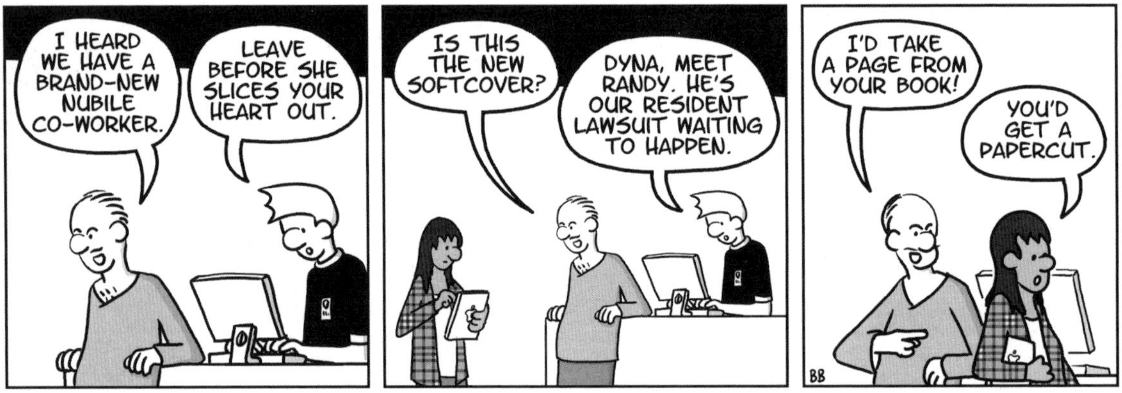
I HEARD WE HAVE A BRAND-NEW NUBILE CO-WORKER.
LEAVE BEFORE SHE SLICES YOUR HEART OUT.
IS THIS THE NEW SOFTCOVER?
DYNA, MEET RANDY. HE'S OUR RESIDENT LAWSUIT WAITING TO HAPPEN.
I'D TAKE A PAGE FROM YOUR BOOK!
YOU'D GET A PAPERCUT.
BB

Too Much Information

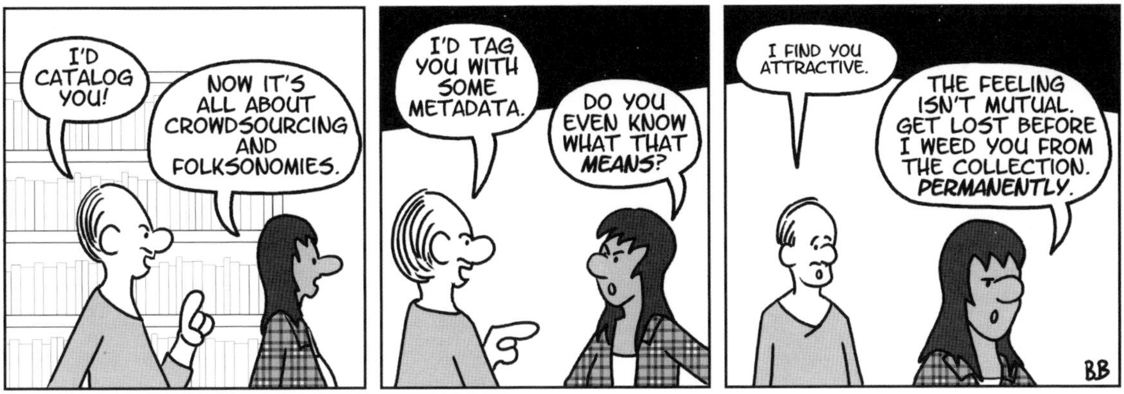
I'D CATALOG YOU!
NOW IT'S ALL ABOUT CROWDSOURCING AND FOLKSONOMIES.
I'D TAG YOU WITH SOME METADATA.
DO YOU EVEN KNOW WHAT THAT MEANS?
I FIND YOU ATTRACTIVE.
THE FEELING ISN'T MUTUAL. GET LOST BEFORE I WEED YOU FROM THE COLLECTION. PERMANENTLY.
BB

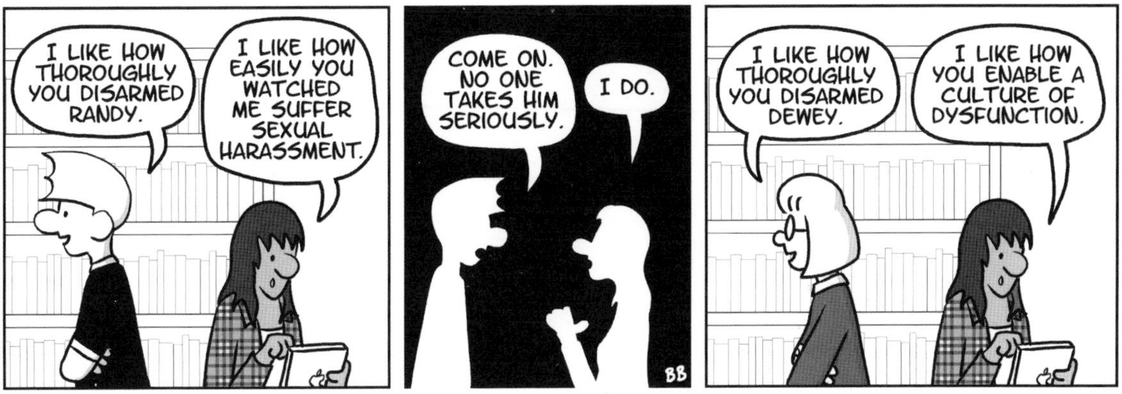
I LIKE HOW THOROUGHLY YOU DISARMED RANDY.
I LIKE HOW EASILY YOU WATCHED ME SUFFER SEXUAL HARASSMENT.
COME ON. NO ONE TAKES HIM SERIOUSLY.
I DO.
I LIKE HOW THOROUGHLY YOU DISARMED DEWEY.
I LIKE HOW YOU ENABLE A CULTURE OF DYSFUNCTION.
BB

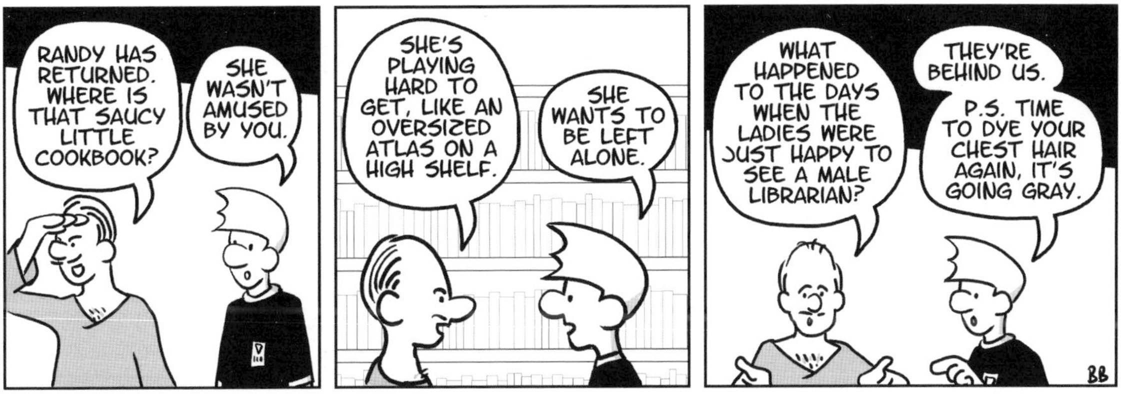
RANDY HAS RETURNED. WHERE IS THAT SAUCY LITTLE COOKBOOK?
SHE WASN'T AMUSED BY YOU.
SHE'S PLAYING HARD TO GET, LIKE AN OVERSIZED ATLAS ON A HIGH SHELF.
SHE WANTS TO BE LEFT ALONE.
WHAT HAPPENED TO THE DAYS WHEN THE LADIES WERE JUST HAPPY TO SEE A MALE LIBRARIAN?
THEY'RE BEHIND US.
P.S. TIME TO DYE YOUR CHEST HAIR AGAIN, IT'S GOING GRAY.
BB

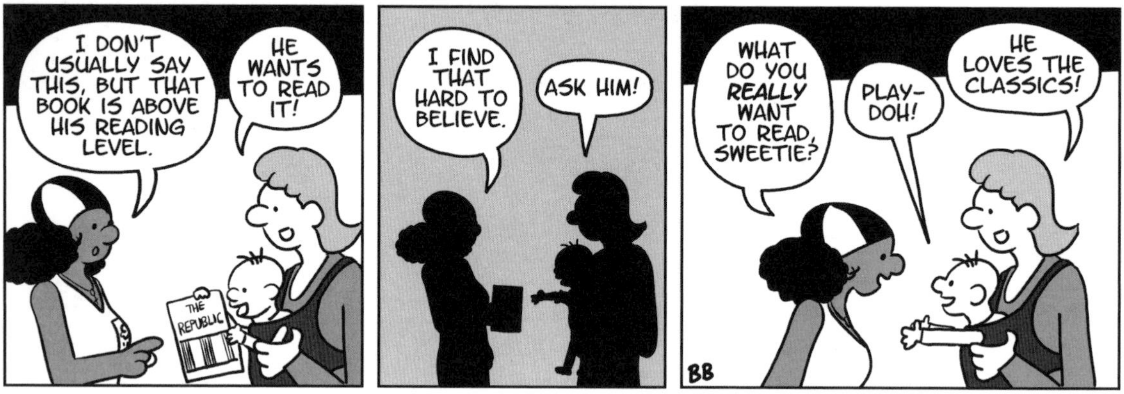
I DON'T USUALLY SAY THIS, BUT THAT BOOK IS ABOVE HIS READING LEVEL.
HE WANTS TO READ IT!
THE REPUBLIC
I FIND THAT HARD TO BELIEVE.
ASK HIM!
WHAT DO YOU *REALLY* WANT TO READ, SWEETIE?
PLAY-DOH!
HE LOVES THE CLASSICS!
BB

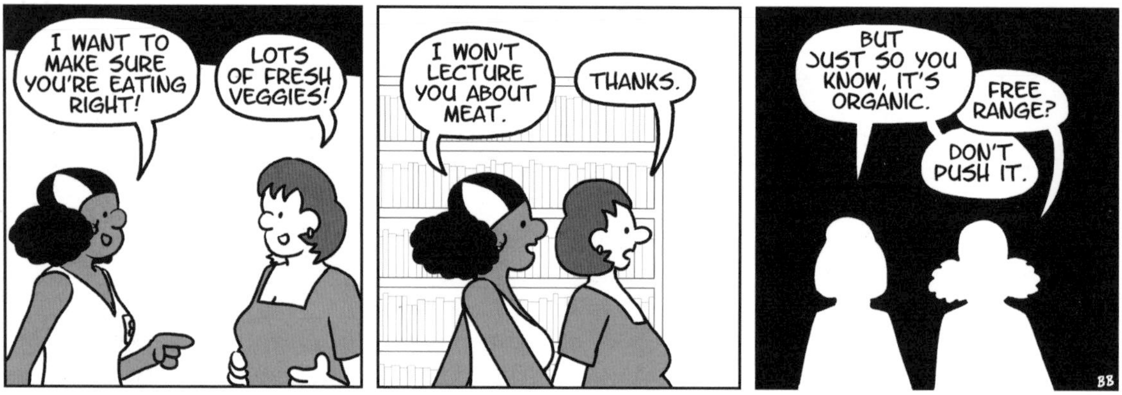
I WANT TO MAKE SURE YOU'RE EATING RIGHT!
LOTS OF FRESH VEGGIES!
I WON'T LECTURE YOU ABOUT MEAT.
THANKS.
BUT JUST SO YOU KNOW, IT'S ORGANIC.
FREE RANGE?
DON'T PUSH IT.
BB

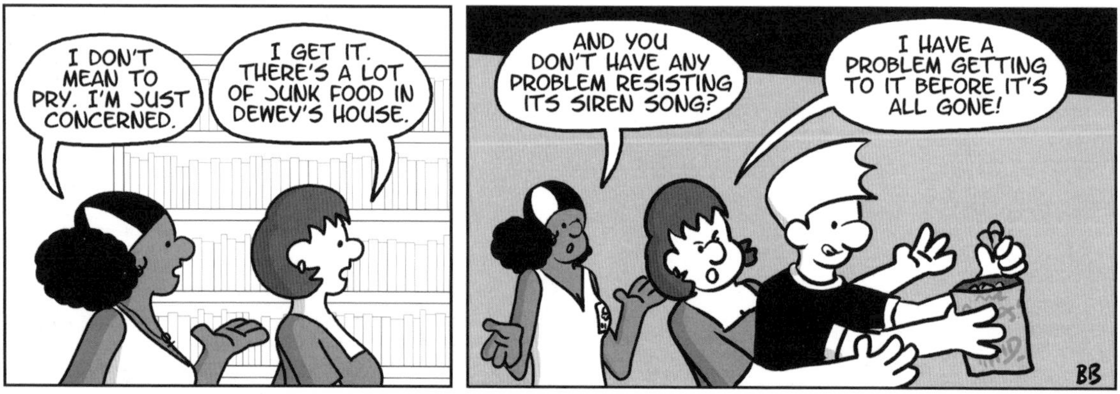
I DON'T MEAN TO PRY. I'M JUST CONCERNED.
I GET IT. THERE'S A LOT OF JUNK FOOD IN DEWEY'S HOUSE.
AND YOU DON'T HAVE ANY PROBLEM RESISTING ITS SIREN SONG?
I HAVE A PROBLEM GETTING TO IT BEFORE IT'S ALL GONE!
BB

Too Much Information

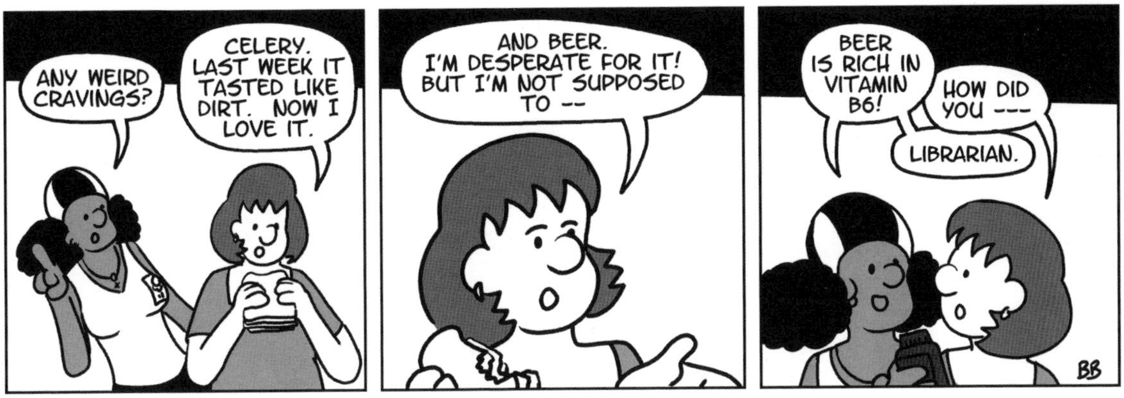
ANY WEIRD CRAVINGS?
CELERY. LAST WEEK IT TASTED LIKE DIRT. NOW I LOVE IT.
AND BEER. I'M DESPERATE FOR IT! BUT I'M NOT SUPPOSED TO --
BEER IS RICH IN VITAMIN B6!
HOW DID YOU ---
LIBRARIAN.
BB

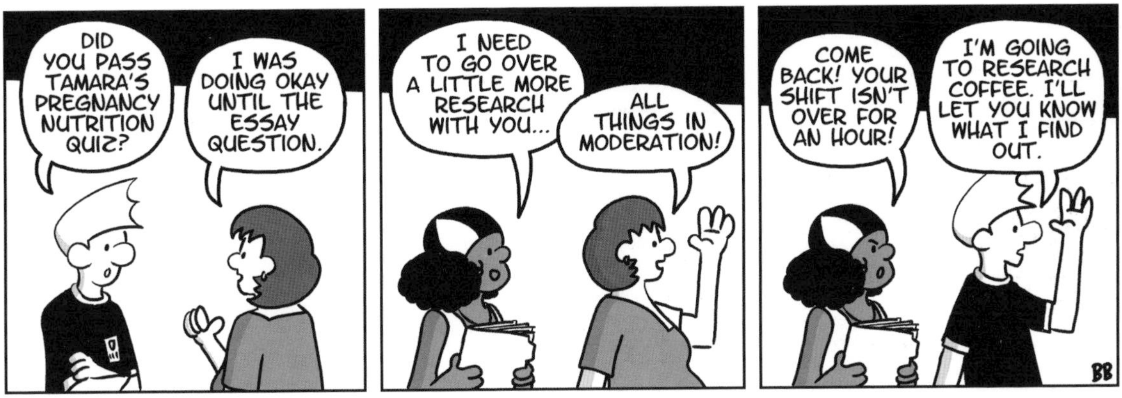
DID YOU PASS TAMARA'S PREGNANCY NUTRITION QUIZ?
I WAS DOING OKAY UNTIL THE ESSAY QUESTION.
I NEED TO GO OVER A LITTLE MORE RESEARCH WITH YOU...
ALL THINGS IN MODERATION!
COME BACK! YOUR SHIFT ISN'T OVER FOR AN HOUR!
I'M GOING TO RESEARCH COFFEE. I'LL LET YOU KNOW WHAT I FIND OUT.
BB

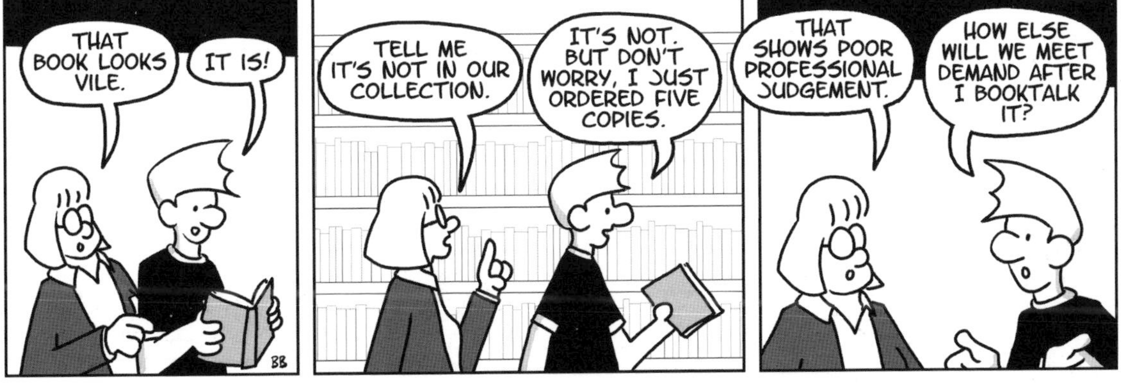
THAT BOOK LOOKS VILE.
IT IS!
BB
TELL ME IT'S NOT IN OUR COLLECTION.
IT'S NOT. BUT DON'T WORRY, I JUST ORDERED FIVE COPIES.
THAT SHOWS POOR PROFESSIONAL JUDGEMENT.
HOW ELSE WILL WE MEET DEMAND AFTER I BOOKTALK IT?

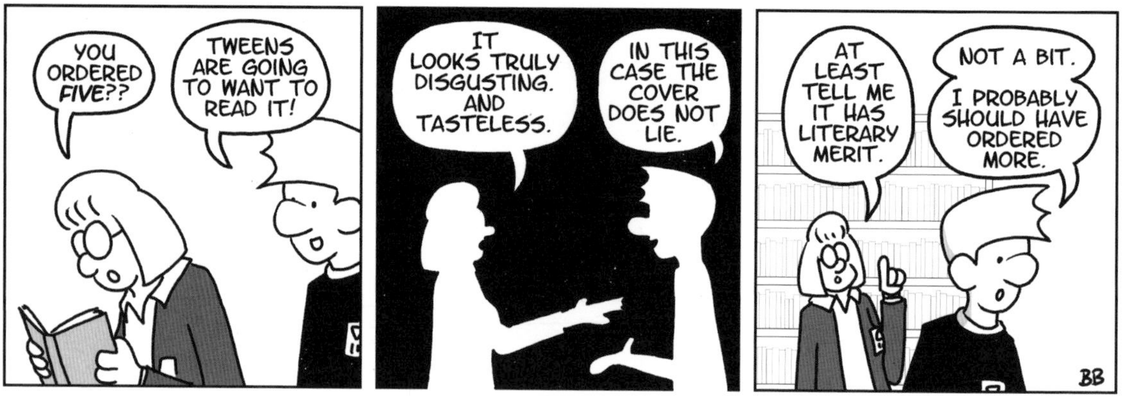
YOU ORDERED *FIVE*??
TWEENS ARE GOING TO WANT TO READ IT!
IT LOOKS TRULY DISGUSTING. AND TASTELESS.
IN THIS CASE THE COVER DOES NOT LIE.
AT LEAST TELL ME IT HAS LITERARY MERIT.
NOT A BIT.
I PROBABLY SHOULD HAVE ORDERED MORE.
BB

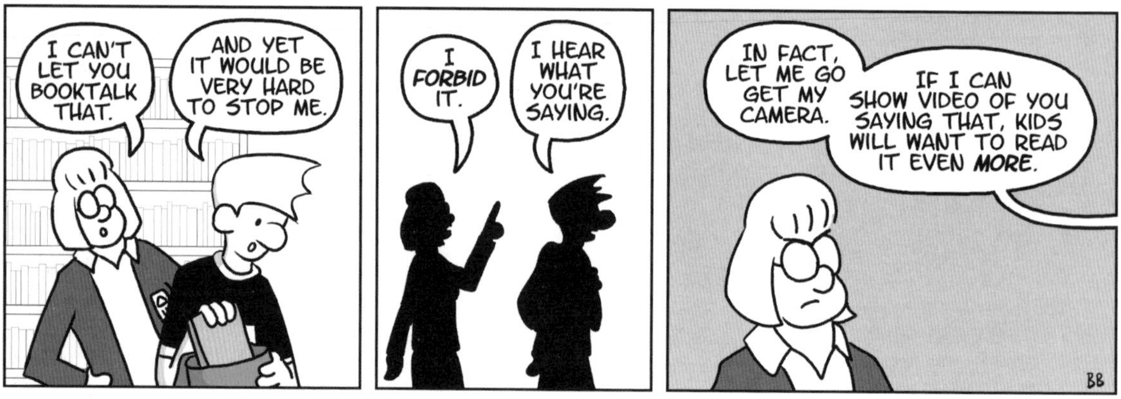
I CAN'T LET YOU BOOKTALK THAT.
AND YET IT WOULD BE VERY HARD TO STOP ME.
I *FORBID* IT.
I HEAR WHAT YOU'RE SAYING.
IN FACT, LET ME GO GET MY CAMERA.
IF I CAN SHOW VIDEO OF YOU SAYING THAT, KIDS WILL WANT TO READ IT EVEN *MORE*.
BB

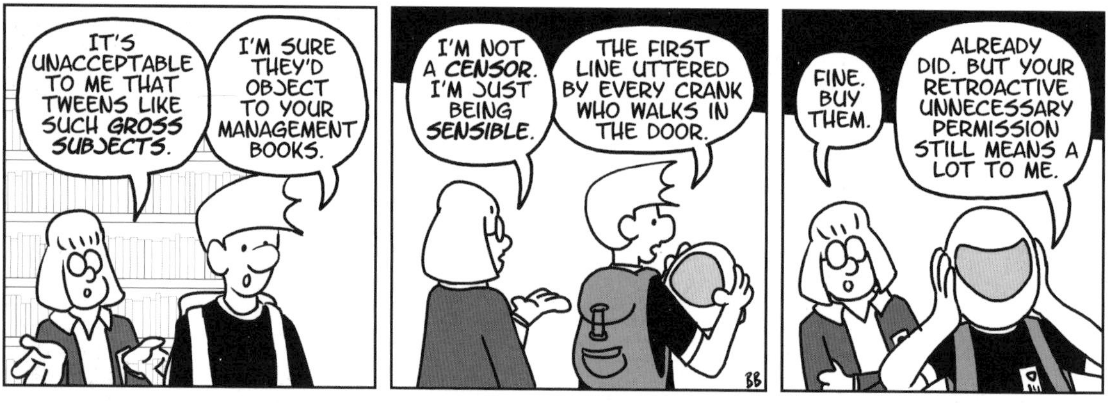
IT'S UNACCEPTABLE TO ME THAT TWEENS LIKE SUCH *GROSS SUBJECTS*.
I'M SURE THEY'D OBJECT TO YOUR MANAGEMENT BOOKS.
I'M NOT A *CENSOR*. I'M JUST BEING *SENSIBLE*.
THE FIRST LINE UTTERED BY EVERY CRANK WHO WALKS IN THE DOOR.
BB
FINE. BUY THEM.
ALREADY DID. BUT YOUR RETROACTIVE UNNECESSARY PERMISSION STILL MEANS A LOT TO ME.

Too Much Information

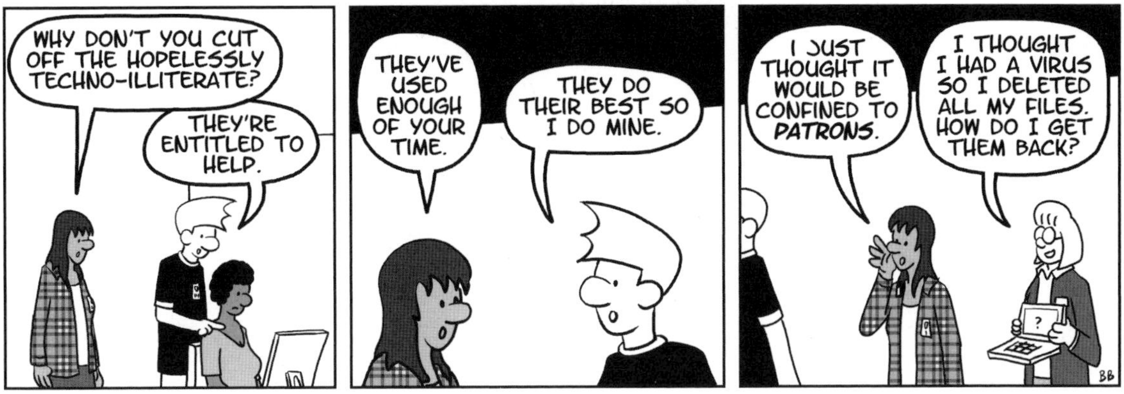
WHY DON'T YOU CUT OFF THE HOPELESSLY TECHNO-ILLITERATE?
THEY'RE ENTITLED TO HELP.
THEY'VE USED ENOUGH OF YOUR TIME.
THEY DO THEIR BEST SO I DO MINE.
I JUST THOUGHT IT WOULD BE CONFINED TO *PATRONS*.
I THOUGHT I HAD A VIRUS SO I DELETED ALL MY FILES. HOW DO I GET THEM BACK?
?
BB

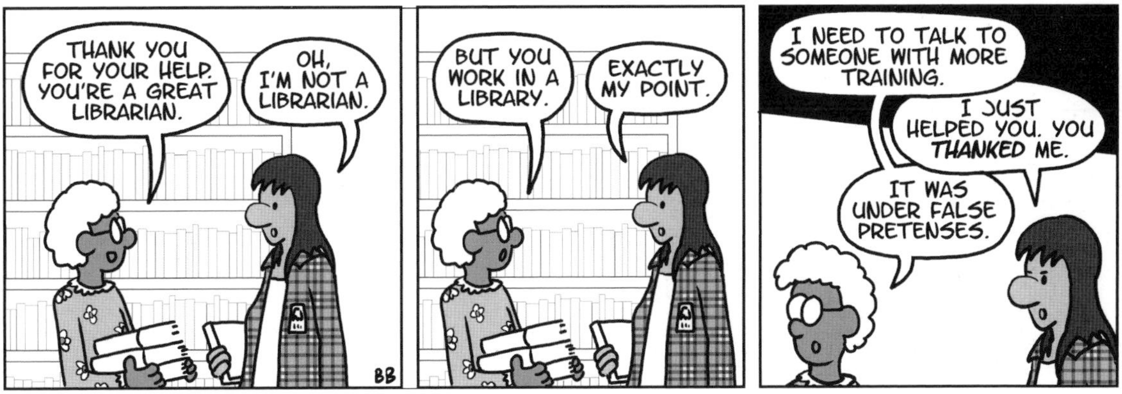
THANK YOU FOR YOUR HELP. YOU'RE A GREAT LIBRARIAN.
OH, I'M NOT A LIBRARIAN.
BB
BUT YOU WORK IN A LIBRARY.
EXACTLY MY POINT.
I NEED TO TALK TO SOMEONE WITH MORE TRAINING.
I JUST HELPED YOU. YOU *THANKED* ME.
IT WAS UNDER FALSE PRETENSES.

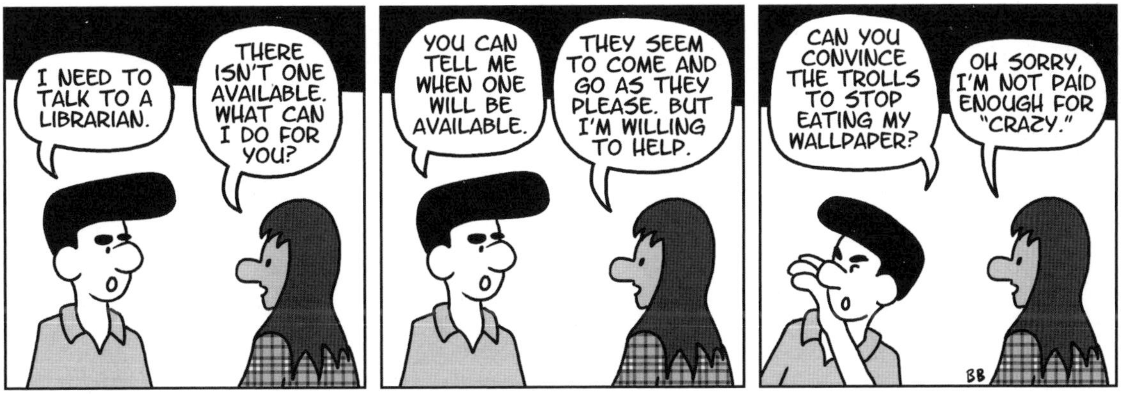
I NEED TO TALK TO A LIBRARIAN.
THERE ISN'T ONE AVAILABLE. WHAT CAN I DO FOR YOU?
YOU CAN TELL ME WHEN ONE WILL BE AVAILABLE.
THEY SEEM TO COME AND GO AS THEY PLEASE. BUT I'M WILLING TO HELP.
CAN YOU CONVINCE THE TROLLS TO STOP EATING MY WALLPAPER?
OH SORRY, I'M NOT PAID ENOUGH FOR "CRAZY."
BB

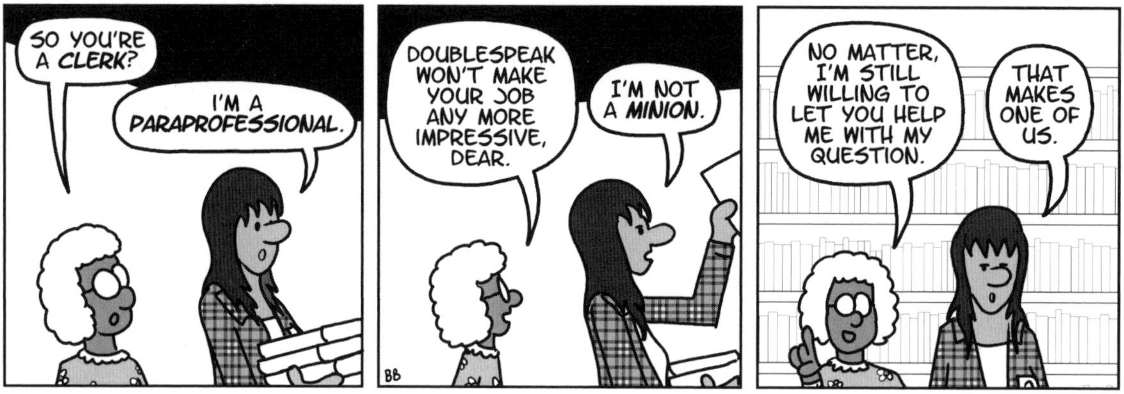
SO YOU'RE A CLERK?
I'M A PARAPROFESSIONAL.
DOUBLESPEAK WON'T MAKE YOUR JOB ANY MORE IMPRESSIVE, DEAR.
I'M NOT A MINION.
NO MATTER, I'M STILL WILLING TO LET YOU HELP ME WITH MY QUESTION.
THAT MAKES ONE OF US.
BB

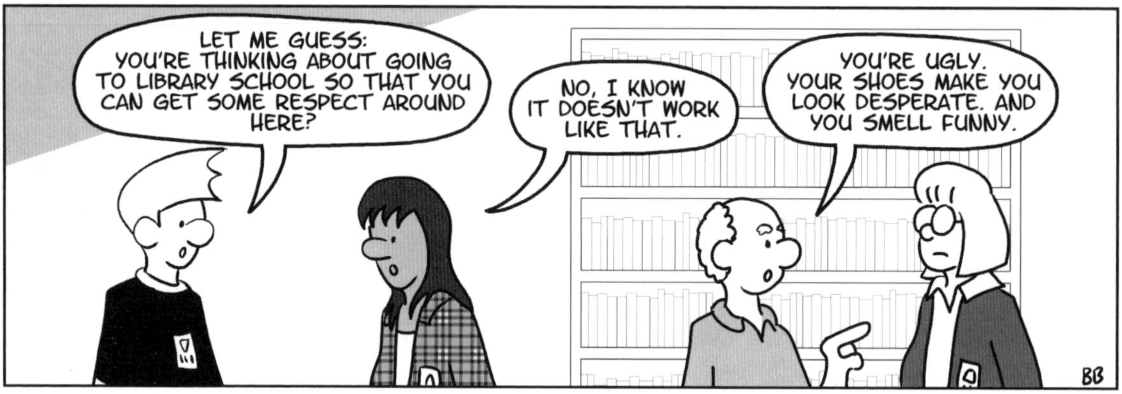
LET ME GUESS: YOU'RE THINKING ABOUT GOING TO LIBRARY SCHOOL SO THAT YOU CAN GET SOME RESPECT AROUND HERE?
NO, I KNOW IT DOESN'T WORK LIKE THAT.
YOU'RE UGLY. YOUR SHOES MAKE YOU LOOK DESPERATE. AND YOU SMELL FUNNY.
BB

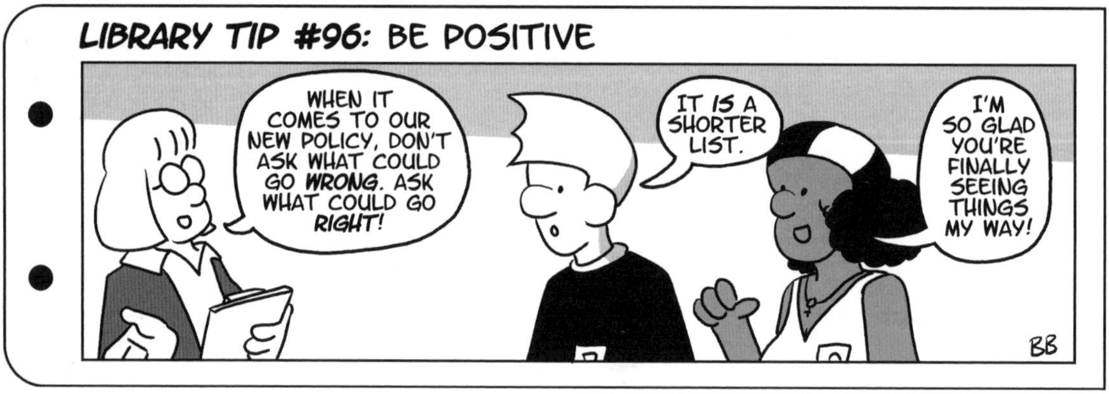
LIBRARY TIP #96: BE POSITIVE
WHEN IT COMES TO OUR NEW POLICY, DON'T ASK WHAT COULD GO WRONG. ASK WHAT COULD GO RIGHT!
IT IS A SHORTER LIST.
I'M SO GLAD YOU'RE FINALLY SEEING THINGS MY WAY!
BB

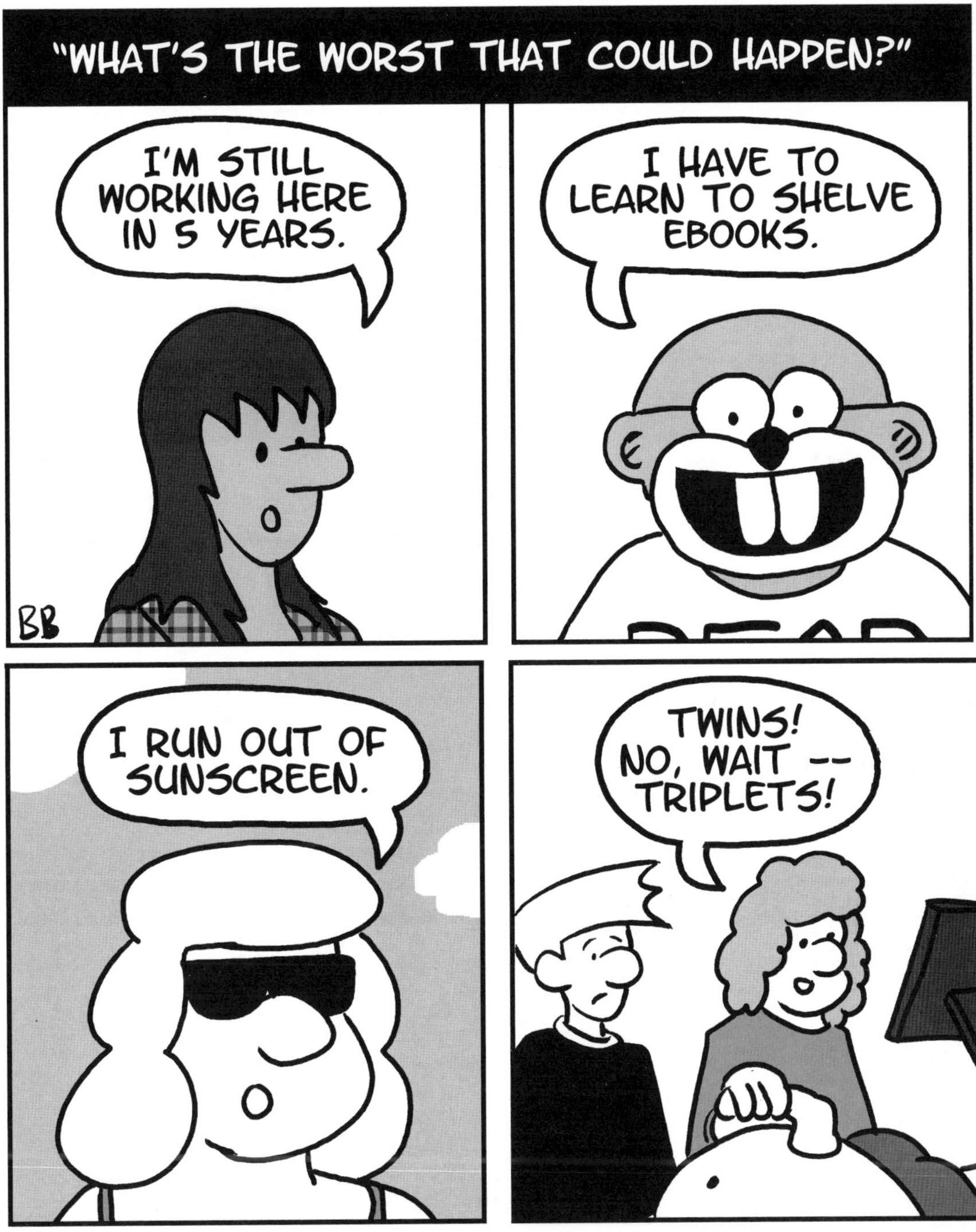
"WHAT'S THE WORST THAT COULD HAPPEN?"
I'M STILL WORKING HERE IN 5 YEARS.
BB
I HAVE TO LEARN TO SHELVE EBOOKS.
I RUN OUT OF SUNSCREEN.
TWINS! NO, WAIT -- TRIPLETS!

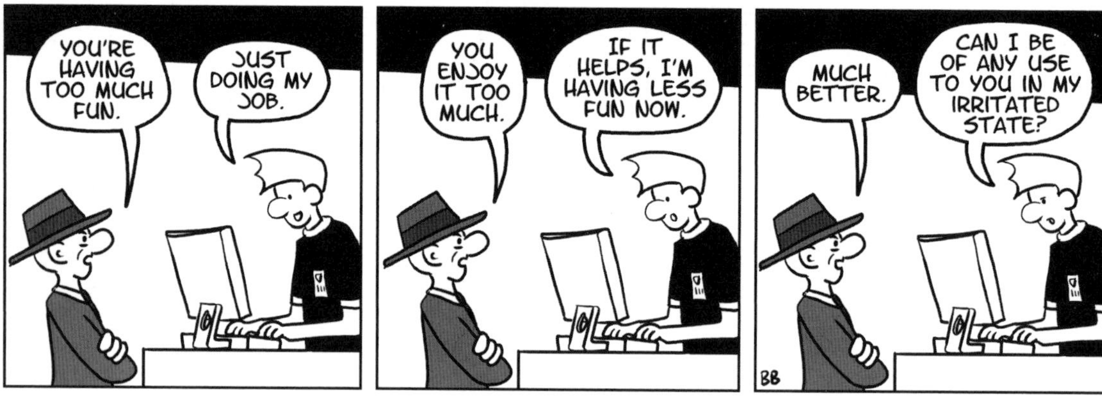
YOU'RE HAVING TOO MUCH FUN.
JUST DOING MY JOB.
YOU ENJOY IT TOO MUCH.
IF IT HELPS, I'M HAVING LESS FUN NOW.
MUCH BETTER.
CAN I BE OF ANY USE TO YOU IN MY IRRITATED STATE?
BB

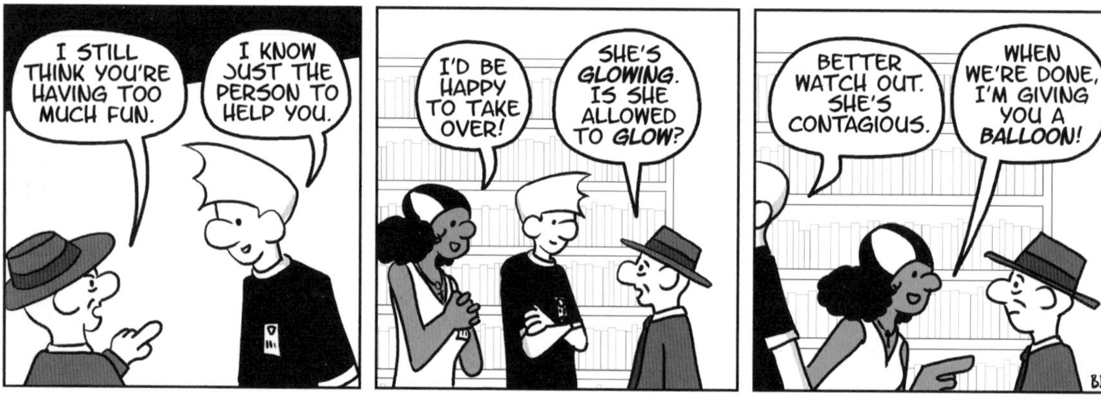
I STILL THINK YOU'RE HAVING TOO MUCH FUN.
I KNOW JUST THE PERSON TO HELP YOU.
I'D BE HAPPY TO TAKE OVER!
SHE'S *GLOWING*. IS SHE ALLOWED TO *GLOW*?
BETTER WATCH OUT. SHE'S CONTAGIOUS.
WHEN WE'RE DONE, I'M GIVING YOU A *BALLOON*!
BB

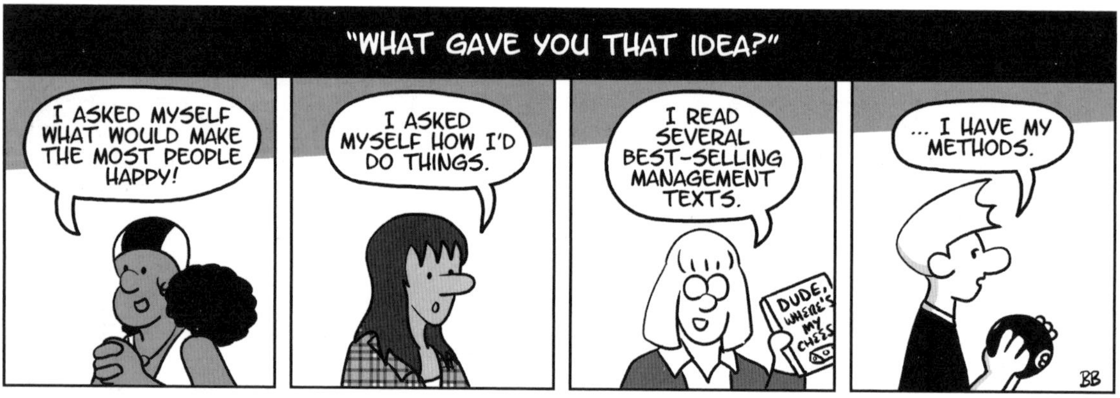
"WHAT GAVE YOU THAT IDEA?"
I ASKED MYSELF WHAT WOULD MAKE THE MOST PEOPLE HAPPY!
I ASKED MYSELF HOW I'D DO THINGS.
I READ SEVERAL BEST-SELLING MANAGEMENT TEXTS.
DUDE, WHERE'S MY
... I HAVE MY METHODS.
BB

Too Much Information

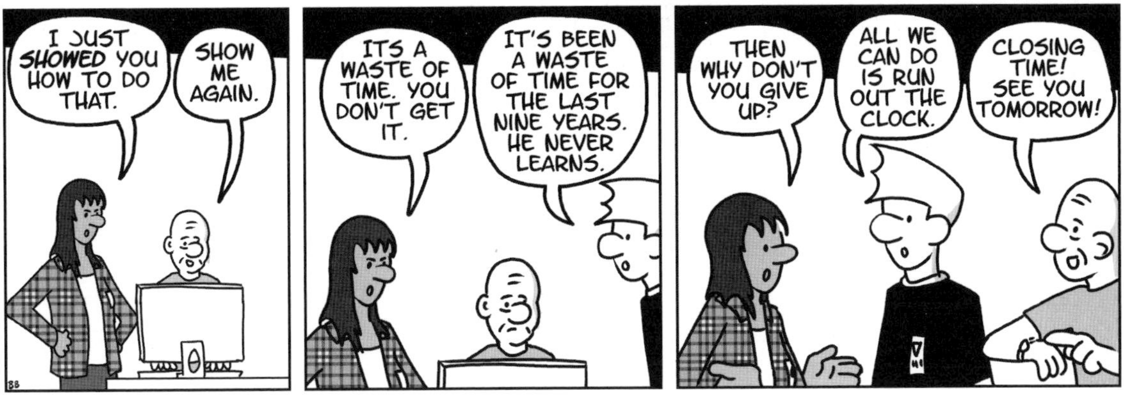
I JUST **SHOWED** YOU HOW TO DO THAT.
SHOW ME AGAIN.
ITS A WASTE OF TIME. YOU DON'T GET IT.
IT'S BEEN A WASTE OF TIME FOR THE LAST NINE YEARS. HE NEVER LEARNS.
THEN WHY DON'T YOU GIVE UP?
ALL WE CAN DO IS RUN OUT THE CLOCK.
CLOSING TIME! SEE YOU TOMORROW!
BB

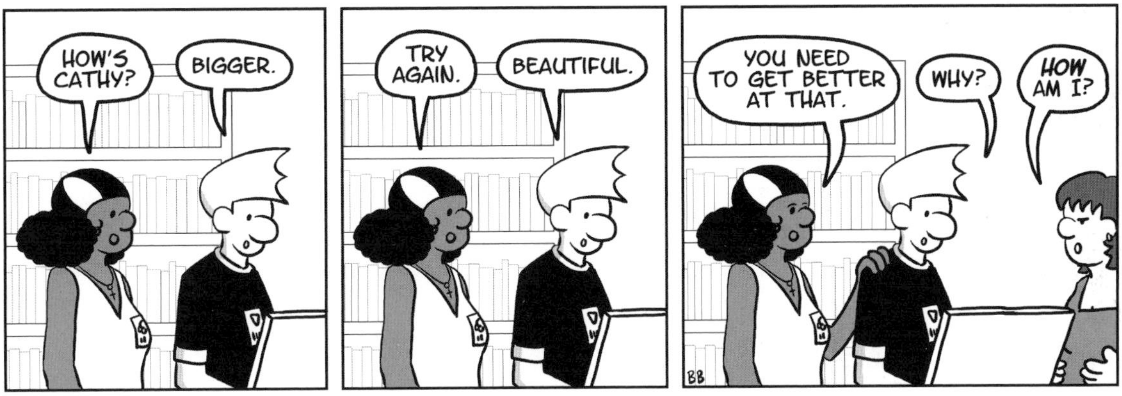
HOW'S CATHY?
BIGGER.
TRY AGAIN.
BEAUTIFUL.
YOU NEED TO GET BETTER AT THAT.
WHY?
HOW AM I?
BB

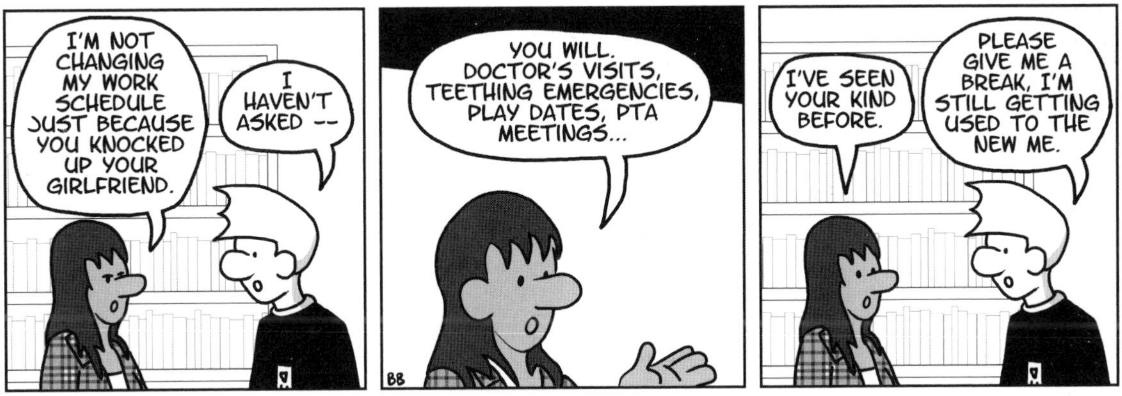
I'M NOT CHANGING MY WORK SCHEDULE JUST BECAUSE YOU KNOCKED UP YOUR GIRLFRIEND.
I HAVEN'T ASKED --
YOU WILL. DOCTOR'S VISITS, TEETHING EMERGENCIES, PLAY DATES, PTA MEETINGS...
BB
I'VE SEEN YOUR KIND BEFORE.
PLEASE GIVE ME A BREAK, I'M STILL GETTING USED TO THE NEW ME.

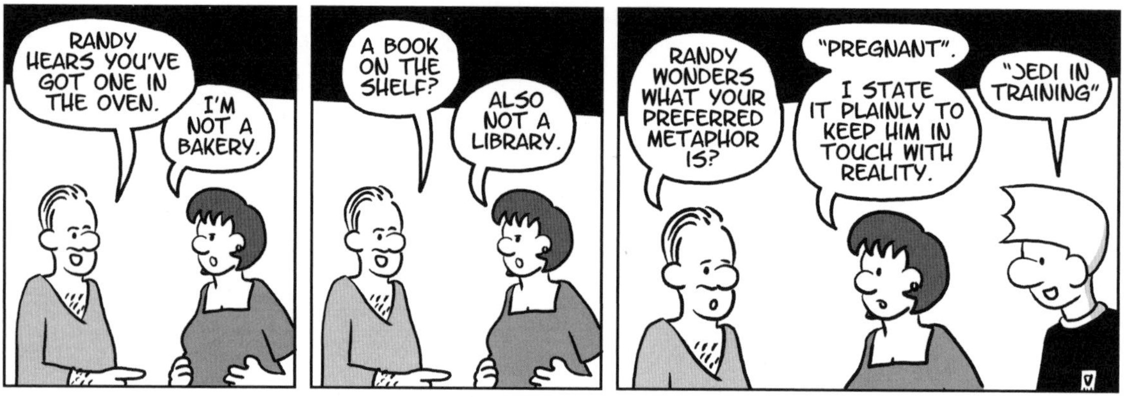
RANDY HEARS YOU'VE GOT ONE IN THE OVEN.
I'M NOT A BAKERY.
A BOOK ON THE SHELF?
ALSO NOT A LIBRARY.
RANDY WONDERS WHAT YOUR PREFERRED METAPHOR IS?
"PREGNANT".
I STATE IT PLAINLY TO KEEP HIM IN TOUCH WITH REALITY.
"JEDI IN TRAINING"

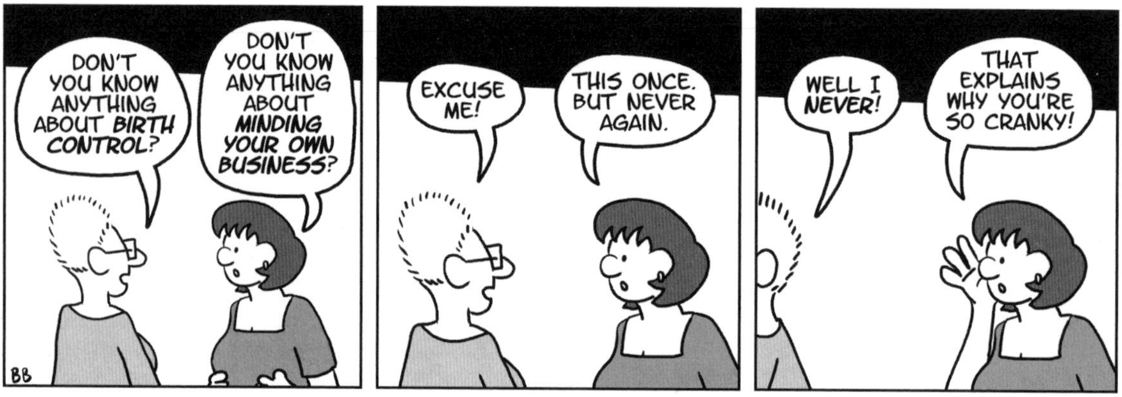
DON'T YOU KNOW ANYTHING ABOUT **BIRTH CONTROL**?
DON'T YOU KNOW ANYTHING ABOUT ***MINDING YOUR OWN BUSINESS***?
EXCUSE ME!
THIS ONCE. BUT NEVER AGAIN.
WELL I ***NEVER***!
THAT EXPLAINS WHY YOU'RE SO CRANKY!

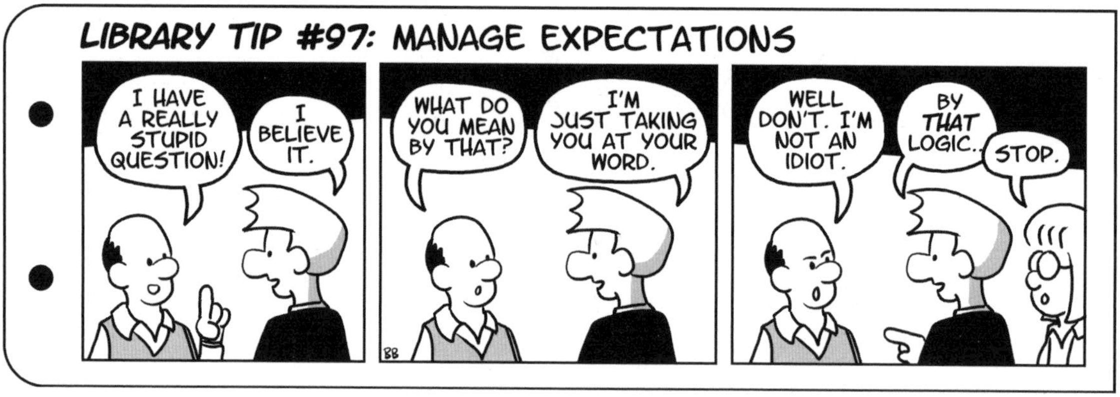
LIBRARY TIP #97: MANAGE EXPECTATIONS
I HAVE A REALLY STUPID QUESTION!
I BELIEVE IT.
WHAT DO YOU MEAN BY THAT?
I'M JUST TAKING YOU AT YOUR WORD.
WELL DON'T. I'M NOT AN IDIOT.
BY ***THAT*** LOGIC...
STOP.

Too Much Information

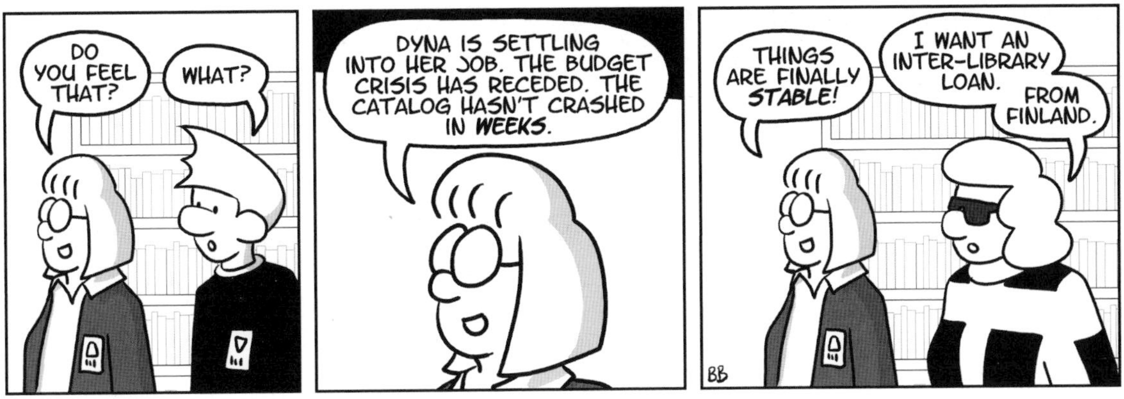
DO YOU FEEL THAT?
WHAT?
DYNA IS SETTLING INTO HER JOB. THE BUDGET CRISIS HAS RECEDED. THE CATALOG HASN'T CRASHED IN WEEKS.
THINGS ARE FINALLY STABLE!
I WANT AN INTER-LIBRARY LOAN.
FROM FINLAND.
BB

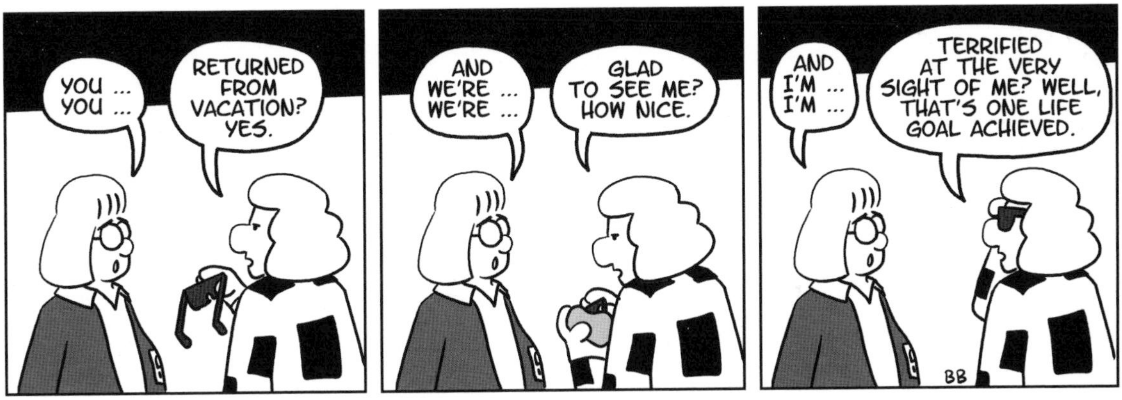
YOU ... YOU ...
RETURNED FROM VACATION? YES.
AND WE'RE ... WE'RE ...
GLAD TO SEE ME? HOW NICE.
AND I'M ... I'M ...
TERRIFIED AT THE VERY SIGHT OF ME? WELL, THAT'S ONE LIFE GOAL ACHIEVED.
BB

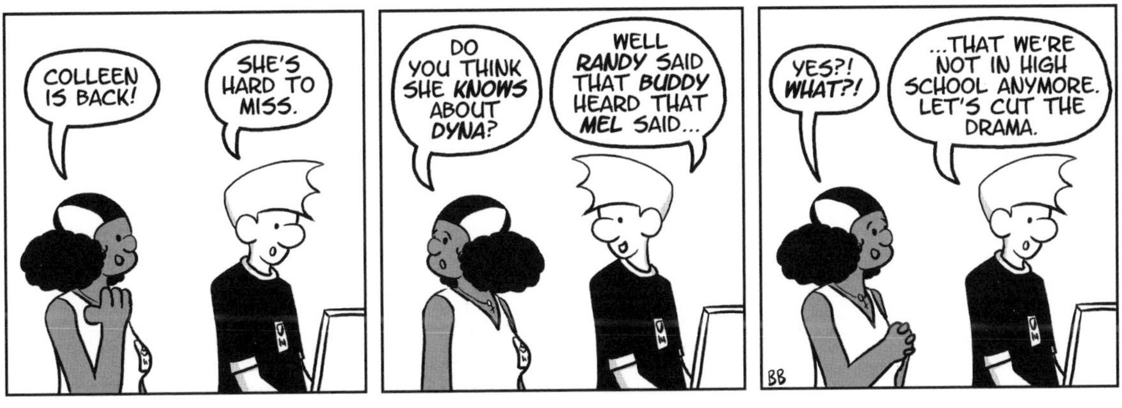
COLLEEN IS BACK!
SHE'S HARD TO MISS.
DO YOU THINK SHE KNOWS ABOUT DYNA?
WELL RANDY SAID THAT BUDDY HEARD THAT MEL SAID...
YES?! WHAT?!
...THAT WE'RE NOT IN HIGH SCHOOL ANYMORE. LET'S CUT THE DRAMA.
BB

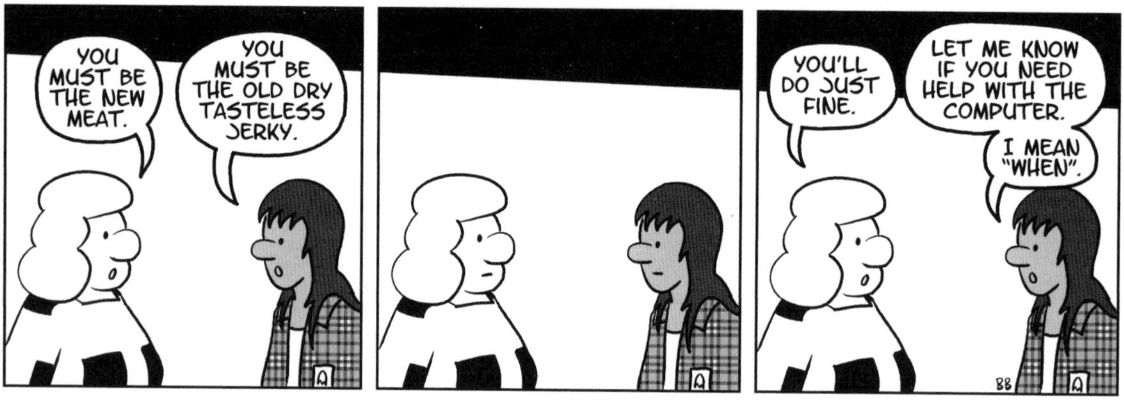
YOU MUST BE THE NEW MEAT.
YOU MUST BE THE OLD DRY TASTELESS JERKY.
YOU'LL DO JUST FINE.
LET ME KNOW IF YOU NEED HELP WITH THE COMPUTER.
I MEAN "WHEN".
BB

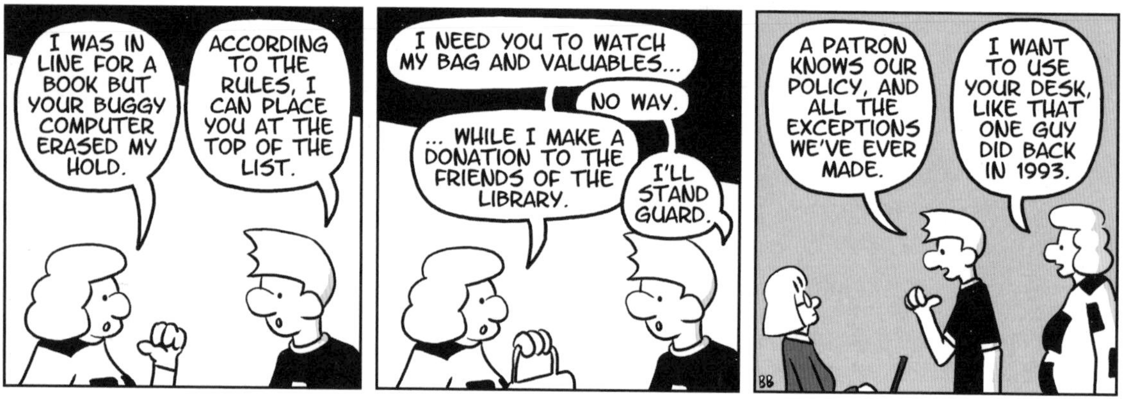
I WAS IN LINE FOR A BOOK BUT YOUR BUGGY COMPUTER ERASED MY HOLD.
ACCORDING TO THE RULES, I CAN PLACE YOU AT THE TOP OF THE LIST.
I NEED YOU TO WATCH MY BAG AND VALUABLES...
NO WAY.
... WHILE I MAKE A DONATION TO THE FRIENDS OF THE LIBRARY.
I'LL STAND GUARD.
A PATRON KNOWS OUR POLICY, AND ALL THE EXCEPTIONS WE'VE EVER MADE.
I WANT TO USE YOUR DESK, LIKE THAT ONE GUY DID BACK IN 1993.
BB

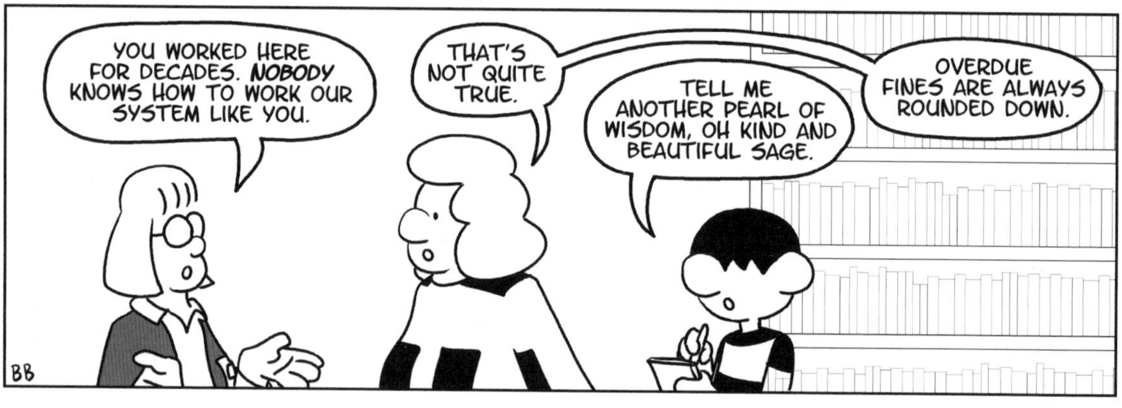
YOU WORKED HERE FOR DECADES. NOBODY KNOWS HOW TO WORK OUR SYSTEM LIKE YOU.
THAT'S NOT QUITE TRUE.
OVERDUE FINES ARE ALWAYS ROUNDED DOWN.
TELL ME ANOTHER PEARL OF WISDOM, OH KIND AND BEAUTIFUL SAGE.
BB

Too Much Information

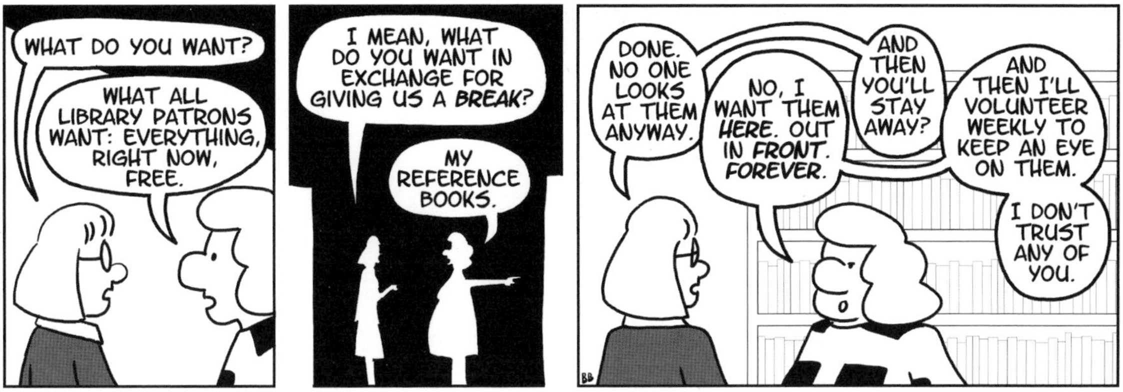

WHAT DO YOU WANT?
WHAT ALL LIBRARY PATRONS WANT: EVERYTHING, RIGHT NOW, FREE.
I MEAN, WHAT DO YOU WANT IN EXCHANGE FOR GIVING US A BREAK?
MY REFERENCE BOOKS.
DONE. NO ONE LOOKS AT THEM ANYWAY.
NO, I WANT THEM HERE. OUT IN FRONT. FOREVER.
AND THEN YOU'LL STAY AWAY?
AND THEN I'LL VOLUNTEER WEEKLY TO KEEP AN EYE ON THEM.
I DON'T TRUST ANY OF YOU.
BB

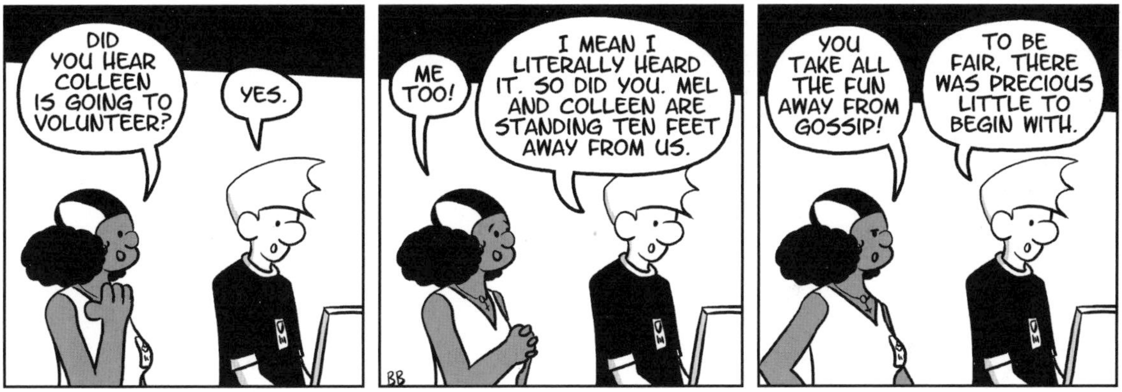

DID YOU HEAR COLLEEN IS GOING TO VOLUNTEER?
YES.
ME TOO!
I MEAN I LITERALLY HEARD IT. SO DID YOU. MEL AND COLLEEN ARE STANDING TEN FEET AWAY FROM US.
BB
YOU TAKE ALL THE FUN AWAY FROM GOSSIP!
TO BE FAIR, THERE WAS PRECIOUS LITTLE TO BEGIN WITH.

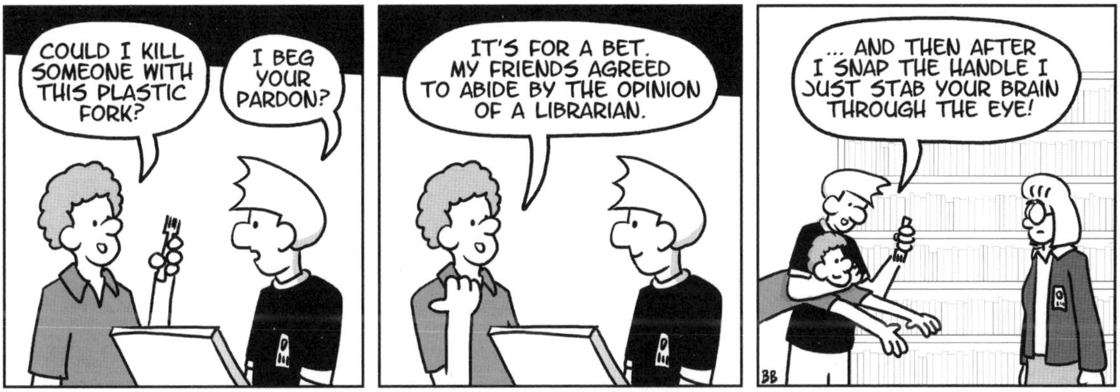

COULD I KILL SOMEONE WITH THIS PLASTIC FORK?
I BEG YOUR PARDON?
IT'S FOR A BET. MY FRIENDS AGREED TO ABIDE BY THE OPINION OF A LIBRARIAN.
... AND THEN AFTER I SNAP THE HANDLE I JUST STAB YOUR BRAIN THROUGH THE EYE!
BB

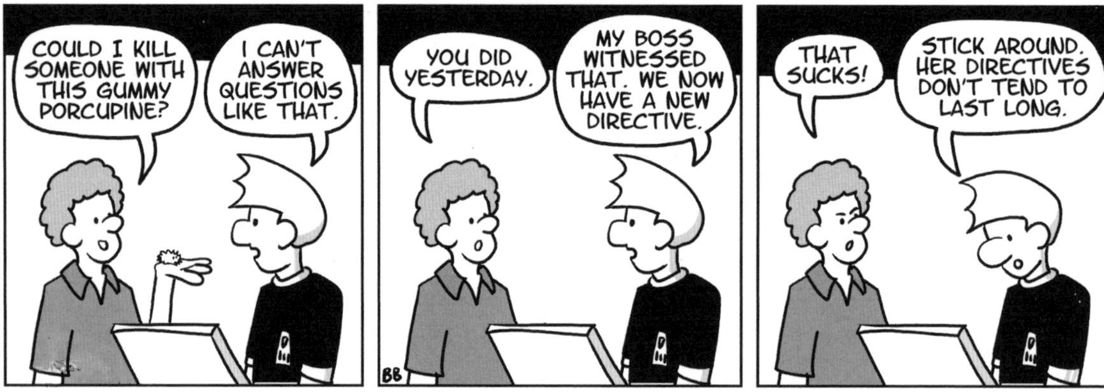
COULD I KILL SOMEONE WITH THIS GUMMY PORCUPINE?
I CAN'T ANSWER QUESTIONS LIKE THAT.
YOU DID YESTERDAY.
MY BOSS WITNESSED THAT. WE NOW HAVE A NEW DIRECTIVE.
THAT SUCKS!
STICK AROUND. HER DIRECTIVES DON'T TEND TO LAST LONG.
BB

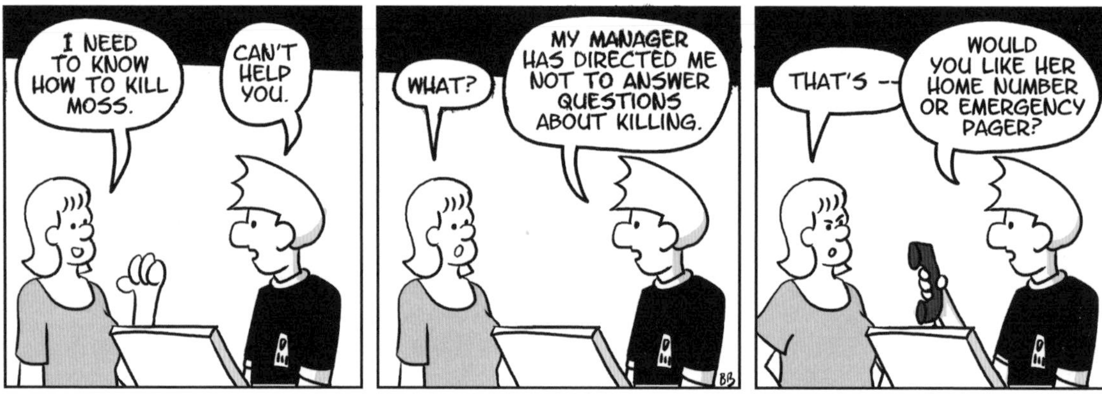
I NEED TO KNOW HOW TO KILL MOSS.
CAN'T HELP YOU.
WHAT?
MY MANAGER HAS DIRECTED ME NOT TO ANSWER QUESTIONS ABOUT KILLING.
THAT'S --
WOULD YOU LIKE HER HOME NUMBER OR EMERGENCY PAGER?
BB

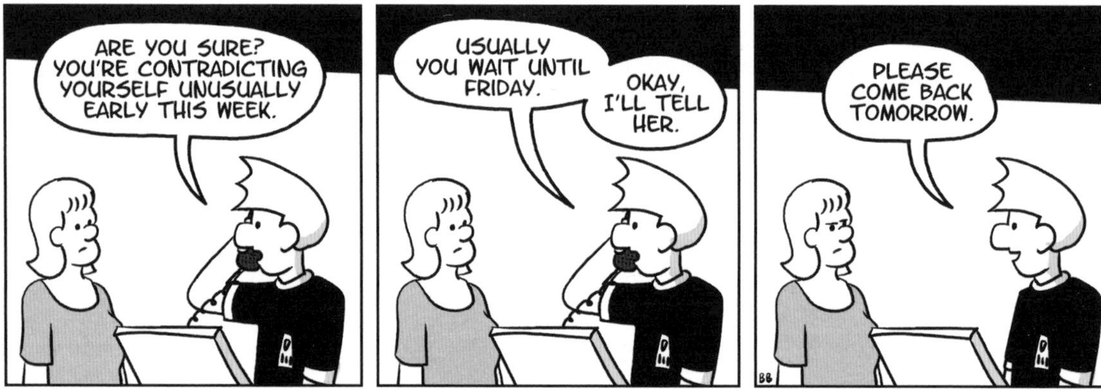
ARE YOU SURE? YOU'RE CONTRADICTING YOURSELF UNUSUALLY EARLY THIS WEEK.
USUALLY YOU WAIT UNTIL FRIDAY.
OKAY, I'LL TELL HER.
PLEASE COME BACK TOMORROW.
BB

Too Much Information

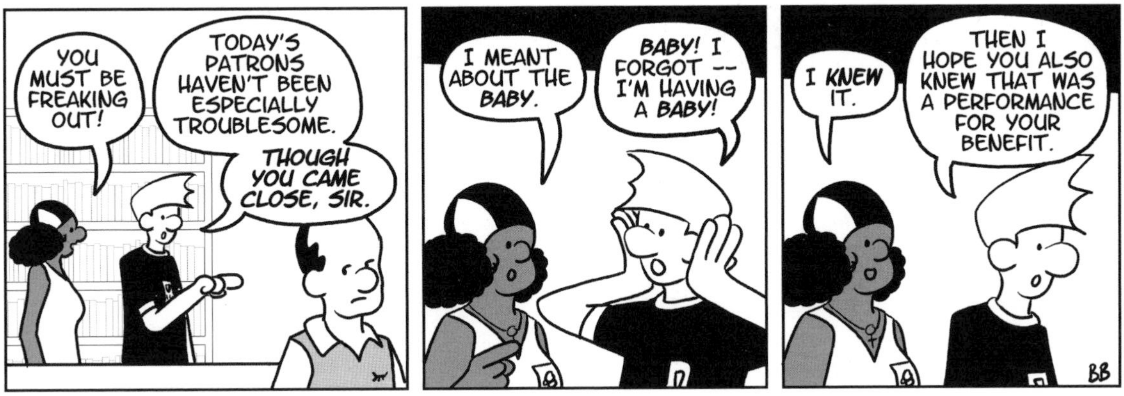
YOU MUST BE FREAKING OUT!
TODAY'S PATRONS HAVEN'T BEEN ESPECIALLY TROUBLESOME.
THOUGH YOU CAME CLOSE, SIR.
I MEANT ABOUT THE BABY.
BABY! I FORGOT -- I'M HAVING A BABY!
I KNEW IT.
THEN I HOPE YOU ALSO KNEW THAT WAS A PERFORMANCE FOR YOUR BENEFIT.
BB

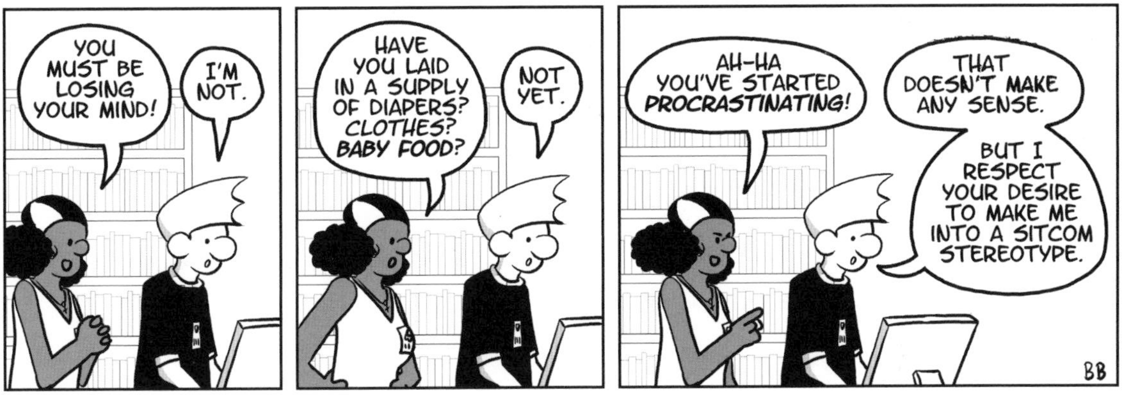
YOU MUST BE LOSING YOUR MIND!
I'M NOT.
HAVE YOU LAID IN A SUPPLY OF DIAPERS? CLOTHES? BABY FOOD?
NOT YET.
AH-HA YOU'VE STARTED PROCRASTINATING!
THAT DOESN'T MAKE ANY SENSE.
BUT I RESPECT YOUR DESIRE TO MAKE ME INTO A SITCOM STEREOTYPE.
BB

Warning to ardent grammarians: the title of the following strip contains sophisticated wordplay.

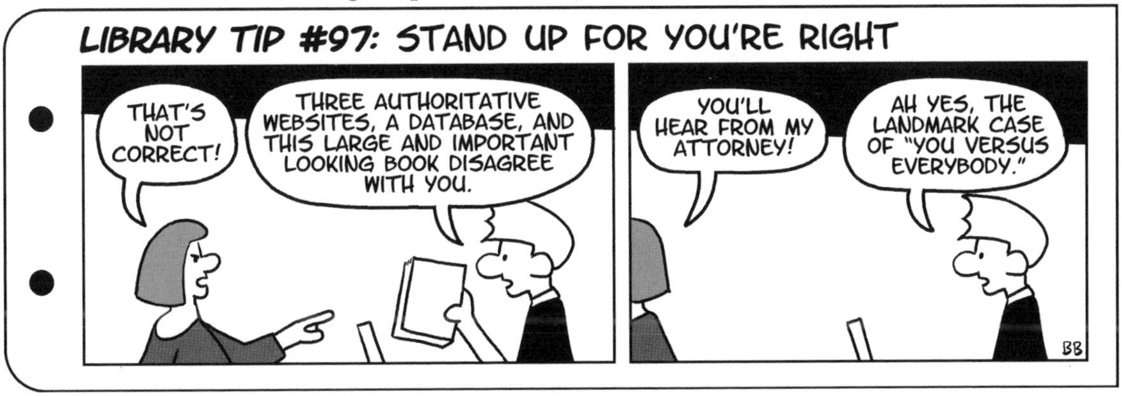
LIBRARY TIP #97: STAND UP FOR YOU'RE RIGHT
THAT'S NOT CORRECT!
THREE AUTHORITATIVE WEBSITES, A DATABASE, AND THIS LARGE AND IMPORTANT LOOKING BOOK DISAGREE WITH YOU.
YOU'LL HEAR FROM MY ATTORNEY!
AH YES, THE LANDMARK CASE OF "YOU VERSUS EVERYBODY."
BB

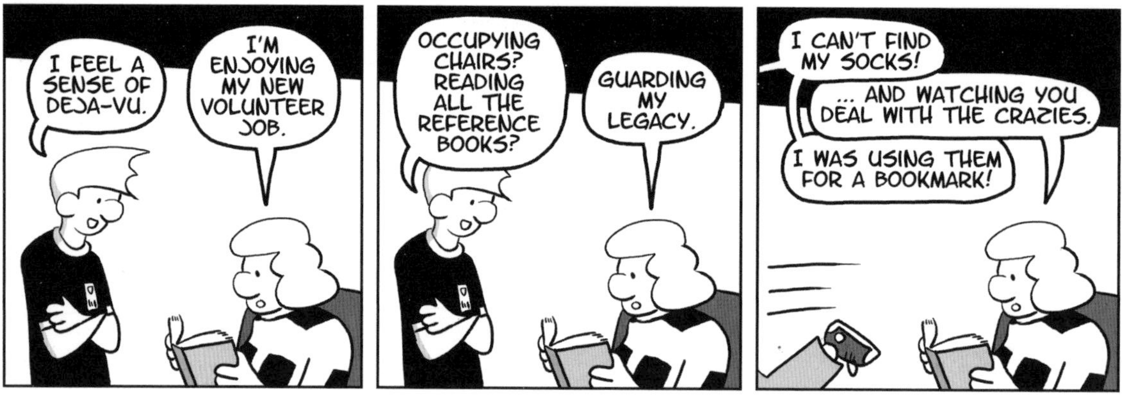
I FEEL A SENSE OF DEJA-VU.
I'M ENJOYING MY NEW VOLUNTEER JOB.
OCCUPYING CHAIRS? READING ALL THE REFERENCE BOOKS?
GUARDING MY LEGACY.
I CAN'T FIND MY SOCKS!
... AND WATCHING YOU DEAL WITH THE CRAZIES.
I WAS USING THEM FOR A BOOKMARK!

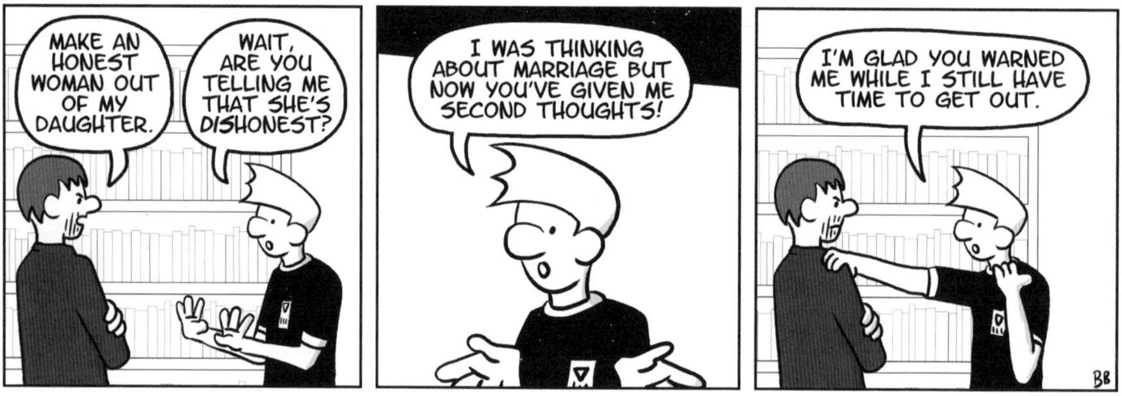
MAKE AN HONEST WOMAN OUT OF MY DAUGHTER.
WAIT, ARE YOU TELLING ME THAT SHE'S DISHONEST?
I WAS THINKING ABOUT MARRIAGE BUT NOW YOU'VE GIVEN ME SECOND THOUGHTS!
I'M GLAD YOU WARNED ME WHILE I STILL HAVE TIME TO GET OUT.
BB

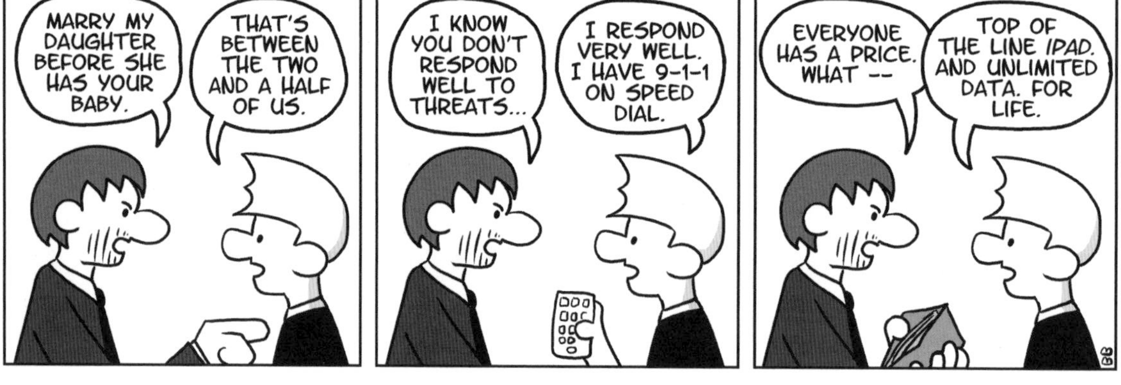
MARRY MY DAUGHTER BEFORE SHE HAS YOUR BABY.
THAT'S BETWEEN THE TWO AND A HALF OF US.
I KNOW YOU DON'T RESPOND WELL TO THREATS...
I RESPOND VERY WELL. I HAVE 9-1-1 ON SPEED DIAL.
EVERYONE HAS A PRICE. WHAT --
TOP OF THE LINE IPAD. AND UNLIMITED DATA. FOR LIFE.
BB

Too Much Information

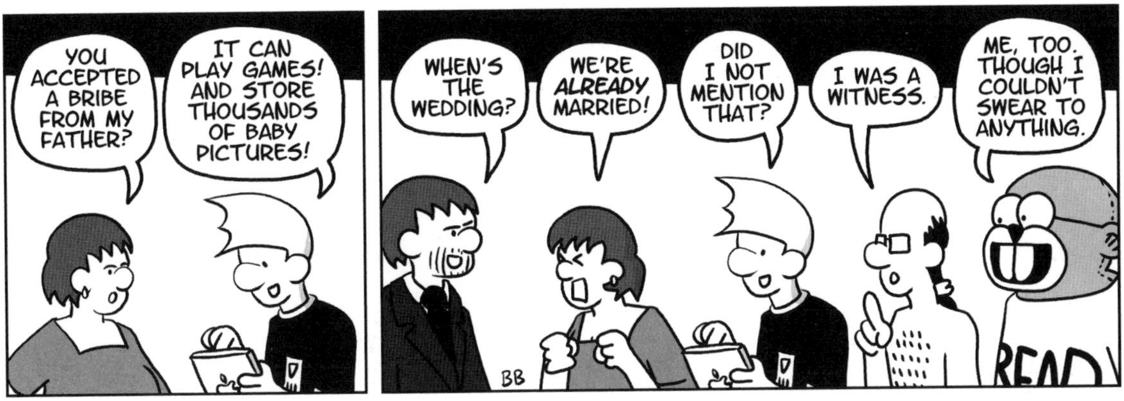

YOU ACCEPTED A BRIBE FROM MY FATHER?
IT CAN PLAY GAMES! AND STORE THOUSANDS OF BABY PICTURES!
WHEN'S THE WEDDING?
WE'RE **ALREADY** MARRIED!
DID I NOT MENTION THAT?
I WAS A WITNESS.
ME, TOO. THOUGH I COULDN'T SWEAR TO ANYTHING.
BB

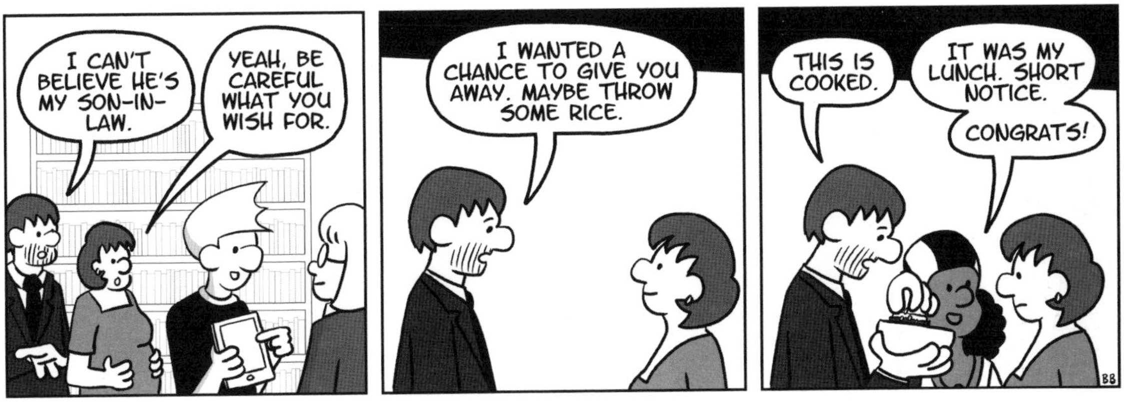

I CAN'T BELIEVE HE'S MY SON-IN-LAW.
YEAH, BE CAREFUL WHAT YOU WISH FOR.
I WANTED A CHANCE TO GIVE YOU AWAY. MAYBE THROW SOME RICE.
THIS IS COOKED.
IT WAS MY LUNCH. SHORT NOTICE.
CONGRATS!
BB

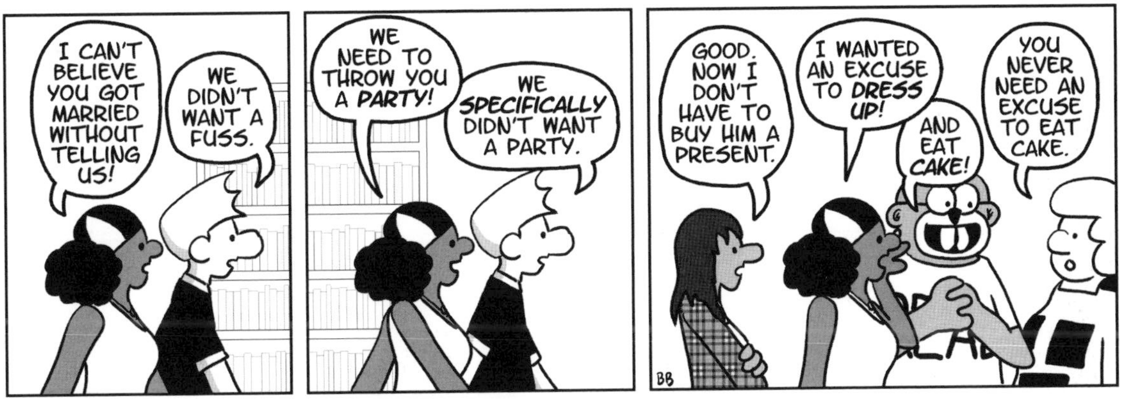

I CAN'T BELIEVE YOU GOT MARRIED WITHOUT TELLING US!
WE DIDN'T WANT A FUSS.
WE NEED TO THROW YOU A **PARTY**!
WE **SPECIFICALLY** DIDN'T WANT A PARTY.
GOOD. NOW I DON'T HAVE TO BUY HIM A PRESENT.
I WANTED AN EXCUSE TO **DRESS UP**!
AND EAT **CAKE**!
YOU NEVER NEED AN EXCUSE TO EAT CAKE.
BB

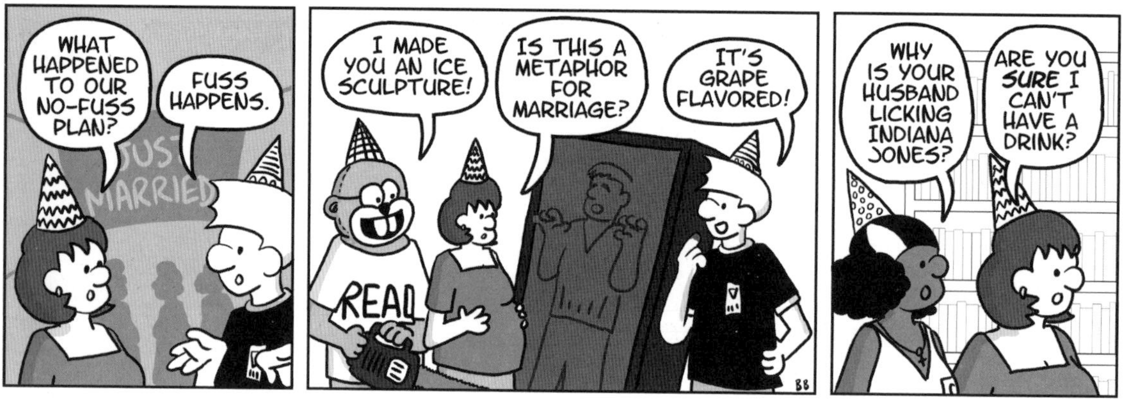
WHAT HAPPENED TO OUR NO-FUSS PLAN?
FUSS HAPPENS.
JUST MARRIED
I MADE YOU AN ICE SCULPTURE!
IS THIS A METAPHOR FOR MARRIAGE?
IT'S GRAPE FLAVORED!
REAL
BB
WHY IS YOUR HUSBAND LICKING INDIANA JONES?
ARE YOU *SURE* I CAN'T HAVE A DRINK?

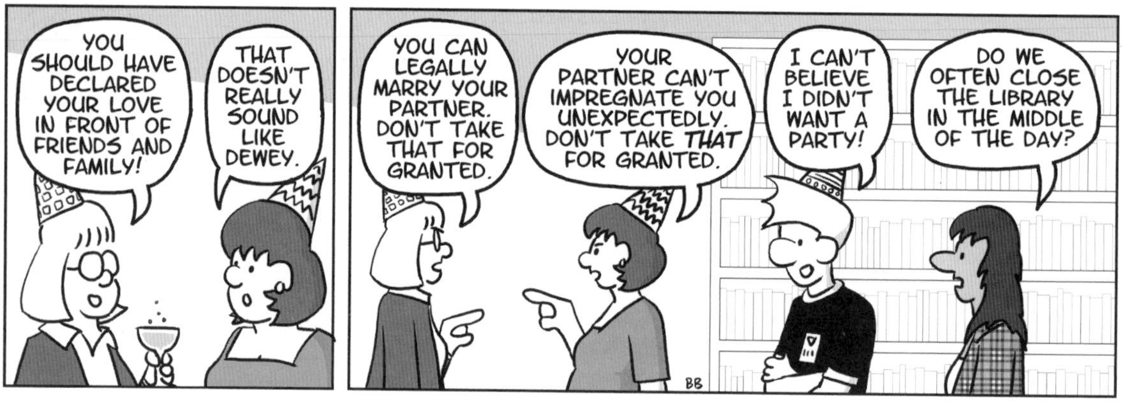
YOU SHOULD HAVE DECLARED YOUR LOVE IN FRONT OF FRIENDS AND FAMILY!
THAT DOESN'T REALLY SOUND LIKE DEWEY.
YOU CAN LEGALLY MARRY YOUR PARTNER. DON'T TAKE THAT FOR GRANTED.
YOUR PARTNER CAN'T IMPREGNATE YOU UNEXPECTEDLY. DON'T TAKE *THAT* FOR GRANTED.
I CAN'T BELIEVE I DIDN'T WANT A PARTY!
DO WE OFTEN CLOSE THE LIBRARY IN THE MIDDLE OF THE DAY?
BB

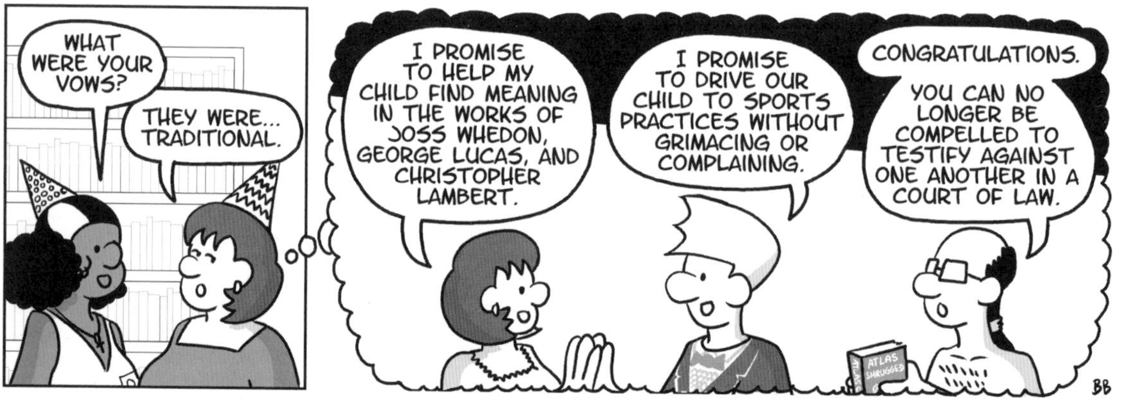
WHAT WERE YOUR VOWS?
THEY WERE... TRADITIONAL.
I PROMISE TO HELP MY CHILD FIND MEANING IN THE WORKS OF JOSS WHEDON, GEORGE LUCAS, AND CHRISTOPHER LAMBERT.
I PROMISE TO DRIVE OUR CHILD TO SPORTS PRACTICES WITHOUT GRIMACING OR COMPLAINING.
CONGRATULATIONS.
YOU CAN NO LONGER BE COMPELLED TO TESTIFY AGAINST ONE ANOTHER IN A COURT OF LAW.
ATLAS SHRUGGED
BB

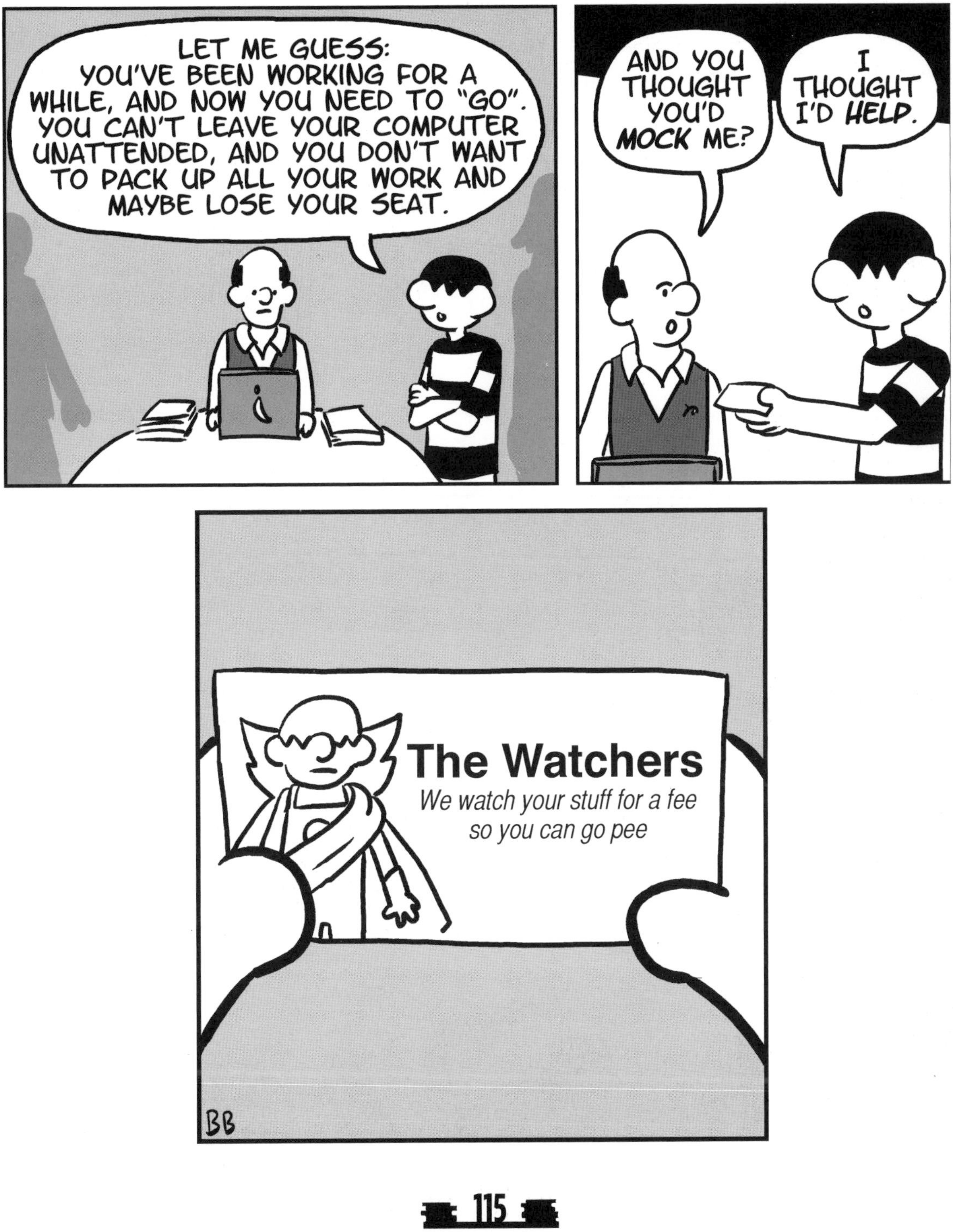
LET ME GUESS: YOU'VE BEEN WORKING FOR A WHILE, AND NOW YOU NEED TO "GO". YOU CAN'T LEAVE YOUR COMPUTER UNATTENDED, AND YOU DON'T WANT TO PACK UP ALL YOUR WORK AND MAYBE LOSE YOUR SEAT.
AND YOU THOUGHT YOU'D MOCK ME?
I THOUGHT I'D HELP.
The Watchers
We watch your stuff for a fee so you can go pee
BB

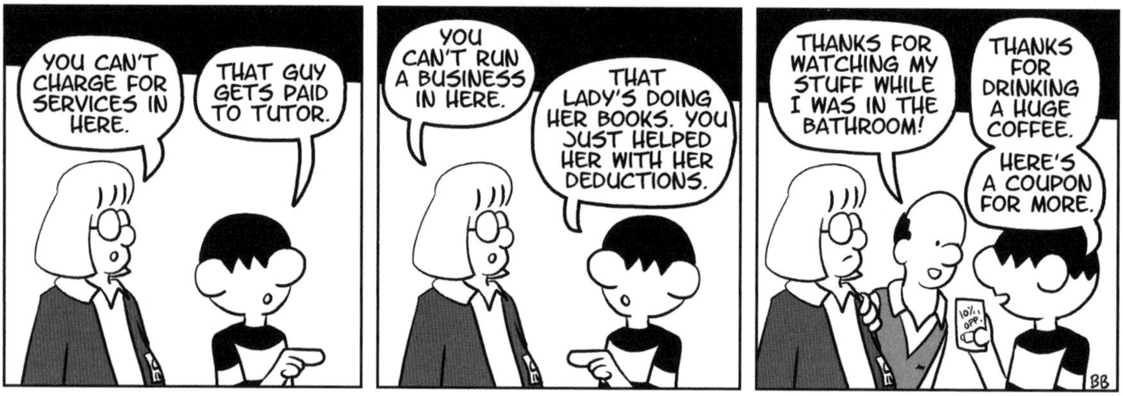
YOU CAN'T CHARGE FOR SERVICES IN HERE.
THAT GUY GETS PAID TO TUTOR.
YOU CAN'T RUN A BUSINESS IN HERE.
THAT LADY'S DOING HER BOOKS. YOU JUST HELPED HER WITH HER DEDUCTIONS.
THANKS FOR WATCHING MY STUFF WHILE I WAS IN THE BATHROOM!
THANKS FOR DRINKING A HUGE COFFEE.
HERE'S A COUPON FOR MORE.
10% OFF
BB

The Internet immediately agreed that such a service was needed in libraries and also cafés.

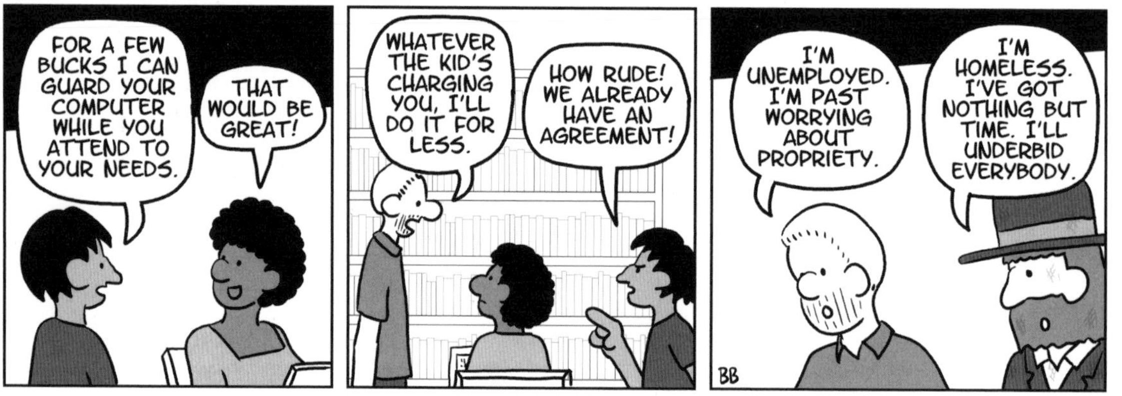
FOR A FEW BUCKS I CAN GUARD YOUR COMPUTER WHILE YOU ATTEND TO YOUR NEEDS.
THAT WOULD BE GREAT!
WHATEVER THE KID'S CHARGING YOU, I'LL DO IT FOR LESS.
HOW RUDE! WE ALREADY HAVE AN AGREEMENT!
I'M UNEMPLOYED. I'M PAST WORRYING ABOUT PROPRIETY.
I'M HOMELESS. I'VE GOT NOTHING BUT TIME. I'LL UNDERBID EVERYBODY.
BB

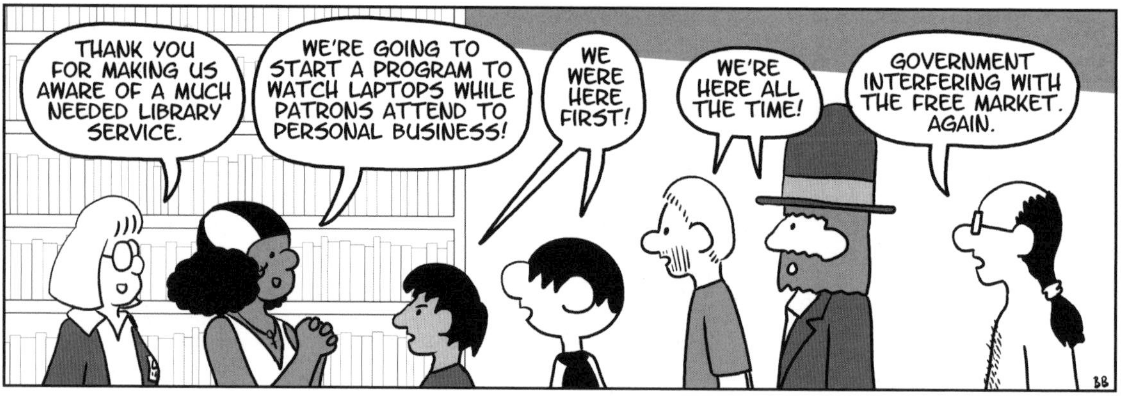
THANK YOU FOR MAKING US AWARE OF A MUCH NEEDED LIBRARY SERVICE.
WE'RE GOING TO START A PROGRAM TO WATCH LAPTOPS WHILE PATRONS ATTEND TO PERSONAL BUSINESS!
WE WERE HERE FIRST!
WE'RE HERE ALL THE TIME!
GOVERNMENT INTERFERING WITH THE FREE MARKET. AGAIN.
BB

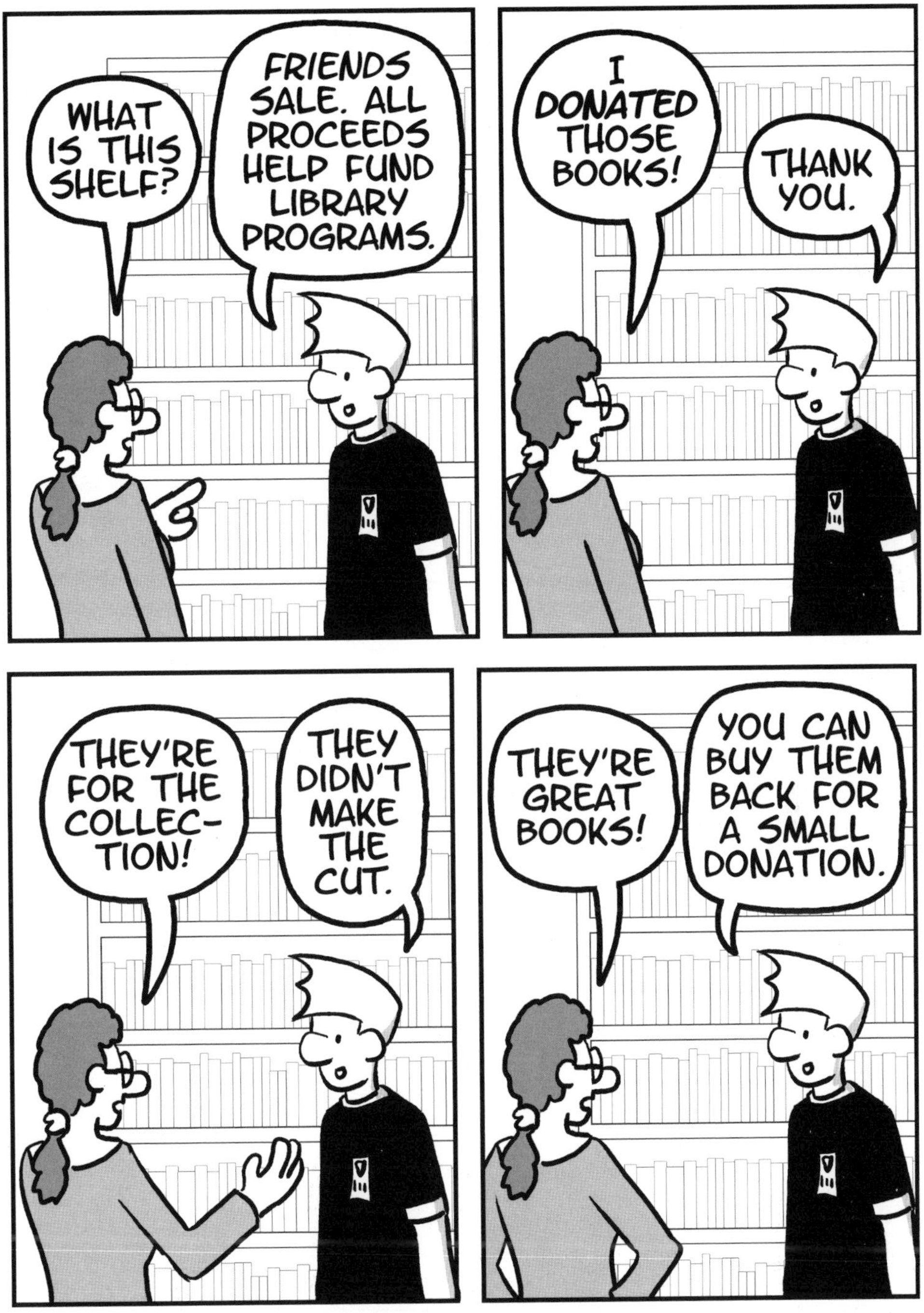
WHAT IS THIS SHELF?
FRIENDS SALE. ALL PROCEEDS HELP FUND LIBRARY PROGRAMS.
I DONATED THOSE BOOKS!
THANK YOU.
THEY'RE FOR THE COLLEC-TION!
THEY DIDN'T MAKE THE CUT.
THEY'RE GREAT BOOKS!
YOU CAN BUY THEM BACK FOR A SMALL DONATION.

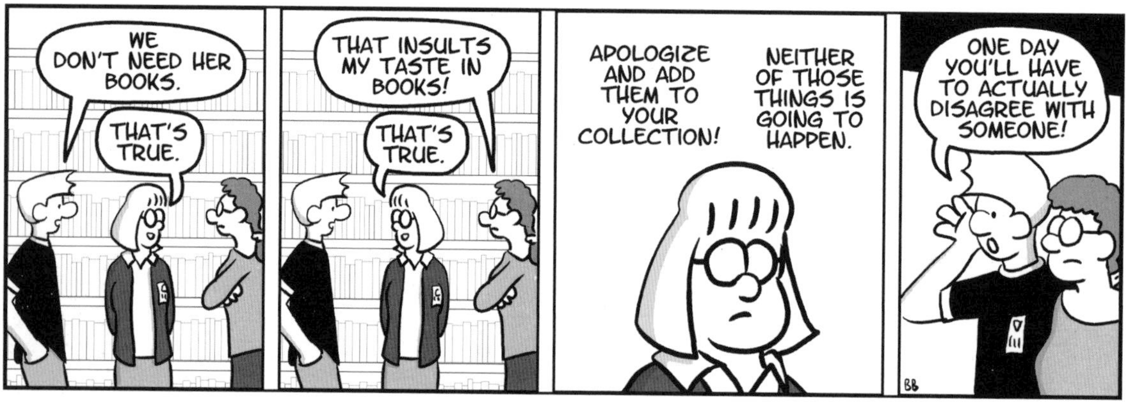
WE DON'T NEED HER BOOKS.
THAT'S TRUE.
THAT INSULTS MY TASTE IN BOOKS!
THAT'S TRUE.
APOLOGIZE AND ADD THEM TO YOUR COLLECTION!
NEITHER OF THOSE THINGS IS GOING TO HAPPEN.
ONE DAY YOU'LL HAVE TO ACTUALLY DISAGREE WITH SOMEONE!

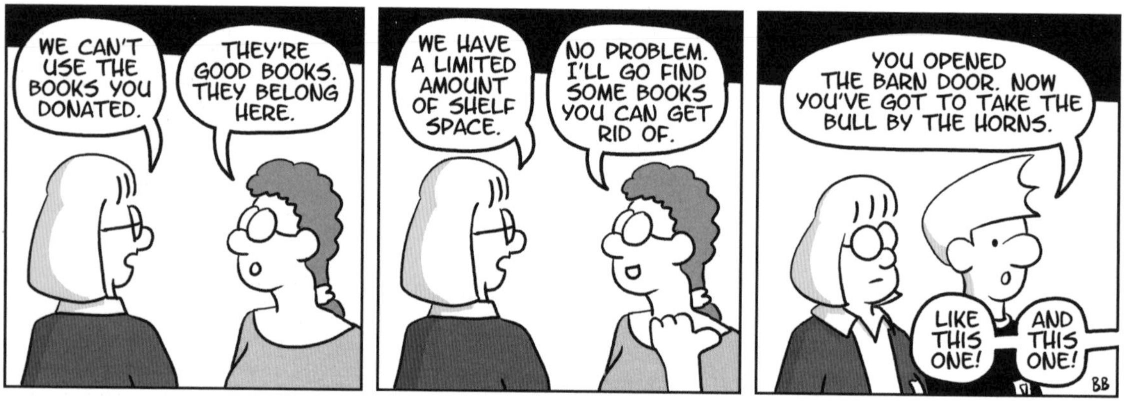
WE CAN'T USE THE BOOKS YOU DONATED.
THEY'RE GOOD BOOKS. THEY BELONG HERE.
WE HAVE A LIMITED AMOUNT OF SHELF SPACE.
NO PROBLEM. I'LL GO FIND SOME BOOKS YOU CAN GET RID OF.
YOU OPENED THE BARN DOOR. NOW YOU'VE GOT TO TAKE THE BULL BY THE HORNS.
LIKE THIS ONE!
AND THIS ONE!

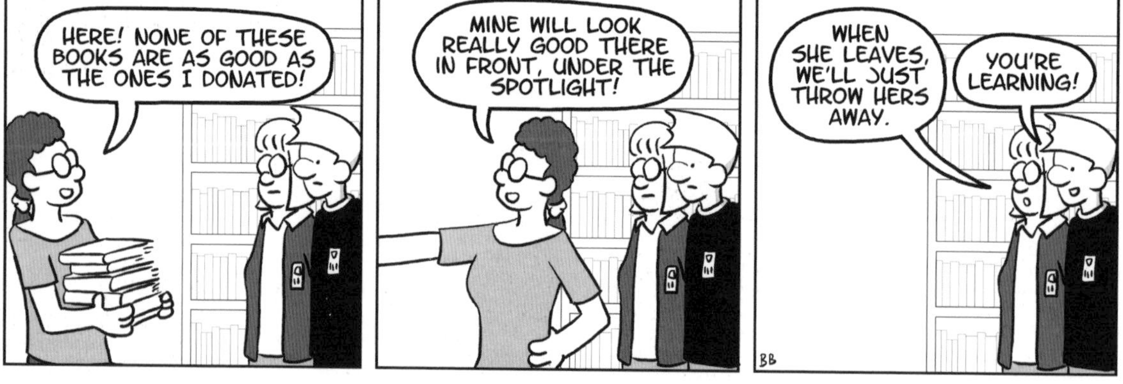
HERE! NONE OF THESE BOOKS ARE AS GOOD AS THE ONES I DONATED!
MINE WILL LOOK REALLY GOOD THERE IN FRONT, UNDER THE SPOTLIGHT!
WHEN SHE LEAVES, WE'LL JUST THROW HERS AWAY.
YOU'RE LEARNING!

Too Much Information

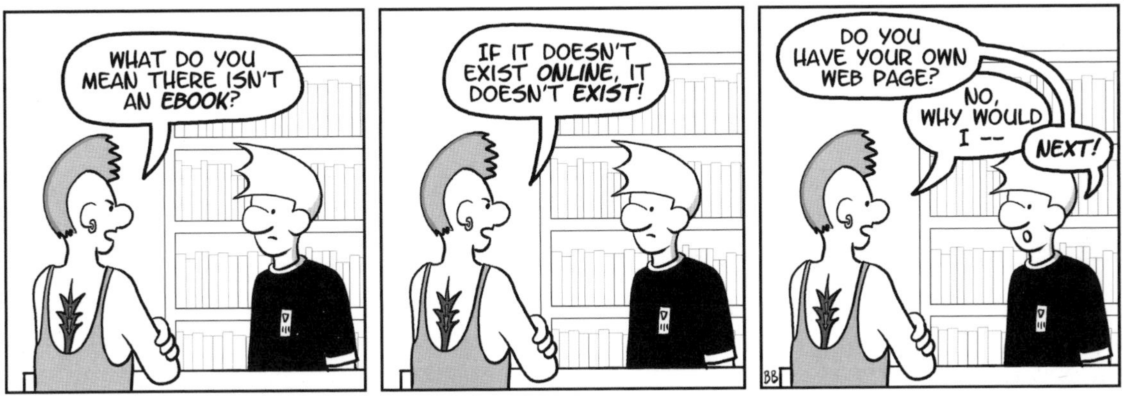
WHAT DO YOU MEAN THERE ISN'T AN EBOOK?
IF IT DOESN'T EXIST ONLINE, IT DOESN'T EXIST!
DO YOU HAVE YOUR OWN WEB PAGE?
NO, WHY WOULD I --
NEXT!
BB

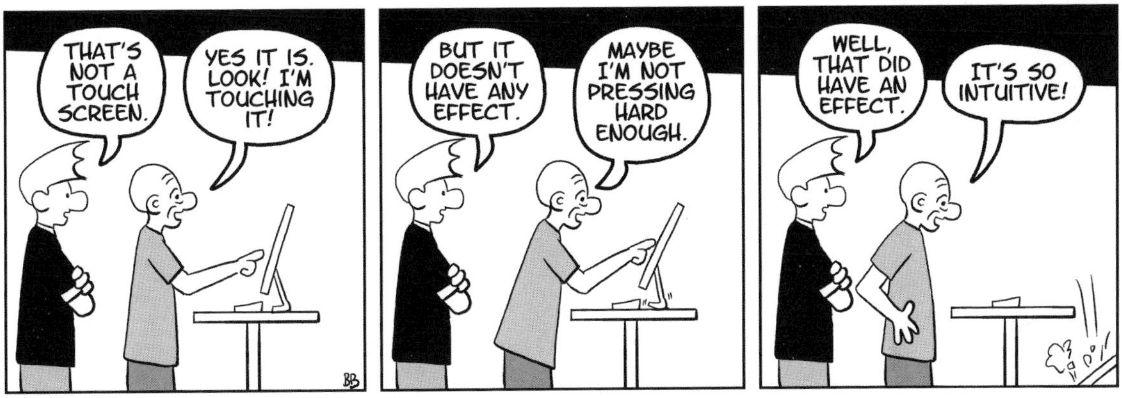
THAT'S NOT A TOUCH SCREEN.
YES IT IS. LOOK! I'M TOUCHING IT!
BB
BUT IT DOESN'T HAVE ANY EFFECT.
MAYBE I'M NOT PRESSING HARD ENOUGH.
WELL, THAT DID HAVE AN EFFECT.
IT'S SO INTUITIVE!

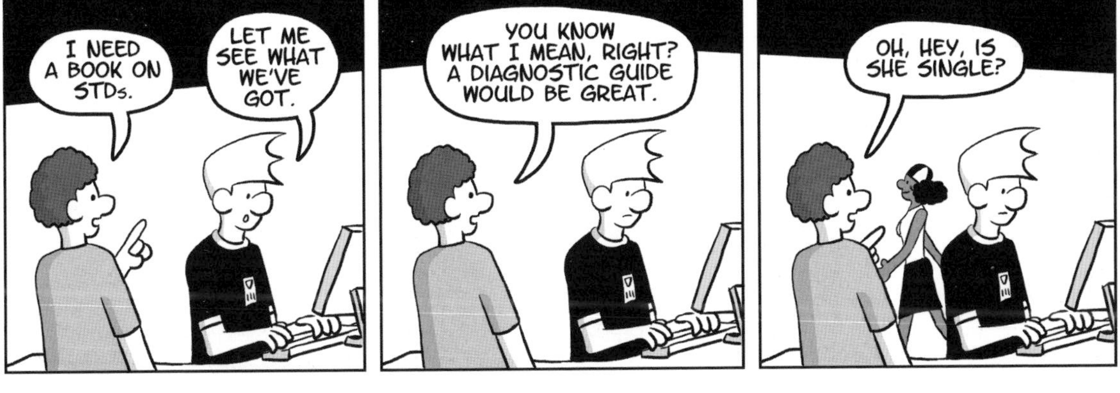
I NEED A BOOK ON STDs.
LET ME SEE WHAT WE'VE GOT.
YOU KNOW WHAT I MEAN, RIGHT? A DIAGNOSTIC GUIDE WOULD BE GREAT.
OH, HEY, IS SHE SINGLE?

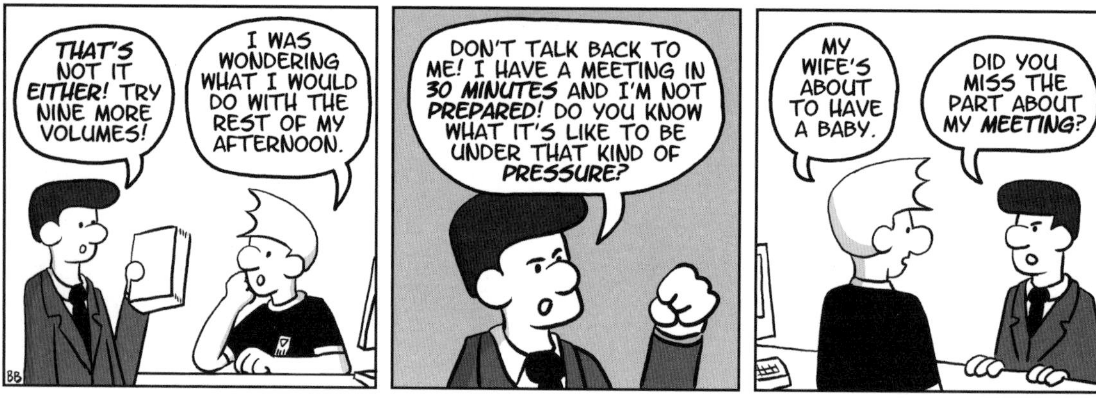
THAT'S NOT IT EITHER! TRY NINE MORE VOLUMES!
I WAS WONDERING WHAT I WOULD DO WITH THE REST OF MY AFTERNOON.
DON'T TALK BACK TO ME! I HAVE A MEETING IN 30 MINUTES AND I'M NOT PREPARED! DO YOU KNOW WHAT IT'S LIKE TO BE UNDER THAT KIND OF PRESSURE?
MY WIFE'S ABOUT TO HAVE A BABY.
DID YOU MISS THE PART ABOUT MY MEETING?
BB

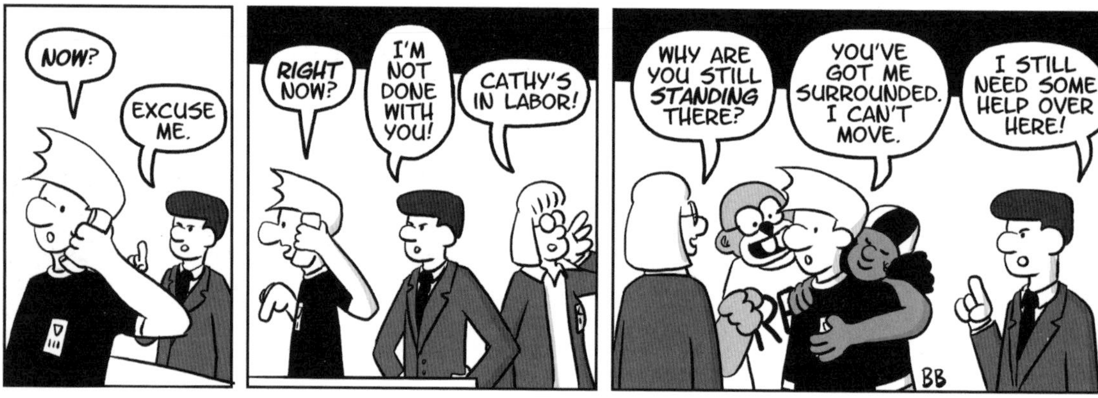
NOW?
EXCUSE ME.
RIGHT NOW?
I'M NOT DONE WITH YOU!
CATHY'S IN LABOR!
WHY ARE YOU STILL STANDING THERE?
YOU'VE GOT ME SURROUNDED. I CAN'T MOVE.
I STILL NEED SOME HELP OVER HERE!
BB

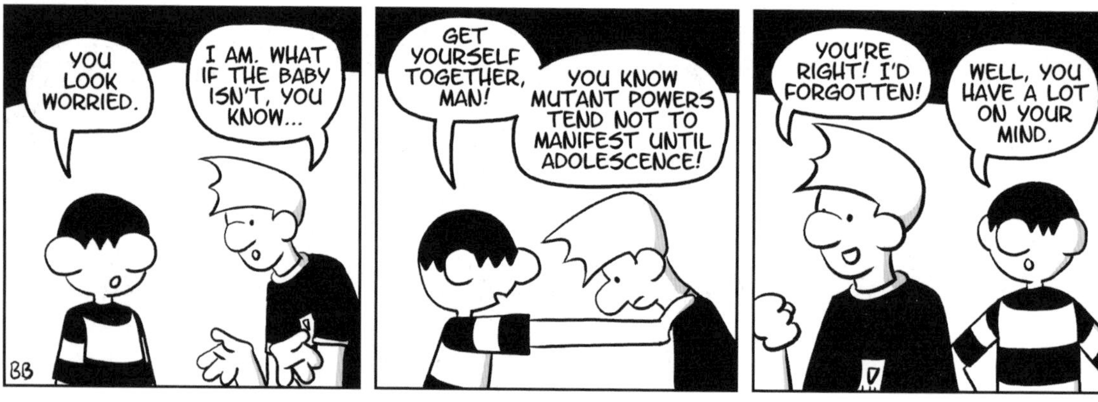
YOU LOOK WORRIED.
I AM. WHAT IF THE BABY ISN'T, YOU KNOW...
GET YOURSELF TOGETHER, MAN!
YOU KNOW MUTANT POWERS TEND NOT TO MANIFEST UNTIL ADOLESCENCE!
YOU'RE RIGHT! I'D FORGOTTEN!
WELL, YOU HAVE A LOT ON YOUR MIND.
BB

Too Much Information

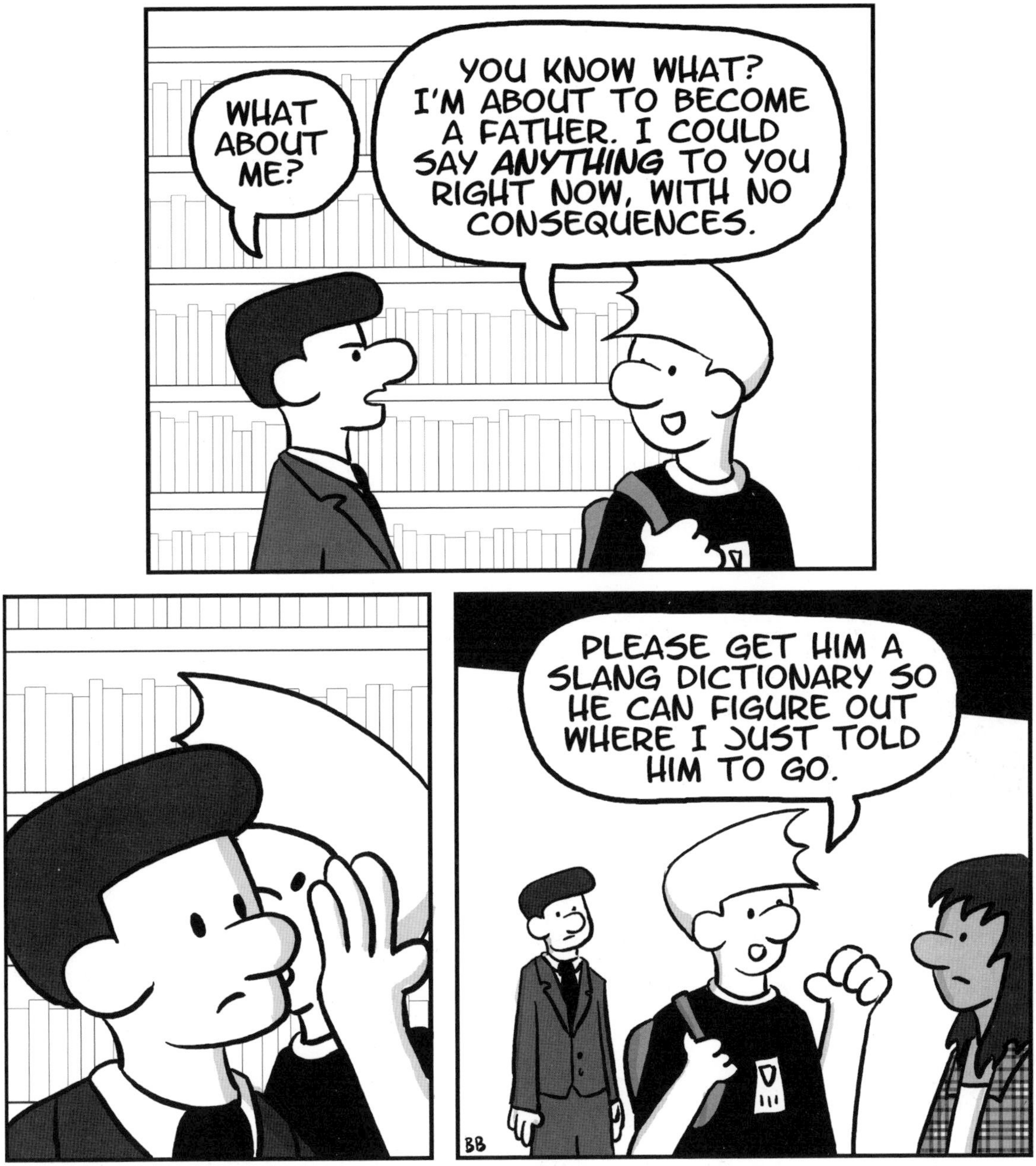
WHAT ABOUT ME?
YOU KNOW WHAT? I'M ABOUT TO BECOME A FATHER. I COULD SAY **ANYTHING** TO YOU RIGHT NOW, WITH NO CONSEQUENCES.
PLEASE GET HIM A SLANG DICTIONARY SO HE CAN FIGURE OUT WHERE I JUST TOLD HIM TO GO.
BB

To Be Continued

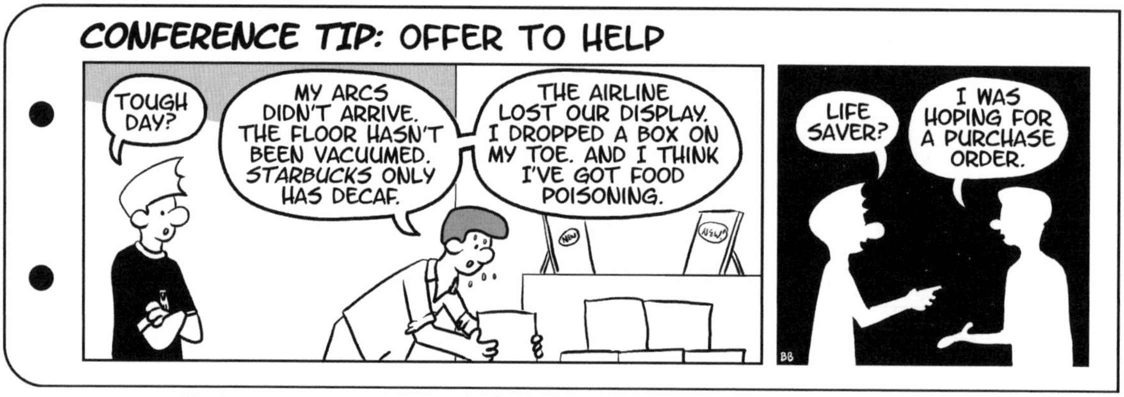
CONFERENCE TIP: OFFER TO HELP
TOUGH DAY?
MY ARCS DIDN'T ARRIVE. THE FLOOR HASN'T BEEN VACUUMED. STARBUCKS ONLY HAS DECAF.
THE AIRLINE LOST OUR DISPLAY. I DROPPED A BOX ON MY TOE. AND I THINK I'VE GOT FOOD POISONING.
LIFE SAVER?
I WAS HOPING FOR A PURCHASE ORDER.

Twice a year we provide helpful advice to attendees at the American Library Association annual conference.

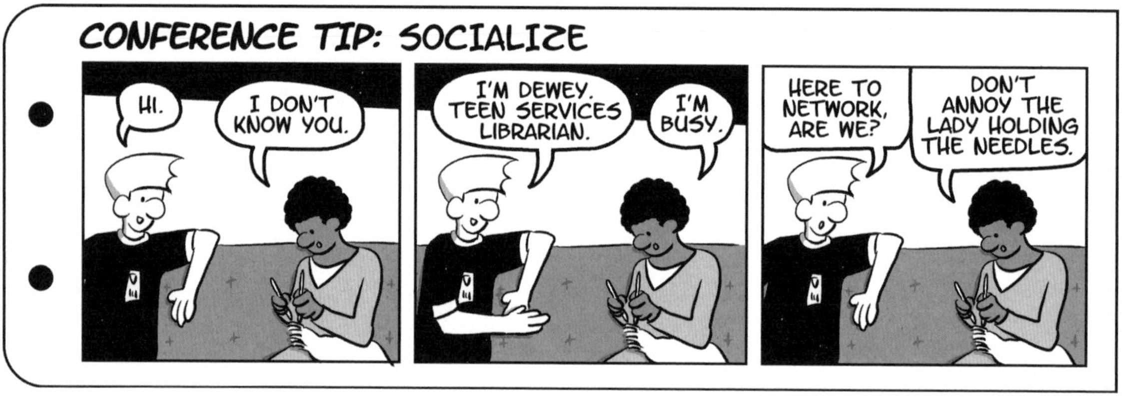
CONFERENCE TIP: SOCIALIZE
HI.
I DON'T KNOW YOU.
I'M DEWEY. TEEN SERVICES LIBRARIAN.
I'M BUSY.
HERE TO NETWORK, ARE WE?
DON'T ANNOY THE LADY HOLDING THE NEEDLES.

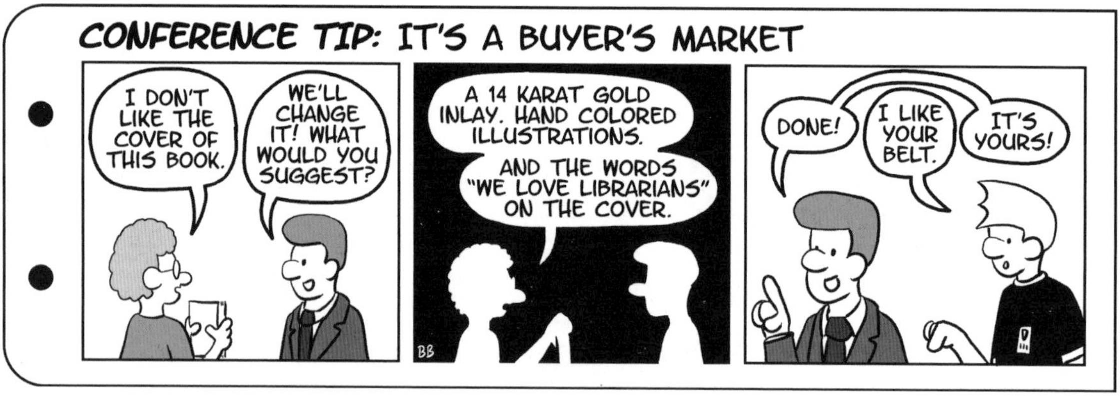
CONFERENCE TIP: IT'S A BUYER'S MARKET
I DON'T LIKE THE COVER OF THIS BOOK.
WE'LL CHANGE IT! WHAT WOULD YOU SUGGEST?
A 14 KARAT GOLD INLAY. HAND COLORED ILLUSTRATIONS.
AND THE WORDS "WE LOVE LIBRARIANS" ON THE COVER.
DONE!
I LIKE YOUR BELT.
IT'S YOURS!

CONFERENCE TIP: SHARE YOUR TRIUMPHS

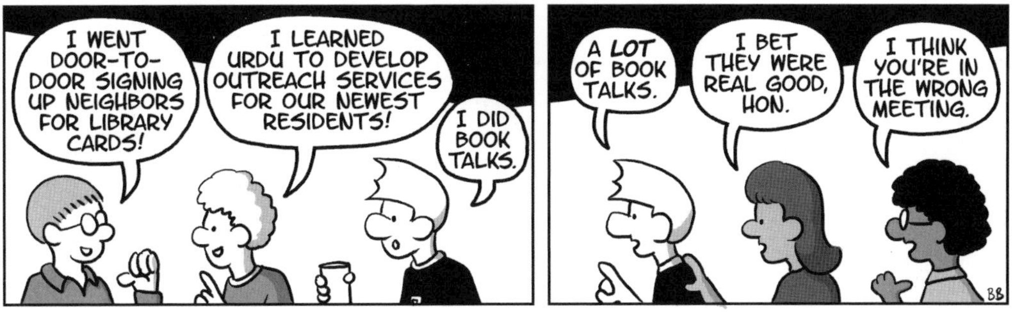
I WENT DOOR-TO-DOOR SIGNING UP NEIGHBORS FOR LIBRARY CARDS!
I LEARNED URDU TO DEVELOP OUTREACH SERVICES FOR OUR NEWEST RESIDENTS!
I DID BOOK TALKS.
A LOT OF BOOK TALKS.
I BET THEY WERE REAL GOOD, HON.
I THINK YOU'RE IN THE WRONG MEETING.
BB

CONFERENCE TIP: LIFT WITH YOUR LEGS

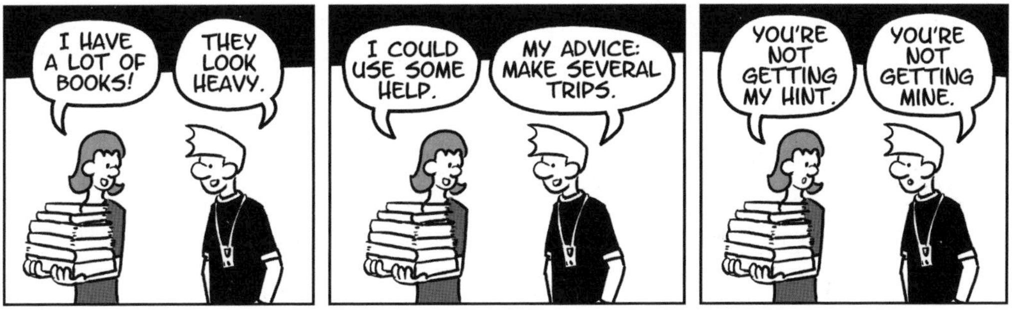
I HAVE A LOT OF BOOKS!
THEY LOOK HEAVY.
I COULD USE SOME HELP.
MY ADVICE: MAKE SEVERAL TRIPS.
YOU'RE NOT GETTING MY HINT.
YOU'RE NOT GETTING MINE.

CONFERENCE TIP: GET SOME REST

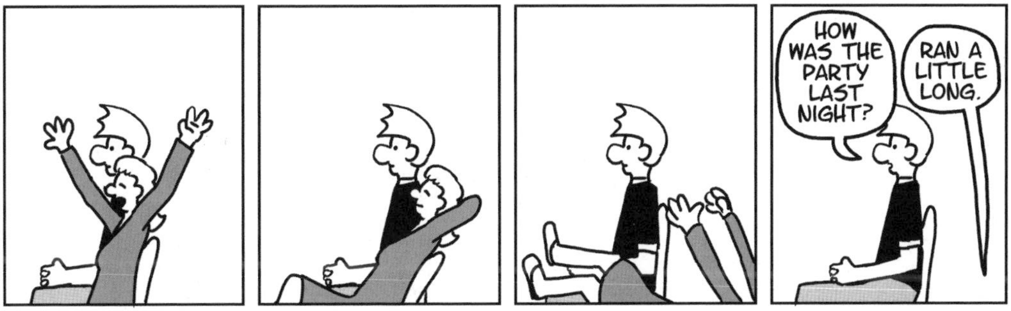
HOW WAS THE PARTY LAST NIGHT?
RAN A LITTLE LONG.

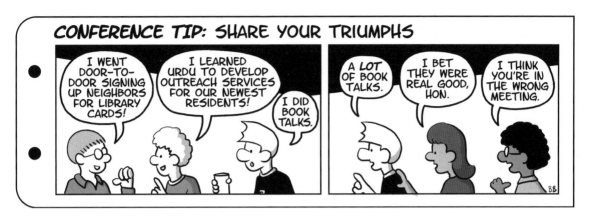

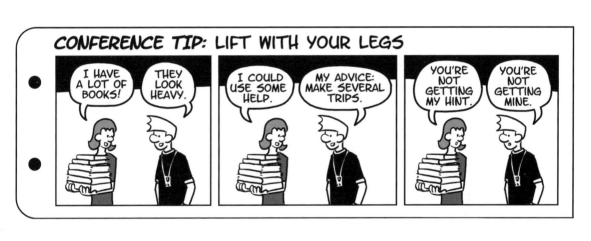

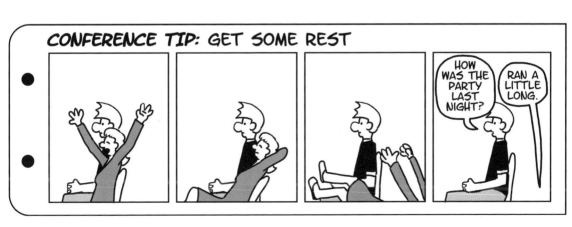

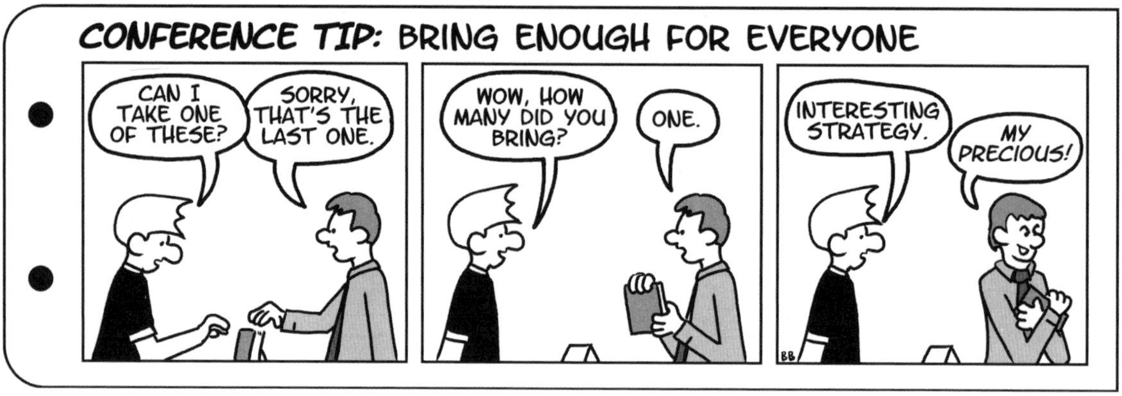
CONFERENCE TIP: BRING ENOUGH FOR EVERYONE
CAN I TAKE ONE OF THESE?
SORRY, THAT'S THE LAST ONE.
WOW, HOW MANY DID YOU BRING?
ONE.
INTERESTING STRATEGY.
MY PRECIOUS!
BB

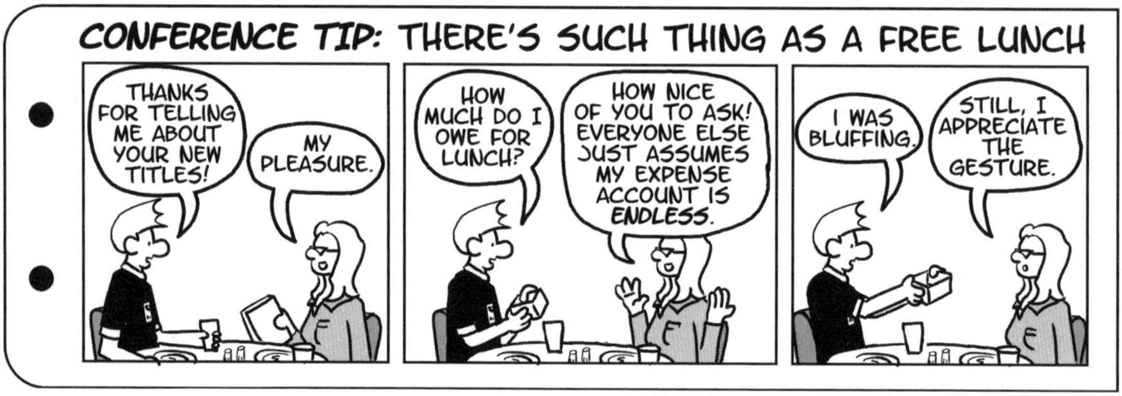
CONFERENCE TIP: THERE'S SUCH THING AS A FREE LUNCH
THANKS FOR TELLING ME ABOUT YOUR NEW TITLES!
MY PLEASURE.
HOW MUCH DO I OWE FOR LUNCH?
HOW NICE OF YOU TO ASK! EVERYONE ELSE JUST ASSUMES MY EXPENSE ACCOUNT IS ENDLESS.
I WAS BLUFFING.
STILL, I APPRECIATE THE GESTURE.

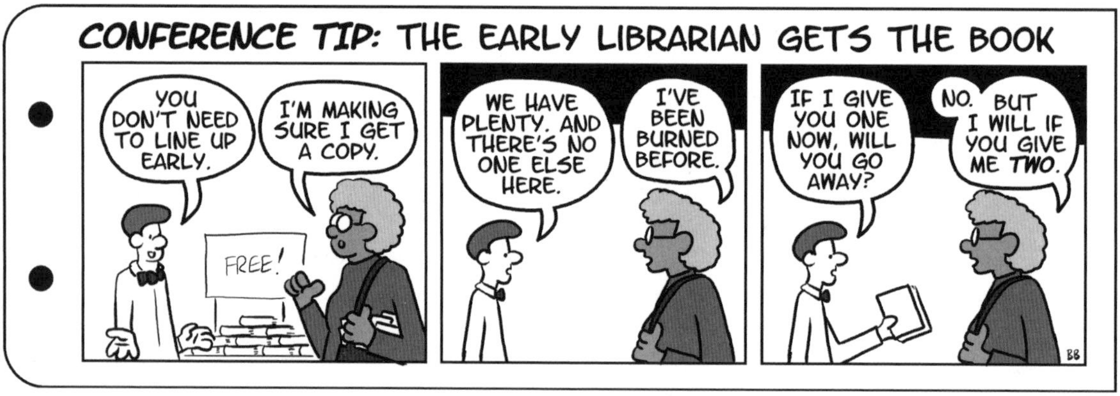
CONFERENCE TIP: THE EARLY LIBRARIAN GETS THE BOOK
YOU DON'T NEED TO LINE UP EARLY.
I'M MAKING SURE I GET A COPY.
FREE!
WE HAVE PLENTY. AND THERE'S NO ONE ELSE HERE.
I'VE BEEN BURNED BEFORE.
IF I GIVE YOU ONE NOW, WILL YOU GO AWAY?
NO. BUT I WILL IF YOU GIVE ME TWO.
BB

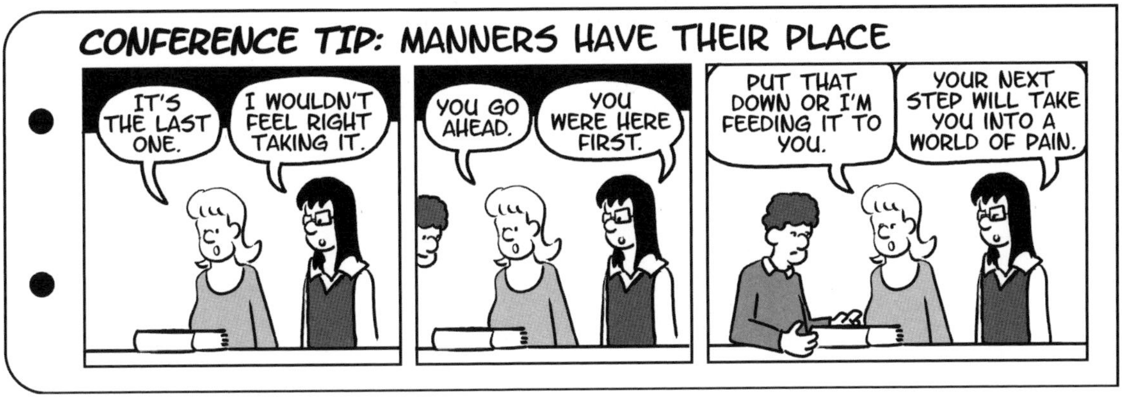
CONFERENCE TIP: MANNERS HAVE THEIR PLACE
IT'S THE LAST ONE.
I WOULDN'T FEEL RIGHT TAKING IT.
YOU GO AHEAD.
YOU WERE HERE FIRST.
PUT THAT DOWN OR I'M FEEDING IT TO YOU.
YOUR NEXT STEP WILL TAKE YOU INTO A WORLD OF PAIN.

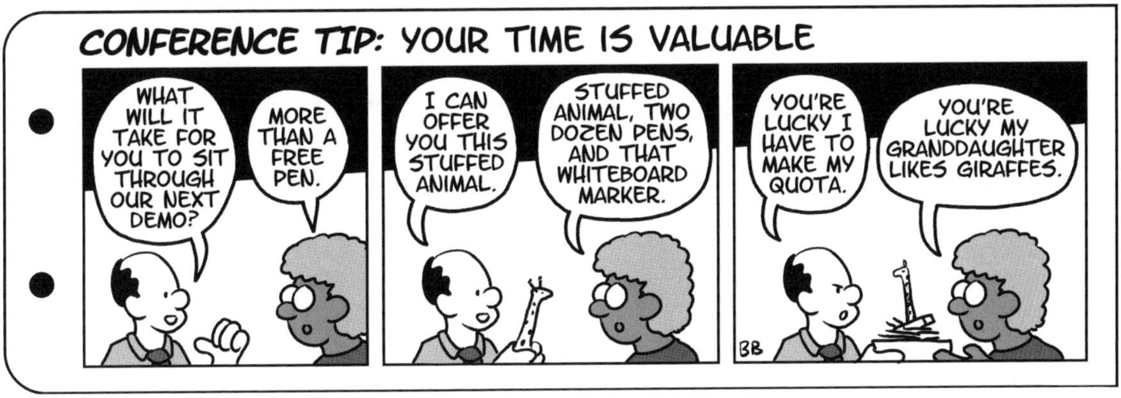
CONFERENCE TIP: YOUR TIME IS VALUABLE
WHAT WILL IT TAKE FOR YOU TO SIT THROUGH OUR NEXT DEMO?
MORE THAN A FREE PEN.
I CAN OFFER YOU THIS STUFFED ANIMAL.
STUFFED ANIMAL, TWO DOZEN PENS, AND THAT WHITEBOARD MARKER.
YOU'RE LUCKY I HAVE TO MAKE MY QUOTA.
YOU'RE LUCKY MY GRANDDAUGHTER LIKES GIRAFFES.
BB

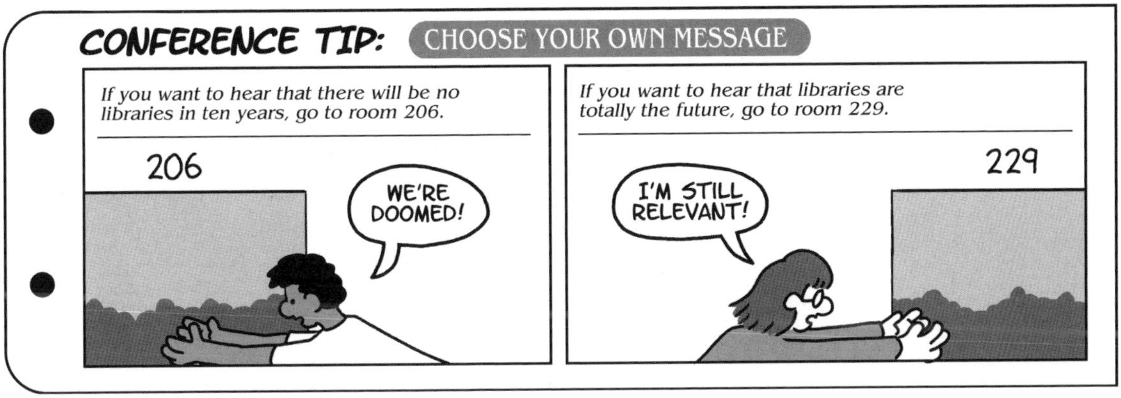
CONFERENCE TIP: CHOOSE YOUR OWN MESSAGE
If you want to hear that there will be no libraries in ten years, go to room 206.
206
WE'RE DOOMED!
If you want to hear that libraries are totally the future, go to room 229.
229
I'M STILL RELEVANT!

Questionable Content guest strip

Cartoonists, by and large, are solitary creatures. But when one of our kind calls out for help, we cannot resist. And so it was when a storm caused *Questionable Content*'s Jeph Jacques to be without power for several days. Bill dashed out this guest strip starring Marten (the protagonist) and Tai (the college library manager).

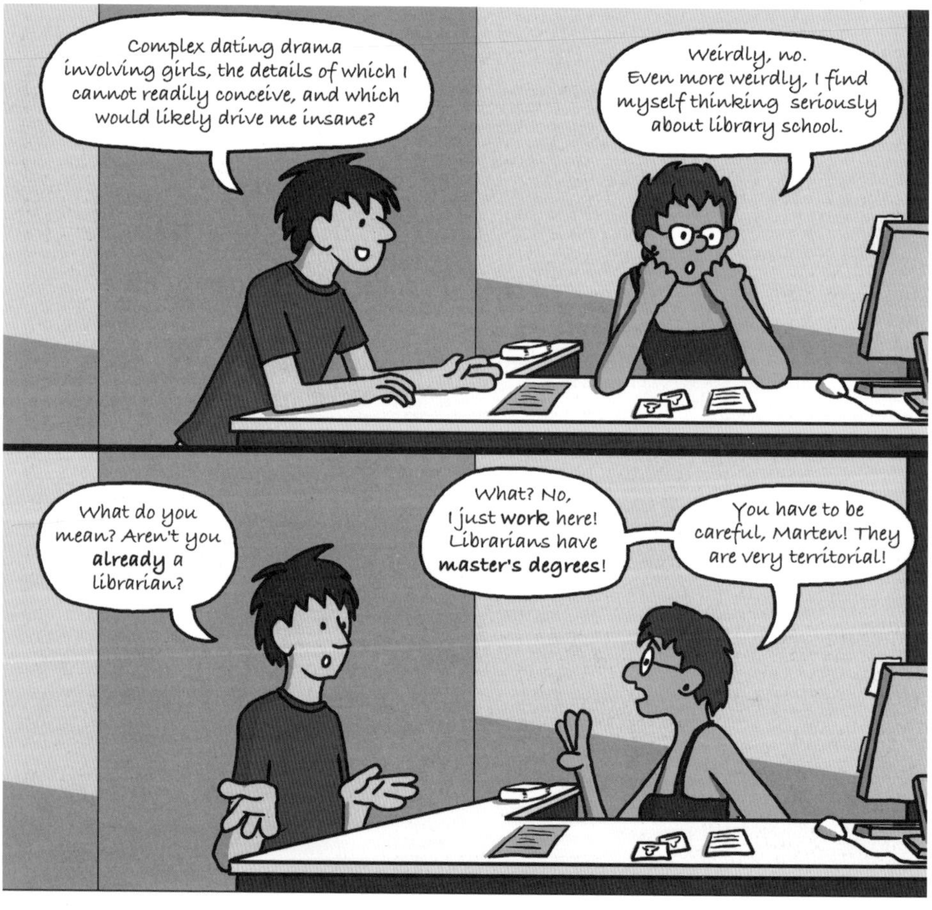
Complex dating drama involving girls, the details of which I cannot readily conceive, and which would likely drive me insane?
Weirdly, no. Even more weirdly, I find myself thinking seriously about library school.
What do you mean? Aren't you **already** a librarian?
What? No, I just **work** here! Librarians have **master's degrees**!
You have to be careful, Marten! They are very territorial!

Too Much Information

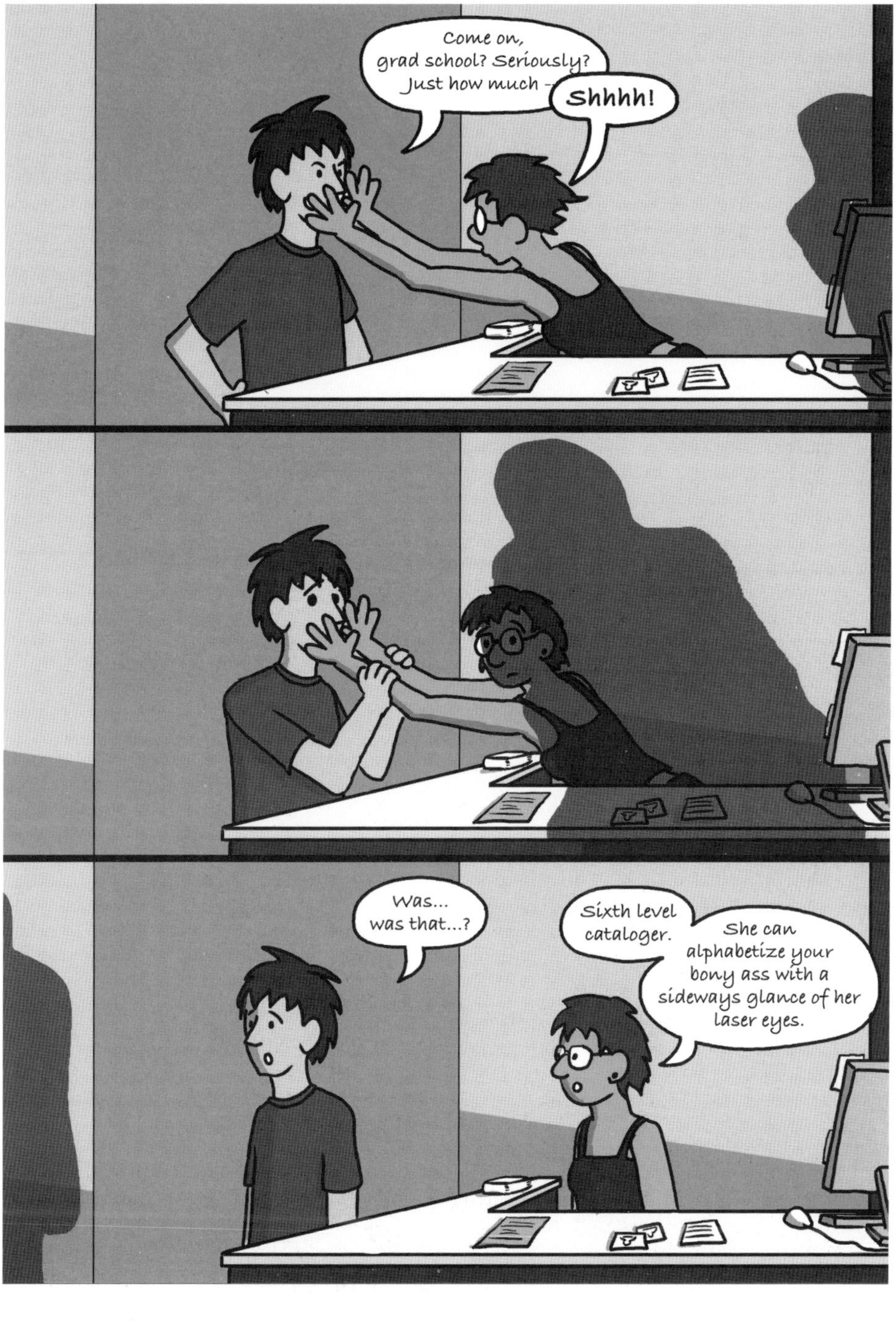

Come on, grad school? Seriously? Just how much --
Shhhh!
Was... was that...?
Sixth level cataloger.
She can alphabetize your bony ass with a sideways glance of her laser eyes.

You'd think if we could put this text here
we could also put some comics here, but
it's not that easy. It's never that easy.